Treasury of the True Dharma Eye

Dōgen's *Shōbōgenzō*

Treasury of the True Dharma Eye
Dōgen's *Shōbōgenzō*

Volume V

The Seventy-five-Chapter Compilation

Part 5

Chapters 61–75

An annotated translation
by the Sōtō Zen Text Project

Sōtōshū Shūmuchō
Tokyo

University of Hawai'i Press
Honolulu

Printed in China

Treasury of the True Dharma Eye: Dōgen's *Shōbōgenzō*

Volume V: The Seventy-five-Chapter Compilation, Part 5, Chapters 61–75

Published in Japan by Sōtōshū Shūmuchō, Tokyo
ISBN: 978-4-911061-00-8

Published for the rest of the world by University of Hawai'i Press, Honolulu

Library of Congress Cataloging-in-Publication Data

Names: Dōgen, 1200–1253, author. | Sōtō Zen Text Project, translator.

Title: Treasury of the true dharma eye : Dōgen's Shōbōgenzō / an annotated translation by the Sōtō Zen Text Project.

Other titles: Shōbō genzō. English

Description: Honolulu : University of Hawai'i Press, [2024] | Published in Japan by Sōtōshū Shūmuchō, 2023. | Includes bibliographical references and index. | Contents: v. 5. The seventy-five-chapter compilation, part 5, chapters 61–75

Identifiers: LCCN 2024004760 (print) | LCCN 2024004761 (ebook) | ISBN 9780824899172 (v. 1 ; paperback) | ISBN 9780824899189 (v. 2 ; paperback) | ISBN 9780824899196 (v. 3 ; paperback) | ISBN 9780824899202 (v. 4 ; paperback) | ISBN 9780824899219 (v. 5 ; paperback) | ISBN 9780824899226 (v. 6 ; paperback) | ISBN 9780824899233 (v. 7 ; paperback) | ISBN 9780824899240 (v. 8 ; paperback) | ISBN 9780824899257 (paperback) | ISBN 9798880700264 (v. 1 ; pdf) | ISBN 9798880700271 (v. 2 ; pdf) | ISBN 9798880700288 (v. 3 ; pdf) | ISBN 9798880700295 (v. 4 ; pdf) | ISBN 9798880700301 (v. 5 ; pdf) | ISBN 9798880700318 (v. 6 ; pdf) | ISBN 9798880700325 (v. 7 ; pdf) | ISBN 9798880700332 (v. 8 ; pdf)

Subjects: LCSH: Sōtōshū—Doctrines—Early works to 1800.

Classification: LCC BQ9449.D653 E5 2024 (print) | LCC BQ9449.D653 (ebook) | DDC 294.3/85—dc23/eng/20240318

LC record available at https://lccn.loc.gov/2024004760
LC ebook record available at https://lccn.loc.gov/2024004761

Cover art: Eihei Dōgen Zenji Gyōjōzu scroll, courtesy of Rev. Ōtani Tetsuo
Cover design by Urs App

University of Hawai'i Press books are printed on acid-free paper and meet the guidelines for permanence and durability of the Council on Library Resources.
Printer-ready copy has been provided by Sōtōshū Shūmuchō

Contents

Volume V

The Seventy-five-Chapter Compilation

Part 5

Conventions

This publication is an annotated translation, in seven volumes, of one hundred three texts of Dōgen's Japanese *Shōbōgenzō,* plus an additional volume containing an introduction, supplementary notes, appendices, and list of works cited. The translation is based on the edition of the *Shōbōgenzō* published in Kawamura Kōdō 河村孝道, ed., *Dōgen zenji zenshū* 道元禅師全集, vols. 1-2 (Tokyo: Shunjūsha, 1991, 1993), cited herein as DZZ.1 and DZZ.2; volume and page numbers of this edition are noted in braces at the corresponding locations in the translation.

The Japanese text accompanying the translation here follows the punctuation and *kanazukai* of the Kawamura edition; for ease of reference to premodern sources, Kawamura's modern Japanese kanji have been replaced with traditional forms. Also, for ease of reference, the sections into which the texts of the Kawamura edition are divided have been assigned numbers in square brackets by the translators. The translation of Kawamura's longer sections is sometimes broken into separate paragraphs, and transitions to new topics between sections are sometimes marked by a string of asterisks.

Though primarily written in Japanese, the *Shōbōgenzō* includes many passages of Chinese, ranging from long quotations of texts to short phrases inserted into the Japanese sentences. Since this inclusion of Chinese is a prominent linguistic feature of the original texts, the translation seeks to indicate such passages by the use of oblique font. The reader is warned that, given the ubiquity in the Japanese language of expressions adopted from Chinese, the identification of the shorter phrases as Chinese, rather than Japanese, is often rather arbitrary.

Much of the *Shōbōgenzō* is devoted to comment on material in other texts. The translation uses quotation marks to indicate terms and passages on which Dōgen is commenting. Here, again, the reader is warned that the distinction between use and mention can often be difficult to draw.

Sanskrit, Chinese, and Japanese terms appearing in the *Oxford English Dictionary* (3rd edition) are considered to have been adopted into English; other such terms are treated as foreign words and rendered in italics. Romanization of all such terms, whether treated as foreign or English, is given with diacritics.

With some exceptions, Chinese transliterations of Sanskrit terms are rendered as romanized Sanskrit. Indic proper nouns, whether transliterated or translated in the Chinese, are rendered as their presumed originals where possible; the reader is warned that some such reconstructions are unattested and speculative.

The proper noun "Zen" is used in reference to (a) the tradition that Dōgen calls the "buddhas and ancestors," and (b) the Japanese instantiation of that tradition; the Chinese name "Chan" is used in reference to the Chinese instantiation of the tradition.

Romanized readings of the Japanese text given in the notes follow wherever possible the ruby in Kawamura's text; readings not provided by Kawamura are based on *Zengaku daijiten* 禅学大辞典 (1978) and/or Katō Shūkō 加藤宗厚, *Shōbōgenzō yōgo sakuin* 正法眼藏用語索引 (1962).

Citations of T (*Taishō shinshū daizōkyō* 大正新脩大藏經) are from the *SAT Daizōkyō Text Database* (https://21dzk.l.u-tokyo.ac.jp/SAT). Citations of ZZ (*Dainihon zokuzōkyō* 大日本続藏經) are from the *CBETA Hanwen dazangjing* 漢文大藏經 (http://tripitaka.cbeta.org). Citations of KR are from *Kanripo* 漢リポ *Kanseki Repository* (https://www.kanripo.org).

The Kawamura edition provides colophons from several sources, some following the relevant chapter, some in the head notes of the chapter, some in the collation notes (*honbun kōi* 本文校異) for that chapter in the end matter of DZZ.1 and DZZ.2. For the convenience of the reader, this translation collects these colophons (and occasionally others omitted by Kawamura) at the end of each chapter. Colophons without attribution are assumed to have been written by Dōgen.

Abbreviations

C Chinese language

DZZ *Dōgen zenji zenshū* 道元禅師全集, Kagamishima Genryū 鏡島元隆 et al., compilers. 7 vols. Tokyo: Shunjūsha, 1988–1993.

ESST *Eihei Shōbōgenzō shūsho taisei* 永平正法眼蔵蒐書大成, Kawamura Kōdō 河村孝道, ed. 27 vols. Tokyo: Taishūkan Shoten, 1974-1982.

J Japanese language

KR Kanseki Repository (Kanseki Ripo 漢籍リポ). Online: https://www.kanripo.org

M *Dai kanwa jiten* 大漢和辞典, Morohashi Tetsuji 諸橋轍次, ed. 13 vols. (plus 2-vol. supplement). Tokyo: Taishūkan Shoten, 1955-1960.

S Sanskrit

SCZ *Shōbōgenzō chūkai zensho* 正法眼藏註解全書, Jinbo Nyoten 神保如天 and Andō Bun'ei 安藤文英, eds. 11 vols. Reprint Tokyo: Nihon Bussho Kankōkai, 1956-1957.

SZ *Sōtōshū zensho* 曹洞宗全書. 20 vols. Tokyo: Kōmeisha, 1929-1938.

T *Taishō shinshū daizōkyō* 大正新脩大藏經, Takakusu Junjirō 高楠順次郎 and Watanabe Kaikyoku 渡邊海旭, eds. 100 vols. Tokyo: Daizōkyōkai, 1924–1935.

ZT *Zengaku taikei* 禪學大系. 8 vols. Tokyo: Kokusho Kankōkai, 1952 (orig. publ. 1910-11).

ZTS *Zengaku tenseki sōkan* 禅学典籍叢刊, Yanagida Seizan 柳田聖山 and Shiina Kōyū 椎名宏雄, eds. 12 vols. Kyoto: Rinsen Shoten, 1999-2001.

ZZ *Dainihon zokuzōkyō* 大日本続藏經. 150 vols. Kyoto: Bussho Kankōkai, 1905-1912.

Treasury of the True Dharma Eye

Number 61

Song of the Dragon

Ryūgin

龍吟

Song of the Dragon

Ryūgin

Introduction

This chapter was composed in the winter of 1243, at Yamashibu 禪師峰 (or Zenji Peak), in Echizen. It occurs as number 61 in the seventy-five-chapter compilation of the *Shōbōgenzō*, number 51 in the sixty-chapter compilation, and number 65 in the Honzan edition.

The text, one of the shortest in the *Shōbōgenzō*, represents a commentary on two sayings on the phrase, "the song of the dragon in the dried-up tree" — a common Zen metaphor for vitality within repose (or the spiritual functions of a Zen master), reflected in similar expressions in our text: "the roar of the lion in the skull," "the eyeball in the skull," "the pregnant column." Dōgen begins his comments by distinguishing the "dried-up tree" in these sayings from the common phrase "dried-up tree and dead ashes," often used to represent a state of mental quiescence. Unlike such a state, Dōgen says, the "dried-up tree" of the buddhas and ancestors can "meet the spring" and "sprout." This "sprouting" is "the song of the dragon," and it is precisely the state of being "dried" that enables one to sing it. He concludes his brief remarks by identifying the Zen masters' talk about "the song of the dragon" with the countless tunes sung by the dragon.

正法眼藏第六十一
Treasury of the True Dharma Eye
Number 61
龍吟

Song of the Dragon

[61:1] {2:151}

舒州投子山慈濟大師、因僧問、枯木裏還有龍吟也無。師曰、我道、髑髏裏有師子吼。

Great Master Ciji of Mount Touzi from Shuzhou was asked by a monk, "Within the dried-up tree, is there the song of the dragon or not?"[1]

The Master said, "I say, within the skull, there's the roar of the lion."[2]

[61:2]

枯木死灰の談は、もとより外道の所教なり。しかあれども、外道のいふところの枯木と、佛祖のいふところの枯木と、はるかにことなるべし。外道は枯木を談すといへども、枯木をしらず、いはんや龍吟をきかんや。外道は、枯木は朽木ならん、とおもへり、不可逢春と學せり。

---

1 **Great Master Ciji of Mount Touzi from Shuzhou** (*Joshū Tōsuzan Jisai daishi* 舒州投子山慈濟大師): I.e., Touzi Datong 投子大同 (819-914), a disciple of Cuiwei Wuxue 翠微無學, in the lineage of Qingyuan Xingsi 青原行思. "Great Master Ciji" 慈濟大師 is a posthumous title. Shuzhou 舒州 is in the vicinity of present-day Anqing 安慶 in Anhui. This conversation can be found at *Jingde chuandeng lu* 景德傳燈錄, T.2076.51:319a29-b1.

"dried-up tree" (*koboku* 枯木): Or "dead tree," "withered tree," etc.; the somewhat infelicitous translation "dried-up" seeks to preserve lexical continuity with Dōgen's other uses of *ko* 枯 ("to dry out," "to be dried out") in this text. The term is regularly used in Zen literature for an immobile state of meditation; see below, Note 3. The phrase "dragon's song in the dried-up tree" (*koboku ryūgin* 枯木龍吟) evokes the sound of the wind in bare branches; often used in Zen to suggest action within repose, or the power of life within the seemingly inanimate.

"song of the dragon" (*ryūgin* 龍吟): The word *gin* (translated here as "song") is used in reference to a range of sounds, both human and animal, from singing, chanting, and reciting, to crying, moaning, sighing, humming, etc. The term *ryūgin* ("dragon song") is used in traditional music to refer both to a type of flute (*ryūteki* 龍笛), and to a melody in court music (*ryūgin chō* 龍吟調).

2 **"skull"** (*dokuro* 髑髏): I.e., of a skeleton; often used in Zen texts in a sense similar to "dried-up tree."

"Roar of the lion" (*shishi ku* 師子吼): S. *siṃha-nāda*; regularly used in Buddhist literature for the preaching of a buddha.

Talk of "dried-up trees and dead ashes" is originally a teaching of an other path.[3] Nevertheless, there should be a big difference between the "dried-up tree" spoken of by other paths and the "dried-up tree" spoken of by the buddhas and ancestors. While the other paths talk of "dried-up trees," they do not know "dried-up trees," much less do they hear "the song of the dragon." The other paths think that the "dried-up tree" is a rotted tree; they study that it *cannot "meet the spring."*[4]

[61:3]

佛祖道の枯木は、海枯の參學なり。海枯は木枯なり、木枯は逢春なり。木の不動著は枯なり。いまの山木・海木・空木等、これ枯木なり。萠芽も枯木龍吟なり、百千萬圍とあるも、枯木の兒孫なり。枯の相・性・體・力は、佛祖道の枯椿なり、非枯椿なり。山谷木あり、田里木あり。山谷木、よのなかに松栢と稱す。田里木、よのなかに人天と稱す。依根葉分布、これを佛祖と稱す。本末須歸宗、すなはち參學なり。かくのごとくなる、枯木の長法身なり、枯木の短法身なり。もし枯木にあらざれば、いまだ龍吟せず、いまだ枯木にあらざれば、龍吟を打失せず。幾度逢春不變心は、渾枯の龍吟なり。宮・商・角・徵・羽に不群なりといへども、宮・商・角・徵・羽は、龍吟の前後二三子なり。

The "dried-up trees" that the buddhas and ancestors speak of is the study of "the ocean drying up."[5] The ocean drying up is the tree drying out; the tree drying out is "meeting the spring." The tree's not moving is "dried." The present mountain trees, ocean trees, sky trees, and

3 **"dried-up trees and dead ashes"** (*koboku shikai* 枯木死灰): Or, as we might say, "dead wood and cold ashes"; a common expression in Zen texts, often used in a pejorative sense, for the mind in trance. A term regularly used in Zen literature for an immobile state of meditation. In his "Shōbōgenzō butsudō" 正法眼藏佛道, Dōgen quotes the passage in the *Linjian lu* 林間錄, by Juefan Huihong 覺範慧洪 (1071-1128), that criticizes those who would treat Bodhidharma as a practitioner of dhyāna, thus locating him among the partisans of "dried-up trees and dead ashes." See Supplementary Notes, s.v. "Dried-up tree" and "Practitioner of dhyāna."

teaching of an other path (*gedō no shokyō* 外道の所教): I.e., something taught in non-Buddhist religious traditions. While the term *gedō* (S. *tīrthika*) is usually used in reference to Hinduism and other Indian religions, Dōgen is no doubt thinking here of Daoist texts like the *Zhuangzi* 莊子. The second book (Qiwu lun 齊物論, KR.5c0126.02.1a) of this work opens with Jiqi of Nanguo 南郭子綦 leaning on his armrest and gazing at the heavens. His companion Yancheng Ziyou 顏成子遊 exclaims,

> 何居乎、形固可使如槁木、而心固可使如死灰乎。
>
> "What's this? Can you actually make the body like a dried-up tree and the mind like dead ashes?"

4 **"meet the spring"** (*hō shun* 逢春): Dōgen here introduces a term from the verse by Damei Fachang 大梅法常 (752-839) that he will quote in the next section. The sense here is likely "revive after the dead of winter."

5 **"the ocean drying up"** (*kaiko* 海枯): Allusion to a saying, drawn from a verse by the poet Du Xunhe 杜荀鶴 (846-907), that occurs often in Zen literature (See, e.g., *Zongjing lu* 宗鏡錄, T.2016.48:564b12):

the rest — these are the "dried-up tree." The "germination of a sprout" is the "song of the dragon in the dried-up tree"; though it may have a circumference measured in hundreds of thousands of myriads, it is the descendant of the dried-up tree.[6] The mark, nature, substance, and power of "dried" is "a dried post" and "not a dried post," spoken of by the buddhas and ancestors.[7]

There are trees of mountains and valleys; there are trees of paddies and villages. The trees of mountains and valleys are known in the world as pines and cypress; the trees of paddies and villages are known in the world as humans and devas. "*The leaves spread based on the root*": this is known as the buddhas and ancestors; "*root and branch return to the source*": this is their study.[8] Being like this is the dried-up tree's long

---

> 海枯終見底、人死不知心。
> When the ocean dries up, we finally see the bottom;
> When a person dies, we do not know his mind.

Dōgen plays with variations on this saying elsewhere in the *Shōbōgenzō* and will return to it in section 7, below.

6 **"germination of a sprout"** (*hōga* 萠芽): Presumably the "sprout" that appears when the dried-up tree "meets the spring." While seemingly not a term of art in Zen literature and not used elsewhere in Dōgen's writings, this expression is somewhat reminscent of the common "before the germination of any portent" (*chinchō mibō* 朕兆未萠), used to represent the "unborn" (*mushō* 無生).

7 **The mark, nature, substance, and power of "dried"** (*ko no sō shō tai riki* 枯の相・性・體・力): Probably here indicating something like "the ultimate meaning of 'dried.'" The phrase draws on a famous line in the *Lotus Sūtra* (*Miaofa lianhua jing* 妙法蓮華經, T.262.9:5c11-13) to which Dōgen often refers; see Supplementary Notes, s.v. "Only buddhas with buddhas can exhaustively investigate the real marks of the dharmas."

"a dried post" (*koshō* 枯椿); **"not a dried post"** (*hi koshō* 非枯椿): Or, we might say, "a rotted stake." Likely a reference to a saying by Shushan Guangren 疏山光仁 (or Kuangren 匡仁, 837-909) included in Dōgen's *shinji Shōbōgenzō* 眞字正法眼藏 (DZZ.5:270, case 285):

> 疏山示衆云、病僧咸通年已前、會法身邊事。咸通年已後、會法身向上事。雲門出問云、如何是法身邊事。師曰、枯椿。曰、如何是法身向上事。師曰、非枯椿。
> Shushan addressed the assembly, saying, "Before the Xiantong years [860-873], I understood things in the vicinity of the dharma body; after the Xiantong years, I understood things beyond the dharma body."
> Yunmen asked, "What are things in the vicinity of the dharma body?"
> The Master said, "A dried post."
> [Yunmen] asked, "What are things beyond the dharma body?"
> The Master said, "Not a dried post."

8 **"The leaves spread based on the root"** (*e kon yō bunpu* 依根葉分布); **"root and branch return to the source"** (*honmatsu shu ki shū* 本末須歸宗): From the famous poem *Cantong qi* 參同契, by Shitou Xiqian 石頭希遷 (700-790) (*Jingde chuandeng lu* 景德傳燈錄, T.2076.51:459b15).

dharma body, the dried-up tree's short dharma body.[9] One who is not a dried-up tree does not yet sing the dragon song; one who is not a dried-up tree does not lose the dragon song.[10] "*How many springs has it met without changing its mind?*" — this is the song of the dragon entirely dried.[11] It does not belong with *kyū shō kaku chi u*; but *kyū shō kaku chi u* are the second or third sons of the song of the dragon.[12]

[61:4] {2:152}

しかあるに、這僧道の枯木裏還有龍吟也無は、無量劫のなかにはじめて問頭に現成せり、話頭の現成なり。投子道の我道髑髏裏有師子吼は、有甚麼掩處なり、屈己推人也未休なり、髑髏遍野なり。

Nevertheless, this monk's saying, "*In the dried-up tree, is there the song of the dragon or not?*" is realized in a question for the first time in innumerable kalpas; it is the realization of a statement.[13] Touzi's saying, "*I say there's the roar of the lion in the skull,*" is, "*is there something*

---

9 **long dharma body** (*chō hosshin* 長法身); **short dharma body** (*tan hosshin* 短法身): From the popular Zen saying, "the long one is a long dharma body; the short one is a short dharma body" (*chōsha chō hosshin tansha tan hosshin* 長者長法身短者短法身); i.e., whether long or short, it is the dharma body of the buddha.

10 **does not lose the dragon song** (*ryūgin o tashitsu sezu* 龍吟を打失せず): Perhaps reflecting the use of *tashitsu* 打失 ("to lose") in the sense "to slough off," "to leave behind" — as in the expression (quoted several times in the *Shōbōgenzō*) "to lose the eyes" (*tashitsu ganzei* 打失眼睛) in reference to awakening.

11 **"How many springs has it met without changing its mind?"** (*kido hō shun fu hen shin* 幾度逢春不變心): Or "without changing its core." From a verse by Damei Fachang 大梅法常 (*Jingde chuandeng lu* 景德傳燈錄, T.2076.51:254c12-13):

摧殘枯木倚寒林、幾度逢春不變心。

Broken dried-up tree keeping to the cold forest.
How many times has it met the spring without changing its mind?

See Supplementary Notes, s.v. "Dried-up tree."

12 **It does not belong with *kyū shō kaku chi u*** (*kyū shō kaku chi u ni fugun nari* 宮・商・角・徵・羽に不群なり): I.e., it is not music as understood through the five notes of the traditional scale of Chinese music: *gong* 宮, *shang* 商, *jue* 角, *zheng* 徵, *yu* 羽. Dōgen is here playing on the common uses of *ryūgin* in reference to music (see above, Note 1) — a play he will continue below.

the second or third sons of the song of the dragon (*ryūgin no zengo nisan shi* 龍吟の前後二三子): Or, perhaps, "two or three former or later sons of the song of the dragon." Taking *shi* 子 here as "child" (as read at *Shōbōgenzō monge* 正法眼藏聞解, SCZ:7:563). The point would seem to be that the musical scale is derivative of the dragon's song.

13 **the realization of a statement** (*watō no genjō* 話頭の現成): I.e., not merely a question but a significant utterance.

concealed?"[14] It is, "*his humbling himself and promoting others never ceases*"; it is, "*skulls fill the fields.*"[15]

* * * * *

[61:5]

香嚴寺襲燈大師、因僧問、如何是道。師云、枯木裏龍吟。僧曰、不會。師云、髑髏裏眼睛。後有僧問石霜、如何是枯木裏龍吟。霜云、猶帶喜在。僧曰、如何是髑髏裏眼睛。霜云、猶帶識在。又有僧問曹山、如何是枯木裏龍吟。山曰、血脈不斷。僧曰、如何是髑髏裏眼睛。山云、乾不盡。僧曰、未審、還有得聞者麼。山云、盡大地未有一箇不聞。僧曰、未審、龍吟是何章句。山云、也不知是何章句。聞者皆喪。

Great Master Xideng of Xiangyan Monastery was asked by a monk, "What is the way?"[16]

The Master said, "The dragon song in the dried-up tree."

The monk said, "I don't understand."

The Master said, "The eyeball in the skull."

Later, a monk asked Shishuang, "What is the dragon song in the dried-up tree?"[17]

Shuang said, "Still harboring joy."

---

14 **"is there something concealed?"** (*u jinmo en sho* 有甚麼掩處): I.e., it is everywhere obvious. Likely reflecting another saying of Touzi 投子 (*Jingde chuandeng lu* 景德傳燈錄, T.2076.51:319b25-26):

> 問、如何是火焰裏藏身。師曰、有什麼掩處。
>
> [Someone] asked, "What is the body hidden within flames?"
> The Master said, "Is there something concealed?"

15 **"his humbling himself and promoting others never ceases"** (*kukko suinin ya mikyū* 屈己推人也未休): The sense here may be simply that Touzi's words are "never ceasing." Likely reflecting another saying of Touzi 投子 (*Jingde chuandeng lu* 景德傳燈錄 (T.2076.51:320a21-22):

> 問、七佛是文殊弟子。文殊還有師也無。師曰、適來恁麼道也、大似屈己推人。
>
> [Someone] asked, "The seven buddhas are the disciples of Mañjuśrī. Does Mañjuśrī have a master?"
> The Master said, "To talk the way you just did looks like humbling yourself and promoting another."

"skulls fill the fields" (*dokuro hen ya* 髑髏遍野): Though this Zen expression might be read in a negative sense, presumably in its context here it is intended to suggest that the roaring skulls Touzi speaks of are ubiquitous. The expression can be found, e.g., attributed to Gushan 鼓山 at *Jingde chuandeng lu* 景德傳燈錄 (T.2076.51:347c11).

16 **Great Master Xideng of Xiangyan Monastery** (*Kyōgenji Shūtō daishi* 香嚴寺襲燈大師): I.e., Xiangyan Zhixian 香嚴智閑 (d. 898). This discussion of the dragon song occurs in several collections, including Dōgen's *shinji Shōbōgenzō* 眞字正法眼藏 (DZZ.5:142, case 28).

17 **Shishuang** (*Sekisō* 石霜): I.e., Shishuang Qingzhu 石霜慶諸 (807-888).

The monk said, "What is the eyeball in the skull?"
Shuang said, "Still harboring consciousness."
Again, a monk asked Caoshan, "What is the dragon song in the dried-up tree?"[18]
Shan said, "The blood vessel not severed."[19]
The monk said, "What is the eyeball in the skull?"
Shan said, "Not entirely dry."
The monk said, "Well, can anyone hear it?"
Shan said, "On all the whole earth, there isn't one who can't hear it."
The monk said, "Well, what verse does the dragon sing?"
Shan said, "I don't know what verse it is. Everyone who hears it loses his life."[20]

[61:6] {2:153}
いま擬道する聞者・吟者は、吟龍吟者に不齊なり、この曲調は龍吟なり。枯木裏・髑髏裏、これ内外にあらず、自他にあらず、而今而古なり。猶帶喜在は、さらに頭角生なり。猶帶識在は、皮膚脱落盡なり。

The hearer and the singer of whom they are trying to speak here are not equal to the singer of the dragon's song; this tune is the dragon's singing.[21] "In the dried-up tree," "in the skull" — these are not about inside

18 **Caoshan** (*Sōzan* 曹山): I.e., Caoshan Benzhi 曹山本寂 (840-901).

19 **"The blood vessel"** (*kechimyaku* 血脈): Or "bloodline"; a standard Zen expression for the lineage of the buddhas and ancestors.

20 **"Everyone who hears it loses his life"** (*monja kai sō* 聞者皆喪): Or "all who hear it are to be mourned"; taking *sō* here as in *sōshitsu* 喪失 ("loss"). See Supplementary Notes, s.v. "Forfeit one's body and lose one's life."

21 **The hearer and the singer they are trying to speak of here are not equal to the singer of the dragon's song** (*ima gidō suru monja ginja wa, gin ryūgin ja ni fusei nari* いま擬道する聞者・吟者は、吟龍吟者に不齊なり): A tentative translation of a passage subject to varied interpretation. The sentence might also be read, "the hearing and singing they are trying to speak of here are not equal to the singing of the singing dragon (*ginryū ginja*)." The commentary of the influential *Shōbōgenzō monge* 正法眼藏聞解 (SCZ.7:566-67) suggests that the point here is that the authentic "song of the dragon" is beyond the active and passive opposites of "singing" and "hearing"; it also offers an alternative opinion to the effect that what the monks are discussing is not the authentic "song of the dragon."

this tune is the dragon's singing (*kono kyokuchō wa ryūgin nari* この曲調は龍吟なり): The antecedent of "this" is unclear; it could refer either to the quoted passage or to Dōgen's comment on it. "Tune" (*kyokuchō* 曲調 here), while playing on the music of the dragon's song, might be taken as the exploration of the theme of the dragon's song — i.e., the study of the dragon's song is the singing of the dragon.

or outside, not about self or other; they are the present and the past.[22] "*Still harboring joy*" is further "horns growing on your head"; "*still harboring consciousness*" is "*skin entirely sloughed off.*"[23]

[61:7]

曹山道の血脈不斷は、道不諱なり、語脈裏轉身なり。乾不盡は、海枯不盡底なり。不盡是乾なるゆえに、乾上又乾なり。聞者ありや、と道著せるは、不得者ありや、といふがごとし。盡大地未有一箇不聞は、さらに聞著すべし、未有一箇不聞は、しばらくおく、未有盡大地時、龍吟在甚麼處、速道速道なり。未審龍吟是何章句は、爲問すべし、吟龍は、おのれづから泥裏の作聲擧拈なり、鼻孔裏の出氣なり。也不知是何章句は、章句裏有龍なり。聞者皆喪は、可惜許なり。

Caoshan's saying, "the blood vessel not severed," is speaking without avoidance; it is "*turning the body in the stream of words.*"[24] "Not entirely dry" is "*when the ocean dries up, it is not entirely to the bottom.*"[25] Since "*not entirely*" *is "dry,"* there is *"dry" beyond "dry."* His saying, "can anyone hear it?" is like saying, "is there anyone who can't?" About "*on all the whole earth, there isn't one who can't hear it,*" we should ask further: leaving aside "*there isn't one who can't hear it,*" *when there isn't any "all the whole earth," where is the song of the dragon? Speak! Speak!* "*Well, what passage does the dragon sing?*" should be questioned. The singing dragon is itself raising its voice and bringing it up within the

22 **the present and the past** (*nikon niko* 而今而古): Probably to be taken in the sense "at once present and past" or, perhaps, "timeless."

23 **"horns growing on your head"** (*zu kaku shō* 頭角生): Perhaps, recalling the saying of Nanquan Puyuan 南泉普願 (748-835), introduced elsewhere in the *Shōbōgenzō*; see Supplementary Note, s.v. "Move among different types."

"skin entirely sloughed off" (*hifu datsuraku jin* 皮膚脱落盡): Likely expressing a positive state. Perhaps reflecting a conversation between Chan masters Mazu Daoyi 馬祖道一 and Yaoshan Weiyan 藥山惟儼 (751-834); see Supplementary Notes, s.v. "Slough off."

24 **speaking without avoidance** (*dō fuki* 道不諱): Or, perhaps, "a saying that does not conceal." A rather unusual expression, in Chinese syntax, not appearing elsewhere in Dōgen's writings.

"turning the body in the stream of words" (*gomyaku ri tenshin* [or *tenjin*] 語脈裏轉身): The translation loses Dōgen's play here with the graph *myaku* 脈 ("stream"), rendered as "vessel" in Caoshan's saying. The expression, variations on which occur elsewhere in the *Shōbōgenzō*, reflects a common Zen usage — as, e.g., in the *Biyan lu* 碧巖錄 (T.2003.48:169a19, case 29):

> 没量大人語脈裏轉却。
>
> The immeasurably great person turns round [or is turned round] within the stream of words.

25 **"when the ocean dries up, it is not entirely to the bottom"** (*kaiko fujin tei* 海枯不盡底): Variation on the saying, "When the ocean dries up, you finally see the bottom"; see above, Note 5.

mud, is breathing it out within its nostrils.[26] "*I don't know what verse it is*" means *there is a dragon within the verse*. "*Everyone who hears it loses his life*": what a pity!

[61:8] {2:154}

いま香嚴・石霜・曹山等の龍吟來、くもをなし、水をなす。不道道、不道眼睛髑髏。只是龍吟の千曲萬曲なり。猶帯喜在也蝦蟇啼、猶帯識在也蚯蚓鳴、これによりて血脈不斷なり、胡蘆嗣胡蘆なり。乾不盡のゆえに、露柱懐胎生なり、燈籠對燈籠なり。

The singing that this dragon of Xiangyan, Shishuang, and Caoshan has been doing forms clouds and forms water.[27] *It does not talk about the way; it does not talk about the eyeball or skull*: it is just a thousand tunes, ten thousand tunes of the song of the dragon.[28] "*Still harboring joy*" is "*the croaking of frogs*"; "*still harboring consciousness*" is "*the singing of worms*."[29] By these, "*the blood vessel is not severed*," "*the*

26 **raising its voice and bringing it up within the mud** (*dei ri no sashō konen* 泥裏の作聲擧拈): The translation supplies the object pronoun "it," assuming the preceding "question" as antecedent. To "bring up" (*konen* 擧拈) is often used for a Zen master's presentation of a topic for comment; the word "mud" (*ni* 泥), while here no doubt suggestive of the "bottom" of the ocean, is often used in Zen for the sphere of the master's teaching activities.

27 **The singing that this dragon of Xiangyan, Shishuang, and Caoshan has been doing** (*ima Kyōgen Sekiso Sōzan tō no ryū gin rai* いま香嚴・石霜・曹山等の龍吟來): An attempt to accommodate in English Dōgen's surprising insertion here of the modal verb *rai* 來 (akin to the present perfect progressive), which would seem to require that *ryūgin* 龍吟 be taken as a subject-predicate construction.

forms clouds and forms water (*kumo o nashi, mizu o nasu* くもをなし、水をなす): Evoking the association of the Chinese dragon with clouds, rain, and bodies of water, no doubt here suggesting spiritual nourishment for those who study the dragon's singing.

28 **It does not talk about the way; it does not talk about the eyeball or skull** (*fudō dō, fudō ganzei dokuro* 不道道、不道眼睛髑髏): Dōgen here shifts into Chinese syntax. The translation takes "song of the dragon" as the unexpressed subject; "the way" (*dō*) here likely refers back to the opening question put by the monk to Xianyan in our quotation, "what is the way?"

29 **"the croaking of frogs"** (*gama tei* 蝦蟇啼); **"the singing of worms"** (*kyūin mei* 蚯蚓鳴): *Gama* ("frogs") is more commonly written 蝦蟆; the reader may supply for the verb *mei* 鳴 whatever sound she would like worms to make. Frogs and worms appear regularly in Zen sayings. The reference here is likely drawn from a verse by Dōgen's teacher, Tiantong Rujing 天童如淨 (1162-1227) (at *Rujing heshang yulu* 如淨和尚語錄, T.2002A.48:124a5-6), quoted in "Shōbōgenzō ganzei" 正法眼藏眼睛 (DZZ.2:122), composed one week before our text:

> 先師古佛上堂云、霖霪大雨、豁達大晴。蝦蟇啼、蚯蚓鳴。古佛不曽過去、発揮金剛眼睛。咄。葛藤葛藤。
>
> In a convocation, my former master, the Old Buddha, said,
> Heavy rain for days on end,
> Opening up to great clear skies.

bottle gourd succeeds the bottle gourd."[30] Since it is "not entirely dry," it is *the pillars conceive and give birth*; it is *the lanterns face the lanterns.*[31]

正法眼藏龍吟第六十一
Treasury of the True Dharma Eye
Song of the Dragon
Number 61

[Ryūmonji MS:]
爾時寬元元年癸卯十二月二十五日、在越宇禪師峰下示衆
Presented to the assembly beneath Yamashibu, Etsuu; twenty-fifth day, twelfth month of the junior water year of the rabbit, the first year of Kangen [5 February 1244][32]

[Tōunji MS:]
弘安二年三月五日、於永平寺書寫之
Copied this at Eihei Monastery; fifth day, third month of the second year of Kōan [17 April 1279][33]

于時文明十二庚子年二月初八日、於于越州吉祥山永平寺承陽庵書寫。
比丘光周
In the Jōyō Hermitage, Eihei Monastery, Mount Kichijō, Esshū; eighth day, second month, senior metal year of the rat, the twelfth year of Bunmei [19 March 1480]. Bhikṣu Kōshū[34]

Frogs croak and worms sing.
The old buddhas have never passed away;
They show their diamond eyes.
Drat!
Entanglements, entanglements.

30 **"the bottle gourd succeeds the bottle gourd"** (*koro shi koro* 葫蘆嗣葫蘆): In Dōgen's usage, the intertwined vines of the bottle gourd can stand for the relationship between master and disciple. Variation on another saying of Rujing 如淨 often cited in the *Shōbōgenzō*; see Supplementary Notes, s.v. "The bottle gourd vine entwines the bottle gourd."

31 **the pillars conceive and give birth** (*rochū kaitai shō* 露柱懷胎生); **the lanterns face the lanterns** (*tōrō tai tōrō* 燈籠對燈籠): The lanterns and free-standing columns of the monastic halls are common topics in Zen conversation, seemingly used especially to represent the concrete reality of the immediate surroundings; "pillars pregnant" (*rochū kaitai* 露柱懷胎), also commonly found in Zen texts, seem to function rather like the "dragon song in the dried-up tree" to suggest vitality within an apparently lifeless object. See Supplementary Notes, s.v. "Pillars and lanterns."

32 The Tōunji 洞雲寺 MS shares an identical colophon.

33 By Ejō 懷奘.

34 **Bhikṣu Kōshū** (*biku Kōshū* 比丘光周): Fifteenth abbot of Eiheiji (1434–1492?).

Treasury of the True Dharma Eye

Number 62

The Intention of the Ancestral Master's Coming from the West

Soshi seirai i

祖師西來意

The Intention of the Ancestral Master's Coming from the West

Soshi seirai i

Introduction

This chapter was composed early in 1244, probably at Kippōji, the monastery in the province of Echizen, where Dōgen was residing at the time. It occurs as number 62 of the seventy-five-chapter compilation of the *Shōbōgenzō* and number 52 in the sixty-fascicle compilation; in the Honzan edition, it represents number 67.

Like several of the *Shōbōgenzō* chapters from this period, the work is rather short. It focuses on a single episode in Zen literature: the famous problem, posed by the ninth-century Chan master Xiangyan Zhixian 香嚴智閑, of the person, hanging by his teeth from the branch of a tree over a thousand-foot precipice, who is asked Bodhidharma's intention in coming to China from India. Though this problem was very well known and often discussed by subsequent masters, Dōgen explicitly rejects the commentarial tradition as rarely having anything significant to say. At the end of his piece, he does, however, offer a remark on one comment, by the eleventh-century figure Xuedou Zhongxian 雪竇重顯.

Dōgen begins his own comments with the advice that the problem should be addressed by thinking of "not thinking" and thinking of "non-thinking" while "sitting fixedly" on the same meditation cushion as its author, Xiangyan — a reference to the famous statement, much admired by Dōgen, of Yaoshan Weiyan 藥山惟儼 (751-834) that his practice was "sitting fixedly," "thinking of not thinking." Dōgen then goes on to question the meaning here of the "person" and the "thousand-foot precipice"; to identify the person's mouth with the branch he bites, and the act of his questioner with biting the branch. In the end, Dōgen "solves" Xiangyan's problem by rejecting the distinction between the man's biting the branch and his opening his mouth to answer the question: both biting the branch and answering the question are Bodhidharma's intention in coming from the west.

正法眼藏第六十二
Treasury of the True Dharma Eye
Number 62

祖師西來意

The Intention of the Ancestral Master's Coming from the West

[62:1] {2:155}

香嚴寺襲燈大師＜嗣大潙、諱智閑＞示衆云、如人千尺懸崖上樹、口啣樹枝、脚不踏樹、手不攀枝、樹下忽有人問、如何是祖師西來意。當恁麼時、若開口答他、即喪身失命、若不答他、又違他所問。當恁麼時、且道、作麼生即得。時有虎頭照上座、出衆云、上樹時即不問、未上樹時、請和尚道、如何。師乃呵呵大笑。

Great Master Xideng of the Xiangyan Monastery (succeeded Dagui; known as Zhixian) addressed the assembly, saying, "A person is up a tree above a thousand-foot precipice.[1] His mouth bites the tree branch; his feet don't stand on the tree; his hands don't hang on a branch. Beneath the tree, all of a sudden, there is a person who asks him, 'What is the intention of the Ancestral Master's coming from the west?'[2] At that time, if he opens his mouth to answer him, he forfeits his body and loses his life; if he doesn't answer him, he fails his question. Tell me, what should he do?"

At that time, the Senior Seat Hutou Zhao came forth from the assembly and said, "I'm not asking about when he's up the tree; please tell us, Reverend, how about when he's not yet up the tree?"[3]

---

1 **Great Master Xideng of the Xiangyan Monastery** (*Kyōgenji Shōtō daishi* 香嚴寺襲燈大師): I.e., Xiangyan Zhixian 香嚴智閑 (d. 898); also written 香巖; disciple of Weishan Lingyou 潙山靈祐, known as Dawei 大潙 (771-853). This famous episode appears in several sources (see, e.g., *Jingde chuandeng lu* 景德傳燈錄 (T.2076.51:284b21-25), including Dōgen's *shinji Shōbōgenzō* 眞字正法眼藏 (DZZ.5:254, case 243). Parentheses in the quotation here are in the original text.

2 **"'the intention of the Ancestral Master's coming from the west'"** (*soshi seirai i* 祖師西來意): A favorite topic in Zen literature, often the subject of lectures and discussions. The "Ancestral Master" here is of course the first ancestor of Chan in China, Bodhidharma, said to have come from India in the sixth century. See Supplementary Notes, s.v. "Intention of the Ancestral Master's coming from the west."

3 **Senior Seat Hutou Zhao** (*Kotō Shō jōza* 虎頭照上座): Biography unknown. In the *Jingde chuandeng lu* version of this story, his name is given as Hutou Zhao 虎頭招; in the *shinji Shōbōgenzō* 眞字正法眼藏 version, he is identified simply as "Senior Seat Hutou" (*kotō jōza* 虎頭上座).

The Master gave a great laugh, "Ha ha."

[62:2] {2:156}

而今の因縁、おほく商量・拈古あれど、道得箇まれなり。おそらくはすべて茫然なるがごとし。しかありといへども、不思量を拈來し、非思量を拈來して思量せんに、おのづから香嚴老と一蒲團の功夫あらん。すでに香嚴老と一蒲團上に兀坐せば、さらに香嚴未開口已前に、この因縁を參詳すべし。香嚴老の眼睛をぬすみて覰見するのみにあらず、釋迦牟尼佛の正法眼藏を拈出して覰破すべし。

Although there have been many discussions and comments on the present episode, those that have said something are rare.[4] Generally speaking, they all seem to be at a loss. Nevertheless, when we take up "not thinking," when we take up "non-thinking," and think about it, we will naturally have concentrated effort on the same cushion as old Xiangyan.[5] Since we are "sitting fixedly" on the same cushion as old Xiangyan, we should go on to a detailed investigation of this episode *before Xiangyan has opened his mouth.*[6] Not only should we steal old Xiangyan's eye and look at it; we should take out "the treasury of the true dharma eye" of Buddha Śākyamuni and look through it.

[62:3]

如人千尺懸崖上樹。この道、しづかに參究すべし。なにをか人といふ、露柱にあらずば、木橛といふべからず。佛面祖面の破顔なりとも、自己他己の相見あやまらざるべし。いま人上樹のところは、盡大地にあらず、百尺竿頭にあらず、これ千尺懸崖なり。たとひ脱落去すとも、千尺懸崖裏なり。落時あり、上時あり。如人千尺懸崖裏上樹といふ、しるべし、上時ありといふこと。しかあれば、向上也千尺なり、向下也千尺なり、左頭也千尺なり、右頭也千尺なり、遮裏也千尺なり、那裏也千尺なり、如人也千尺なり、上樹也千尺なり。向來の千尺は、恁麼なるべし。且問すらくは、千尺量多少。いはく、如古鏡量なり、如火爐量なり、如無縫塔量なり。

"*A person is up a tree above a thousand-foot precipice*": we should quietly investigate these words. What is the "person"? If it is not a pillar,

---

4 **those that have said something** (*dōtoku ko* 道得箇): I.e. "those that are able to offer a meaningful remark."

5 **when we take up "not thinking," when we take up "non-thinking," and think about it** (*fushiryō o nenrai shi, hishiryō o nenrai shite shiryō sen ni* 不思量を拈來し、非思量を拈來して思量せんに): Allusion to the words of Yaoshan Weiyan 藥山惟儼 (751-834), in a dialogue found in the *shinji Shōbōgenzō* 眞字正法眼藏 (DZZ.5:196, case 129) and much cited by Dōgen; see Supplementary Notes, s.v. "Yaoshan's not thinking."

the same cushion (*ichi futon* 一蒲團): I.e., the same meditation cushion; in Zen usage, *futon* typically refers to a round cushion stuffed with rushes or cattails (*kama* 蒲).

6 **"sitting fixedly"** (*gotsuza* 兀坐): From the conversation, alluded to just above, on "thinking of not thinking"; see Supplementary Notes, s.v. "Sit fixedly."

we should not call it a stake.[7] Though it be the face of a buddha and the face of an ancestor breaking into a smile, we should not be mistaken about the meeting of self and other.[8] This place where the "person" is "up a tree" is not all the whole earth, not "the tip of a hundred-foot pole"; it is "a thousand-foot precipice."[9] Even if he drops off, he is within "a thousand-foot precipice."[10] There is a time of dropping, a time of climbing. Where he says, "*A person is up a tree above a thousand-foot precipice*," we should realize that this is saying there is a time of climbing. Consequently, *ascent is a thousand feet, descent is a thousand feet; left is a thousand feet, right is a thousand feet; here is a thousand feet, there is a thousand feet.*[11] "*A person" is a thousand feet; "up a tree" is a thousand*

---

7 **If it is not a pillar, we should not call it a stake** (*rochū ni arazuba, bokuketsu to iu bekarazu* 露柱にあらずば、木橛といふべからず): Likely, an allusion to a saying of Linji Yixuan 臨濟義玄 (d. 866) (see *Linji lu lu* 臨濟錄, T.1985.47:503c3-6; *Tiansheng guangdeng lu* 天聖廣燈錄, ZZ.135:687b17-688a2):

> 師因入軍營赴齋。門首見員僚。師指露柱問、是凡是聖。員僚無語。師打露柱云、直饒道得、也秖是箇木橛。便入去。
>
> The Master [Linji] once entered a military camp to attend a meal offering. At the entrance, he saw an officer. Pointing to a pillar, the Master asked, "Is this a commoner or a sage?"
> The officer said nothing.
> Hitting the pillar, the Master said, "Even if you had something to say, it's still just a wooden stake." Then, he went in.

See Supplementary Notes, s.v. "Pillars and lanterns," "Wooden stake."

8 **the face of a buddha and the face of an ancestor breaking into a smile** (*butsumen somen no hagan* 佛面祖面の破顏): Allusion to the famous story of the first transmission of the "treasury of the true dharma eye" (*shōbōgenzō* 正法眼藏) from Śākyamuni to Mahākāśyapa at an assembly on Vulture Peak. See Supplementary Notes, s.v. "Buddha faces, ancestor faces," "Break into a smile," and "Treasury of the true dharma eye."

we should not be mistaken about the meeting of self and other (*jiko tako no shōken ayamarazaru beshi* 自己他己の相見あやまらざるべし): The implication is unclear; perhaps simply that, even the accord between buddhas and ancestors, should be understood as a "person" meeting a "person."

9 **"the tip of a hundred-foot pole"** (*hyakushaku kantō* 百尺竿頭): A common expression in Chan literature for the extreme limit of religious practice, as in the saying, "proceed one step beyond the tip of a hundred-foot pole" (*hyakushaku kantō shin ippō* 百尺竿頭進一步).

10 **Even if he drops off** (*tatoi datsuraku ko su tomo* たとひ脱落去すとも): Taking *datsuraku* as an intransitive verb. Dōgen here seems to be playing with this term, more commonly used as a transitive verb meaning to "drop," or "slough off," something — as in Dōgen's well-known expression "body and mind sloughed off" (*shinjin datsuraku* 身心脱落); see Supplementary Notes, s.v. "Slough off," and "Body and mind sloughed off."

11 **ascent is a thousand feet, descent is a thousand feet** (*kōjō ya senjaku nari, kōge ya senjaku nari* 向上也千尺なり、向下也千尺なり): Dōgen switches into Chinese syntax for these and the following members of this list. The terms *kōjō* 向上 ("ascent") and *kōge* 向下 ("descent") can also be read as "above" and "below" — a sense suggested here by

feet. So far, a thousand feet should be like this. Now, what I ask is, "*what size is a thousand feet?*" It is the size of "the old mirror"; it is the size of "the brazier"; it is the size of "the seamless stūpa."[12]

[62:4]
口喃樹枝。いかにあらんかこれ口。たとひ口の全闊全口をしらずといへども、しばらく樹枝より尋枝摘葉しもてゆきて、口の所在しるべし。しばらく樹枝を把拈して、口をつくれるあり。このゆえに、全口是枝なり、全枝是口なり、通身口なり、通口是身なり。樹自踏樹、ゆえに脚不踏樹といふ、脚自踏脚のごとし。枝自攀枝、ゆえに手不攀枝といふ、手自攀手のごとし。しかあれども、脚跟、なほ進歩退歩あり、手頭、なほ作拳開拳あり。自他の人家、しばらくおもふ、掛虚空なり、と。しかあれども、掛虚空、それ喃樹枝にしかむや。

"*His mouth bites the tree branch.*" What is the "mouth"? Even though we do not know the whole mouth, the whole vastness of the mouth, we will know the location of the mouth by starting from "the tree branch" and "searching the branches and plucking at the leaves" for a while.[13] There is making a mouth by grasping the branch for a while. Therefore, *the whole mouth is the branch; the whole branch is the mouth.* It is the mouth throughout the body; it is *the mouth throughout is the body.*[14]

their pairing with the following "left" (*satō* 左頭) and "right" (*utō* 右頭). The two terms are sometimes used to indicate the two phases of the bodhisattva path: "ascending" toward liberation, and "descending" into the world for the sake of sentient beings.

12 **"the old mirror"** (*kokyō* 古鏡); **"the brazier"** (*karo* 火爐): Allusion to a conversation between Xuefeng Yicun 雪峰義存 (822-908) and his disciple Xuansha Shibei 玄沙師備 (835-908); recorded in Dōgen's *shinji Shōbōgenzō* 眞字正法眼藏 (DZZ.5:184, case 109) and treated in his "Shōbōgenzō kokyō" 正法眼藏古鏡 (DZZ.1:234); see Supplementary Notes, s.v. "Old mirror."

"the seamless stūpa" (*muhō tō* 無縫塔): I.e., a stone memorial for a deceased monk. Likely an allusion to another story of Xuefeng and Xuansha, found in the *shinji Shōbōgenzō* 眞字正法眼藏 (DZZ.5:158, case 60) and treated in "Shōbōgenzō juki" 正法眼藏授記; see Supplementary Notes, s.v. "Seven or eight feet."

13 **"searching the branches and plucking at the leaves"** (*jinshi tekiyō* 尋枝摘葉): Probably indicating something like "examining the particulars." Recalls lines from the famous poem *Zhengdao ge* 證道歌, attributed to the early Chan figure Yongjia Xuanjue 永嘉玄覺 (d. 723) (T.2014.48:395c21-22):

直截根源佛所印。摘葉尋枝我不能。

Just cutting off the root source — this is sealed by the Buddha;
Plucking at the leaves and searching the branches — this I can't do.

14 **It is the mouth throughout the body; it is the mouth throughout is the body** (*tsūshin ku nari, tsūku ze shin nari* 通身口なり、通口是身なり): The first clause could also be read "throughout the body is the mouth." Dōgen is likely recalling here the dialogue between Yunyan Tansheng 雲巖曇晟 (782-841) and fellow disciple Daowu Yuanzhi 道吾圓智 (769-835) regarding the thousand-armed, thousand-eyed Bodhisattva Avalokiteśvara (*senju sengen Kannon* 千手千眼觀音); quoted at *shinji Shōbōgenzō* 眞字正法眼藏 (DZZ.5:182, case 105) and discussed in "Shōbōgenzō Kannon" 正法眼藏觀

The tree itself stands on the tree; therefore, it says, "*his feet don't stand on the tree*," as if *his feet themselves stand on his feet. The branch itself hangs on the branch*; therefore, it says, "*his hands don't hang on a branch*," as if *his hands themselves hang on his hands*. Nevertheless, his feet still step forward and step back; his hands still make a fist and open a fist. We and others think at first he is "hanging in empty space"; but, can "hanging in empty space" compare with "biting the tree branch"?[15]

[62:5] {2:157}

樹下忽有人問、如何是祖師西來意。この樹下忽有人は、樹裏有人といふがごとし、人樹ならんがごとし。人下忽有人問、すなはちこれなり。しかあれば、樹問樹なり、人問人なり。擧樹擧問なり、擧西來意、問西來意なり。問著人、また口喻樹枝して問來するなり。口喻枝にあらざれば、問著することあたはず。滿口の音聲なし、滿言の口あらず。西來意を問著するときは、喻西來意にて問著するなり。

"*Beneath the tree, all of a sudden, there is a person who asks him, 'What is the intention of the Ancestral Master's coming from the west?'*" This "*beneath the tree, all of a sudden, there is a person*" is like saying "there is a person within the tree," as if it were a person tree. "*Beneath the person, all of a sudden, there is a person who asks him*"— this is what this is. Therefore, it is *the tree asks the tree*; it is *the person asks the person*. It is, *they raise the tree and raise the question*; it is, *they raise "the intention of coming from the west" and question "the intention of coming from the west.*" The questioner also asks the question with "*his mouth biting the tree branch*." If his mouth were not biting the branch, he could not be questioning: he would have no sound filling his mouth; he would have no mouth filled with words.[16] When he asks about "the intention of coming from the west," he asks while biting "the intention of coming from the west."

音. See Supplementary Notes, s.v. "His body throughout is hands and eyes."

15 **"hanging in empty space"** (*ka kokū* 掛虛空): Perhaps reflecting a verse on the wind chime by Dōgen's teacher, Tiantong Rujing 天童如淨 (1162-1227), cited in "Shōbōgenzō maka hannya haramitsu" 正法眼藏摩訶般若波羅蜜 and elsewhere in Dōgen's writings:

> 渾身似口掛虛空、不問東西南北風、一等爲他談般若、滴丁東了滴丁東。
>
> Its whole body, like a mouth, hanging in empty space,
> Without asking if the winds are from north, south, east, or west.
> Equally, for them, it talks of prajñā:
> *Di dingdong liao di dingdong.*

16 **he would have no sound filling his mouth; he would have no mouth filled with words** (*manku no onjō nashi, mangon no ku arazu* 滿口の音聲なし、滿言の口あらず): Dōgen is here playing with the colloquial expression *manku* ("filling the mouth"), which carries the sense "to speak at length" or, as we might say, "to say a mouthful." He will return to this term below.

[62:6]
若開口答他、即喪身失命。いま若開口答他の道、したしくすべし。不開口答他もあるべし、ときこゆ。もししかあらんときは、不喪身失命なるべし。たとひ開口・不開口ありとも、口喻樹枝をさまたぐべからず。開・閉、かならずしも全口にあらず、口に開・閉もあるなり。しかあれば、喻枝は全口の家常なり、開閉口をさまたぐべからず。開口答他といふは、開樹枝答他するをいふか、開西來意答他するをいふか。もし開西來意答他にあらずば、答西來意にあらず。すでに答他あらず、これ全身保命なり、喪身失命といふべからず。さきより喪身失命せば、答他あるべからず。しかあれども、香嚴のこころ、答他を辞せず、ただおそらくは喪身失命のみなり。しるべし、未答他時、護身保命なり。忽答他時、　翻身活命なり。はかりしりぬ、人人滿口是道なり。答他すべし、答自すべし、問他すべし、問自すべし。これ口喻道なり、口喻道を口喻枝といふなり。若答他時、口上更開一隻口なり。若不答他、違他所問なりといへども、不違自所問なり。

"*If he opens his mouth to answer him, he forfeits his body and loses his life.*" We should get familiar with the words here, "*if he opens his mouth to answer him.*" It sounds as if there must also be "*not opening his mouth to answer him.*" If such is the case, he should not "*forfeit his body and lose his life.*" Whether there is opening the mouth or not opening the mouth, they should not prevent "*his mouth biting the tree branch.*" Opening and closing are not necessarily the whole mouth, though the mouth does have opening and closing. Therefore, biting the branch is the everyday routine of the whole mouth; it should not prevent opening and closing the mouth.[17] Does saying "*he opens his mouth to answer him*" mean he *opens "the tree branch" to answer him*? He *opens "the intention in coming from the west" to answer him?* If it is not *opening "the intention of coming from the west" to answer him,* it is not *answering [the question of] "the intention of coming from the west."* And, since it is not answering him, this is "*his whole body protecting his life*"; we cannot say that "*he forfeits his body and loses his life.*" If he had already "*forfeited his body and lost his life,*" he would not answer him. Nevertheless, in Xiangyan's mind, he does not avoid answering him; it seems he has simply "*forfeited his body and lost his life.*" We should realize that *before he has answered him, he is guarding his body and protecting his life; once he suddenly answers him, he is flipping his body and saving his life.*[18] Thus, we know that *each person with a mouth full is the way:*

17 **everyday routine** (*kajō* 家常): A loose translation of a colloquial expression, meaning more literally something like "usual at home," most often associated with the daily fare of the household (what we might call "home-style" cooking) — as in the expression, often encountered in Zen texts, "everyday tea and rice" (*kajō sahan* 家常茶飯; see Supplementary Notes). Dōgen seems to be playing here with the notion that the branch is the everyday fare of the "whole mouth."

18 **flipping his body and saving his life** (*honshin katsumyō* 翻身活命): To "flip one's

he should answer him; he should answer himself; he should ask him; he should ask himself.[19] This is *the mouth biting the way*; *the mouth biting the way* is called "*his mouth bites the branch.*" *If he answers him, he opens a mouth on top of his mouth*; if *he does not answer him, "he fails his question,"* but *he does not fail his own question.*

[62:7] {2:158}

しかあればしるべし、答西來意する一切の佛祖は、みな上樹口啣樹枝の時節にあひあたりて、答來するなり。問西來意する一切の佛祖は、みな上樹口啣樹枝の時節にあひあたりて、答來せるなり。

Therefore, we should realize that all the buddhas and ancestors who answer [the question of] "the intention of coming from the west" answer it as they encounter the moment of "*up a tree, his mouth biting the tree branch*"; all the buddhas and ancestors who ask about "the intention of coming from the west" have been answering it as they encounter the moment of "*up a tree, his mouth biting the tree branch.*"[20]

[62:8]

雪竇明覺禪師重顯和尚云、樹上道即易、樹下道即難。老僧上樹也、致將一問來。

Chan Master Mingjue of Xuedou, Reverend Zhongxian , said, "To say something up a tree is easy; to say something down a tree is hard.[21] *This old monk is up a tree. Bring me a question."*

---

body" (*honshin* 翻身; also written 飜身) is a common Zen expression for spiritual transformation.

19 **each person with a mouth full is the way** (*ninnin manku ze dō* 人人滿口是道): A phrase in Chinese syntax that might also be rendered "each person with a mouth full is a saying." Similarly, the phrase translated below as "the mouth biting the way" (*ku kan dō* 口啣道) can be read "the mouth biting the saying." Dōgen seems to be playing here with two common Zen expressions: (1) "X is the way" (as in, e.g., "the ordinary mind is the way" [*byōjō shin ze dō* 平常心是道]); and (2) "though his mouth is full, he can't say it" (*manku dō futoku* 滿口道不得).

he should answer him (*tō ta su beshi* 答他すべし): The unexpressed subject of this and the following three imperatives could also be taken as "we."

20 **have been answering it** (*tōrai seru* 答來せる): Following Kawamura's edition here; some texts read *monrai seru* 問來せる ("have been asking it").

21 **Chan Master Mingjue of Xuedou, Reverend Zhongxian** (*Setchō Myōkaku zenji Jūken oshō* 雪竇明覺禪師重顯和尚): I.e., Xuedou Zhongxian 雪竇重顯 (980-1052). The saying here appears as a comment (*nenko* 拈古) on Xiangyan's case in the *Mingjue chanshi yulu* 明覺禪師語錄, T.1996.47:685c19-20.

[62:9]
いま致將一問來は、たとひ盡力來すとも、この問、きたることおそくして、うらむらくは、答よりものちに問來せることを。あまねく古今の老古錐にとふ、香嚴呵呵大笑する、これ、樹上道なりや、樹下道なりや、答西來意なりや、不答西來意なりや。試道看。

About this "*bring me a question,*" though we bring it with all our might, the question will arrive too late; regrettably, we will have brought the question after the answer [has been given]. I ask the venerable old awls everywhere in past and present: *Xiangyan's great laugh, "ha ha"* — is this "*saying something up a tree,*" or is it "*saying something down a tree*"?[22] Is it *answering "the intention of coming from the west,"* or is it *not answering "the intention of coming from the west"*? *Try saying something.*

正法眼藏祖師西來意第六十二
Treasury of the True Dharma Eye
The Intention of the Ancestral Master's Coming from the West
Number 62

[Ryūmonji MS:]
爾時寛元二年甲辰二月四日、在越宇深山裡示衆
Presented to the assembly in the deep mountains of Etsuu; fourth day, second month of the senior wood year of the dragon, the second year of Kangen [14 March 1244][23]

[Tōunji MS:]
弘安二年己卯六月二十二日、在吉祥山永平寺書寫之
Copied this at Eihei Monastery, Mount Kichijō; twenty-second day, sixth month of the junior earth year of the rabbit, the second year of Kōan [1 August 1279][24]

22 **venerable old awls** (*rō kosui* 老古錐): A common expression in Zen texts for a master. The term "old awl" may indicate a dull awl and, hence, represent ironic praise.

23 The Tōunji 洞雲寺 MS shares an identical colophon.

24 By Ejō 懷奘.

Treasury of the True Dharma Eye

Number 63

Bringing Forth the Mind of Bodhi

Hotsu bodai shin

發菩提心

Bringing Forth the Mind of Bodhi

Hotsu bodai shin

Introduction

This work was composed in the spring of 1244, at Kippōji, in the province of Echizen (present-day Fukui prefecture). It appears as number 63 in the seventy-five-chapter compilation of the *Shōbōgenzō*. The work is perhaps more often known as "Hotsu mujō shin" 發無上心 ("bringing forth the mind of the unsurpassed [bodhi]"), the title supplied in the sixty-chapter *Shōbōgenzō*, where it occurs as number 53, and used in the ninety-five chapter Honzan edition, where it represents number 69 (number 70 in the Iwanami and Shūmuchō versions). This text is not be confused with a second, undated essay bearing the title "Hotsu bodai shin" that is also found in the sixty-chapter compilation, as number 34, and reproduced as number 4 in the twelve-chapter *Shōbōgenzō*: despite the identical title, there is no overlap of its content with our text here.

The term *hotsu bodai shin* 發菩提心 refers to the aspiration of the bodhisattva to attain the supreme awakening of a buddha. In his treatment of this theme, Dōgen expands the sense of the term in two directions. On the one hand, from the very outset, he identifies the bodhisattva's aspiration with "trees and rocks," with "the whole earth," with the mind that is the reality of all things. On the other hand, he associates this aspiration with the concrete acts of Buddhist piety and practice — from offering alms, reciting a buddha's name, and sponsoring temple building, to entering the clerical order, practicing meditation, and preaching the dharma. Dōgen describes such acts as "unconditioned" and "unproduced," and strongly criticizes those Buddhists who dismiss them as merely good deeds generating merit for the agent. Fashioning an icon or erecting a stūpa, he says, is itself "making a buddha and practicing buddhahood."

The celebration here of the common acts of Buddhist ritual practice seems something of a departure from a teaching Dōgen elsewhere attributes to his master Tiantong Rujing 天童如淨: that offering incense, bowing, invoking the buddhas, practicing repentance, and reading scriptures are all unnecessary in the study of Zen. Some interpreters have suggested that the message of the "Hotsu bodai shin" was intended especially for the lay supporters of Dōgen's new temple, Daibutsuji, the ground-breaking ceremony for which took place only five days after the date of the text.

正法眼藏第六十三
Treasury of the True Dharma Eye
Number 63

發菩提心

Bringing Forth the Mind of Bodhi

[63:1] {2:160}
西國高祖曰、雪山喩大涅槃。

The Eminent Ancestor of the Western Land said, "The Snowy Mountains are comparable to the great nirvāṇa."[1]

---

1 **Bringing Forth the Mind of Bodhi** (*hotsu bodai shin* 發菩提心): Or "producing the thought of bodhi"; S. *bodhi-cittotpāda*. A standard expression in the literature of the Mahāyāna for the aspiration of the bodhisattva to become a buddha; often abbreviated, as in our text, to the expression "bringing forth the mind (or thought)" (*hosshin* 發心). The translation of *shin* 心 (S. *citta*) as "mind" (rather than "thought") here seeks to maintain lexical continuity with Dōgen's other uses of this term and reflects the common theological practice of treating *bodhi-citta*, not only as an aspiration for awakening, but as an inherent quality of awakening in the mind that the bodhisattva seeks to activate, or manifest. See Supplementary Notes, s.v. "Bring forth the mind."

The Eminent Ancestor of the Western Land (*Saigoku kōso* 西國高祖): A saying attributed to Baizhang Huaihai 百丈懷海 (749-814); see *Guzunsu yulu* 古尊宿語錄, ZZ.118:179b9; *Tiansheng guangdeng lu* 天聖廣燈錄, ZZ.135:682b5-6. "Eminent ancestor" here refers to Buddha Śākyamuni; the title is not a common epithet of the Buddha and is typically used rather for the founder of a lineage. "Western Land" is a standard term for India.

"The Snowy Mountains are comparable to the great nirvāṇa" (*Sessen yu dai nehan* 雪山喩大涅槃): Or, we might say, "the Snowy Mountains represent the great nirvāṇa." The term *Sessen* 雪山 ("snowy mountains") usually refers to the Himalayas; *dai nehan* 大涅槃 ("the great nirvāṇa") here, though likely indicating the *mahā-parinirvāṇa* of the Buddha, could also be taken as a reference to the sūtra of the same name (*Da banniepan jing* 大般涅槃經).

This saying, though attributed by Baizhang to the Buddha, does not seem to occur in any Buddhist sūtra. The most likely source would seem to be a parable in the *Nirvāṇa Sūtra* (T.374.12:554a27ff) in which seven men enter the Ganges River. Six of them for various reasons fail to cross, but the seventh crosses to the other shore of the river, climbs a great mountain, and attains bliss without fear. The sūtra then relates the seven men to seven types of *icchantika* (those who have "cut off their good roots" [*dan zenkon* 斷善根]) who seek to cross "the great river of birth and death," adding at the end (T.374.12:555a20-21),

> 善男子、彼岸山者喩於如來。受安樂者喩佛常住。大高山者喩大涅槃。
>
> Sons of good family, the mountain of the other shore is comparable to the tathāgata;

[63:2]

しるべし、たとふべきをたとふ。たとふべき、といふは、親曾なるなり、端的なるなり。いはゆる雪山を拈來するは、喩雪山なり。大涅槃を拈來する、大涅槃にたとふるなり。

We should realize that this compares what should be compared. To say that they should be compared is [to say] they are personally once, they are immediately obvious.[2] To take up "the Snowy Mountains" is "comparable to the Snowy Mountains"; to take up the great nirvāṇa is to compare it to the great nirvāṇa.[3]

[63:3]

震旦初祖曰、心心如木石。

The First Ancestor of Cīnasthāna said, "Each mind is like trees and rocks."[4]

---

attaining ease and joy is comparable to the buddha's permanently abiding; the great high mountain is comparable to the great nirvāṇa.

2 **personally once** (*shinzō* 親曾): An adverbial expression that Dōgen likes to use as a noun expressing intimate relationship; probably derived from a verse by Dōgen's teacher, Tiantong Rujing 天童如淨 (1162-1227), quoted more than once in the *Shōbōgenzō*.

3 **To take up "the Snowy Mountains" is "comparable to the Snowy Mountains"** (*iwayuru Sessen o nenrai suru wa, yu sessen nari* いはゆる雪山を拈來するは、喩雪山なり): This and the following odd sentence presumably represent the explanation of what Dōgen means here by "personally once" and "immediately obvious": i.e., that the Snowy Mountains and the great nirvāṇa are comparable to each other because they are "comparable" to themselves — or, we might say, each is just what it is.

4 **The First Ancestor of Cīnasthāna** (*Shintan shoso* 晨旦初祖): A continuation of the quotation from Baizhang Huaihai 百丈懷海, *Guzunsu yulu* 古尊宿語錄, ZZ.118:179b10; *Tiansheng guangdeng lu* 天聖廣燈錄, ZZ.135:682b6; the Chinese texts have "the First Ancestor of this land" (*cidu chuzu* 此土初祖). The reference is to Bodhidharma, the first Chinese ancestor in the Chan lineage; the term *Shintan* 晨旦 represents a transliteration of a Sanskrit term for China, *Cīnasthāna* ("Land of the Qin").

"Each mind is like trees and rocks" (*shinjin nyo bokuseki* 心心如木石): Or "each thought is like wood and stone"; though somewhat awkward, the translation "mind" here seeks to retain a consistent English rendering of *shin* 心 throughout. The expression "a mind like trees and rocks" (*shin nyo bokuseki* 心如木石) occurs often in Zen literature, including in the appended material to the *Erru sixing lun* 二入四行論 attributed to Bodhidharma. (Yanagida Seizan 柳田聖山, *Daruma no goroku: Ninyū shigyō ron* 達磨の語録:二入四行論, *Zen no goroku* 禅の語録 1:98.) Baizhang himself uses it in a description of the Chan teaching of sudden awakening (*Jingde chuandeng lu* 景德傳燈錄, T.2076.51:250a17-21):

> 僧問、如何是大乘頓悟法門。師曰、汝等先歇諸緣休息萬事。善與不善世出世間、一切諸法莫記憶莫緣念。放捨身心令其自在。心如木石無所辯別。心無所行心地若空。慧日自現如雲開日出。
>
> A monk asked, "What is the dharma gate of the sudden awakening of the great vehicle?" The Master answered, "First put to rest the various involvements and stop the myriad affairs. Do not recall, do not think about any dharmas, good or not good, mundane or

[63:4]

いはゆる心は、心如なり、盡大地の心なり、このゆえに、自他の心なり。盡大地人、および盡十方界の佛祖、および天龍等の心心は、これ木石なり、このほかさらに心あらざるなり。この木石、おのれづから有・無・空・色等の境界に籠籮せられず。この木石心をもて、發心・修證するなり、心木・心石なるがゆえなり。この心木・心石のちからをもて、而今の思量箇不思量底は現成せり。心木・心石の風聲を見聞するより、はじめて外道の流類を超越するなり。それよりさきは、佛道にあらざるなり。

"Mind" here is "mind is like."[5] It is the mind of all the whole earth. Therefore, it is the mind of self and other. Each mind of the humans of all the whole earth, as well as of the buddhas and ancestors, and of the devas and dragons of all the worlds in the ten directions — these are "trees and rocks"; there is no mind apart from them.[6] These "trees and rocks" are by their nature not cooped up in the realm of being and non-being, emptiness and form.[7]

With this mind of trees and rocks, we bring forth the mind [of bodhi], practice and verify; for they are trees of mind, rocks of mind.[8] Through

---

transmundane. Cast aside body and mind, and set them free, so the mind is like trees and rocks, without disputation or distinction. When the mind is without activity, the ground of the mind is as the sky; the sun of wisdom appears of its own, like the sun emerging when the clouds part."

Dōgen is likely alluding to Baizhang's text elsewhere in the *Shōbōgenzō*, in remarks such as "[the spiritual powers (*jinzu* 神通)] are the same as the Snowy Mountains, are like trees and rocks" (*dō Sessen nari nyo bokuseki nari* 同雪山なり如木石なり) ("Shōbōgenzō jinzū" 正法眼藏神通, DZZ.1:392), or "the Snowy Mountains have great awakening because of the Snowy Mountains; trees and rocks have great awakening through trees and rocks" (*Sessen no Sessen no tame ni daigo suru ari bokuseki wa bokuseki o karite daigo su* 雪山の雪山のために大悟するあり木石は木石をかりて大悟す) ("Shōbōgenzō daigo" 正法眼藏大悟, DZZ.1:97). For the association between "Snowy Mountains" and "trees and rocks," see Supplementary Notes, s.v. "Whether on trees or on rocks."

5 **"mind is like"** (*shinnyo* 心如): Dōgen is here playfully creating a compound expression from the subject and predicate of Bodhidharma's saying, the sense of which might be something like "mind as such," "mind as it is."

6 **as well as of the buddhas and ancestors, and of the devas and dragons of all the worlds in the ten directions** (*oyobi jin jippō kai no busso, oyobi ten ryū nado* および盡十方界の佛祖、および天龍等): The phrase might also be parsed, "as well as of the buddhas and ancestors of all the worlds in the ten directions, and of the devas and dragons." The "ten directions" (the four cardinal and four ordinal points, plus the zenith and nadir) is standard Buddhist usage for "everywhere."

7 **not cooped up** (*rōra serarezu* 籠籮せられず): A loose translation of a variant of the more common *rarō* 籮籠 ("nets and cages"), here put in a passive verbal form; see Supplementary Notes, s.v. "Nets and cages."

8 **we bring forth the mind [of bodhi], practice and verify** (*hosshin shushō* 發心・修證): I.e., we develop the aspiration for bodhi, practice on the bodhisattva path, and realize buddhahood.

the power of these trees of mind and rocks of mind, the present "*thinking of not thinking*" is realized.[9] Upon hearing the "sound of the wind" in the trees of mind and rocks of mind, we first transcend the followers of other paths; before that, it is not the way of the buddhas.[10]

[63:5] {2:161}
大證國師曰、牆壁瓦礫、是古佛心。

The National Teacher Dazheng said, "Fences, walls, tiles, and pebbles — these are the old buddha mind."[11]

[63:6]
いまの牆壁瓦礫、いづれのところにかある、と參詳看あるべし、是什麼物恁麼現成と問取すべし。古佛心、といふは、空王那畔にあらず、粥足飯足なり、草足水足なり。

We should try studying in detail: "where are these "fences, walls, tiles, and pebbles"; we should ask: "*what thing is it that appears like this?*"[12]

---

for they are trees of mind, rocks of mind (*shin boku shin seki naru ga yue nari* 心木・心石なるがゆえなり): Or "they are mind trees, mind rocks." The grammatical subject is unexpressed here; presumably, the activities of "bringing forth the mind, practicing and verifying" (*hosshin shushō* 發心修證) in the previous sentence.

9 **"thinking of not thinking"** (*shiryō ko fushiryō tei* 思量箇不思量底): An expression for meditation practice appearing prominently in Dōgen's writings; see Supplementary Notes, s.v. "Yaoshan's not thinking."

10 **the "sound of the wind" in the trees of mind and rocks of mind** (*shinboku shinseki no fūshō* 心木・心石の風聲): The translation seeks to preserve the concrete image of wind among the trees and rocks. The term *fūshō* 風聲, translated here as "sound of the wind," while sometimes understood as the "ways (*fū* 風) and words (*shō* 聲)" of the masters, is perhaps more simply taken as the "good news" (of the mind trees and rock trees). The term does not appear elsewhere in the *Shōbōgenzō*.

followers of the other paths (*gedō no rurui* 外道の流類): I.e., those of non-Buddhist religious traditions (S. *tīrthika*), a common pejorative in Dōgen's writings.

11 **National Teacher Dazheng** (*Daishō kokushi* 大證國師): I.e., Nanyang Huizhong 南陽慧忠 (d. 775), disciple of the Sixth Ancestor and the subject of a number of famous kōans. While a source of this exact phrasing has not been identified, the content reflects a well-known saying by Nanyang occurring in several Chan texts; see Supplementary Notes, s.v. "Fences, walls, tiles, and pebbles."

"the old buddha mind" (*kobutsushin* 古佛心): A common expression in Zen texts, it plays on the ambiguity between "the mind of the ancient buddhas (leading to Śākyamuni)" and "the ancient (i.e., eternal) buddha mind." See "Shōbōgenzō kobutsushin" 正法眼藏古佛心 for Dōgen's treatment of the term.

12 **"what thing is it that appears like this?"** (*ze jūmo butsu inmo genjō* 是什麼物恁麼現成): A variation on the question, in one of Dōgen's favorite stories, posed by the Sixth Ancestor, Huineng 慧能, upon the approach of his disciple Nanyue Huairang 南嶽懷讓 (677-744). Quoted at *shinji Shōbōgenzō* 眞字正法眼藏, DZZ.5:178, case 101; see Supplementary Notes, s.v. "What thing is it that comes like this?"

"The old buddha mind" is not on that side of King of Emptiness: it is "*the gruel is enough, the rice is enough*"; it is "*the grass is enough, the water is enough.*"[13]

[63:7]

かくのごとくなるを拈來して、坐佛し作佛するを、發心と稱す。おほよそ發菩提心の因緣、ほかより拈來せず、菩提心を拈來して、發心するなり。菩提心を拈來する、といふは、一莖草を拈して造佛し、無根樹を拈じて造經するなり。いさごをもて供佛し、漿をもて供佛するなり。一摶の食を衆生にほどこし、五莖の華を如來にたてまつるなり。他のすすめによりて片善を修し、魔に嬈せられて禮佛する、また發菩提心なり。しかのみにあらず、知家非家捨家出家、入山・修道、信行・法行するなり、造佛・造塔するなり、讀經・念佛するなり、爲衆説法するなり、尋師訪道するなり、結跏坐するなり、一禮三寶するなり、一稱南無佛するなり。

Taking it up like this, "sitting as a buddha" and "making a buddha" are called "bringing forth the mind."[14] Generally speaking, in the cases of [those] bringing forth the mind of bodhi, rather than taking it up from elsewhere, they bring forth the mind by taking up the mind of bodhi [itself]. To "take up the mind" means to take up "one blade of grass" and construct a buddha, to take up "a tree without roots" and construct

---

13 **that side of King of Emptiness** (*Kūō nahan* 空王那畔): An unusual expression, found only here and in the "Sansui kyō" 山水經 chapter; presumably derived from the common Zen saying, "that side of King Majestic Voice" (*Ion'ō nahan* 威音王那畔), used in reference to what precedes all differentiation; see Supplementary Notes, s.v. "Before King of Emptiness."

"the gruel is enough, the rice is enough" (*shuku soku han soku* 粥足飯足); **"the grass is enough, the water is enough"** (*sōsoku suisoku* 草足水足): The first phrase is a fairly common Zen expression meaning that the monk's meals are sufficient and suggesting, by metaphorical extension, that the monk's practice is complete. The second, somewhat less common phrase extends the image to provisions for cattle; its source here may be a verse by Haihui Shouduan 海會守端 (1025-1072) (*Chanlin paoxun* 禪林寶訓, T.2022.48:1019b25-26):

> 牛來山中、水足草足。牛出山去、東觸西觸。
>
> The ox enters the mountain;
> The water is enough, the grass is enough.
> The ox leaves the mountain;
> Butting to the east, butting to the west.

Dōgen also uses these two phrases together in a lecture (*jōdō* 上堂) in his *Eihei kōroku* 永平廣錄 (DZZ.3:200, no. 305).

14 **Taking it up like this** (*kaku no gotoku naru o nenrai shite* かくのごとくなるを拈來して): The grammatical object here is unexpressed; presumably, "the old buddha mind" of the preceding passage.

"sitting as a buddha" and "making a buddha" (*zabutsu shi sabutsu su* 坐佛し作佛す): More literally, given the double predicates in each phrase, something like "do a sitting buddha and do a making buddha." References to seated meditation, alluding to the story known as "Nanyue polishes a tile"; see Supplementary Notes.

a sūtra.[15] It is to offer sand to a buddha, to offer slop to a buddha.[16] It is to provide one ball of food to a living being, to offer five flowers to a tathāgata.[17] To practice a bit of good when encouraged by another, to bow to a buddha when charmed by a demon, are also to bring forth the mind of bodhi.[18] Not only this: [to bring forth the mind is] *to recognize that one's home is not a home, abandon the home and leave the home, enter the mountains and practice the way, proceeding by faith and pro-*

---

15 **"one blade of grass"** (*ikkyō sō* 一莖草): Likely reflecting a well-known Zen trope, invoked elsewhere in the *Shōbōgenzō*, that equates a single blade of grass with the sixteen-foot tall body of the buddha; see Supplementary Notes, s.v. "One blade of grass."

"a tree without roots" (*mu kon ju* 無根樹): A popular expression in Zen texts. Here, probably reflecting its use as a metaphor for the *bodhi-citta* in the *Avataṃsaka-sūtra* (*Huayen jing* 華嚴經, T.279.10:434a19-23):

> 非餘衆生善根處生。善男子、譬如有樹名曰無根。不從根生、而枝葉華果悉皆繁茂。菩薩摩訶薩菩提心樹、亦復如是無根可得。
>
> [The *bodhi-citta*] is not born from the good roots (S. *kuśula-mūla*) of beings. Good men, it is like the tree called "without roots": it is not born from roots, yet its branches, leaves, flowers, and fruit all flourish. Similarly, the tree of the mind of bodhi of the bodhisattva, the *mahāsattva*, is attained without roots.

16 **offer sand to a buddha** (*isago o mote kubutsu shi* いさごをもて供佛し): Likely an allusion to the story of a prior life of King Aśoka, when, as a boy, he offered sand to Buddha Śākyamuni; see, e.g., *Ayu wang jing* 阿育王經 (T.2043.50:131c9ff).

offer slop to a buddha (*shō o mote kubutsu su* 漿をもて供佛す): The term *shō* ("starch," "paste," "thick fluid") here is generally thought to refer to the water left from washing rice. Perhaps an allusion to a story recorded in the *Dazhidu lun* 大智度論 (T.1509.25:115a14ff), in which an old servant woman offers Buddha Śākyamuni "foul slops" (*chou pan dian* 臭潘澱) from the kitchen.

17 **provide one ball of food to a living being** (*ittan no jiki o shujō ni hodokoshi* 一摶の食を衆生にほどこし): A common expression in Buddhist texts for a simple act of charity; see, e.g., the *Dasheng bensheng xindi guan jing* 大乘本生心地觀經 (T.159.3:306a6-7):

> 於末法中善男子、一摶之食施衆生、以是善根見彌勒、當得菩提究竟道。
>
> During the final dharma, if a son of good family
> Provides one ball of food to a living being,
> By these good roots, he will see Maitreya
> And attain the ultimate path of bodhi.

offer five flowers to a tathāgata (*gokyō no ke o nyorai ni tatematsuru* 五莖の華を如來にたてまつる): Perhaps alluding to the story of Buddha Śākyamuni in a previous life as the Bodhisattva Māṇava, who offered five flowers to Buddha Dīpaṃkara and received a prediction of his eventual buddhahood; see, e.g., *Taizi ruiying benqi jing* 太子瑞應本起經 (T.185.3:472c18-473a22-23).

18 **To practice a bit of good when encouraged by another, to bow to a buddha when charmed by a demon** (*ta no susume ni yorite henzen o shu shi, ma ni nyō serarete raibutsu suru* 他のすすめによりて片善を修し、魔に嬈せられて禮佛する): While some commentators have tried to identify scriptural sources for these remarks, none seems particularly apt; and it may well be that here, as is likely the case in the succeeding examples of bringing forth the mind in this section, Dōgen has no specific passages in mind.

ceeding by dharma.[19] It is to build buddhas and build stūpas; it is to recite sūtras and recollect the buddhas.[20] It is to preach the dharma for the multitude. It is to seek a master and inquire of the way. It is to sit with legs crossed.[21] It is to make one bow to the three treasures.[22] It is to make one call, "*namo buddhāya.*"[23]

[63:8] {2:162}

かくのごとく、八萬法蘊の因縁、かならず發心なり。あるいは夢中に發心するもの、得道せるあり、あるいは酔中に發心するもの、得道せるあり、あるいは飛華・落葉のなかより、發心・得道するあり、あるいは桃華・翠竹のなかより、發心・得道するあり、あるいは天上にして、發心・得道するあり、あるいは海中にして、發心・得道するあり。これみな發菩提心中にして、さらに發菩提心するなり、身心のなかにして、發菩提心するなり。諸佛の身心中にして、發菩提心するなり、佛祖の皮肉骨髓のなかにして、發菩提心するなり。

In this way, the cases in the eighty-thousandfold aggregate of dharmas

---

19 **recognize that one's home is not a home** (*chi ke hi ke* 知家非家): This and the following three clauses represent variation on a standard trope in Buddhist literature describing the process by which one "leaves home" (*shukke* 出家) to enter the order. This same four-character phrase appears elsewhere in Dōgen's writings, but the more common expression is "believing that one's home is not a home" (*shin ke hi ke* 信家非家).

proceeding by faith and proceeding by dharma (*shingyō hōgyō* 信行・法行): Or "engaging in the practices of faith and the practices of dharma." The translation takes the two terms here as abbreviations of *zuishingyō* 隨信行 (S. *śraddhānusāra*) and *zuihōgyō* 隨法行 (S. *dharmānusāra*) respectively, a common distinction between two approaches to Buddhist spiritual development.

20 **build buddhas and build stūpas; recite sūtras and recollect the buddhas** (*zōbutsu zōtō suru nari, dokyō nenbutsu suru nari* 造佛・造塔するなり、讀經・念佛するなり): I.e., the standard practices of the pious Buddhist laity: to sponsor the making of icons and building of monuments, to read and recite scripture and invoke the name of a buddha. The last practice here, *nenbutsu*, may refer merely to recollection of a buddha but most often implies the vocal invocation of a buddha's name (*shōmyō* 稱名) mentioned just below.

21 **sit with legs crossed** (*kekka za* 結跏坐): I.e., in the traditional posture of meditation (S. *paryaṅka*), sometimes called the "lotus posture" (S. *padmāsana*); more commonly given as *kekkafuza* 結跏趺坐.

22 **make one bow to the three treasures** (*ichirai sanbō* 一禮三寶): I.e., pay obeisance to the three treasures (or "jewels"; S. *triratna*) of buddha, dharma, and saṃgha.

23 **make one call, "*namo buddhāya*"** (*isshō namu butsu* 一稱南無佛): I.e., an invocation of a buddha. The phrase here may reflect a passage in the *Lotus Sūtra* (T.262.9:9a24-25):

若人散亂心、入於塔廟中、一稱南無佛、皆已成佛道。

If any people, with distracted mind,
Enter a stūpa or shrine
And make one call, "*namo buddhāya,*"
They will all have attained the way of the buddhas.

are without exception bringing forth the mind.[24] There are those who gained the way having brought forth the mind in a dream; there are those who gained the way having brought forth the mind while drunk.[25] Or they bring forth the mind and gain the way amidst flying blossoms and falling leaves; or they bring forth the mind and gain the way amidst peach blossoms and jade bamboo.[26] Or they bring forth the mind and gain the way while being in the heavens; or they bring forth the mind

---

24 **the cases in the eighty-thousandfold aggregate of dharmas** (*hachiman hōun no innen* 八萬法蘊の因緣): I.e., the instances cited in Buddhist scripture. The term *hachiman* 八萬 is here likely an abbreviation for the more common *hachiman shisen* 八萬四千 ("eighty-four thousand"); *hōun* 法蘊 (S. *dharma-skandha*) is a standard expression for the collection of the Buddha's teachings.

25 **brought forth the mind in a dream** (*muchū ni hosshin su* 夢中に發心す): See Supplementary Notes, s.v. "Bring forth the mind." It is not clear that Dōgen had a particular case in mind here. If he did, one possibility might be a passage in the *Lotus Sūtra* (*Miaofa lianhua jing* 妙法蓮華經, T.262.9:39b20-c15), quoted in "Shōbōgenzō muchū setsumu" 正法眼藏夢中說夢, that offers the dream of a bodhisattva career as one of the benefits promised devotees of the scripture.

> 又夢作國王、捨宮殿眷屬、及上妙五欲。行詣於道場、在菩提樹下、而處師子座、求道過七日、得諸佛之智。
>
> They also dream of becoming the king of a country,
> Who abandons his palace and his entourage,
> And the most marvelous pleasures of the five senses;
> And, going to the place of awakening,
> There, beneath the bodhi tree,
> Then sits upon the lion throne
> And, seeking the way for seven days,
> Attains the wisdom of the buddhas.

brought forth the mind while drunk (*suichū ni hosshin su* 醉中に發心す): Perhaps an allusion to a story, retold in "Shōbōgenzō shukke" 正法眼藏出家, found in the *Dazhidu lun* 大智度論 (T.1509.25:161b17-23); see Supplementary Notes, s.v. "Bring forth the mind."

26 **amidst flying blossoms and falling leaves** (*hike rakuyō no naka yori* 飛華・落葉のなかより): The term *hike rakuyō* 飛華落葉 (more often read *hika rakuyō*) is a fixed expression in Japanese literature for the evidence of evanescence that prompts a turn to Buddhism. In Buddhist literature, it is especially associated with the "conditions" (*en* 緣; S. *pratyāya*) by which the *pratyeka-buddha* (*engaku* 緣覺) awakens.

amidst peach blossoms and jade bamboo (*tōke suichiku no naka yori* 桃華・翠竹のなかより): Likely allusion to two popular stories in the Chan corpus, which appear together in Dōgen's "Shōbōgenzō keisei sanshoku" 正法眼藏溪聲山色. The first concerns the monk Lingyun Zhiqin 靈雲志勤 (dates unknown), a student of Dawei Lingyou 大潙靈祐 (771-853), who gained an understanding upon seeing peach trees in bloom; see Supplementary Notes, s.v. "Peach blossoms." The reference to "jade (i.e., jade green) bamboo" recalls the famous story of the Chan monk Xiangyan Zhixian 香嚴智閑 (d. 898), who is said to have gained an understanding upon hearing the sound of a bit of debris strike a bamboo stalk; see Supplementary Notes, s.v. "A painted cake can't satisfy hunger."

and gain the way while being in the ocean.[27] All of these bring forth the mind of bodhi while being within bringing forth the mind of bodhi. They bring forth the mind of bodhi while being within body and mind; they bring forth the mind of bodhi while being within the body and mind of the buddhas; they bring forth the mind of bodhi while being within the skin, flesh, bones, and marrow of the buddhas and ancestors.[28]

[63:9]

しかあれば、而今の造塔・造佛等は、まさしくこれ發菩提心なり、直至成佛の發心なり、さらに中間に破廢すべからず。これを無爲の功德とす、これを無作の功德とす。これ眞如觀なり、これ法性觀なり、これ諸佛集三昧なり、これ得諸佛陀羅尼なり、これ阿耨多羅三藐三菩提心なり、これ阿羅漢果なり、これ佛現成なり。このほか、さらに無爲・無作等の法なきなり。

Thus, the present building stūpas, building buddhas, and the like, are surely bringing forth the mind of bodhi.[29] They are bringing forth the mind of "*directly attaining buddhahood*"; [they] should not be aban-

---

27 **while being in the heavens** (*tenjō ni shite* 天上にして): There are many accounts of Buddhism in the deva realms, and it seems impossible to say from this brief reference which, if any, particular story Dōgen may have been thinking of here. Elsewhere in the *Shōbōgenzō*, he mentions two unusual examples of teaching Buddhism in the deva realms. In the "Gyōbutsu iigi" 行佛威儀 (DZZ.1:65), he remarks:

> 祖宗いはく、釋迦牟尼佛、自從迦葉佛所傳正法往兜率天、化兜率陀天、于今有在。
>
> The ancestors say, "The Buddha Śākyamuni, after receiving transmission of the true dharma from Buddha Kāśyapa, went to the Tuṣita Heaven and converted the devas of Tuṣita, where he remains even now."

In the "Kobutsushin" 古佛心 (DZZ.1:89), he reports of Chan Master Nanyang Huizhong 南陽慧忠:

> いはんやまた帝釋宮の請をえて、はるかに上天す。諸天衆のなかにして、帝釋のために説法す。
>
> Moreover, receiving an invitation to Lord Śakra's palace, he ascended to the distant heavens, where amidst the devas, he preached the dharma for Lord Śakra.

while being in the ocean (*kaichū ni shite* 海中にして): Undoubtedly the most famous case of aquatic awakening is that of the daughter of the dragon king Sāgara presented in Chapter 12 of the *Lotus Sūtra* (*Miaofa lianhua jing* 妙法蓮華經, T.262.9:35b12-19).

28 **while being within the skin, flesh, bones, and marrow of the buddhas and ancestors** (*busso no hi niku kotsu zui no naka ni shite* 佛祖の皮肉骨髓のなかにして): The expression "skin, flesh, bones, and marrow" (*hi niku kotsu zui* 皮肉骨髓) occurs repeatedly throughout Dōgen's writings to indicate the essence or entirety of something or someone. The phrase derives from the famous story of Bodhidharma's testing of four disciples, to whom he said of each in turn that he (or, in one case, she) had gotten his skin, flesh, bones, and marrow. See Supplementary Notes, s.v. "Skin, flesh, bones, and marrow."

29 **the present building stūpas, building buddhas** (*nikon no zōtō zōbutsu* 而今の造塔・造佛): The implication of *nikon* 而今 ("the present") here is unclear: it may well mean simply "here, in the above"; but it is at least possible that it refers to such activities "nowadays," or specifically to the activities involved in the founding of Dōgen's Daibutsuji 大佛寺 at the time this text was composed.

doned halfway.[30] They represent unconditioned merit; they represent unproduced merit.[31] They are the contemplation of suchness; they are the contemplation of the dharma nature.[32] They are the samādhi of the assembly of the buddhas; they are acquiring the *dhāraṇī* of the buddhas.[33]

---

30 **bringing forth the mind of "directly attaining buddhahood"** (*jikishi jōbutsu no hosshin* 直至成佛の發心): An ambiguous expression that could be interpreted as "the aspiration directly to become a buddha," "the aspiration that leads directly to becoming a buddha," or "the aspiration that directly becomes a buddha." The expression "directly attain buddhahood" (*jikishi jōbutsu* 直至成佛) is commonly used in Buddhist literature in reference to the bodhisattva who will proceed to buddhahood without further rebirths in undesirable states.

should not be abandoned halfway (*chūgen ni hahai su bekarazu* 中間に破廢すべからず): Or "will not be abandoned halfway." Given the discussion that follows here, the translation takes *zōtō zōbutsu tō* 造塔造佛等 ("constructing of stūpas, constructing of buddhas, and the like") as the unexpressed subject here, a reading that suggests that these devotional practices should be continued throughout one's spiritual career. It is also possible to supply *hosshin* 發心 ("bringing forth the mind") as the subject.

31 **unconditioned merit** (*mui no kudoku* 無爲の功德); **unproduced merit** (*musa no kudoku* 無作の功德): Or, perhaps, the "merit (or virtue) of not doing"; the "merit of not making." Tentative translations of somewhat ambiguous phrases that can be understand either as "the merit (i.e., good karma; S. *puṇya*) that is without conditions (or production)," or as "the virtue (i.e., attribute; S. *guṇa*) of being without conditions (or production)."

32 **the contemplation of suchness** (*shinnyo kan* 眞如觀): I.e., the contemplation of things as they ultimately are. The term *shinnyo* 眞如 ("truly such") can represent the Sanskrit *tathatā* ("thusness"), often associated with the "emptiness" (S. *śūnyatā*) of things. This contemplation is not commonly mentioned in Zen literature and does not appear elsewhere in Dōgen's writings.

the contemplation of the dharma nature (*hosshō kan* 法性觀): I.e, the contemplation of *dharmatā*, the ultimate nature of things; roughly synonymous with the *shinnyo kan* 眞如觀, immediately above. As seen in our text, below, the terms *shinnyo* 眞如 and *hosshō* 法性 often occur together as a single concept, "the dharma nature of suchness."

33 **samādhi of the assembly of the buddhas** (*shobutsu shū zanmai* 諸佛集三昧): Presumably a contemplative state in which the buddhas are assembled before one. Perhaps reflecting a line in Chapter 27 of the *Lotus Sūtra* (*Miaofa lianhua jing* 妙法蓮華經, T.262.9:60b7-8):

> 其王夫人得諸佛集三昧、能知諸佛祕密之藏。
>
> The queen attained the samādhi of the assembly of the buddhas and was able to know the treasury of the secrets of the buddhas.

acquiring the *dhāraṇī* of the buddhas (*toku shobutsu darani* 得諸佛陀羅尼): Presumably one or more *dhāraṇī* preached by the buddhas. Possibly recalling the *dhāraṇī* acquired by the daughter of the dragon king alluded to above (section 8). Such spells taught by the buddhas are described in Chapter 26 of the *Lotus Sūtra* — e.g., at *Miaofa lianhua jing* 妙法蓮華經, T.262.9:58c4-5:

> 世尊、是陀羅尼神咒、六十二億恒河沙等諸佛所說。
>
> World-Honored One, this *dhāraṇī* spell has been preached by buddhas [equal to] the sands of sixty-two *koṭis* of Ganges Rivers.

They are the mind of *anuttara-samyak-saṃbodhi*; they are the fruit of the arhat; they are the realization of the buddha.[34] Beyond these, there is no unconditioned or unproduced dharma.

[63:10]

しかるあるに、小乘愚人いはく、造像・起塔は有爲の功業なり、さしおきていとなむべからず、息慮凝心、これ無爲なり、無生・無作、これ眞實なり、法性・實相の觀行、これ無爲なり。かくのごとくいふを、西天東地の古今の習俗とせり。これによりて重罪・逆罪をつくるといへども、造像・起塔せず。塵勞稠林に染汚すといへども、念佛・讀經せず。これただ人天の種子を損壞するのみにあらず、如來の佛性を撥無するともがらなり。まことにかなしむべし、佛法僧の時節にあひながら、佛法僧の怨敵となりぬ。三寶の山にのぼりながら、空手にしてかへり、三寶の海にいりながら、空手にしてかへらんことは、たとひ千佛萬祖の出世にあふとも、得度の期なく、發心の方を失するなり。これ、經巻にしたがはず、知識にしたがはざるによりて、かくのごとし。おほく外道・邪師にしたがふによりて、かくのごとし。造塔等は發菩提にあらず、といふ見解、はやくなげすつべし。こころをあらひ、身をあらひ、みみをあらひ、めをあらうて、見聞すべからざるなり。まさに、佛經にしたがひ、知識にしたがひて、正法に歸し、佛法を修學すべし。

Nevertheless, stupid people of the Small Vehicle say that constructing images and erecting stūpas are conditioned meritorious deeds; one should leave off and not perform them.[35] "To stop thinking and congeal the mind" — this is the unconditioned; the unborn, the unproduced — this is the true reality; the contemplations of the dharma nature and the

34 **mind of *anuttara-samyak-saṃbodhi*** (*anokutara sanmyaku sanbodai shin* 阿耨多羅三藐三菩提心): "The mind of unsurpassed, perfect awakening" — i.e., the perfect wisdom attained by a buddha.

fruit of the arhat (*arakan ka* 阿羅漢果): I.e., the last of the "four fruits" (*shika* 四果) of the *śrāvaka* path to nirvāṇa.

realization of the buddha (*butsu genjō* 佛現成): Or "the appearance of a buddha"; an expression not occurring elsewhere in the *Shōbōgenzō*, it could be taken to mean either "the attainment of buddhahood" or "the manifestation of buddhahood (or of a buddha)." The last reading is suggested by the line in the text below, "making buddha after buddha appear" (*butsu butsu o genjō seshimete* 佛佛を現成せしめて).

35 **stupid people of the Small Vehicle** (*shōjō gunin* 小乘愚人): The reference here to the "Small Vehicle" does not necessarily reflect the standard divisions between the Mahāyāna and non-Mahāyāna literature: Dōgen regularly uses the term *shōjō* 小乘 (S. *hīnayāna*) in pejorative reference to those versions of Buddhism that do not accord with what he considers the ultimate teachings of the tradition. Indeed, while it is not clear just whom he may have had in mind here, views of the sort he attributes to the "stupid people" can be found in the literature of the Mahāyāna (including Chan).

conditioned meritorious deeds (*ui no kugō* 有爲の功業): Also read *ui no kugyō* (or *kōgyō*). I.e., acts bringing forth good karma.

real marks — this is the unconditioned.[36] They have made this kind of talk their custom throughout past and present in Sindh in the West and the Land of the East. Accordingly, though they commit grave offenses and heinous offenses, they do not construct images or erect stūpas; though they are defiled in the thicket of the afflictions, they do not recollect the buddhas or read the sūtras.[37] This is a bunch that not only damages the seeds of humans and devas but discards the buddha nature of the tathāgatas.[38] It is truly sad that, though they have encountered the time of buddha, dharma, and saṃgha, they have become enemies of buddha, dharma, and saṃgha. While climbing the mountain of the three treasures, they have returned empty handed; while entering the ocean of the

---

36 **"To stop thinking and congeal the mind"** (*soku ryo gyō shin* 息慮凝心): Two terms implying a concentrated state of meditation, as in common expressions such as "stop thinking and forget objects" (*soku ryo bō en* 息慮忘緣) or "congeal the mind and enter samādhi" (*gyō shin nyū jō* 凝心入定). The terms occur as positive descriptions of meditation but are also used pejoratively in Zen texts to dismiss such practice. In his "Shōbōgenzō zazen shin" 正法眼藏坐禪箴, Dōgen strongly rejects what he calls there "the enterprise of stopping thinking and congealing in tranquility" (*soku ryo gyō jaku no keiei* 息慮凝寂の經營).

the unborn, the unproduced (*mushō musa* 無生・無作): "The unborn" (or "unarisen") is an exceedingly common term in Buddhism and Zen for the ultimate, "empty" nature of things; a near synonym for "the unproduced" and "the unconditioned" with, perhaps, the added connotation of "that which exists before anything arises."

contemplations of the dharma nature and the real marks (*hosshō jissō no kangyō* 法性・實相の觀行): Or "contemplation of the real marks of the dharma nature." I.e., meditation on the ultimate reality of phenomena. The translation follows Kawamura's punctuation, which suggests that *hosshō jissō* 法性實相 refers to two well-known meditations, *hosshō kan* 法性觀 and *jissō kan* 實相觀; alternatively, it could be read as a single expression, occurring often in Buddhist texts, for the ultimate truth.

37 **grave offenses and heinous offenses** (*jūzai gyakuzai* 重罪・逆罪): The former term is often associated with violations of the ten grave precepts of the Chinese *Fanwang jing* 梵網經: killing, stealing, adultery, lying, using immoral language, slandering, equivocating, coveting, anger, and false views. The latter term can refer most specifically to the five offenses (*gogyaku* 五逆; S. *pañcānantarya*) leading to the *avīci* hell: matricide, patricide, killing an arhat, injuring a buddha, and disrupting the saṃgha.

the thicket of the afflictions (*jinrō chūrin* 塵勞稠林): More literally, "the dense grove of dust and toil." The term *jinrō* 塵勞 is regularly used for the *kleśa* (*bonnō* 煩惱), or "defilements," that keep beings in saṃsāra. See Supplementary Notes, s.v. "Dust."

they do not recollect the buddhas or read the sūtras (*nenbutsu dokyō sezu* 念佛・讀經せず): Dōgen's dismissal here of those who do not engage in these practices seems in some tension with a remark by his teacher, Rujing 如淨, that Dōgen quotes with approval in several places; see Supplementary Notes, s.v. "Body and mind sloughed off."

38 **the seeds of humans and devas** (*ninten no shūji* 人天の種子): I.e., the karmic potential (S. *bīja*) for birth in the favorable states of human and deva.

three treasures, they have returned empty handed.[39] Thus, though they encounter the appearance in the world of a thousand buddhas and ten thousand ancestors, they have no prospect of attaining deliverance and have lost the means to bring forth the mind.[40] They are like this because they do not follow the sūtra scrolls and do not follow wise friends; they are like this because many of them follow other paths and false teachers.[41] We should quickly discard the opinion that constructing stūpas and the like is not bringing forth bodhi. Washing our minds, washing our bodies, washing our ears, washing our eyes, we should not listen to it. Following the sūtras of the buddhas and following wise friends, we should return to the true dharma and study the buddha dharma.

[63:11] {2:163}

佛法の大道は、一塵のなかに大千の經巻あり、一塵のなかに無量の諸佛ましします。一草一木、ともに身心なり。萬法不生なれば、一心も不生なり、諸法實相なれば、一塵實相なり。しかあれば、一心は諸法なり、諸法は一心なり、全身なり。造塔等、もし有爲ならんときは、佛果菩提・眞如佛性も、また有爲なるべし。眞如佛性、これ有爲にあらざるゆえに、造像・起塔、すなはち有爲にあらず、無爲の發菩提心なり、無爲・無漏の功德なり。ただまさに、造像・起塔等は發菩提心なり、と決定信解すべきなり。億劫の行願、これより生長すべし、億億萬劫、くつべからざる發心なり。これを見佛聞法といふなり。

In the great way of the buddha dharma, there is a chiliocosm of sūtra scrolls within a single dust mote; there are incalculable buddhas within a single dust mote.[42] One blade of grass and one tree are both body and

39 **the three treasures** (*sanbō* 三寶): I.e., the "buddha, dharma, and saṃgha" mentioned in the preceding sentence of the text.

40 **attaining deliverance** (*tokudo* 得度): Taken here in its sense "be able to cross over (to the other shore of nirvāṇa)," rather than its common use in reference to taking the precepts.

41 **they do not follow the sūtra scrolls and do not follow wise friends** (*kyōkan ni shitagawazu, chishiki ni shitagawazaru* 經巻にしたがはず、知識にしたがはざる): I.e., they do not learn from either Buddhist texts or Buddhist teachers; reflecting the fixed expression, occurring often in Dōgen's writings, "whether from a wise friend, whether from a sūtra scroll" (*waku jū chishiki waku jū kyōkan* 或從知識或從經卷). See Supplementary Notes, s.v. "Whether from a wise friend, whether from a *sūtra* scroll."

other paths and false teachers (*gedō jashi* 外道・邪師): Following Kawamura's punctuation, which treats the four glyphs as two separate terms; alternatively, they may be read as "false teachers of other paths" (*gedō jashi* 外道邪師): i.e., non-Buddhist teachers (S. *tīrthika*).

42 **a chiliocosm of sūtra scrolls** (*daisen no kyōkan* 大千の經巻): Or, as we might say, "a universe of scriptures." The term *daisen* 大千 is generally used as an abbreviation for *sanzen daisen sekai* 三千大千世界 (S. *trisāhasra-mahāsāhasra-lokadhātu*), the "three-thousandfold great thousandfold" that constitutes the domain of a buddha. A great chiliocosm equals one billion worlds (1000^3).

mind.[43] Where "the myriad dharmas do not arise," the one mind also does not arise; where it is "the real marks of the dharmas," it is the real marks of a single dust mote.[44] Therefore, the one mind is the dharmas; the dharmas are the one mind, are the entire body.[45] Were constructing stūpas and so on conditioned, the bodhi of the buddha fruit and the buddha nature of true suchness would also be conditioned.[46] Since suchness and buddha nature are unconditioned, constructing images, erecting stūpas and so on are not conditioned: they are the unconditioned bringing forth of the mind of bodhi; they are merit unconditioned and uncontaminated.[47] We should firmly believe that constructing images and erecting stūpas are bringing forth the mind of bodhi. From them will grow a vow [to last] *koṭis* of kalpas; they are bringing forth the mind that will not decay for

---

a single dust mote (*ichijin* 一塵): I.e., the tiniest particle, a "grain," an "atom" (S. *aṇu*). The term *jin* 塵 is also used to indicate a sense object (*kyō* 境; S. *viṣaya*); hence, this expression could also be rendered "a single object [of perception]." See Supplementary Notes, s.v. "Dust."

43 **One blade of grass and one tree are both body and mind** (*issō ichiboku tomo ni shinjin nari* 一草一木ともに身心なり): An odd claim that should probably be interpreted through the statement just below that "the dharmas are the one mind, are the entire body." See Supplementary Notes, s.v. "Body and mind."

44 **"the myriad dharmas do not arise"** (*manbō fushō* 萬法不生): Probably to be taken in the sense, all things are "empty" of real arising and ceasing; seen in a common saying in Zen texts, "When the mind is without concerns, the myriad dharmas do not arise" (*shin nyaku buji manbō fushō*). The translation here of *fushō* 不生 as "not arise" obscures its close semantic relationship with *mushō* 無生, rendered above (section 10) as "unborn."

the one mind also does not arise (*isshin mo fushō* 一心も不生): Or "a single thought also does not arise." A conclusion no doubt reflecting the common notion that the myriad dharmas all arise as the content of experience.

"the real marks of the dharmas" (*shohō jissō* 諸法實相): A popular phrase occurring widely throughout the Chinese Buddhist canon. The translation here takes it to mean simply "what the dharmas really are," but there is a long tradition of reading the phrase as "the dharmas are the real mark"—i.e., the phenomena of our experience are the ultimate reality.

45 **the dharmas are the one mind, are the entire body** (*shohō wa isshin nari, zenshin nari* 諸法は一心なり、全身なり): Presumably, a rephrasing of the previous claim that each grass and tree is the body and mind.

46 **the bodhi of the buddha fruit and the buddha nature of true suchness** (*bukka bodai shinnyo busshō* 佛果菩提・眞如佛性): Two common expressions for ultimate wisdom and reality; alternatively, the four glyphs can be read separately as "buddhahood, bodhi, suchness, and buddha nature."

47 **merit unconditioned and uncontaminated** (*mui muro no kudoku* 無爲・無漏の功德): The term *muro* 無漏 (S. *anāsrava*) refers to the undefiled states of the advanced adept (*sheng* 聖; S. *ārya*).

koṭis of *koṭis* of myriads of kalpas. This is called "*seeing the buddha and hearing the dharma.*"[48]

[63:12]
しるべし、木石をあつめ、泥土をかさね、金銀七寶をあつめて造佛・起塔する、すなはち一心をあつめて造塔・造像するなり。空空をあつめて作佛するなり、心心を拈じて造佛するなり、塔塔をかさねて造塔するなり、佛佛を現成せしめて造佛するなり。

We should realize that to construct a buddha or erect a stūpa by collecting wood and stone, piling up mud, or collecting gold, silver, and the seven treasures is to construct a stūpa or construct an image by collecting the one mind.[49] It is to make a buddha by collecting emptiness after emptiness; it is to construct a buddha by taking up mind after mind.[50] It is to construct a stūpa by piling up stūpa after stūpa; it is to construct a buddha by making buddha after buddha appear.

[63:13] {2:164}
かるがゆえに、經にいはく、作是思惟時、十方佛皆現。しるべし、一思惟の作佛なるときは、十方思惟佛皆現なり。一法の作佛なるときは、諸法作佛なり。

Hence, it is said in the sūtra, "*When I had this thought, the buddhas of the ten directions all appeared.*"[51] We should understand that, when one thought is making a buddha, *the "thought buddhas of the ten directions" all appear.* When one dharma is making a buddha, all the dharmas are making a buddha.

---

48 **"seeing the buddha and hearing the dharma"** (*kenbutsu monpō* 見佛聞法): A standard expression found throughout the Buddhist canon. The antecedent of *kore* これ ("this") here is unclear; presumably, "constructing images and erecting stūpas."

49 **gold, silver, and the seven treasures** (*kin gin shippō* 金銀七寶): A standard expression meaning "the seven treasures beginning with gold and silver." Lists in Buddhist scriptures of the seven precious substances (S. *sapta-ratna*) vary somewhat; a popular version in East Asia is that given in the *Lotus Sūtra* (*Miaofa lianhua jing* 妙法蓮華經, T.262.9:21b20-21): gold, silver, beryl, moonstone, agate, pearl, and cornelian.

50 **emptiness after emptiness** (*kūkū* 空空): Here, and in the following three clauses, Dōgen simply duplicates the glyph. The implied syntactical relationships are unclear; hence, the expression could be interpreted as "various emptinesses" ("minds," "stūpas," "buddhas"), "each individual instance of emptiness (etc.)," "emptiness upon emptiness (etc.)."

51 **"When I had this thought, the buddhas of the ten directions all appeared"** (*sa ze shiyui ji, jippō butsu kai gen* 作是思惟時、十方佛皆現): The speaker here is Buddha Śākyamuni. Reference to a passage in Chapter 2 of the *Lotus Sūtra* (*Miaofa lianhua jing* 妙法蓮華經, T.262.9:9c17-20), in which Śākyamuni explains why he decided to preach the three vehicles as an expedient device.

[63:14]
釋迦牟尼佛言、明星出現時、我與大地有情、同時成道。

Buddha Śākyamuni said, "When the dawn star appeared, I, together with the whole earth and sentient beings, simultaneously attained the way."[52]

[63:15]
しかあれば、發心・修行・菩提・涅槃は、同時の發心・修行・菩提・涅槃なるべし。佛道の身心は、草木瓦礫なり、風雨水火なり。これをめぐらして佛道ならしむる、すなはち發心なり。虚空を撮得して造塔・造佛すべし、渓水を掬啗して造佛・造塔すべし、これ發阿耨多羅三藐三菩提なり。一發菩提心を、百千萬發するなり、修證もまたかくのごとし。

Thus, bringing forth the mind [of bodhi], practice, bodhi, and nirvāṇa must be a "simultaneous" bringing forth the mind, practice, bodhi, and nirvāṇa.[53] The body and mind on the way of the buddhas is grass and trees, tiles and pebbles, is wind and rain, water and fire. To turn these into the way of the buddhas — this is bringing forth the mind. We should grab hold of empty space and construct a stūpa, construct a buddha; we should swallow a handful of the valley stream and construct a buddha, construct a stūpa.[54] This is bringing forth *anuttara-samyak-saṃbodhi*. It

---

52 **Buddha Śākyamuni** (*Shakamuni butsu* 釋迦牟尼佛): A description of the Buddha's awakening under the bodhi tree. This line is quoted in several chapters of the *Shōbōgenzō*, as well as in Dōgen's *Eihei kōroku* 永平廣錄 (DZZ.3:28, no. 37). Although the passage does appear in Chan texts from this period (see, e.g, *Jianzhong Jingguo xudeng lu* 建中靖國續燈錄, ZZ.136:36b17-18), it has not been located in any extant sūtra, and Dōgen's source for it is unknown.

"dawn star" (*myōjō* 明星): I.e., the planet Venus.

"the whole earth and sentient beings" (*daichi ujō* 大地有情): The translation follows a common interpretation of this phrase; it could also be parsed "sentient beings of the great earth."

53 **"simultaneous" bringing forth the mind, practice, bodhi, and nirvāṇa** (*dōji no hosshin shugyō bodai nehan* 同時の發心・修行・菩提・涅槃): Dōgen is here borrowing the term *dōji* 同時 ("simultaneous") from the passage just above and seems, in the process, to be shifting (or, perhaps, extending) its sense from the claim that all things achieve awakening with the Buddha to the view that all stages of the bodhisattva path occur at the same time.

54 **grab hold of empty space** (*kokū o sattoku shi* 虚空を撮得し): Perhaps reflecting the words of the Tang-dynasty monk Shigong Huizang 石鞏慧藏 (dates unknown), in a conversation recorded at *Shōbōgenzō* 眞字正法眼藏, DZZ.5:256, case 248, and discussed in the "Shōbōgenzō kokū" 正法眼藏虚空; see Supplementary Notes, s.v. "Nose."

swallow a handful of the valley stream (*keisui o kikutan shi* 渓水を掬啗し): Stream water figures in two sources much appreciated by Dōgen. One is the story, found in the *shinji Shōbōgenzō* 眞字正法眼藏 (DZZ.5:218, case 183) and discussed in "Shōbōgenzō dōtoku" 正法眼藏道得, of a hermit who drank from a stream. See Supplementary Notes, s.v. "Intention of the Ancestral Master's coming from the west." The notion of making is a hundred thousand myriad instances of bringing forth one instance of bringing forth the mind of bodhi. Practice and verification are also like this.

[63:16]

しかあるに、發心は一發にしてさらに發心せず、修行は無量なり、證果は一證なり、とのみきくは、佛法をきくにあらず、佛法をしれるにあらず、佛法にあふにあらず。千億發の發心は、さだめて一發心の發なり、千億人の發心は、一發心の發なり、一發心は、千億の發心なり。修證・轉法もまたかくのごとし。草木等にあらずば、いかでか身心あらん、身心にあらずば、いかでか草木あらん、草木にあらずば、草木にあらざるがゆえに、かくのごとし。

Despite this, to hear only that bringing forth the mind is one bringing forth without further instances of bringing forth the mind, or that the practices are incalculable while the fruit of verification is one verification — this is not hearing the buddha dharma, is not knowing the buddha dharma, is not encountering the buddha dharma.[55] The bringing forth the mind of a thousand million instances of bringing forth is definitely bringing forth one instance of bringing forth the mind. A thousand million people's bringing forth the mind is bringing forth one bringing forth the mind; one bringing forth the mind is a thousand million instances of bringing forth the mind. Practice and verification and turning the dharma are also like this.[56] Were they not grass, trees, and the rest, how could there be body and mind?[57] Were they not body and mind, how could there be grass and trees? This is so because, were they not grass and trees, they would not be grass and trees.

---

a buddha with mountain stream water is also reminiscent of a verse by the famed poet Su Shi 蘇軾 (Su Dongpo 蘇東坡, 1037-1101) that provides the title theme for Dōgen's "Shōbōgenzō keisei sanshoku" 正法眼藏溪聲山色 (DZZ.1:274):

溪聲便是廣長舌、山色無非清淨身、夜來八萬四千偈、他日如何擧似人。

The sound of the stream is his long, broad tongue;
The mountain form, his pristine body.
This evening's 84,000 gāthās —
How will I tell them tomorrow?

55 **one bringing forth without further instances of bringing forth the mind** (*ichihotsu ni shite sara ni hosshin sezu* 一發にしてさらに發心せず): The argument here is likely against the common use of "bringing forth the mind" in reference specifically to the initial aspiration of the bodhisattva.

56 **Practice and verification and turning the dharma** (*shushō tenbō* 修證轉法): I.e., the entire bodhisattva spiritual career, from practice, through awakening, to teaching as a buddha.

57 **Were they not grass, trees, and the rest** (*sōmoku tō ni arazuba* 草木等にあらずば): The subject here is unexpressed; presumably, "practice and verification" (as well, perhaps, as "bringing forth the mind"). The argument here points back to the statement in the preceding section, "the body and mind on the way of the buddhas is grass and trees," etc.

[63:17] {1:165}

坐禪辨道、これ發菩提心なり。發心は一異にあらず、坐禪は一異にあらず、再三にあらず、處分にあらず、頭頭みな、かくのごとく參究すべし。草木・七寶をあつめて造塔・造佛する始終、それ有爲にして成道すべからずば、三十七品菩提分法も有爲なるべし。三界・人天の身心を拈じて修行せん、ともに有爲なるべし、究竟地あるべからず。草木瓦礫と四大五蘊と、おなじくこれ唯心なり、おなじくこれ實相なり。盡十方界・眞如佛性、おなじく法住法位なり。眞如佛性のなかに、いかでか草木等あらん、草木等、いかでか眞如佛性ならざらん。諸法は有爲にあらず、無爲にあらず、實相なり。實相は如是實相なり、如是は而今の身心なり。この身心をもて、發心すべし、水をふみ、石をふむを、きらふことなかれ。一莖草を拈じて丈六金身を造作し、一微塵を拈じて古佛塔廟を建立する、これ發菩提心なるべし。見佛なり、聞佛なり、見法なり、聞法なり。作佛なり、行佛なり。

Pursuing the way in seated meditation — this is bringing forth the mind of bodhi. Bringing forth the mind is neither one with nor different from it; seated meditation is neither one with nor different from it; they are not at two or three times; they are not arranged.[58] Each should be investigated in this way.[59] If collecting grass and trees and the seven treasures to construct stūpas and construct buddhas were conditioned throughout and were not attaining the way, the thirty-seven factors of bodhi would also be conditioned.[60] Humans and devas of the three realms taking up body and mind to practice would all be conditioned and would have no ultimate stage.[61] Grass and trees, tiles and pebbles, and the four elements

---

58 **Bringing forth the mind is neither one with nor different from it** (*zazen wa ichii ni arazu* 坐禪は一異にあらず): The translation supplies "it," assuming the antecedent to be "pursuing the way in seated meditation" (and "bringing forth the mind" in the next clause); but this passage might also be translated in more abstract terms: "Bringing forth the mind is not [a matter of] oneness or difference. Sitting in meditation is not oneness or difference, is not two or three times, is not an arrangement. Each thing should be studied in this way."

not at two or three times; not arranged (*saisan ni arazu, shobun ni arazu* 再三にあらず、處分にあらず): The sense here is likely "do not occur one after the other, are not distinguishable as separate categories." The term *shobun* 處分, rendered here "arranged," typically means to "deal with," or "handle."

59 **Each** (*tōtō* 頭頭): The antecedent is not clear; presumably "seated meditation" and "bringing forth the mind," but it is also possible to take this as a more general reference: "each thing (or topic)."

60 **attaining the way** (*jōdō* 成道): A term typically referring to the attainment of bodhi, perhaps especially in the context of Śākyamuni's attainment under the bodhi tree.

the thirty-seven factors of bodhi (*sanjūshichi hon bodai bunpō* 三十七品菩提分法): A Buddhist technical term for a common list of factors in the attainment of bodhi. Dōgen discusses the list in the *Shōbōgenzō* chapter of this name.

61 **Humans and devas of the three realms** (*sangai ninten* 三界・人天): Or, as Kawamura punctuates, "the three realms, humans and devas."

and five aggregates, are equally only mind, are equally the real mark.[62] All the worlds in the ten directions, the buddha nature of true suchness, are all the "*dharmas abiding in their dharma positions*."[63] How could grass and trees, and the like, be within the buddha nature of true suchness? How could grass and trees, and the like, not be the buddha nature of true suchness? The dharmas are not conditioned, not unconditioned; they are the real marks.[64] The real marks are the real marks of suchness; suchness is the present body and mind.[65] We should bring forth the mind with this body and mind. Do not dislike walking on water and walking on rocks.[66] Just taking up one blade of grass and constructing a sixteen-foot golden body, taking up a single infinitesimal dust mote

---

would have no ultimate stage (*kukyō chi aru bekarazu* 究竟地あるべからず): I.e., would not culminate in buddhahood. "Ultimate stage" is a standard Buddhist term referring to the culmination (S. *niṣṭha*) of the bodhisattva path.

62 **four elements and five aggregates** (*shidai goun* 四大五蘊): I.e., the four primary forms of matter (S. *mahābhūta*), earth, water, fire, and wind, of which the physical world is composed; and the five "heaps" (S. *skandha*), form, sensation, perception, formations, and consciousness, into which the psychophysical organism can be analyzed. See Supplementary Notes, s.v. "Four elements and five aggregates."

only mind (*yui shin* 唯心): A version of the common claim, found throughout Zen (and other Buddhist) texts, that "the three realms are only mind" (*sangai yui shin* 三界唯心) or "the three realms are only one mind" (*sangai yui isshin* 三界唯一心). See Supplementary Notes, s.v. "The three realms are only mind."

63 **All the worlds in the ten directions, the buddha nature of true suchness** (*jin jippō kai shinnyo busshō* 盡十方界眞如佛性): The grammatical relationship between these two phrases is unclear. Perhaps the most likely choice is to read them with an implied conjunction; it is also possible to take them in apposition or to treat them as a single phrase ("the buddha nature of the true suchness of all the worlds in the ten directions").
"dharmas abiding in their dharma positions" (*hō jū hō i* 法住法位): Invoking a line in the *Lotus Sūtra* often cited by Dōgen. See Supplementary Notes, s.v. "Dharmas abide in their dharma positions."

64 **the real marks** (*jissō* 實相): I.e., are ultimately real. See above, Note 44.

65 **the real marks of suchness** (*nyoze jissō* 如是實相): Or "such real marks." No doubt a variant of the common *nyoze sō* 如是相 ("such marks" or "such a mark"). Though seemingly not particularly popular in Chan, this expression is not uncommon in Tiantai texts. It likely reflects the famous passage in Kumārajīva's translation of the *Lotus Sūtra*, from which Tiantai derives its characteristic teaching of the "ten suchnesses" (*jū nyoze* 十如是); see Supplementary Notes, s.v. "Only buddhas with buddhas can exhaustively investigate the real marks of the dharmas."

66 **Do not dislike walking on water and walking on rocks** (*mizu o fumi, ishi o fumu o, kirau koto nakare* 水をふみ、石をふむを、きらふことなかれ): The suggestion would seem to be, "do not disdain action in the world of grass and trees, tiles and pebbles." "Walking on water" (*risui* 履水) is commonly associated with the spiritual powers (*jinsoku* 神足; S. *ṛddhi-pāda*) of the contemplative adept, often occurring in the expression "walking on water as if it were earth; walking on earth as if it were water" (*risui nyo chi richi nyo sui* 履水如地履地如水).

and building a stūpa shrine for an old buddha — this is bringing forth the mind of bodhi.[67] It is seeing the buddha; it is seeing the dharma; it is hearing the dharma; it is making a buddha; it is practicing buddhahood.[68]

[63:18]

釋迦牟尼佛言、優婆塞・優婆夷・善男子・善女人、以妻子肉供養三寶、以自身肉、供養三寶。諸比丘既受信施、云何不修。

Buddha Śākyamuni said,[69]

Upāsakas and upāsikās, good sons and good daughters, offer the flesh of wives and children to the three treasures, offer the flesh of their own bodies to the three treasures.[70] *How could bhikṣus who have received*

67 **taking up one blade of grass and constructing a sixteen-foot golden body** (*ikkyō sō o nenjite jōroku konjin o zōsa shi* 一茎草を拈じて丈六金身を造作し): "A sixteen-foot golden body" refers to the body of a buddha (or an image of the buddha). The phrase reflects a well-known Zen saying; see above, Note 15.

68 **it is making a buddha; it is practicing buddhahood** (*sabutsu nari, gyōbutsu nari* 作佛なり、行佛なり: The second phrase might also be rendered "it is a practicing buddha," an expression appearing often in Dōgen's writings and the title theme of his "Shōbōgenzō gyōbutsu iigi" 正法眼藏行佛威儀. The rendering here tries to retain the verb-object construction of the preceding statements.

69 **Buddha Śākyamuni** (*Shakamuni butsu* 釋迦牟尼佛): The source of this quotation is unknown.

70 ***Upāsakas* and *upāsikās*, good sons and good daughters** (*ubasoku ubai zennanshi zennyonin* 優婆塞・優婆夷・善男子・善女人): I.e., the Buddhist laity. The terms "*upāsakas*" and "*upāsikās*" refer to observant laymen and laywomen respectively; "good sons" (S. *kula-putra*) and "good daughters" (S. *kula-duhitṛ*) are standard forms of polite address to the laity in Buddhist texts. Note that, though the compound grammatical subject here is gender inclusive, the offering of wives assumes a male donor. The practice of offering wives and children, as well as one's own body, for the sake of awakening is celebrated in various Buddhist texts. One example occurs in the *Lotus Sūtra* (*Miaofa lianhua jing* 妙法蓮華經, T.262.9:3a13-14), in a speech by the Bodhisattva Maitreya to which Dōgen will allude below (section 25):

> 復見菩薩、身肉手足、及妻子施、求無上道。
>
> Again, I see bodhisattvas,
Donating the flesh of their bodies, their arms and legs,
As well as their wives and children,
In their quest for the unsurpassed way.

The most famous example of the offering of wives and children occurs in the story of Śākyamuni's own previous life as the Bodhisattva Prince Sudāna (Xudana taizi 須達拏太子; better known in the Pali accounts as Vessantara), who practiced the virtue of charity by giving away his wife and children. (See, e.g., *Taizi xudana jing* 太子須大拏經, T.171.3:422a6ff.) The offering of one's own flesh is reminiscent of the well-known story in the *Prajñā-pāramitā-sūtra* of the Bodhisattva Sadāprarudita (*Changti pusa* 常啼菩薩), who offered to sell his body parts to a brahman in the course of his quest for the perfection of wisdom. (See, e.g., *Mohe bore boluomi jing* 摩訶般若波羅蜜經, T.223.8:419a1-10.)

these donations of the faithful not practice?[71]

[63:19] {2:166}
しかあればしりぬ、飲食・衣服・臥具・医藥、僧房・田林等を三寶に供養するは、自身および妻子等の身肉皮骨髓を供養したてまつるなり。すでに三寶の功徳海にいりぬ、すなはち一味なり。すでに一味なるがゆえに三寶なり。三寶の功徳、すでに自身およべ妻子の皮肉骨髓に現成する、精勤の辦道功夫なり。いま世尊の性相を擧して、佛道の皮肉骨髓を參取すべきなり。いまこの信施は、發心なり、受者比丘、いかでか不修ならん、頭正尾正なるべきなり。

Therefore, we know that making offerings to the three treasures of food and robes, bedding and medicines, monastic lodgings, fields and woodlands, and the like, is making offerings of the flesh, skin, bones, and marrow of "one's own body" and of the bodies of "one's wife and children."[72] Entered into the ocean of the merit of the three treasures, they are of one taste.[73] Since they are of one taste, they are the three treasures. The merit of the three treasures appearing in the skin, flesh, bones, and marrow of "one's own body" and that of one's "wife and children" is our exertion's concentrated effort in pursuit of the way. Now, taking up the nature and marks of the World-Honored One, we should study the skin, flesh, bones, and marrow of the way of the buddhas.[74] These "donations of the faithful" are bringing forth the mind; how could the bhikṣus who receive them not practice? They must be correct from head to tail.

[63:20]
これによりて、一塵たちまちに發すれば、一心したがひて發するなり。一心はじめて發すれば、一空わづかに發するなり。おほよそ有覺・無覺の發心するとき、はじめて一佛性を種得するなり。四大五蘊をめぐらして誠心に修行すれば、得道す、草木牆壁をめぐらして誠心に修行せん、得道すべし。四大五蘊と草木牆壁と、同參なるがゆえなり、同性なるがゆえなり。同心同命なるがゆえなり、同身同機なるがゆえなり。

---

flesh of their own bodies (*jishin niku* 自身肉): Or, "offer their own flesh." Here and below, the glyphs *jishin* 自身 may be taken either as "one's own" or as "own body."

71 **donations of the faithful** (*shinse* 信施): Or "donations [given] in faith."

72 **flesh, skin, bones, and marrow** (*niku hi kotsu zui* 肉皮骨髓): Here and below, Dōgen is playing on the expression *hi niku kotsu zui* associated with Bodhidharma; see above, Note 28.

73 **they are of one taste** (*ichi mi nari* 一味なり): From the common Buddhist metaphor that the Buddha's teachings are all of a single purport, as the waters of the ocean all have the single taste (S. *eka-rasa*) of salt. The grammatical subject here is unexpressed; presumably, the "offerings" of the preceding sentence.

74 **nature and marks of the World-Honored One** (*seson no shōsō* 世尊の性相): I.e., the essential nature (S. *svabhāva*) and phenomenal characteristics (S. *lakṣana*) of the Buddha.

Hence, as soon as one dust mote is brought forth, one mind is brought forth in accordance with it; once one mind is first brought forth, one emptiness is just barely brought forth.[75] In sum, it is when the conscious and non-conscious bring forth the mind that they can first plant one buddha nature.[76] When, turning the four elements and five aggregates, they practice with a sincere mind, they will gain the way; when, turning the grass and trees, fences and walls, they practice with a sincere mind, they will gain the way; for the four elements and five aggregates and the grass and trees, fences and walls, have the same study, for they have the same nature, for they have the same mind, the same life, for they have the same body, the same function.[77]

---

75 **one mind** (*isshin* 一心): The term seems multivalent here : "a single thought [of the dust mote]," "one mind [of bodhi]," "the one mind," "the whole mind," etc. The rather awkward translation seeks to preserve the text's play with the verb *hotsu* 發, as both "to produce" and "to occur," and with the terms *jin* 塵, as both "particle" and "object," and *shin* 心, as both "mind" and "thought." For *jin* 塵, see above, Note 42.

one emptiness (*ikkū* 一空): Perhaps, one of the multiple emptinesses taken up to make a buddha in section 12; perhaps, the whole of empty space pinched to make a buddha or stūpa in section 15. The sense of *wazuka ni* わづかに (tentatively rendered "just barely") here is uncertain.

76 **conscious and non-conscious** (*ukaku mukaku* 有覺・無覺): Read here as equivalent to "sentient and insentient" (*ujō mujō* 有情無情) (as, e.g., at *Zongjing lu* 宗鏡錄, T.2016.48:853a6-7) — perhaps in reference to the "mind" and "dust mote," respectively. This pair of terms occurs several times in the *Shōbōgenzō*, usually in the sense "awakened and non-awakened." Some manuscript witnesses read here *ugaku mugaku* 有學無學 ("student and non-student" — i.e., one in training on the Buddhist path and one who has completed training).

can first plant one buddha nature (*hajimete ichi busshō o shutoku su* はじめて一佛性を種得す): The figure of "planting" the buddha nature here likely serves to introduce the examples of horticultural practice in the following paragraph. The notion that the buddha nature is "planted" both before and after completion of training seems akin to Dōgen's treatment of the concept elsewhere in the *Shōbōgenzō* — e.g., in "Hakujushi" 柏樹子 (DZZ.1:442):

> 佛性は成佛以後の莊嚴なり、さらに成佛と同生同參する佛性もあるべし。
>
> The buddha nature is an adornment after one attains buddhahood; further, there must be a buddha nature that is born together and studies together with attaining buddhahood.

77 **the same study** (*dōsan* 同參): Or "study together"; a term usually referring to fellow students. The translation seeks to retain the parallel with the following nominal forms, "same nature" (*dōshō* 同性), etc.

the same function (*dōki* 同機): A tentative translation of an unusual expression, not occurring elsewhere in Dōgen's writing. The glyph *ki* 機 may also refer to the "faculties" or "abilities" of students.

[63:21]

これによりて、佛祖の會下、おほく拈草木心の辦道あり、これ發菩提心の様子なり。五祖は、一時の栽松道者なり、臨濟は、黄檗山の栽杉松の功夫あり、洞山には、劉氏翁あり、栽松す。かれこれ、松栢の操節を拈じて、佛祖の眼睛、抉出するなり。これ弄活眼睛のちから、開明眼睛なることを見成するなり。

Accordingly, in the communities of the buddhas and ancestors, there are many who pursued the way by taking up the mind of grass and trees; this is the form of bringing forth the mind of bodhi.[78] The Fifth Ancestor was once a practitioner who grew pines.[79] Linji worked at planting fir and pine on Mount Huangbo.[80] On Dongshan, there was old Mr. Liu, who planted pines.[81] In this, they take up the discipline of pine and cypress and gouge out the eye of the buddhas and ancestors; in this, they show that the power to play with the living eye is opening the clear eye.[82]

---

78 **this is the form of bringing forth the mind of bodhi** (*kore hotsu bodai shin no yōsu nari* これ發菩提心の様子なり): Or "this is a form of bringing forth the mind of bodhi." The term *yōsu* 様子, occurring often in Dōgen's writing, carries the sense both of the "shape" of something and a "model" of something.

79 **The Fifth Ancestor was once a practitioner who grew pines** (*goso wa, ichiji no saishō dōsha nari* 五祖は、一時の栽松道者なり): Reference to a story about the Fifth Ancestor of Chan in China, Daman Hongren 大滿弘忍 (602-675), recounted in "Shōbōgenzō busshō" 正法眼藏佛性. The term *dōsha* 道者 ("person of the way") may refer to any Buddhist (or Daoist) practitioner or to a Buddhist acolyte.

80 **Linji worked at planting fir and pine on Mount Huangbo** (*Rinzai wa, Ōbakusan no sai sanshō no kufū ari* 臨濟は、黄檗山の栽杉松の功夫あり): Reference to a story about the famed Chan master Linji Yixuan 臨濟義玄 (d. 866), recounted in "Shōbōgenzō gyōji" 正法眼藏行持. The term *sanmatsu* 杉松 ("fir [or cedar] and pine") may also be taken simply as a generic term for conifers.

81 **On Dongshan, there was old Mr. Liu, who planted pines** (*Tōzan ni wa, Ryū shi ō ari, saishō su* 洞山には、劉氏翁あり、栽松す): Old man Liu figures in the life of Chan master Dongshan Siqian 洞山師虔 (d. 904), as recorded in the *Jingde chuandeng lu* 景德傳燈錄 (T.2076.51:338b24-27):

> 師在洞山栽松。有劉翁者從師求偈。師作偈曰、長長三尺餘、鬱鬱覆荒草、不知何代人、得見此松老。
>
> The Master [Dongshan Siqian] was on Mt. Dong planting pines. A certain old man Liu asked the Master for a gāthā. The Master composed a gāthā saying,
>
> Tall, tall, more than three feet;
> Dense, dense, covered with weeds.
> Who knows what generation
> Will see these pines grow old.

82 **discipline of pine and cypress** (*shō haku no sōsetsu* 松栢の操節): The term *sōsetsu* 操節 ("discipline") does not occur elsewhere in Dōgen's writings; likely synonymous with the more common *sōgyō* 操行 ("restrained conduct"). The notion of a discipline of cypress is reminiscent of Zhaozhou's 趙州 famous "cypress at the front of the garden" (*teizen hakujushi* 庭前柏樹子), which Dōgen treats at length in his "Shōbōgenzō hakujushi" 正法眼藏柏樹子. See Supplementary Notes, s.v. "Cypress tree at the front of the garden."

[63:22]

造塔・造佛等は、弄眼睛なり、喫發心なり、使發心なり。造塔等の眼睛をえざるがごときは、佛祖の成道あらざるなり。造佛の眼睛をえてのちに、作佛作祖するなり。造塔等はつひに塵土に化す、眞實の功德にあらず、無生の修練は堅牢なり、塵埃に染汚せられず、といふは、佛語にあらず。塔婆、もし塵土に化すといはば、無生もまた塵土に化するなり。無生、もし塵土に化せずば、塔婆また塵土に化すべからず。遮裡是甚麼處在、說有爲說無爲なり。

To construct stūpas, construct buddhas, and the like, is to play with the eye, is to taste bringing forth the mind, is to deploy bringing forth the mind.[83] Those who have not acquired the eye of constructing stūpas and the like have not attained the way of the buddhas and ancestors. It is after we acquire the eye of constructing buddhas that we make a buddha and make an ancestor. To say that constructing stūpas and the like will eventually turn to dust, that it is not the true merit; to say that training in the unborn is firm and stable, that it is not defiled by dust — these are not the words of a buddha.[84] If we say that stūpas turn to dust, then the unborn will also turn to dust. If the unborn does not turn to dust, the

---

gouge out the eye of the buddhas and ancestors (*busso no ganzei kesshutsu su* 佛祖の眼睛抉出す): An idiomatic expression for getting the point of Zen, used interchangeably with the more common *tosshutsu ganzei* 突出眼睛 ("poke out the eye"); see Supplementary Notes, s.v. "Eye," and "Gouge out Bodhidharma's eye."

in this, they show that the power to play with the living eye is opening the clear eye (*kore rō katsu ganzei no chikara, kai mei ganzei naru koto o genjō suru nari* これ弄活眼睛のちから、開明眼睛なることを見成するなり). This sentence might also be parsed, "This reveals the power to play with the living eye, the opening of the clear eye." The expression "to open the eye" (*kaigen* 開眼) typically refers to the final act of consecrating a buddhist icon, though Chan masters regularly use it as a metaphor for spiritual awakening.

83 **taste bringing forth the mind** (*kitsu hosshin* 喫發心); **deploy bringing forth the mind** (*shi hosshin* 使發心): Tentative translations of two odd expressions. The verbs *kitsu* 喫 ("to eat" or "to drink"; "to endure") and *shi* 使 ("to use," "to employ," "to send off," etc.) might be taken as passive and causative markers respectively; hence "to suffer bringing forth the mind"; "to cause bringing forth the mind."

84 **not defiled by dust** (*jin'ai ni zenna serarezu* 塵埃に染汚せられず): The image shifts here from the "dust" (*jindo* 塵土) that remains from the ruined stūpa to the "dust" (*jin'ai* 塵埃) that defiles the mind; possibly recalling the famous verse attributed to the Sixth Ancestor, Huineng 慧能; see, e.g., *Tiansheng guangdeng lu* 天聖廣燈錄, ZZ.135:645a6-7:

菩提本無樹、明鏡亦非臺。本來無一物、何處有塵埃。

Bodhi originally has no tree,
The bright mirror, no stand.
From the beginning, not one thing;
Where is there any dust?

See Supplementary Notes, s.v. "Bright mirror," and "Dust."

stūpas also will not turn to dust. *Where are we here, that we're talking about "conditioned" and talking about "unconditioned"?*[85]

[63:23] {2:167}
經曰、菩薩於生死、最初發心時、一向求菩提、堅固不可動。彼一念功德、深廣無涯際、如來分別説、窮劫不能盡。

It is said in a sūtra,[86]

When the bodhisattva, in the midst of birth and death,
First brings forth the mind,
Solely seeking bodhi,
Firmly and immovably,
The merit of that one thought
Is so deep, broad, and boundless that,
Were the Tathāgata to explain its particulars,
He could not exhaust them by the end of the kalpa.

[63:24]
あきらかにしるべし、生死を拈來して發心する、これ一向求菩提なり。彼一念は、一草一木とおなじかるべし、一生一死なるがゆえに。しかあれども、その功德の深も無涯際なり、廣も無涯際なり。窮劫を言語として、如來、これを分別すとも、盡期あるべからず。海かれてなほ底のこり、人は死すとも心のこるべきがゆえに、不能盡なり。彼一念の深廣無涯際なるがごとく、一草一木・一石一瓦の深廣も、無涯際なり。一草一石、もし七尺八尺なれば、彼一念も七尺八尺なり、發心もまた七尺八尺なり。

We should clearly recognize that taking up birth and death and bringing forth the mind is "solely seeking bodhi." "That one thought" must be the same as one blade of grass, one tree; for it is one "birth," one "death." Nevertheless, the "depth" of its "merit" is "boundless," the "breadth" of its "merit" is "boundless." Even if "the Tathāgata" were to "describe its particulars" in the language of the "end of the kalpa," he could not expect to exhaust them.[87] He could not exhaust them because, "when the ocean dries up," the bottom remains; "though a person dies," the mind

85 **Where are we here, that we're talking about "conditioned" and talking about "unconditioned"?** (*shari ze jinmo shozai, setsu ui setsu mui nari* 遮裡是甚麼處在、説有爲説無爲なり): Dōgen here slips into Chinese to ask a common form of Chan rhetorical question.

86 **a sūtra** (*kyō* 經): From the *Avataṃsaka-sūtra* (*Huayan jing* 華嚴經, T.278.9:432c29-433a3).

87 **in the language of the "end of the kalpa"** (*gūgō o gongo toshite* 窮劫を言語として): A tentative translation of an odd play on the sūtra passage; literally, "taking 'the end of the kalpa' as his words." Dōgen seems to want to parse the Chinese phrase *rulai fenbie shuo qiong jie bu neng jin* 如來分別説窮劫不能盡 ("Were the Tathāgata to explain its particulars, he could not exhaust them by the end of the kalpa") as if *qiong jie* 窮劫 ("end of the kalpa") were the object of the predicate *shuo* 説 ("to explain"). Possibly the sense is, "to speak from the ultimate position."

remains.[88] Just as the depth and breadth of "that one thought" are boundless, so the depth and breadth of one blade of grass, one tree, one rock, one tile, are also boundless. When one blade of grass, one rock, is seven feet or eight feet, "that one thought" is also seven feet or eight feet, and bringing forth the mind is likewise seven feet or eight feet.[89]

[63:25] {2:168}

しかあればすなはち、入於深山、思惟佛道は、容易なるべし、造塔・造佛は、甚難なり。ともに精進無怠より成熟すといへども、心を拈來すると、心に拈來せらるると、はるかにことなるべし。かくのごとくの發菩提心、つもりて佛祖現成するなり。

Therefore, "*entering the deep mountains and thinking on the way of the buddhas*" is easy; building stūpas and building buddhas is extremely difficult.[90] Both may be developed from vigor and perseverance, but there is a great difference between taking up the mind and being taken up by the mind. As this kind of bringing forth the mind of bodhi builds up, the buddhas and ancestors appear.

---

88 **"when the ocean dries up," the bottom remains; "though a person dies," the mind remains** (*kai karete nao soko nokori, hito wa shisu tomo shin nokoru beki* 海かれてなほ底のこり、人は死すとも心のこるべき): Presumably, we are to understand "mind" here as "the mind of bodhi." Dōgen is playing here, as he does elsewhere in the *Shōbōgenzō*, with a saying, drawn from a verse by the poet Du Xunhe 杜荀鶴 (846-907), that occurs often in Chan literature. See, e.g., *Zongjing lu* 宗鏡錄, T.2016.48:564b12:

海枯終見底、人死不知心。

When the ocean dries up, we finally see the bottom;
When a person dies, we do not know his mind.

89 **seven feet or eight feet** (*shichi shaku hachi shaku* 七尺八尺): The use of this measurement occurs regularly in the *Shōbōgenzō*, generally in ironic reference to something immeasurable. Given his identification of bringing forth the mind with constructing a stūpa, Dōgen may here be recalling in particular Chan Master Xuansha's 玄沙 proposal, cited in the *shinji Shōbōgenzō* 眞字正法眼藏 (DZZ.5:158, case 60) for a seamless stūpa of seven or eight feet; see Supplementary Notes, s.v. "Seven feet or eight feet."

90 **"entering the deep mountains and thinking on the way of the buddhas"** (*nyū o shinzan, shiyui butsudō* 入於深山、思惟佛道): I.e., the practices of the renunciant. From the *Lotus Sūtra* (*Miaofa lianhua jing* 妙法蓮華經, T.262.9:3a20-22):

又見菩薩、勇猛精進、入於深山、思惟佛道。又見離欲、常處空閑、深修禪定、得五神通。

And I [Maitreya] see bodhisattvas,
Courageous and vigorous,
Entering the deep mountains
And thinking on the way of the buddhas.
And I see them, free from desire,
Dwelling always in the wild,
Deeply cultivating meditation
And attaining the five spiritual powers.

正法眼藏發菩提心第六十三
Treasury of the True Dharma Eye
Bringing Forth the Mind of Bodhi
Number 63

[Ryūmonji MS:]

爾時寛元二年甲辰二月十四日、在越州吉峰精舍示衆
Presented to the assembly at Kippō Vihāra, Esshū; fourteenth day, second month of the senior wood year of the dragon, the second year of Kangen [24 March 1244][91]

[Tōunji MS:]
弘安二年己卯三月十日、在永平寺書寫之。懷奘
Copied this at Eihei Monastery; tenth day, third month of the junior earth year of the rabbit, the second year of Kōan [22 April 1279]. Ejō

于時文明十二庚子年三月初五日、於于越州永平寺承陽庵書寫之。比丘光周
Copied this in the Jōyō Hermitage, Eihei Monastery, Esshū; fifth day, third month, senior metal year of the rat, the twelfth year of Bunmei [14 April 1480]. Bhikṣu Kōshū[92]

---

91 The Tōunji 洞雲寺 MS shares an almost identical colophon.

92 **Bhikṣu Kōshū** (*biku Kōshū* 比丘光周): Fifteenth abbot of Eiheiji (1434–1492?).

Treasury of the True Dharma Eye

Number 64

The Udumbara Flower

Udonge

優曇華

The Udumbara Flower

Udonge

Introduction

This short text was composed in the early spring of 1244, at Kippōji, in Echizen province. Number 64 in the seventy-five-chapter *Shōbōgenzō*, it occurs as number 54 in the sixty-chapter compilation and number 68 in the Honzan edition.

The title theme is the rare *udumbara* flower said (in Dōgen's version of the story) to have been held up by Buddha Śākyamuni on Vulture Peak at the time he transmitted his treasury of the true dharma eye to his disciple Mahākāśyapa, the First Ancestor of the Zen lineage. Dōgen opens with the famous legend, and then proceeds to comment on the meaning of "holding up the flower" and other elements of the tale. In closing, he introduces two poems by his own teacher, Tiantong Rujing 天童如淨, on plum and peach blossoms.

正法眼藏第六十四
Treasury of the True Dharma Eye
Number 64
優曇華
The Udumbara Flower

[64:1] {2:169}

靈山百萬衆前、世尊拈優曇華瞬目。于時摩訶迦葉、破顔微笑。世尊云、我有正法眼藏涅槃妙心、附囑摩訶迦葉。

On Vulture Peak, before an assembly of a million, the World-Honored One held up an udumbara flower and blinked his eyes.[1] *At that time, Mahākāśyapa broke into a smile. The World-Honored One said, "I have the treasury of the true dharma eye, the wondrous mind of nirvāṇa; I now bequeath it to Mahākāśyapa.*

[64:2]

七佛・諸佛は、おなじく拈華來なり。これを向上の拈華と修證現成せるなり、直下の拈華と裂破開明せり。

The seven buddhas, all the buddhas, have similarly been holding up a flower. They have practiced and verified it and realized it as a higher holding up a flower; they have broken it open and revealed it as the immediate holding up the flower.[2]

---

1 **Vulture Peak** (*Ryōzen* 靈山): I.e., Sacred Vulture Peak (*Ryōjusen* 靈鷲山; S. *Gṛdhrakūta-parvata*), the mountain near Rājagṛha in Magadha said to be the site of the legendary first transmission of Zen, described here, from Śākyamuni to Mahākāśyapa. The legend occurs often in Chan literature, but Dōgen's version here (variations of which occur elsewhere in his writings), while given in Chinese as if quoting a source, does not seem to have any extant Chinese precedent.

the World-Honored One held up an *udumbara* flower and blinked his eyes (*Seson nen undonge shunmoku* 世尊拈優曇華瞬目): See Supplementary Notes, s.v. "Holding up a flower and blinking the eyes." The *udumbara* flower (*udonge* 優曇華), often identified as the cluster fig (*ficus glomerata*), is said to bloom only rarely (by some accounts, only once every three thousand years) and, hence, used in Buddhist literature to represent a rare and precious event. While mention of the flower (and occasionally of the "blink," or "wink") occurs in other accounts of the first transmission, the identification of the flower as an *udumbara* blossom seems to lack extant precedent.

2 **a higher holding up a flower** (*kōjō no nenge* 向上の拈華); **the immediate holding up the flower** (*jikige no nenge* 直下の拈華): Perhaps meaning something like, "an act that is at once beyond the historical buddhas and yet immediately present in history."

[64:3]

しかあればすなはち、拈華裏の向上下、向自他、向表裏等、ともに渾華拈なり。華量・佛量・心量・身量なり。いく拈華も、面面の嫡嫡なり、附嘱有在なり。世尊拈華來、なほ放下著いまだし。拈華世尊來、ときに嗣世尊なり。拈華時すなはち盡時のゆえに、同參世尊なり、同拈華なり。

Thus, within holding up a flower, toward higher and lower, toward self and other, toward surface and interior, and so on, are all the holding up of the entire flower.[3] It is the measure of the flower, the measure of the buddha, the measure of the mind, the measure of the body.[4] However many [instances of] holding up a flower there may be, they are successor after successor, one after another; they are the continued existence of the bequest. The World-Honored One has been holding up a flower; he has never let it go. When the World-Honored One comes holding up a flower, that is succeeding the World-Honored One.[5] Because the time of holding up a flower is all time, it is studying together with the World-Honored One; it is holding up the flower together.

[64:4] {2:170}

いはゆる拈華といふは、華拈華なり、梅華・春華・雪華・蓮華等なり。いはくの梅華の五華は、三百六十餘會なり、五千四十八巻なり、三乘十二分教なり、三賢十聖なり。これによりて、三賢十聖およばざるなり。大藏あり、奇特あり、これを華開世界起といふ。一華開五葉、結果自然成とは、渾身是已掛渾身なり。桃華をみて眼睛を打失し、翠竹をきくに耳處を不現ならしむる、拈華の而今なり。腰雪斷臂、禮拜得髓する、華自開なり。石碓米白、夜半傳衣する、華已拈なり。これら世尊手裏の命根なり。

"Holding up a flower" means a flower holding up a flower; it means plum flowers, spring flowers, snow flowers, lotus flowers, and so on. What we speak of as the five petals of the plum blossom are the three hundred sixty-four plus assemblies; they are the five thousand forty-eight

---

The English "higher" and "immediate" mask the directional parallelism of *kōjō* 向上 ("toward up") and *jikige* 直下 ("straight down") with which Dōgen will open his next sentence.

3 **the holding up of the entire flower** (*kon ge nen* 渾華拈): Or "the entire holding up of the flower."

4 **It is the measure of the flower, the measure of the buddha, the measure of the mind, the measure of the body** (*keryō butsuryō shinryō shinryō nari* 華量・佛量・心量・身量なり): Presumably, meaning that the dimensions of the flower, buddha, mind, and body are all equivalent to "holding up a flower." See Supplementary Notes, s.v. "Measure of the buddha."

5 **The World-Honored One has been holding up a flower** (*Seson nenge rai* 世尊拈華來); **the World-Honored One comes holding up a flower** (*nenge Seson rai* 拈華世尊來): Dōgen plays here with the syntax of the Chinese phrase, in the process shifting the sense of the glyph *rai* 來 from a present perfect progressive marker to the verb "to come."

scrolls; they are the three vehicles and twelvefold teachings; they are the three worthies and ten sages.[6] Accordingly, the three worthies and ten sages do not reach them.[7]

There is the great treasury; there is the extraordinary — these are called "*a flower opens, and the world arises.*"[8] "A *single flower opens five pet-*

---

6 **What we speak of as the five petals of the plum blossom** (*iwaku no baika no goke* いはくの梅華の五華): Reading *goyō* 五葉 ("five petals") for Kawamura's *goke* 五華 ("five blossoms"). The plum blossom is in fact composed of five petals, though here Dōgen is no doubt alluding to a line in the transmission verse attributed to Bodhidharma, in which the "five petals" are generally taken as a prediction of the five generations of ancestors after Bodhidharma (or, sometimes, of the five houses into which the lineage would develop after the Sixth Ancestor); see *Jingde chuandeng lu* 景德傳燈錄, T.2076.51:219c17-18:

> 吾本來茲土、傳法救迷情、一華開五葉、結果自然成。
>
> I originally came to this land
> To transmit the dharma and save deluded sentient beings.
> A single flower opens five petals;
> The fruit forms, ripening naturally of itself.

For more on this verse, see Supplementary Notes, s.v. "A single flower opens five petals."

the three hundred sixty-four plus assemblies (*sanbyaku rokujū yo e* 三百六十餘會): The number of gatherings at which Buddha Śākyamuni is said to have preached during the course of his ministry (see, e.g., *Biyan lu* 碧巖錄, T.2003.48:146c3).

five thousand forty-eight scrolls (*gosen shijūhachi kan* 五千四十八巻): The number of fascicles in the imperially-sponsored catalog of Buddhist scriptures, the *Kaiyuan shijiao lu* 開元釋教錄 (T.2154), compiled in 730 by Zhisheng 智昇.

the three vehicles and twelvefold teachings (*sanjō jūnibun kyō* 三乘十二分教): I.e., the vehicles of *śrāvaka*, *pratyeka-buddha*, and bodhisattva; and the twelve genres into which the literature of the Buddhist canon is sometimes divided (discussed by Dōgen in "Shōbōgenzō bukkyō" 正法眼藏佛教); see Supplementary Notes, s.v. "Three vehicles and twelvefold teachings."

the three worthies and ten sages (*sanken jisshō* 三賢十聖): A common reference to those on the bodhisattva path: the three levels of "worthies" (*ken* 賢; S. *bhadra*), and the ten higher stages, or "grounds" (*ji* 地; S. *bhūmi*) of the sage (*sheng* 聖; S. *ārya*).

7 **the three worthies and ten sages do not reach them** (*sanken jisshō oyobazaru nari* 三賢十聖およばざるなり): Presumably meaning that the petals of the plum blossom include but go beyond the bodhisattva path. That the tradition of the buddhas and ancestors transcends even the most advanced stages of the bodhisattva path is a common refrain in Dōgen's writing.

8 **There is the great treasury; there is the extraordinary** (*daizō ari, kitoku ari* 大藏あり、奇特あり): Probably meaning that the petals of the plum blossom contain both the complete teachings of Buddhism (the "great treasury" of the Buddhist canon) and the practices of the Buddhist adepts (the extraordinary matter of Chan life). The expression "the extraordinary" (or "weird"; *kitoku* 奇特) here may recall the saying, quoted in "Shōbōgenzō kajō" 正法眼藏家常, of Baizhang Huaihai 百丈懷海 (749-814) that the "extraordinary matter" (*kitoku ji* 奇特事) was "sitting alone on Daxiong Peak." (See, e.g. *Biyan lu* 碧巖錄, T.2003.48:166c26-27.)

als; the fruit forms, ripening naturally of itself" means "*the whole body is the self hanging on the whole body.*"[9] Seeing the peach blossoms and losing the eyes; making the ears disappear upon hearing the jade bamboo — these are the present of holding up a flower.[10] *Hip-deep in snow and cutting off an arm; making a bow and getting the marrow* — these are a flower opening of itself.[11] *A stone pestle and whitened rice, transmitting the robe in the middle of the night* — these are the flower already held up.[12] They are the root of life in the hand of the World-Honored One.

"a flower opens, and the world arises" (*ke kai sekai ki* 華開世界起): The final line of the dharma transmission verse attributed to Bodhidharma's master, Prajñātāra. See Supplementary Notes, s.v. "A flower opens, and the world arises."

9 **"A single flower opens five petals; the fruit forms, ripening naturally of itself"** (*ikke kai goyō, kekka jinen jō* 一華開五葉、結果自然成): Two lines of the transmission verse attributed to Bodhidharma (*Jingde chuandeng lu* 景德傳燈錄, T.2076.51:219c17-18); see above, Note 6.

"the whole body is the self hanging on the whole body" (*konjin ze ko ka konjin* 渾身是已掛渾身): Variation on a line from a verse on the wind chime by Tiantong Rujing 天童如淨 (1162-1227), quoted elsewhere in the *Shōbōgenzō* (from *Rujing heshang yulu* 如淨和尚語錄, T.2002A.48:132b15-16):

> 渾身似口掛虛空、不問東西南北風、一等爲他談般若、滴丁東了滴丁東。
> The whole body, like a mouth, hanging in empty space,
> Without asking if the winds are from east, west, south, or north,
> Equally, for them, it talks of prajñā:
> *Di dingdong liao di dingdong.*

10 **Seeing the peach blossoms and losing the eyes** (*tōka o mite ganzei o tashitsu shi* 桃華をみて眼睛を打失し): These two clauses seem to combine allusions to two different passages in Chan literature to which Dōgen will return below: the former, treated in sections 14 and 15, recalls the case of Lingyun Zhiqin 靈雲志勤 (dates unknown), who is said to have attained an awakening from seeing peach trees in bloom; the latter, quoted in section 12, suggests lines of a verse by Tiantong Rujing. See Supplementary Notes, s.v. "Peach blossoms," "Eye."

making the ears disappear upon hearing the jade bamboo (*suichiku o kiku ni nisho o fugen narashimuru* 翠竹をきくに耳處を不現ならしむる): Allusion to the famous story of Xiangyan Zhixian 香嚴智閑 (died 898) (cited in *shinji Shōbōgenzō* 眞字正法眼藏, DZZ.5:134, case 17, and discussed in "Shōbōgenzō keisei sanshoku" 正法眼藏溪聲山色), who attained an understanding when he heard the sound of a bit of debris striking a bamboo stalk.

11 **Hip-deep in snow and cutting off an arm; making a bow and getting the marrow** (*yōsetsu danpi, raihai tokuzui* 腰雪斷臂、禮拜得髓): Reference, in Chinese, to two famous incidents, appearing often in the *Shōbōgenzō*, in the hagiography of the Second Ancestor, Huike 慧可: the first recalls the legend that Huike stood all night in a snowstorm waiting to be recognized by Bodhidharma and finally cut off one of his arms as an offering to the Indian master (see Supplementary Notes, s.v. "Cut off an arm"); the second evokes the transmission of the ancestral lineage to Huike when Bodhidharma acknowledged his silent bow with the words, "You've gotten my marrow" (see Supplementary Notes, s.v. "Skin, flesh, bones, and marrow").

12 **A stone pestle and whitened rice, transmitting the robe in the middle of the**

[64:5]
おほよそ拈華は、世尊成道より已前にあり、世尊成道と同時なり、世尊成道よりものちにあり。これによりて、華成道なり。拈華、はるかにこれらの時節を超越せり。諸佛諸祖の發心・發足・修證・保任、ともに拈華の春風を蝶舞するなり。しかあれば、いま瞿曇世尊、はなのなかに身をいれ、空のなかに身をかくせるによりて、鼻孔をとるべし、虚空をとれり、拈華と稱す。拈華は眼睛にて拈ず、心識にて拈ず、鼻孔にて拈ず、華拈にて拈ずるなり。

In sum, "holding up a flower" is before the World-Honored One attained the way, is at the same time that the World-Honored One attained the way, is after the World-Honored One attained the way. Consequently, it is the flower attaining the way. "Holding up the flower" has far transcended these times. The buddhas and ancestors' bringing forth the mind, setting out, practicing and verifying, and maintaining [bodhi] are all the flowers they hold dancing like butterflies in the spring wind. Thus, since now Gautama, the World-Honored One, has put himself inside the flower, has hidden himself in the sky, that we should grab his nose, that we have grabbed empty space, is called "holding up a flower."[13] "Holding up a flower" is holding it up with the eye, holding it up with the consciousness, holding it up with the nose, holding it up with holding up the flower.

---

night (*sekitai bei haku, yahan den'e* 石碓米白、夜半傳衣): Reference to the famous story, mentioned often in the *Shōbōgenzō*, of the transmission of the ancestral lineage to the Sixth Ancestor, Huineng 慧能. The layman Huineng is working pounding rice at the monastery of the Fifth Ancestor, Hongren 弘忍 (602-675); when his verse is recognized, he is invited into the master's quarters and given the ancestral robe of Bodhidharma during the night.

13 **now Gautama, the World-Honored One, has put himself inside the flower, has hidden himself in the sky** (*ima Kudon Seson, hana no naka ni mi o ire, kū no naka ni mi o kakuseru* いま瞿曇世尊、はなのなかに身をいれ、空のなかに身をかくせる): Or, perhaps, "has hidden himself in emptiness." The translation assumes that Dōgen has in mind here the expression "sky flowers" (*kūge* 空華; S. *khapuṣpa*), the optical illusion of spots appearing to the diseased eye, used as metaphor for what is mere appearance without objective reality. See Supplementary Notes, s.v. "Clouded eyes and sky flowers."

that we should grab his nose, that we have grabbed empty space (*bikū o toru beshi, kokū o toreri* 鼻孔をとるべし、虚空をとれり): Likely reflecting a story, included in the *shinji Shōbōgenzō* 眞字正法眼藏 (DZZ.5:256, case 248) and discussed in the "Shōbōgenzō kokū" 正法眼藏虚空, in which grabbing hold of a nose is taken as grabbing hold of space; see Supplementary Notes, s.v. "Nose."

[64:6]
おほよそこの山河・大地・日月風雨・人畜草木のいろいろ、角角拈來せる、すなはちこれ拈優曇華なり。生死去來も、はなのいろいろなり、はなの光明なり。いまわれら、かくのごとく參學する、拈華來なり。

In sum, the holding up at every turn of this assortment of mountains, rivers, and the whole earth, sun, moon, wind, and rain, humans, beasts, grass, and trees — this is precisely "holding up the *udumbara* flower." Birth and death, coming and going are an assortment of flowers, are the radiance of the flower. Our study like this here has been "holding up a flower."

[64:7]
佛言、譬如優曇華、一切皆愛樂。

Buddha said, "It is like the udumbara, in which everyone delights."[14]

[64:8] {2:171}
いはくの一切は、現身藏身の佛祖なり、草木昆蟲の自有光明在なり。皆愛樂とは、面面の皮肉骨髓、いまし活鱍鱍なり。

"Everyone" refers to the buddhas and ancestors who show themselves and hide themselves, to the radiance naturally possessed by the grass, trees, and insects.[15] "Everyone delights" means the skin, flesh, bones, and marrow of each one is brisk and lively right now.

[64:9]
しかあればすなはち、一切はみな優曇華なり。かるがゆえに、すなはちこれを、まれなり、といふ。瞬目とは、樹下に打坐して、明星に眼睛を換却せしときなり。このとき、摩訶迦葉、破顔微笑するなり。顔容、はやく破して、拈華顔に換却せり。如來、瞬目のときに、われらが眼睛、はやく打失しきたれり。この如來瞬目、すなはち拈華なり。優曇華のこころ、おのづからひらくるなり。

Thus, "everyone" is the *udumbara* flower; precisely for this reason it is said to be rare. "Blinked his eyes" refers to the time that, sitting under the tree, he exchanged his eye for the dawn star.[16] At this time,

14 **The Buddha** (*butsu* 佛): From a verse in the *Lotus Sūtra* (*Miaofa lianhua jing* 妙法蓮華經, T.262.9:10a28); the antecedent of "it" here is the teaching of the sūtra.

15 **the radiance naturally possessed by the grass, trees, and insects** (*sōmoku konchū no ji u kōmyō zai* 草木昆蟲の自有光明在): Perhaps variation on words attributed to Yunmen Wenyan 雲門文偃 (864–949), recorded in the *shinji Shōbōgenzō* 眞字正法眼藏 (DZZ.5:166, case 81), probably from the *Yuanwu yulu* 圓悟語錄 (T.1997.47:803a25-26):

> 人人盡有光明在。看時不見暗昏昏。
>
> People all have a radiance,
> But when they look for it, they can't see it in the dark.

16 **sitting under the tree, he exchanged his eye for the dawn star** (*juge ni taza*

Mahākāśyapa broke into a smile. His countenance had long since broken and changed into the face holding up the flower.[17] When the Tathāgata blinked, our eyes were lost from the start. The Tathāgata's blinking is itself his holding up the flower. The heart of the *udumbara* flower opens of itself.

[64:10]

拈華の正當恁麼時は、一切の瞿曇、一切の迦葉、一切の衆生、一切のわれら、ともに一隻の手をのべて、おなじく拈華すること、只今までもいまだやまざるなり。さらに手裏藏身三昧あるがゆえに、四大五蘊といふなり。

At the very moment that he holds up the flower, all Gautamas, all Kāśyapas, all living beings, all of us together extend a hand and similarly hold up a flower, without interruption even to the present.[18] And further, because they have the samādhi of concealing oneself in the hand, they are called "the four elements and five aggregates."[19]

[64:11]

我有は附嘱なり、附嘱は我有なり。附嘱は、かならず我有に罣礙せらるるなり。我有は、頂䫌なり。その參學は、頂䫌量を巴鼻して參學するなり。我有を拈じて附嘱に換却するとき、保任正法眼藏なり。祖師西來、これ拈華來なり。拈華を弄精魂といふ。弄精魂とは、祇管打坐、脱落身心なり。佛となり祖となるを、弄精魂といふ、著衣喫飯を、弄精魂といふなり。おほよそ佛祖極則の事、かならず弄精魂なり。佛殿に相見せられ、僧堂を相見する、はなに、いろ・いろ、いよいよそなはり、いろに、ひかりますま

---

shite, myōjō ni ganzei o kankyaku seshi 樹下に打坐して、明星に眼睛を換却せし): Reference to the Buddha's awakening experience; seated at the foot of the bodhi tree, he achieved buddhahood upon seeing Venus rising in the dawn sky.

17 **His countenance had long since broken** (*gan'yō, hayaku hashite* 顔容、はやく破して): A play on the expression *hagan bishō* 破顔微笑 (literally, "his face broke into a slight smile"). See Supplementary Notes, s.v. "Break into a smile."

18 **together extend a hand** (*tomo ni isseki no shu o nobete* ともに一隻の手をのべて): A fixed expression occurring elsewhere in the *Shōbōgenzō*; best known from a story recorded in Dōgen's *shinji Shōbōgenzō* 眞字正法眼藏 (DZZ.5:175-176, case 97): A monk asked Luoshan Daoxian 羅山道閑 how much he should pay to have a stūpa built. Luoshan said,

> 若將三文錢與匠人、和尚此生決定不得塔。若將兩文錢與匠人、和尚與匠人共出一隻手。若將一文錢與匠人、帶累匠人眉鬚墮落。
>
> If you offer the artisan three cash, the Reverend will definitely not get a stūpa in this lifetime. If you offer the artisan two cash, the Reverend and the artisan will each put out one hand. If you offer the artisan one cash, you'll so perplex him that the artisan's eyebrows and beard will fall off.

19 **"four elements and five aggregates"** (*shidai goun* 四大五蘊): Likely reflecting a saying by Zhaozhou Congshen 趙州從諗 (778-897), which Dōgen quotes in his *shinji Shōbōgenzō* 眞字正法眼藏 (DZZ.5:270, case 88) and elsewhere; see Supplementary Notes, s.v. "Four elements and five aggregates."

すかさなるなり。さらに僧堂、いま板をとりて雲中に拍し、佛殿、いま笙をふくむで水底にふく。

"I have" is to "bequeath it"; to "bequeath it" is "I have." To "bequeath it" is invariably impeded by "I have."[20] "I have" is the crown of the head; in studying it, we study with the dimensions of the crown of the head as our nose grip.[21] When we take up "I have" and change it to "bequeath it," we maintain the treasury of the true dharma eye. "The Ancestral Master's coming from the west" — this is to come holding up the flower.[22]

"Holding up the flower" is called "playing with the spirit."[23] "Playing with the spirit" means "*just sitting, sloughing off body and mind.*"[24] Becoming a buddha, becoming an ancestor, is called "playing with the spirit"; wearing clothes and taking meals is called "playing with the spirit." In general, the matter of the ultimate standard of the buddhas and ancestors is invariably "playing with the spirit." In being met by the buddha hall, in meeting with the saṃgha hall, their flowers are endowed with ever more colors, their colors accumulate more and more brilliance.[25]

---

20 **To "bequeath it" is invariably impeded by "I have"** (*fuzoku wa, kanarazu ga u ni keige seraruru nari* 附囑は、かならず我有に罣礙せらるるなり): The use of *keige* 罣礙 ("to obstruct," "to hinder") here follows a familiar pattern in Dōgen's writings, in which the term is used to mean "to define," "to identify."

21 **we study with the dimensions of the crown of the head as our nose grip** (*sono sangaku wa, chōnei ryō o habi shite sangaku suru nari* その參學は、頂顮量を巴鼻して參學するなり): Perhaps meaning something like, "to understand the meaning of 'I have' we need to grasp the dimensions of the true person." "Nose grip" renders *habi* 巴鼻 (also written 把鼻), to have a "hold" or "handle" on something, from the nose rope or ring for leading livestock; see Supplementary Notes, s.v. "Crown of the head," "Nose."

22 **"The Ancestral Master's coming from the west"** (*soshi seirai* 祖師西來): I.e., Bodhidharma's advent in China; see Supplementary Notes, s.v. "Intention of the Ancestral Master's coming from the west."

23 **"playing with the spirit"** (*rō zeikon* 弄精魂): A fixed expression occurring often in Chan literature for a distracted, or "possessed," state of mind; sometimes, as likely here, used in ironic reference to meditation.

24 **"just sitting, sloughing off body and mind"** (*shikan taza, datsuraku shinjin* 祗管打坐、脱落身心): Variation on an expression Dōgen famously attributes in several places to his teacher, Tiantong Rujing 天童如淨; see Supplementary Notes, s.v. "Just sit," and "Body and mind sloughed off."

25 **In being met by the buddha hall, in meeting with the saṃgha hall** (*butsuden ni shōken serare, sōdō o shōken suru* 佛殿に相見せられ、僧堂を相見する): Play likely inspired by the saying, cited elsewhere in the *Shōbōgenzō*, of Xuefeng Yicun 雪峰義存 (822-908), e.g., at *shinji Shōbōgenzō* 眞字正法眼藏 (DZZ.5:272, case 290):

> 雪峰示衆云、望州亭與諸人相見了也、烏石嶺與諸人相見了也、僧堂前與諸人相見了也。
>
> Xuefeng addressed the assembly, saying, "I met everyone at Wangzhou Pavilion. I met everyone at Wushi Ridge. I met everyone in front of the saṃgha hall."

Further, now the saṃgha hall "takes the board and strikes it amidst the clouds"; now the buddha hall "holds the panpipe and plays it at the bottom of the water."[26]

[64:12] {2:172}
到恁麼のとき、あやまりて梅華引を吹起せり。いはゆる先師古佛いはく、
瞿曇打失眼睛時、雪裏梅華只一枝、而今到處成荊棘、却笑春風繚亂吹。

When it comes to this, they have mistakenly started playing a plum blossom tune.[27] That is, my former master, the Old Buddha, said,[28]

At the time that Gautama lost his eye,
It was just one branch of plum blossoms in the snow.
Now, it's a thicket wherever you go;
Yet we laugh as the spring wind swirls them about.

[64:13]
いま如來の眼睛、あやまりて梅華となれり、梅華、いま彌綸せる荊棘をなせり。如來は眼睛に藏身し、眼睛は梅華に藏身す、梅華は荊棘に藏身せり。いまかへりて春風をふく。

Now, "the eye" of the Tathāgata has mistakenly become "plum blossoms"; now, the "plum blossoms" form "a thicket" spreading everywhere. The Tathāgata has hidden himself in the eye; the eye has hidden itself in the plum blossoms; the plum blossoms have hidden themselves in the thicket. And, now, instead, they blow "the spring wind."

---

26 **"takes the board and strikes it amidst the clouds"** (*han o torite unchū ni hakushi* 板をとりて雲中に拍し); **"holds the panpipe and plays it at the bottom of the water"** (*shō o fukumude suitei ni fuku* 笙をふくむで水底にふく): Dōgen plays here in Japanese with a couplet found (in slightly variant forms) in a number of Chan texts (e.g., at *Rujing heshang yulu* 如淨和尚語錄, T.2002A.48:122c13):

木人執板雲中拍、石女含笙水底吸。
The wooden man takes the board and strikes it amidst the clouds;
The stone woman holds the panpipe and plays it at the bottom of the water.

27 **they have mistakenly started playing a plum blossom tune** (*ayamarite baika in o suiki seri* あやまりて梅華引を吹起せり): Ironic reference to the verse by Rujing 如淨 that Dōgen is about to quote.

28 **my former master, the Old Buddha** (*senshi kobutsu* 先師古佛): From the *Rujing heshang yulu* 如淨和尚語錄, T.2002A.48:122c29-123a1. Dōgen also quotes this verse in his "Shōbōgenzō ganzei" 正法眼藏眼睛 and "Baika" 梅華 chapters.

[64:14]
しかもかくのごとくなりといへども、桃華樂を慶快す。先師天童古佛云、靈雲見處桃華開、天童見處桃華落。

Nevertheless, while this may be so, he enjoys the music of the peach blossom.[29] My former master, the Old Buddha of Tiantong said,[30]

What Lingyun sees is the peach blossoms opening;
What Tiantong sees is the peach blossoms falling.[31]

[64:15]
しるべし、桃華開は、靈雲の見處なり、直至如今更不疑なり。桃華落は、天童の見處なり。桃華のひらくるは、春のかぜにもよほされ、桃華のおつるは、春のかぜににくまる。たとひ春風ふかく桃華をにくむとも、桃華おちて身心脱落せん。

We should understand that "the peach blossoms opening" is "what Lingyun sees;" it is "*I'm like this now, without further doubts.*"[32] "The peach blossoms falling" is "what Tiantong sees." The peach blossoms open at the urging of the spring wind; the peach blossoms fall hated by the spring wind. The spring wind may deeply hate the peach blossoms, but, as the peach blossoms fall, "body and mind are sloughed off."

正法眼藏優曇華第六十四
Treasury of the True Dharma Eye
The Udumbara Flower
Number 64

[Ryūmonji MS:]
爾時寬元二年甲辰二月十二日、越宇吉峰精藍示衆
Presented to the assembly at Yoshimine Monastic Complex, Etsuu; twelfth day, second month of the senior wood year of the dragon, the second year of Kangen [22 March 1244]

---

29 **he enjoys the music of the peach blossom** (*tōka gaku o keikai su* 桃華樂を慶快す): Presumably, a reference to Rujing's composition of the verse that Dōgen is about to quote.

30 **My former master, the Old Buddha** (*senshi kobutsu* 先師古佛): Quoting a couplet from a verse by Rujing 如淨 appearing at *Rujing heshang hoshang* 如淨和尚語錄, T.2002A.48:127b29.

31 **What Lingyun sees** (*Reiun kenjo* 靈雲見處): Reference to the story of Lingyun's 靈雲 awakening upon seeing peach trees in bloom; see above, Note 10.

32 **"I'm like this now, without further doubts"** (*jikishi nyokon kō fugi* 直至如今更不疑): Final line of Lingyun's verse expressing his awakening upon seeing peach blossoms; found at *shinji Shōbōgenzō* 眞字正法眼藏, DZZ.5:206, case 155; and see Supplementary Notes, s.v. "Peach blossoms."

[Tōunji MS:]

正和三年甲寅二月六日、書寫之

Copied this on the sixth day, second month of the senior wood year of the tiger, the third year of Shōwa [20 February 1314][33]

于時文明十二庚子年三月初六日、於于越之永平寺承陽庵書寫之。比丘光周

Copied this in the Jōyō Hermitage, Eihei Monastery, Etsu; sixth day, third month, senior metal year of the rat, the twelfth year of Bunmei [15 April 1480],
Bhikṣu Kōshū[34]

33 Copyist unknown.

34 **Bhikṣu Kōshū** (*biku Kōshū* 比丘光周): Fifteenth abbot of Eiheiji (1434–1492?).

Treasury of the True Dharma Eye

Number 65

The Entire Body of the Tathāgata

Nyorai zenshin

如來全身

The Entire Body of the Tathāgata

Nyorai zenshin

Introduction

This work bears a colophon identical to that of the "Zanmai ō zanmai" 三昧王三昧 chapter, stating that it was presented to the assembly on 25 March 1244, at Kippōji in Echizen. Number 65 in the seventy-five-chapter *Shōbōgenzō*, it occurs as number 55 in the sixty-chapter compilation and number 70 in the Honzan edition (or 71 in the Iwanami and Shūmuchō versions).

The text is a brief discussion of a passage from the *Lotus Sūtra*, in which the Buddha says that, "wherever the sūtra is preached, read, recited, or copied," a stūpa should be built and worshiped as if it contained a *śarīra*, a sacred relic of the Buddha; for the sūtra represents "the entire body of the Tathāgata." In his remarks, Dōgen identifies the sūtra with the "real marks of the dharmas" (i.e., the ultimate reality of all things), and the preaching, reading, reciting, and copying of the sūtra with "the entire body of the Tathāgata."

正法眼藏第六十五
Treasury of the True Dharma Eye
Number 65

如來全身

The Entire Body of the Tathāgata

[65:1] {2:173}

爾時、釋迦牟尼佛、住王舍城耆闍崛山。　告藥王菩薩摩訶薩言、藥王、在在處處、若説、若讀、若誦、若書、若經卷所住之處、皆應起七寶塔、極令高廣嚴飾。不須復安舍利、所以者何。此中已有如來全身。此塔應以一切華香・瓔珞・繒蓋・幢旛・妓樂・歌頌、供養・恭敬、尊重・讚歎。若有人得見此塔、禮拜供養、當知、是等皆近阿耨多羅三藐三菩提。

At that time, Buddha Śākyamuni was staying on Mount Gṛdhrakūṭa at Rājagṛha.[1] *He addressed the Bodhisattva-mahāsattva Bhaiṣajyarāja, saying,*

> *Bhaiṣajyarāja, wherever it is preached, read, recited, or copied, wherever a sūtra scroll resides, there should be erected a seven-jeweled stūpa, made exceedingly tall and wide, and richly adorned. There need not be a śarīra placed within it.*[2] *Why? Within it there is already the entire body of the Tathāgata. This stūpa should be given offerings, honored, venerated, and praised with all kinds of flowers and incense, jeweled necklaces, silk canopies, banners and pennants, music, song, and verse. If there are people able to see this stūpa, to pay obeisance and make offerings to it, you should know that they are all close to anuttara-samyak-saṃbodhi.*

[65:2] {2:174}

いはゆる經卷は、若説、これなり、若讀、これなり、若誦、これなり、若書、これなり。經卷は、實相、これなり。應起七寶塔は、實相を塔といふ。極令の高廣、その量、かならず實相量なり。此中已有如來全身は、經卷、これ全身なり。

"The sūtra scroll" spoken of here is the "preaching" itself, is the "reading" itself, is the "reciting" itself, is the "copying" itself. "The sūtra

---

1 **At that time** (*ni ji* 爾時): Dōgen here provides his own Chinese introduction to a passage from the *Lotus Sūtra* (*Miaofa lianhua jing* 妙法蓮華經, T.262.9:31b26-c3).

2 **There need not be a *śarīra* placed within it** (*fusu bu an shari* 不須復安舍利): Reflecting the typical practice of interring a physical relic of the Buddha's body in stūpas.

scroll" is "the real mark" itself.[3] "*There should be erected a seven-jeweled stūpa*" is saying that "the real mark" is a "stūpa." "Made exceedingly tall and wide": its size will invariably be the size of "the real mark." "*Within it there is already the entire body of the Tathāgata*": "the sūtra scroll" — this is "the entire body."

[65:3]

しかあれば若説・若讀・若誦・若書等、これ如來全身なり。一切の華香・瓔珞・繒蓋・幢旛・妓樂・歌頌をもて、供養、恭敬、尊重、讃歎すべし。あるいは天華・天香・天繒蓋等なり、みなこれ實相なり。あるいは人中上華・上香・名衣・名服なり、これらみな實相なり。供養・恭敬、これ實相なり。

Thus, "preaching, reading, reciting, and copying" — this is the "entire body of the Tathāgata." [It] "should be given offerings, honored, venerated, and praised with all kinds of flowers and incense, jeweled necklaces, silk canopies, banners and pennants, music, song and verse."[4] They may be heavenly flowers, heavenly incense, heavenly silk canopies, and the like; all of them are "the real mark." Or they may be the best flowers and best incense, the finest robes and finest garments; they are all "the real mark." "Giving offerings and venerating" — these are "the real mark."

[65:4]

起塔すべし、不須復安舍利といふ。しりぬ、經巻はこれ如來舍利なり、如來全身なり、といふことを。まさしく佛口の金言、これを見聞するよりもすぎたる大功德あるべからず。いそぎて功をつみ、德をかさぬべし。もし人ありて、この塔を禮拜供養するは、まさにしるべし、皆近阿耨多羅三藐三菩提なり。この塔をみんとき、この塔を、誠心に禮拜供養すべし。すなはち阿耨多羅三藐三菩提に皆近ならん。近は、さりて近なるにあらず、きたりて近なるにあらず、阿耨多羅三藐三菩提を、皆近といふなり。而今われら、受持・讀誦・解說・書寫をみる、得見此塔なり。よろこぶべし、皆近阿耨多羅三藐三菩提なり。

It says a stūpa should be erected, and "*there need not be a śarīra placed*" in it. We know from this, it is saying that "the sūtra scroll" is itself the *śarīra* of the Tathāgata, is "the entire body of the Tathāgata." Truly, golden words from the mouth of the Buddha — there can be no

3 **"The sūtra scroll" is "the real mark" itself** (*kyōkan wa, jissō, kore nari* 經巻は、實相、これなり): I.e., the sūtra in question here is just the reality of all things. From a line in the *Lotus Sūtra*; see Supplementary Notes, s.v. "Only buddhas with buddhas can exhaustively investigate the real marks of the dharmas."

4 **[It] "should be given offerings, honored, venerated, and praised"** (*kuyō, kugyō, sonjū, santan su beshi* 供養、恭敬、尊重、讃歎すべし): Dōgen here translates the sūtra sentence into Japanese. His omission of the original subject ("this stūpa") makes it seem likely he wants us to read "the entire body of the Tathāgata" as the subject.

greater merit than seeing and hearing them. We should hurry to accumulate merit and pile up virtue. "If there are people who pay obeisance and make offerings to this stūpa, you should know that *they are all close* to anuttara-samyak-saṃbodhi."[5] When we see this stūpa, we should sincerely pay obeisance and make offerings to this stūpa. This itself should be "all close" to "*anuttara-samyak-saṃbodhi*."[6] "Close" does not mean [somewhere] is close from here or here is close [to somewhere]: "*anuttara-samyak-saṃbodhi*" is called "all close." Our present seeing of receiving and keeping, reading and reciting, interpreting, and copying [the sūtra] is being "able to see this stūpa." We should rejoice: it is "*all close to anuttara-samyak-saṃbodhi*."

[65:5]

しかあれば、經巻は、如來全身なり。經巻を禮拜するは、如來を禮拜したてまつるなり。經巻にあひたてまつれるは、如來にまみえたてまつるなり、經巻は、如來舍利なり。かくのごとくなるゆえに、舍利は此經なるべし。たとひ、經巻はこれ舍利なり、としるといふとも、舍利はこれ經巻なり、としらずば、いまだ佛道にあらず。而今諸法實相は、經巻なり。人間・天上、海中・虛空、此土・他界、みなこれ實相なり、經巻なり、舍利なり。舍利を受持・讀誦・解説・書寫して、開悟すべし、これ、或從經卷なり。古佛舍利あり、今佛舍利あり、辟支佛舍利あり、轉輪王舍利あり、獅子舍利あり、あるいは木佛舍利あり、繪佛舍利あり、あるいは人舍利あり。現在大宋國諸代の佛祖、いきたるとき、舍利を現出せしむるあり、闍維ののち、舍利を生ぜる、おほくあり、これみな經巻なり。

Thus, the sūtra scroll is "the entire body of the Tathāgata." To pay obeisance to the sūtra scroll is to pay obeisance to the Tathāgata. To encounter the sūtra scroll is to meet the Tathāgata. The sūtra scroll is the *śarīra* of the Tathāgata; since such is the case, the *śarīra* must be the sūtra. Though one may know that the sūtra scroll is the *śarīra*, if one does not know that the *śarīra* is the sūtra scroll, it is not yet the way of the buddhas. The present "real marks of the dharmas" are the sūtra scroll; among humans and in the heavens above, in the ocean and empty space, this land and other worlds — all are the real marks, are the *śarīra*. We should awaken by receiving and keeping, reading and reciting, interpreting, and copying the *śarīra*; this is *whether from a sūtra scroll*.[7]

---

5 **"If there are people who pay obeisance and make offerings to this stūpa"** (*moshi hito arite, kono tō o raihai kuyō suru* もし人ありて、この塔を禮拜供養する): This sentence represents a partial Japanese rendering of the line from the sūtra quotation.

6 **This itself should be "all close" to "*anuttara-samyak-saṃbodhi*"** (*sunawachi anokutara sanmyaku sanbodai ni kai gon naran* すなはち阿耨多羅三藐三菩提に皆近ならん): Dōgen plays here with Chinese, treating the pronoun "all" (*kai* 皆) as an adverb modifying "close"; presumably, meaning something like "completely close" or, perhaps "close to everything."

7 **this is whether from a sūtra scroll** (*kore, waku jū kyōkan nari* これ、或從經卷な

There are the *śarīra* of the ancient buddhas; there are the *śarīra* of the present buddhas; there are the *śarīra* of *pratyeka-buddhas*; there are the *śarīra* of the wheel-turning kings; there are the *śarīra* of lions. Or there are the *śarīra* of wooden buddhas; there are the *śarīra* of painted buddhas. Or there are the *śarīra* of humans. At present among the buddhas and ancestors in the Land of the Great Song, there are those who manifest *śarīra* during their lifetimes, and there are many who produce *śarīra* after their *jhyāpita*.[8] These are all the sūtra scroll.

[65:6] {2:175}
釋迦牟尼佛、告大衆言、我本行菩薩道、所成壽命、今猶未盡、復倍上數。

Buddha Śākyamuni addressed the great assembly, saying, "The lifespan I attained by my original practice of the bodhisattva path is even now still not exhausted; it is twice the above number."[9]

[65:7]
いま八斛四斗の舍利は、なほしこれ佛壽なり。本行菩薩道の壽命は、三千大千世界のみにあらず、そこばくなるべし。これ如來全身なり、これ經卷なり。

The present eight bushels four pecks of *śarīra* are precisely the lifespan of the Buddha.[10] The lifespan of his "originally practicing the bodhisattva path" is not just trichiliocosms; it must be a lot.[11] This is "the entire

り): From the expression, "whether from a wise friend, whether from a sūtra scroll" (*waku jū chishiki waku jū kyōkan* 或從知識或從經卷), occurring often in Dōgen's writings; see Supplementary Notes.

8 **after their *jhyāpita*** (*jai no nochi* 闍維ののち): I.e., "upon cremation"; Dōgen uses a transliteration of the Indic term (also rendered *dabi* 荼毘, *jabi* 闍毘, etc.)

9 **Buddha Śākyamuni** (*Shakamuni butsu* 釋迦牟尼佛): Quoting the *Lotus Sūtra* (*Miaofa lianhua jing* 妙法蓮華經, T.262.9:42c19-23):

> 如是我成佛已來甚大久遠。壽命無量阿僧祇劫、常住不滅。諸善男子。我本行菩薩道所成壽命、今猶未盡、復倍上數。
>
> In this way, since I attained buddhahood, it has been a very long time. My lifespan is incalculable *asaṃkhyeya* kalpas, constantly abiding without extinction. Good sons, the lifespan attained by my original practice of the bodhisattva path is even now still not exhausted; it is twice the above number.

10 **The present eight bushels four pecks of *śarīra*** (*ima hachikoku shitō no shari* いま八斛四斗の舍利): From the tradition that the cremation of the Buddha's body yielded eighty-four pecks of relics.

11 **not just trichiliocosms** (*sanzen daisen sekai nomi ni arazu* 三千大千世界のみにあらず): A trichiliocosm, or "three-thousandfold great thousandfold," equaling one billion Mount Sumeru world systems. Here, likely recalling the *Lotus Sūtra* passage (*Miaofa lianhua jing* 妙法蓮華經, T.262.9:42b13-16) in which the Buddha likens the length of his lifespan to the total distance traveled by one who took all the atoms of an incalculable number of trichiliocosms and, traveling eastward, dropped one of the atoms each time he passed an incalculable number of lands, until he had exhausted the lot.

body of the Tathāgata"; this is "the sūtra scroll."

[65:8]

智積菩薩言、我見釋迦如來、於無量劫、難行苦行、積功累德、求菩薩道、未曾止息。觀三千大千世界、乃至無有如芥子許、非是菩薩捨身命處、爲衆生故。然後乃得成菩提道。

> *Bodhisattva Prajñākūṭa said,*[12]
>
> *I see that Tathāgata Śākyamuni for innumerable kalpas has engaged in difficult practices and painful practices, accumulating merit and amassing virtue, seeking the bodhisattva path without ever stopping. I see that in the trichiliocosm, there is not a single place, even the size of a mustard seed, in which the Bodhisattva has not abandoned his life for the sake of living beings. Only after this did he attain the way of bodhi.*

[65:9]

はかりしりぬ、この三千大千世界は、赤心一片なり、虚空一隻なり、如來全身なり、捨・未捨にかかはるべからず。舍利は、佛前佛後にあらず、佛とならべるにあらず。無量劫の難行苦行は、佛胎佛腹の活計消息なり、佛皮肉骨髓なり。すでに未曾止息といふ、佛にいたりてもいよいよ精進なり、大千界に化しても、なほすすむなり。全身の活計、かくのごとし。

It is obvious that this "trichiliocosm" is a single piece of bare mind, is a single bit of empty space, is the entire body of the Tathāgata; it has nothing to do with his "abandoning" or not "abandoning."[13] The *śarīra* are not before the Buddha nor after the Buddha; they are not alongside the Buddha.[14] The "difficult practices and painful practices" of "innumerable kalpas" are the circumstances of the life of the womb of the Buddha and the belly of the Buddha, are the skin, flesh, bones, and marrow of the Buddha.[15] Since it says, "*without ever stopping,*" even after reaching buddhahood, he exerts himself all the more; even having converted the trichiliocosm, he still proceeds. Such is the life of the "entire body."

---

12 **Bodhisattva Prajñākūṭa** (*Chishaku bosatsu* 智積菩薩): Quoting the *Lotus Sūtra* (*Miaofa lianhua jing* 妙法蓮華經, T.262.9:35b21-25).

13 **a single piece of bare mind** (*sekishin ippen* 赤心一片); **a single bit of empty space** (*kokū isseki* 虚空一隻): The former expression is a fixed phrase; the latter is unusual. A "bare (or 'red') mind" (*sekishin* 赤心) is a common Chinese idiom for a sincere, or straightforward, mind (or heart). Chan texts often speak of "a bare mind in pieces" (*sekishin henpen* 赤心片片); see Supplementary Notes, s.v. "Bare mind in pieces."

14 **The *śarīra* are not before the Buddha nor after the Buddha** (*shari wa, butsuzen butsugo ni arazu* 舍利は、佛前佛後にあらず): Perhaps indicating that the Buddha's relics are not only spatially but also temporally coterminous with the "entire body of the Tathāgata" (and, hence, with the "trichiliocosm").

15 **the circumstances of the life of the womb of the Buddha and the belly of the Buddha** (*buttai buppuku no kakkei shōsoku* 佛胎佛腹の活計消息): An unusual expression, perhaps meaning something like "the inner, or personal, life of the Buddha."

正法眼藏如來全身第六十五
Treasury of the True Dharma Eye
The Entire Body of the Tathāgata
Number 65

[Ryūmonji MS:]
爾時寬元二年甲辰二月十五日、在越州吉田縣吉峰精舍示衆
Presented to the assembly at Kippō Vihāra, Yoshida District, Esshū; fifteenth day, second month of the senior wood year of the dragon, the second year of Kangen [25 March 1244]

[Tōunji MS:]
弘安二年六月二十三日、在永平禪寺衆寮書寫之
Copied in the common quarters of the Eihei Zen Monastery; twenty-third day, sixth month, second year of Kōan [2 August 1279][16]

于時文明十二庚子年三月十日、於于越州吉祥山永平寺承陽庵書寫。比丘光周
Copied this in the Jōyō Hermitage, Eihei Monastery, Mount Kichijō, Esshū; tenth day, third month, senior metal year of the rat, the twelfth year of Bunmei [19 April 1480]. Bhikṣu Kōshū[17]

16 Copyist unknown.

17 **Bhikṣu Kōshū** (*biku Kōshū* 比丘光周): Fifteenth abbot of Eiheiji (1434–1492?).

Treasury of the True Dharma Eye

Number 66

The King of Samādhis Samādhi

Zanmai ō zanmai

三昧王三昧

The King of Samādhis Samādhi

Zanmai ō zanmai

Introduction

This short chapter was composed early in 1244 at Kippōji, the monastery where Dōgen taught in the period from his arrival in Echizen (present-day Fukui prefecture) till the opening of the Daibutsuji (later renamed Eiheiji). The work appears as number 66 in the seventy-five-chapter compilation of the *Shōbōgenzō* and number 71 in the Honzan edition (or 72 in the Iwanami and Shūmuchō versions); it is not included in the sixty-chapter compilation but is found in the twenty-eight-text *Himitsu* collection, where it is listed as number 10 of fascicle 1.

The notion of a samādhi (i.e., state of mental concentration) that is the king of samādhis (S. *samādhi-rāja-samādhi*) occurs with some frequency throughout the Buddhist literature, without consistent reference to a specific spiritual practice or state of mind. Dōgen's essay here draws on a passage from the influential *Dazhidu lun* 大智度論 (*Treatise on the Great Perfection of Wisdom*), a commentary, traditionally attributed to Nāgārjuna, on the 25,000-line *Prajñā-pāramitā-sūtra*. A line in the sūtra reads, "At that time, the World-Honored One spread his lion seat and, sitting with legs crossed, straightening his body and binding his thoughts before him, entered into the king of samādhis samādhi, in which all samādhis are included." The commentary on this line in the *Treatise* extols the spiritual advantages of cross-legged sitting and goes on to explain that this samādhi is first among samādhis because it is "freely able to take innumerable dharmas as its object."

Dōgen's own comments here focus especially on the practice of sitting with legs crossed (*kekkafu za* 結跏趺坐; S. *paryaṅka*), the posture sometimes known as the "lotus position" (S. *padmāsana*). This practice, he associates with a famous teaching he attributes to his Chinese master, Tiantong Rujing 天童如淨, that the study of Zen is "just sitting" (*shikan taza* 祇管打坐), with "body and mind sloughed off" (*shinjin datsuraku* 身心脱落). Through this association, Dōgen is able to claim that sitting with legs crossed is itself the king of samādhis, is itself the complete practice and teaching of the Buddha, is itself the spiritual lineage of the first Chinese Chan ancestor, Bodhidharma. The emphasis on such claims makes this short text one of the more important sources for understanding Dōgen's approach to zazen practice.

正法眼藏第六十六
Treasury of the True Dharma Eye
Number 66

三昧王三昧
The King of Samādhis Samādhi

[66:1] {2:177}

驀然として盡界を超越して、佛祖の屋裏に大尊貴生なるは、結跏趺坐なり、外道・魔儻の頂𩕳を踏翻して、佛祖の堂奥に箇中人なることは、結跏趺坐なり。佛祖の極之極を超越するは、ただこの一法なり。このゆえに、佛祖、これをいとなみて、さらに餘務あらず。

Abruptly transcending all the worlds, to be greatly honored within the house of the buddhas and ancestors — this is sitting with legs crossed.[1] Trampling the heads of the followers of other paths and the minions of Māra, to be the one here within the halls of the buddhas and ancestors — this is sitting with legs crossed.[2] Transcending the extreme of the extreme of the buddhas and ancestors is just this one dharma.[3] Therefore, the buddhas and ancestors engage in it, without any further task.

1 **greatly honored within the house of the buddhas and ancestors** (*busso no okuri ni tai sonki sei* 佛祖の屋裏に太尊貴生): Possibly reflecting a description by Dongshan Liangjie 洞山良价 (807-869) (*Dongshan dashi yulu* 洞山大師語錄, T.1986A.47:509a26-b6) of the "greatly honored" (*tai zungui sheng* 太尊貴生) official (*guanchashi* 觀察使), without name or duties, who simply remains within his chambers (*langmu* 廊幕), never going in or out. The Chinese envelope construction *tai . . . sheng* 太生 here functions as an intensive. The term *okuri* 屋裏 (also written 屋裡) can be understood as a reference either to the "house" (i.e., lineage) of the buddhas and ancestors or to their "rooms" (i.e., innermost dwelling place). See Supplementary Notes, s.v. "Buddhas and ancestors."

sitting with legs crossed (*kekkafu za* 結跏趺坐): A standard Buddhist term for the traditional meditation posture (S. *paryaṅka*) sometimes called the "lotus position" (S. *padmāsana*).

2 **followers of other paths and the minions of Māra** (*gedō matō* 外道・魔黨): The former expression refers to members of non-Buddhist traditions (S. *tīrthika*); the latter expression indicates the followers of Māra, the Evil One (S. *papīyān*), lord of the sixth heaven of the realm of desire (S. *kāma-loka*), who seeks to obstruct Buddhist awakening.

the one here within the halls of the buddhas and ancestors (*busso no dōō ni kochūnin* 佛祖の堂奥に箇中人): I.e., an authentic representative of the tradition. "Within the halls of the buddhas and ancestors" is a common expression virtually synonymous with *busso no okuri* 佛祖の屋裏, above; "the one here" (*kochūnin* 箇中人) is a common term for the real or accomplished person.

3 **the extreme of the extreme of the buddhas and ancestors** (*busso no kyoku shi kyoku* 佛祖の極之極): An unusual expression, not found elsewhere in the *Shōbōgenzō*,

[66:2]

まさにしるべし、坐の盡界と餘の盡界と、はるかにことなり。この道理をあきらめて、佛祖の發心・修行・菩提・涅槃を辨肯するなり。正當坐時は、盡界、それ竪なるか、横なるか、と參究すべし。正當坐時、その坐、それいかん。翻筋斗なるか、活鱍鱍地なるか、思量か、不思量か、作か、無作か。坐裏に坐すや、身心裏に坐すや、坐裏・身心裏等を脱落して坐すや。恁麼の千端萬端の參究あるべきなり。身の結跏趺坐すべし、心の結跏趺坐すべし、身心脱落の結跏趺坐すべし。

We should realize that there is a vast difference between all the worlds of sitting and all the other worlds.[4] Clarifying this principle, we confirm the bringing forth of the mind [of bodhi], the practice, the bodhi, and the nirvāṇa of the buddhas and ancestors.[5] We should investigate: at the very moment we are sitting, are all the worlds vertical?[6] Are they horizontal? At the very moment we are sitting, what about that sitting? Is it a flip? Is it brisk and lively?[7] Is it thinking? Is it not thinking?[8] Is it making? Is

---

presumably suggesting the "highest reaches" or "outermost limits" of the tradition — an image in contrast to the innermost recesses of the "quarters" and "halls" in the previous two sentences.

this one dharma (*kono ippō* この一法): Or "this one method," "this one truth," or simply "this one thing"; as is so often the case in Buddhist usage, the term *hō* 法, translated here as "dharma," is multivalent.

4 **all the worlds of sitting** (*za no jinkai* 坐の盡界): The translation seeks to preserve Dōgen's repetition here of *jinkai* (rendered as "all the worlds" above), but one might well take this expression simply as "the world of sitting."

5 **we confirm** (*benkō su* 辨肯す): A predicate, common in Dōgen's writing, carrying the sense "to discern and assent." The grammatical subject is unclear in the original and could be taken not as "we" (or "one") but as the "buddhas and ancestors."

the bringing forth of the mind [of bodhi], the practice, the bodhi, and the nirvāṇa (*hosshin shugyō bodai nehan* 發心・修行・菩提・涅槃): I.e., the spiritual career of the bodhisattva, from the initial aspiration for unsurpassed bodhi (S. *bodhi-cittotpāda*), through training on the path and the attainment of buddhahood, to final extinction. The point here would seem to be that, when one clarifies the principle of sitting, one comprehends the entirety of the Buddhist spiritual life. See Supplementary Notes, s.v. "Bring forth the mind."

6 **at the very moment we are sitting** (*shōtō za ji* 正當坐時): It is unclear whether this adverbial phrase governs the verb "to investigate" (*sankyū* 參究). Hence, though the form of the following passage suggests otherwise, the sentence could also be parsed, "At the very moment we are sitting, we should investigate: are all the worlds vertical? Are they horizontal?"

7 **a flip** (*honkinto* 翻筋斗); **brisk and lively** (*kappatsupatchi* 活鱍鱍地): Two terms, common in Chan texts, expressing unimpeded freedom and vigorous energy. For the latter, see Supplementary Notes, s.v. "Brisk and lively."

8 **Is it thinking? Is it not thinking?** (*shiryō ka, fushiryō ka* 思量か、不思量か): Likely an allusion to one of Dōgen's favorite dialogues about seated meditation; see Supplementary Notes, s.v. "Yaoshan's not thinking."

it without making?[9] Are we sitting within sitting? Are we sitting within body and mind? Are we sitting having sloughed off "within sitting," "within body and mind," and the like? We should investigate one thousand points, ten thousand points, such as these. We should do cross-legged sitting of the body; we should do cross-legged sitting of the mind; we should do cross-legged sitting of "body and mind sloughed off."[10]

[66:3] {2:178}

先師古佛云、參禪者、身心脱落也、祇管打坐始得。不要燒香・禮拜・念佛・修懺・看經。

My former master, the Old Buddha, said,[11]

Studying Chan is body and mind sloughed off. You only get it when you just sit; you don't need to offer incense, make bows, recollect the buddha, practice repentance, or read scripture.[12]

---

9 **Is it making? Is it without making?** (*sa ka, musa ka* 作か、無作か): While one need not assume a specific source for these questions, given the juxtaposition elsewhere in Dōgen's writing of "Yaoshan's not thinking" with the story known as "Nanyue polishes a tile" (*Nangaku ma sen* 南嶽磨甎), they are suggestive of the famous episode involving Mazu Daoyi 馬祖道一 (709-788) and his teacher, Nanyue Huairang 南嶽懷讓 (677-744). When Mazu says that he is practicing seated meditation to "make a buddha" (*sabutsu* 作佛), Nanyue likens this to trying to make a mirror by polishing a clay tile. See Supplementary Notes, s.v. "Nanyue polishes a tile"; for Dōgen's treatment of the story, see, e.g., "Shōbōgenzō zazen shin" 正法眼藏坐禪箴.

10 **we should do cross-legged sitting of "body and mind sloughed off"** (*shinjin datsuraku no kekkafu za subeshi* 身心脱落の結跏趺坐すべし): Dōgen here introduces the expression "body and mind sloughed off" (*shinjin datsuraku* 身心脱落) from the saying attributed to Rujing that he will quote immediately following this passage.

11 **My former master, the Old Buddha** (*senshi kobutsu* 先師古佛): An epithet, occurring often in Dōgen's writings, for his teacher Tiantong Rujing 天童如淨 (1162-1227). This saying, variant versions of which appear elsewhere in Dōgen's writings, has no known source in extant Chinese texts and is generally assumed to be the private recollection of Dōgen.

12 **body and mind sloughed off** (*shinjin datsuraku* 身心脱落); **just sit** (*shikan taza* 祇管打坐; also written 只管打坐): Two unusual expressions, not found in Chan literature (including that of Rujing 如淨); occurring several times in Dōgen's writings and much used in subsequent Sōtō tradition as technical terms for correct seated meditation. See Supplementary Notes, s.v. "Just sit" and "Body and mind sloughed off."

offer incense, make bows, recollect the buddha, practice repentance, or look at scripture (*shōkō raihai nenbutsu shusan kankin* 燒香・禮拜・念佛・修懺・看經): Standard Buddhist devotional practices. In Dōgen's day, recollection of the buddha (*nenbutsu* 念佛) typically referred to the recitation of the name of a buddha, especially Buddha Amitābha. The term *kankin* 看經, translated here as "look at scripture," is used in Chan and Zen to refer either to the reading or chanting of texts.

[66:4]
あきらかに佛祖の眼睛を抉出しきたり、佛祖の眼睛裏に打坐すること、四五百年よりこのかたは、ただ先師ひとりなり、震旦國に齊肩すくなし。打坐の佛法なること、佛法は打坐なることをあきらめたる、まれなり。たとひ打坐を佛法と體解すといふとも、打坐を打坐としれる、いまだあらず。いはんや佛法を佛法と保任するあらんや。

For the last four or five hundred years, clearly my former master is the only one who has plucked out the eye of the buddhas and ancestors, who sits within the eye of the buddhas and ancestors. There are few of equal stature in the Land of Cīnasthāna.[13] It is rare to have clarified that sitting is the buddha dharma, that the buddha dharma is sitting. Even if [some] realize sitting as the buddha dharma, they have not understood sitting as sitting — let alone maintained the buddha dharma as the buddha dharma.[14]

[66:5]
しかあれべすなはち、心の打坐あり、身の打坐とおなじからず。身の打坐あり、心の打坐とおなじからず。身心脱落の打坐あり、身心脱落の打坐とおなじからず。既得恁麼ならん、佛祖の行解相應なり。この念想觀を保任すべし。この心意識を參究すべし。

This being the case, there is the sitting of the mind, which is not the same as the sitting of the body. There is the sitting of the body, which is not the same as the sitting of the mind. There is the sitting of "body and mind sloughed off," which is not the same as the sitting of "body and mind sloughed off." To have got such is the accordance of practice and understanding of the buddhas and ancestors.[15] We should maintain this thought, idea, and perception; we should investigate this mind, mentation, and consciousness.[16]

13 **Land of Cīnasthāna** (*Shintan koku* 震旦國): A Buddhist term for China derived from the transliterated Sanskrit name.

14 **realize** (*taige* 體解): A loose translation for a term suggesting something like "to understand with one's body" — i.e., to have direct personal experience. The only instance of its use in the *Shōbōgenzō*.

15 **To have got such** (*ki toku inmo* 既得恁麼): Dōgen here uses the Chinese phrase *de renmo* (literally, "get such"), often encountered in Chan texts in casual reference to spiritual attainment — as in the well-known saying attributed to Yunju Daoying 雲居道膺 (d. 902); see Supplementary Notes, s.v. "Such a person."

16 **thought, idea, and perception** (*nen sō kan* 念想觀); **mind, mentation, and consciousness** (*shin i shiki* 心意識): A paired set of six types of mental activity appearing elsewhere in Dōgen's writings, where — contrary to his injunction here to "maintain" and "investigate" them — they are dismissed as irrelevant to zazen. (See "Shōbōgenzō zazen gi" 正法眼藏坐禪儀, DZZ.1:100.)

* * * * *

[66:6]

釋迦牟尼佛、告大衆言、若結跏趺坐、身心證三昧、威德衆恭敬、如日照世界。除睡懶覆心、身輕不疲懈、覺悟亦輕便、安坐如龍蟠。見畫跏趺坐、魔王亦驚怖、何況證道人、安坐不傾動。

Buddha Śākyamuni addressed the great assembly, saying,[17]
When sitting with legs crossed,
Body and mind realizing samādhi,
One's majesty, the multitudes respect,
Like the sun illumining the world.
Removed, the lethargy clouding the mind,
The body light, without pain or fatigue;
The awareness similarly light and easy,
One sits calmly, like the dragon coiled.
King Māra is startled and fearful
On seeing depicted one sitting with legs crossed,
How much more [on seeing] one who realizes the way,
Sitting calmly without stirring.

[66:7] {2:179}

しかあれば、跏趺坐を畫圖せるを見聞するを、魔王なほおどろき、うれへおそるるなり。いはんや眞箇に跏趺坐せん、その功德、はかりつくすべからず。しかあればすなはち、よのつねに打坐する福德無量なり。

Thus, King Māra is startled and frightened to perceive the depiction of [someone] sitting with legs crossed — how much more [someone] really sitting with legs crossed; the merit cannot be fully reckoned.[18] This being the case, the merit of our ordinary sitting is immeasurable.[19]

[66:8]

釋迦牟尼佛、告大衆言、以是故、結跏趺坐。復次如來世尊、教諸弟子應如是坐。或外道輩、或常翹足求道、或常立求道、或荷足求道。如是狂狷心、没邪海、形不安穩。以是故、佛教弟子結跏趺坐直心坐。何以故。直身心易正故。其身直坐、則心不懶。端心正意、繋念在前。若心馳散、若身傾動、攝之令還。欲證三昧、欲入三昧、種種馳念、種種散亂、皆悉攝之。如此修習、證入三昧王三昧。

17 **Buddha Śākyamuni** (*Shakamuni butsu* 釋迦牟尼佛): A slightly variant version of a verse appearing in the *Dajidu lun* 大智度論 (T.1509.25:111b-c). Dōgen's introductory clause here is not in the original passage, which does not in fact represent the words of the Buddha but occurs in the commentary on a line in the *Dapin bore jing* 大品般若經.

18 **really sitting with legs crossed** (*shinko ni kafu za* 眞箇に跏趺坐): The sense of *shinko ni* 眞箇に here could be taken either as "truly" (i.e., authentically) or as "actually" (as opposed to a depiction).

19 **our ordinary sitting** (*yo no tsune ni taza* よのつねに打坐): The exact implication is not clear; presumably, the routine practice of the monk sitting with legs crossed.

Buddha Śākyamuni addressed the great assembly, saying,[20]

Therefore, [the Buddha] sits with legs crossed. Further, the Thus Come One, the World-Honored One, instructs his disciples that they should sit like this. Followers of other paths seek the way while always keeping [one] leg raised, or seek the way while always standing, or seek the way with their legs on their shoulders.[21] *Thus, their minds are crazed, sinking in the sea of falsity, and their bodies are ill at ease. Therefore, the Buddha instructs his disciples to sit with legs crossed, to sit with mind upright. Why? Because, when the body is upright, the mind is easily corrected. When one's body is sitting upright, the mind will not slacken. With straightforward mind and correct attention, one fastens thought in front of one. If the mind wanders, if the body leans, one controls them and brings them back. Wishing to realize samādhi, wishing to enter samādhi, one collects the multiple wandering thoughts, the multiple distractions. Training in this way, one enters verification of the king of samādhis samādhi.*

[66:9] {2:180}

あきらかにしりぬ、結跏趺坐、これ三昧王三昧なり、これ證入なり。一切の三昧は、この王三昧の眷属なり。結跏趺坐は、直身なり、直心なり、直身心なり、直佛祖なり、直修證なり。直頂顊なり、直命脈なり。

It is clear from this that sitting with legs crossed is the king of samādhis samādhi, is entering verification. All the samādhis are the attendants of this king samādhi. Sitting with legs crossed is upright body, is upright mind, is upright body and mind, is upright buddha and ancestor, is upright practice and realization; it is upright crown of the head, upright vital artery.

[66:10]

いま人間の皮肉骨髓を結跏して、三昧中王三昧を結跏するなり。世尊、つねに結跏坐を保任しまします、諸弟子にも結跏趺坐を正傳しまします、人天にも結跏趺坐ををしへましますなり。七佛正傳の心印、すなはちこれなり。

Now crossing the legs of the human skin, flesh, bones, and marrow, one crosses the legs of the king of samādhis samādhi. The World-Honored One always maintains sitting with legs crossed; and to the disciples he correctly transmits sitting with legs crossed; and to the humans and

20 **Buddha Śākyamuni** (*Shakamuni butsu* 釋迦牟尼佛): Dōgen is here quoting (with some variation) the prose immediately following the *Dajidu lun* 大智度論 verse cited above (T.1509.25:111b22-29). Again, he has added the line, "Buddha Śākyamuni addressed the great assembly, saying," to what in the original is part of the commentary.

21 **Followers of other paths** (*gedō hai* 外道輩): Reference to non-Buddhist yogis.

devas he teaches sitting with legs crossed. The mind seal directly transmitted by the seven buddhas is this.[22]

[66:11]
釋迦牟尼佛、菩提樹下に跏趺坐しましまして、五十小劫を經歷し、六十劫を經歷し、無量劫を經歷しまします。あるひは三七日、あるひは結跏趺坐、時間の跏坐、これ轉妙法輪なり、これ一代の佛化なり。さらに虧缺せず、これすなはち黄卷朱軸なり。ほとけの、ほとけをみる、この時節なり。これ、衆生成佛の正當恁麼時なり。

Buddha Śākyamuni, sitting with legs crossed under the bodhi tree, passed fifty small kalpas, passed sixty kalpas, passed innumerable kalpas.[23] Or sitting with legs crossed for twenty-one days, sitting cross-legged for one time — this is turning the wheel of the wondrous dharma; this is the buddha's proselytizing of a lifetime.[24] There is nothing lacking. This is the yellow roll and vermilion roller.[25] Buddha meeting buddha is this time. This is precisely the time when beings attain buddhahood.

[66:12]
初祖菩提達磨尊者、西來のはじめより、嵩嶽少室峰少林寺にして面壁跏趺坐禪のあひだ、九白を經歷せり。それより頂𩕳眼睛、いまに震旦國に遍界せり。初祖の命脈、ただ結跏坐のみなり。初祖西來よりさきは、東土の衆生、いまだかつて結跏趺坐をしらざりき、祖師西來よりのち、これをしれり。

Upon coming from the west, the First Ancestor, the worthy Bodhidharma, passed nine autumns in seated meditation with legs crossed fac-

22 **The mind seal directly transmitted by the seven buddhas** (*shichi butsu shōden on shin'in* 七佛正傳の心印): "The seven buddhas" refers to the series of ancient buddhas ending with Buddha Śākyamuni; see Supplementary Notes, s.v. "Seven buddhas." "The mind seal" (*shin'in* 心印), or "buddha mind seal" (*busshin'in* 佛心印), is a common Chan expression for the state of mind of a buddha transmitted from master to disciple or for the verification of that transmission.

23 **fifty small kalpas** (*gojū shōkō* 五十小劫); **sixty kalpas** (*rokujū kō* 六十劫): Accounts of Śākyamuni's time under the bodhi tree do not typically reckon it in fifty or sixty kalpas. Rather, these periods of sitting may reflect two scenes in the *Lotus Sūtra* in which the Buddha and his community pass fifty and sixty small æons sitting without moving (*Miaofa lianhua jing* 妙法蓮華經, T.262.9:39c19-21 and T.262.9:4a23-26, respectively).

24 **twenty-one days** (*san shichi nichi* 三七日): Literally "three [times] seven days"; reference to the legend that the Buddha sat for three weeks under the bodhi tree.

turning the wheel of the wondrous dharma (*ten myōhō rin* 轉妙法輪): I.e., the promulgation of the buddha dharma.

25 **yellow roll and vermilion roller** (*ōkan shujiku* 黄卷朱軸): Reference to the paper and spindle of a roll of text; i.e., a scripture or, by extension here, the teachings of the buddha.

ing a wall at the Shaolin Monastery at Shaoshi Peak on Mount Song.[26] Thereafter, till now, the crown of his head and his eyes have been in realms everywhere throughout the Land of Cīnasthāna.[27] The vital artery of the First Ancestor is just sitting with legs crossed. Prior to the First Ancestor's coming from the west, beings in the Land of the East had not known of sitting with legs crossed; after the Ancestral Master came from the west, they knew of it.[28]

[66:13] {2:181}

しかあればすなはち、一生萬生、把尾収頭、不離叢林、晝夜祇管跏趺坐して餘務あらざる、三昧王三昧なり。

Therefore, for one life or ten thousand lives, grasping the tail and taking in the head, without leaving the grove, just sitting with legs crossed day and night, without other business — this is the king of samādhis samādhi.[29]

---

26 **nine autumns** (*kuhaku* 九白): Literally, "nine whites," taking "white" in the sense of "autumn," from its association with this season in the Chinese system of the five phases (*wuxing* 五行). Reference to the famous legend that Bodhidharma sat for nine years "facing a wall" (*menpeki* 面壁). The question of whether the term *menpeki* should be taken literally or metaphorically (as, for example, sitting with a "wall-like mind") is debated.

Shaolin Monastery at Shaoshi Peak on Mount Song (*Sōgaku Shōshippō* [or *Shitsuhō*] *Shōrinji* 嵩嶽少室峰少林寺): Monastery in the present Chengfeng District 澄封縣 of Henan prefecture, where Bodhidharma is said to have resided.

27 **crown of his head and his eyes** (*chōnei ganzei* 頂𩕳眼睛): Terms often used in Chan texts as synecdoche for a Chan master's wisdom or essential message; see Supplementary Notes, s.v. "Crown of the head" and "Nose."

have been in realms everywhere throughout the Land of Cīnasthāna (*Shintan koku ni henkai seri* 震旦國に遍界せり): I.e., have been pervasive in China. The translation attempts to preserve Dōgen's unusual use of *henkai* 遍界 ("realms everywhere") as a verb.

28 **Prior to the First Ancestor's coming from the west, beings in the Land of the East had not known of sitting with legs crossed** (*shoso seirai yori saki wa, Tōdo no shujō, imada katsute kekkafu za o shirazariki* 初祖西來よりさきは、東土の衆生、いまだかつて結跏趺坐をしらざりき): An odd claim, since of course Chinese Buddhists had been practicing seated meditation for centuries before the sixth century, when Bodhidharma was said to have arrived; perhaps Dōgen has in mind here some distinction between authentic and inauthentic cross-legged sitting, or between sitting and knowing the meaning of sitting.

29 **grasping the tail and taking in the head** (*ha bi shu tō* 把尾収頭): I.e., "from head to tail," "from start to finish."

without leaving the grove (*furi sōrin* 不離叢林): "The grove" is a common idiom for the monastic institution. The expressions "for one life" and "without leaving the grove" seem to reflect a saying of Zhaozhou Congshen 趙州從諗 (778-897) that is referred to in several of Dōgen's writings:

> 儞若一生不離叢林、不語十年五載、無人喚儞作啞漢、已後佛也不奈儞何.
>
> If for a lifetime you don't leave the grove and don't talk for ten years or five years,

正法眼藏三昧王三昧第六十六
Treasury of the True Dharma Eye
The King of Samādhis Samādhi
Number 66

[Ryūmonji MS:]
爾時寛元二年甲辰二月十五日、在越宇吉峰精舍示衆
Presented to the assembly at Kippō Vihāra, Etsuu; fifteenth day, second month of the senior wood year of the dragon, the second year of Kangen [25 March 1244][30]

---

no one will call you a mute; after that, even the Buddha won't know what to make of you.

For sources of the saying, see Supplementary Notes, s.v. "For a lifetime not leaving the grove."

30 The *Himitsu* 秘密 MS shares an identical colophon.

Treasury of the True Dharma Eye

Number 67

Turning the Dharma Wheel

Ten hōrin

轉法輪

Turning the Dharma Wheel

Ten hōrin

Introduction

This short work was produced in the spring of 1244, at Kippōji in Echizen. Number 67 in the seventy-five-chapter *Shōbōgenzō* and number 73 in the Honzan edition (or 74 in the Iwanami and Shūmuchō versions), it is not included in the sixty-chapter compilation but appears as number 5 in fascicle 2 of the twenty-eight-text *Himitsu Shōbōgenzō*.

The work deals with a passage from the *Śūraṃgama-sūtra* and the comments on it of several Chan masters, including Dōgen's own teacher, Tiantong Rujing 天童如淨. Our author himself adds a comment, but, in fact, he is less interested here in the content of the passage and the comments on it than in the canonical status of the passage and the effect of the comments on that status.

The *Śūraṃgama-sūtra*, although a popular work in Dōgen's day, was widely suspected to have been composed in China and, hence, to be an apocryphal scripture. In the *Hōkyō ki* 寶慶記, the record of his interviews with Rujing, Dōgen himself expresses his doubts about the text's authenticity and the quality of its teachings. Yet he argues here that the fact that Chan masters have taken up the sūtra passage for comment has rendered it authentic. Not only textual passages, he goes on to say, but everything taken up by the buddhas and ancestors of the tradition becomes thereby an authentic turning of the dharma wheel.

正法眼藏第六十七
Treasury of the True Dharma Eye
Number 67

轉法輪

Turning the Dharma Wheel

[67:1] {2:182}

先師天童古佛上堂、擧、世尊道、一人發眞歸源、十方虛空、悉皆消殞。師拈云、既是世尊所説、未免盡作奇特商量。天童則不然、一人發眞歸源、乞兒打破飯椀。

My former master, the Old Buddha of Tiantong, in a convocation, raised [the following]:[1]

The World-Honored One said, "When someone reveals the truth and returns to the source, space throughout the ten directions completely vanishes."

The Master took this up, saying, "Since this was spoken by the World-Honored One, inevitably, there have been endless extraordinary deliberations about it. Tiantong is not like this. When someone reveals the truth and returns to the source, the beggar breaks his rice bowl."

[67:2]

五祖山法演和尚道、一人發眞歸源、十方虛空、築著磕著。佛性法泰和尚道、一人發眞歸源、十方虛空、只是十方虛空。夾山円悟禪師克勤和尚云、一人發眞歸源、十方虛空、錦上添華。大佛道、一人發眞歸源、十方虛空、發眞歸源。

Reverend Fayan of Mount Wuzu said, "When someone reveals the truth and returns to the source, space throughout the ten directions "hits and bangs."[2]

1 **My former master, the Old Buddha of Tiantong** (*senshi Tendō kobutsu* 先師天童古佛): I.e., Dōgen's teacher, Tiantong Rujing 天童如淨 (1162-1227). The passage is quoted from the *Rujing heshang yulu* 如淨和尚語錄 (T.2002A.48:128b5-8). Rujing's quotation of the Buddha is based on a passage in the *Śūraṃgama-sūtra* (*Shoulengyan jing* 首楞嚴經, T.945.19:147b10-11). The material in this and the following section appears in a slightly different form in Dōgen's *Eihei kōroku* 永平廣錄 (DZZ.3:118, no. 179).

2 **Reverend Fayan of Mount Wuzu** (*Gosozan Hōen oshō* 五祖山法演和尚): I.e., Wuzu Fayan 五祖法演 (d. 1104), teacher to Yuanwu Keqin 圜悟克勤 (whose words appear just below). His saying here can be found in the *Fayan chanshi yulu* 法演禪師語錄 (T.1995.47:650a7-9). "Hits and bangs" translates *chikujaku katsujaku* 築著磕著, a

Reverend Foxing Fatai said, "When someone reveals the truth and returns to the source, space throughout the ten directions is just space throughout the ten directions."[3]

Chan Master Yuanwu of Jiashan, Reverend Keqin, said, "When someone reveals the truth and returns to the source, space throughout the ten directions adds flowers to brocade."[4]

Daibutsu says, "When someone reveals the truth and returns to the source, space throughout the ten directions reveals the truth and returns to the source."[5]

[67:3] {2:182}

いま擧するところの、一人發眞歸源、十方虛空、悉皆消殞は、首楞嚴經のなかの道なり。この句、かつて數位の佛祖、おなじく擧しきたれり。いまよりこの句、まことに佛祖骨髓なり、佛祖眼睛なり。しかいふこころは、首楞嚴經一部拾軸、あるいはこれを僞經といふ、あるいは僞經にあらずといふ、兩説すでに往古よりいまにいたれり。舊譯有り、新譯ありといへども、疑著するところ、神龍年中の譯をうたがふなり。しかあれども、いますでに五祖の演和尚・佛性泰和尚・先師天童古佛、ともにこの句を擧しきたれり。ゆえにこの句、すでに佛祖の法輪に轉ぜられたり、佛祖法輪轉なり。このゆえに、この句、すでに佛祖を轉じ、この句、すでに佛祖をとく。佛祖に轉ぜられ、佛祖を轉ずるがゆえに、たとひ僞經なりとも、佛祖、もし轉擧しきたらば、眞箇の佛經・祖經なり、親曾の佛祖法輪なり。たとひ瓦礫なりとも、たとひ黄葉なりとも、たとひ優曇華なりとも、たとひ金襴衣なりとも、佛祖すでに拈來すれば佛法輪なり、佛正法眼藏なり。

What is taken up here — "*When someone reveals the truth and returns to the source, space throughout the ten directions completely vanishes*" — are words from the *Śūraṃgama-sūtra*. This passage has previously been taken up by several buddhas and ancestors. So now, the passage is truly the bones and marrow of the buddhas and ancestors, the eyes of buddhas and ancestors. I speak of this because, from long ago till today, there have been two opinions [on the text], some holding that the *Śūraṃgama-sūtra* in ten rolls is an apocryphal sūtra and some saying that it is not an apocryphal sūtra. There is an older translation and a new-

---

common expression in Zen texts for things colliding or bumping together; see Supplementary Notes, s.v. "Hitting and banging."

3 **Reverend Foxing Fatai** (*Busshō Hōtai oshō* 佛性法泰和尚): I.e., Dawei Fatai 大潙法泰 (dates unknown), another disciple of Yuanwu Keqin 圜悟克勤. His saying appears in the *Jiatai pudeng lu* 嘉泰普燈錄, ZZ.137:371a8-11.

4 **Chan Master Yuanwu of Jiashan, Reverend Keqin** (*Kassan Engo zenji Kokugon oshō* 夾山円悟禪師克勤和尚): I.e., Yuanwu Keqin 圜悟克勤 (1063–1135). His saying can be found in the *Yuanwu chanshi yulu* 圓悟禪師語錄 (T.1997.47:748a25-28).

5 **Daibutsu** (*Daibutsu* 大佛): I.e., Dōgen, who was at this time abbot of Daibutsuji 大佛寺, the monastery subsequently renamed Eiheiji 永平寺.

er translation; but the one about which there are doubts is the translation done during the Shenlong years.[6]

Nevertheless, now Reverend Yan of Wuzu, Reverend Foxing Tai, and my former master, the Old Buddha of Tiantong have all taken up this passage. Hence, this passage has been turned by the dharma wheel of the buddhas and ancestors; it is a turning of the dharma wheel of the buddhas and ancestors. For this reason, this passage has turned the buddhas and ancestors; this passage has preached the buddhas and ancestors. Because it has been turned by the buddhas and ancestors and has turned the buddhas and ancestors, even if it is [found in] an apocryphal sūtra, if the buddhas and ancestors have been turning it and taking it up, it is an authentic sūtra of the buddhas and sūtra of the ancestors; it is a dharma wheel of the buddhas and ancestors personally experienced.[7] Even tiles and pebbles, even yellow leaves, even the *udumbara* flower, even the gold brocade robe — since the buddhas and ancestors have taken them up, they are the dharma wheel of the buddhas, the treasury of the true dharma eye of the buddhas.[8]

---

6 **There is an older translation and a newer translation** (*kyūyaku ari, shinyaku ari* 舊譯有り、新譯あり): Likely a reference to two different sūtras, with similar titles, that are often confused: (a) the *Shoulengyan sanmei jing* 首楞嚴三昧經 (*Śūraṃgama-samādhi-sūtra*), in two rolls, known in Dōgen's day from the early fifth-century translation of Kumārajīva (T.642); and (b) the *Shoulengyan jing* 首楞嚴經 (*Śūraṃgama-sūtra*; T.945), in ten rolls, said to have been translated in 705 by someone named Bolamidi 般剌蜜帝 but generally thought to have been composed in China. "The Shenlong years" (*Jinryū nenchū* 神龍年中) in the next clause refers to the Chinese era, 705-707.

Interestingly, given what he says here, Dōgen himself seems to have shared the doubts about the Indian provenance of the *Śūraṃgama-sūtra*. In his *Hōkyō ki* 寶慶記 (DZZ.7:12, section 6), the work purporting to record his conversations with Tiantong Rujing 天童如淨, Dōgen expresses his doubts about the authenticity of the sūtra (as well as another sūtra of Chinese origin, the *Yuanjue jing* 圓覺經) and receives assurance from Rujing that he is right to question it.

7 **dharma wheel of the buddhas and ancestors personally experienced** (*shinzō no busso hōrin* 親曾の佛祖法輪): Or, perhaps, "a dharma wheel of the buddhas and ancestors who have personally experienced it." "Personally experienced" is a loose rendering of the unusual expression *shinzō* 親曾 (literally, "once personally"), appearing several times in the *Shōbōgenzō* to indicate what is personal or intimate; probably adopted by Dōgen from a line in a poem by his teacher, Rujing 如淨: "He [Piṇḍola] once personally saw the Buddha" (*shin zō ken butsu* 親曾見佛).

8 **tiles and pebbles** (*ga ryaku* 瓦礫): Likely recalling the well-known definition of the buddha mind first attributed to Nanyang Huizhong 南陽慧忠 (d. 775); see Supplementary Notes, s.v. "Fences, walls, tiles, and pebbles."

yellow leaves (*kōyō* 黄葉): Likely recalling the well-known case, found in the *Nirvāṇa Sūtra* (*Da banniepan jing* 大般涅槃經, T.375.12:729a3-6) of the yellow willow leaf that is given to a crying child, who takes it for gold and is thereby consoled.

[67:4]

しるべし、衆生、もし超出成正覺すれば、佛祖なり、佛祖の師資なり、佛祖の皮肉骨髓なり。さらに從來の兄弟衆生を兄弟とせず、佛祖これ兄弟なるがごとく、拾軸の文句たとひ僞なりとも、而今の句は超出の句なり、佛句・祖句なり、餘文・餘句に群すべからず。たとひこの句は超越の句なりとも、一部の文句・性相を佛言祖語に擬すべからず、參學眼睛とすべからず。

We should recognize that, when living beings transcend themselves and attain correct awakening, they are buddhas and ancestors; they are the teachers and disciples of the buddhas and ancestors; they are the skin, flesh, bones, and marrow of the buddhas and ancestors. Furthermore, they do not regard as brothers their former brother living beings; the buddhas and ancestors are their brothers. Similarly, even if the text of the ten rolls is apocryphal, the present passage is a transcendent passage, is a buddha passage, an ancestor passage, not to be grouped with the other texts or other passages. Although this passage is a transcendent passage, we should not judge the nature and marks of the entire text to be the speech of the buddhas and words of the ancestors; we should not take them as the eye of study.

[67:5] {2:184}

而今の句を諸句に比論すべからざる道理おほかる、そのなかに、一端を擧拈すべし。いはゆる、轉法輪は佛祖儀なり、佛祖いまだ不轉法輪あらず。その轉法輪の樣子、あるいは聲色を擧拈して聲色を打失す、あるいは聲色を跳脱して轉法輪す、あるいは眼睛を抉出して轉法輪す、あるいは拳頭を擧起して轉法輪す、あるいは鼻孔をとり、あるいは虚空をとるところに、法輪自轉なり。而今の句をとる、いましこれ明星をとり、鼻孔をとり、桃華をとり、虚空をとる、すなはちなり。佛祖をとり、法輪をとる、すなはちなり。この宗旨、あきらかに轉法輪なり。

Among the many reasons why the present passage should not be compared with the other passages, we should take up one point. Turning the dharma wheel is the praxis of the buddhas and ancestors; there have never been buddhas and ancestors who did not turn the dharma wheel. In their manner of turning the dharma wheel, they may take up sound and form to lose sound and form; they may turn the dharma wheel by jumping out of sound and form; they may turn the dharma wheel by

---

***udumbara* flower** (*udonge* 優曇華): A flower said to bloom only rarely (in some accounts, only once every three thousand years) and, hence, used in Buddhist literature to represent a rare and precious event; often identified as the cluster fig (*ficus glomerata*). Here, the reference is likely to the *udumbara* flower that, in Dōgen's telling of the story, the Buddha held up when he transmitted the dharma to Mahākāśyapa on Vulture Peak.

gold brocade robe (*kinran e* 金襴衣): Likely recalling the legend that Buddha Śākyamuni bestowed a gold brocade robe on Mahākāśyapa, to be handed on to the next buddha, Maitreya (see, e.g., *Jingde chuandeng lu* 景德傳燈錄, T.2076.51:205c3-5).

gouging out the eye; they may turn the dharma wheel by holding up a fist; or the dharma wheel may turn by itself where they grab a nose or grab empty space.[9] Grabbing the present passage — this is immediately to grab the dawn star, to grab the nose, to grab the peach blossoms, to grab space, exactly; it is to grab the buddhas and ancestors, to grab the dharma wheel, exactly.[10] Clearly, the essential point of this is turning the dharma wheel.

[67:6]

轉法輪といふは、功夫參學して一生不離叢林なり、長連牀上に請益辦道するをいふ。

"Turning the dharma wheel" means making concentrated effort and studying, "for a lifetime without leaving the grove"; it means seeking instruction and pursuing the way on the long platform.[11]

正法眼藏轉法輪第六十七
The Treasury of True Dharma Eye
Turning the Dharma Wheel
Number 67

---

9 **grab a nose** (*bikū o tori* 鼻孔をとり); **grab empty space** (*kokū o toru* 虛空をとる): Likely allusion to the story, recorded in Dōgen's *shinji Shōbōgenzō* 眞字正法眼藏 (DZZ.5:256, case 248) and discussed in the "Shōbōgenzō kokū" 正法眼藏虛空, in which grabbing hold of a nose is taken as grabbing hold of space; see Supplementary Notes, s.v. "Nose."

10 **grab the dawn star** (*myōjō o tori* 明星をとり): Reference to the tradition that Prince Siddhārtha achieved buddhahood upon seeing Venus in the morning sky.

grab the peach blossoms (*tōka o tori* 桃華をとり): Likely an allusion to the story, cited several times in the *Shōbōgenzō*, of Lingyun Zhiqin 靈雲志勤 (dates unknown), who was awakened upon seeing peach trees in bloom; see Supplementary Notes, s.v. "Peach blossoms."

11 **"for a lifetime without leaving the grove"** (*isshō furi sōrin* 一生不離叢林): "The grove" is a common idiom for the monastic institution. Perhaps, recalling a saying of Zhaozhou Congshen 趙州從諗 (778-897) that is referred to in several of Dōgen's writings.

> 儞若一生不離叢林、不語十年五載、無人喚儞作啞漢、已後佛也不奈儞何.
>
> If for a lifetime you don't leave the grove and don't talk for ten years or five years, no one will call you a mute; after that, even the Buddha won't know what to make of you.

For sources of the saying, see Supplementary Notes, s.v. "For a lifetime not leaving the grove."

long platform (*chōrenshō* 長連牀): The extended daises in the saṃgha hall (*sōdō* 僧堂) on which monks of the great assembly (*daishu* 大衆) sat in meditation, chanted sūtras in prayer services, took their meals, and slept at night.

爾時寬元二年甲辰二月二十七日、在越宇吉峰精舍示衆

Presented to the assembly at the Yoshimine Vihāra, Etsuu, Twenty-seventh day, second month of the senior wood year of the dragon, the second year of Kangen [6 April 1244]

同三月一日、在同精舍侍者寮書寫之

Copied at the acolyte's quarters, in the same vihāra, first day, third month of the same year [9 April 1244]

後以御再治本校勘、書寫之畢

Collation and copying subsequently completed from his revised text[12]

12 **his revised text** (*gosaijibon* 御再治本): The honorific prefix suggests that the copy was made from a version revised by Dōgen himself.

Treasury of the True Dharma Eye

Number 68

Great Practice

Dai shugyō

大修行

Great Practice

Dai shugyō

Introduction

This work was composed in the spring of 1244, at Dōgen's Kippōji in Echizen. Occurring as number 68 in the seventy-five-chapter *Shōbōgenzō*, it represents number 75 in the Honzan edition (or 76 in the Iwanami and Shūmuchō versions); it is not included in the sixty-chapter compilation but appears as number 7 in fascicle 2 of the twenty-eight-text *Himitsu* collection.

The work is a commentary on the famous kōan of Baizhang Huaihai 百丈懷海 and a fox, with which the essay opens. The kōan turns on the question of whether the person of "great practice" (*dai shugyō* 大修行) is subject to the laws of cause and effect. The fox was once a monk on Mount Baizhang who taught that such a person is not subject to cause and effect, as a consequence of which he has been reborn as a fox for five hundred lifetimes. He is liberated from his fox body upon hearing Baizhang say that the person of great practice is "not in the dark about cause and effect." The corpse of the fox is then given the funeral rites of a monk.

In his comments, Dōgen identifies "great practice" with "great cause and effect" and goes on to criticize those who think that the monk was wrong and Baizhang right in their answers. Indeed, he is strongly critical more generally of what he considers naive readings of the story, pointing out a variety of interpretive issues arising from a literal reading. Among these, he is particularly dismissive of the notion that a fox corpse could be given a monastic funeral, a dangerous precedent, he warns, for lay householders expecting the same.

It is instructive to compare Dōgen's comments in this essay with his remarks on the fox kōan in the "Jinshin inga" 深信因果 essay in the twelve-chapter *Shōbōgenzō*.

正法眼藏第六十八
Treasury of the True Dharma Eye Number 68

大修行
Great Practice

[68:1] {2:185}

洪州百丈山大智禪師＜嗣馬祖諱懷海＞、凡參次、有一老人、常隨衆聽法、大衆若退、老人亦退。忽一日不退。師遂問、面前立者、復是何人。老人對曰、某甲是非人也。於過去迦葉佛時、曾住此山、因學人問、大修行底人、還落因果也無。某甲答他云、不落因果。後五百生、墮野狐身。今請和尚代一轉語、貴脱野狐身。遂問曰、大修行底人、還落因果也無。師云、不昧因果。老人於言下大悟、作禮曰、某甲已脱野狐身、住此山後、敢告和尚、乞依亡僧事例。師令維那白槌告衆曰、食後送亡僧。大衆言議、一衆皆安、涅槃堂又無病人、何故如是。食後只見師領衆、至山後巖下、以杖指出一死野狐。乃依法火葬。師至晩上堂、擧前因緣。黄檗便問、古人錯對一轉語、墮五百生野狐身、轉轉不錯、合作箇什麼。師云、近前來、與儞道。檗遂近前、與師一掌。師拍手笑云、將爲胡鬚赤、更有赤鬚胡。

Whenever Chan Master Dazhi of Mount Baizhang in Hongzhou (succeeded Mazu, named Huaihai) held a convocation, there was an old man who always joined the assembly to hear the dharma and who also withdrew when the great assembly withdrew.[1] *One day, unexpectedly, he did not withdraw. Whereupon, the Master asked him, "Just who are you, standing there?"*

The old man answered, "I'm not a human. At the time of the past Buddha Kāśyapa, I once lived on this mountain.[2] *A student asked me,*

---

1 **Chan Master Dazhi of Mount Baizhang in Hongzhou (succeeded Mazu, named Huaihai)** (*Kōshū Hyakujōzan Daichi zenji* [*shi Baso ki Ekai*] 洪州百丈山大智禪師＜嗣馬祖諱懷海＞): Parenthetical matter is in the original. I.e., Baizhang Huaihai 百丈懷海 (749-814). This famous story of Baizhang and the fox occurs in many sources, including Dōgen's *shinji Shōbōgenzō* 眞字正法眼藏 (DZZ.5:178, case 102). Dōgen also quotes and comments on the story in his "Shōbōgenzō jinshin inga" 正法眼藏深信因果.

2 **"At the time of the past Buddha Kāśyapa"** (*o kako Kashō butsu ji* 於過去迦葉佛時): Or "in the past, at the time of Buddha Kāśyapa." Kāśyapa is the sixth in the series of seven buddhas of the past culminating with Buddha Śākyamuni; see Supplementary Notes, s.v. "Seven buddhas."

"I once lived on this mountain" (*sō jū shi san* 曾住此山): The suggestion is that he served as abbot of a monastery on Mount Baizhang 百丈山; hence, below he will be referred to as "the former Baizhang."

'Does the person of great practice fall into cause and effect?' I answered him saying, 'He doesn't fall into cause and effect.' Thereafter, for five hundred lives, I have descended into the body of a fox. Now I beg the Reverend to say a turning word in my stead and let me shed this fox body." Whereupon, he asked, "Does the person of great practice fall into cause and effect?"

The Master said, "He's not in the dark about cause and effect."[3]

At these words, the old man had a great awakening. He made a prostration and said, "I've shed the body of the fox, which lived behind this mountain. May I be so bold as to beg the Reverend for the rites for a deceased monk?"

The Master had the rector strike the mallet and announce to the assembly, "After the meal, we send off a deceased monk."[4]

The great assembly expressed doubt, [saying] "The assembly is all well, and there is no one ill in the nirvāṇa hall.[5] *So, what is this?"*

But after the meal, the Master led the assembly beneath a cliff behind the mountain, where he uncovered a dead fox with his staff. They then cremated it in accordance with the dharma.

In a convocation that evening, the Master raised the above incident. Huangbo then asked, "The man of old, with the single turning word of a mistaken response, descended for five hundred lives into the body of a fox.[6] *What would happen if he turned and turned without a mistake?"*[7]

The Master said, "Come forward and I'll tell you."

Po thereupon came forward and gave the Master a blow.

---

3 **"He's not in the dark about cause and effect"** (*fumai inga* 不昧因果): The predicate *fumai* 不昧 is variously interpreted as "not blind to," "not oblivious to," "not ignorant of (or about)," "not confused by (or about)," etc.

4 **had the rector strike the mallet** (*rei ino byakutsui* 令維那白椎): The rector (*ino* 維那) is the administrator in charge of the assembly of monks, one of the six principle monastic offices (*roku chiji* 六知事). "Strike the mallet" translates *byakutsui* 白椎 (also written 白槌), the "announcement mallet" with the sound of which the *ino* signals the assembly.

5 **"nirvāṇa hall"** (*nehan dō* 涅槃堂): I.e., the monastic infirmary, also called the "life-prolonging hall" (*enju dō* 延壽堂); the designation "nirvāṇa hall" comes from the fact that it also served as a hospice for dying monks.

6 **Huangbo** (*Ōbaku* 黄檗): I.e., Huangbo Xiyun 黄檗希運 (dates unknown), famous disciple of Baizhang 百丈.

7 **"turned and turned without a mistake"** (*tenden fushaku* 轉轉不錯): "Turned and turned" (*tenden* 轉轉) here is generally taken to mean "through lifetime after lifetime."

The Master clapped his hands and laughed, saying, "Here, I thought the foreigner's beard is red, but now here's a red-bearded foreigner."[8]

[68:2] {2:186}

而今現成の公案、これ大修行なり。老人道のごときは、過去迦葉佛のとき洪州百丈山あり、現在釋迦牟尼佛のとき洪州百丈山あり。これ現成の一轉語なり。かくのごとくなりといへども、過去迦葉佛時の百丈山と、現在釋迦牟尼佛時の百丈山と、一にあらず、異にあらず、前三三にあらず、後三三にあらず。過去の百丈山きたりて、而今の百丈山となれるにあらず、いまの百丈山、さきだちて、迦葉佛時の百丈山にあらざれども、曾住此山の公案あり。爲學人道、それ今百丈の爲老人道のごとし。因學人問、それ今老人問のごとし。擧一不得擧二、放過一著、落在第二なり。

The kōan realized here is "the great practice."[9] What the old man said is that, at the time of "the past Buddha Kāśyapa," there was Mount Baizhang in Hongzhou; at the time of the present Buddha Śākyamuni, there is Mount Baizhang in Hongzhou.[10] This is a realized "turning word."[11] Although this is the case, Mount Baizhang at the time of the past Buddha Kāśyapa and Mount Baizhang at the time of the present Buddha Śākyamuni are not one, not different, not three three in front, not three three in back.[12] It is not that the past Mount Baizhang has come down to become the present Mount Baizhang; it is not that the present Mount Baizhang existed before and was the Mount Baizhang at the time of Buddha Kāśyapa. Nevertheless, there is the kōan of "*I once lived on*

8 **"Here, I thought the foreigner's beard is red, but now here's a red-bearded foreigner"** (*shō i koshu shaku, kō u shakushu ko* 將爲胡鬚赤、更有赤鬚胡): A saying often used in the sense of a distinction without a difference, but here perhaps meaning something like, "while I knew that foreigners had red beards, I didn't expect to encounter such a person." The term *hu* (*ko* 胡), often translated "barbarian," is used to refer to non-Han people to the north and west of the Chinese heartland.

9 **The kōan realized here** (*nikon genjō no kōan* 而今現成の公案): I.e., "the present case," "the case occurring here." Dōgen uses here a version of the famous expression "the realized kōan" (*genjō kōan* 現成公案); see Supplementary Notes, s.v. "Realized kōan."

10 **the time of the present Buddha Śākyamuni** (*genzai Shakamuni butsu no toki* 現在釋迦牟尼佛のとき): Presumably, the reference here is to the present age, of which Śākyamuni is the buddha (not the time in which Śākyamuni lived).

11 **This is a realized "turning word"** (*kore genjō no itten go nari* これ現成の一轉語なり): I.e., the old man's saying that Mount Baizhang in Hongzhou existed at both the time of Kāśyapa and the time of Śākyamuni is "an obvious turning word" —a statement that expresses what is at stake in the case.

12 **three three in front** (*zen sansan* 前三三); **three three in back** (*go sansan* 後三三): Or, perhaps, "three three of the former"; "three three of the latter." From a dialogue included in the *shinji Shōbōgenzō* 眞字正法眼藏 (DZZ.5:194-195, case 127) and cited elsewhere in the *Shōbōgenzō*; see Supplementary Notes, s.v. "Three three in front, three three in back."

this mountain." His *saying something for the student* is like Baizhang here saying something for the old man.[13] *A student once asked* is like the old man here asking. "*If you take up one, you can't take up a second; if you let the first move go, you fall into the second.*"[14]

[68:3] {2:187}

過去學人問、過去百丈山の大修行底人、還落因果也無。この問、まことに卒爾に容易會すべからず。そのゆえは、後漢永平のなかに、佛法東漸よりのち、梁代普通のなか、祖師西來ののち、はじめて老野狐の道より、過去の學人問をきく。これよりさきは、いまだあらざるところなり。しかあれば、まれにきくといふべし。

The past student asked, "Does the person of great practice on the past Mount Baizhang *fall into cause and effect?*" Truly, we should not easily understand this question too quickly. For, only after the buddha dharma progressed eastward in the Yongping [era] of the Later Han, after the Ancestral Master came from the west in the Putong [era] of the Liang dynasty, do we hear of the past student's question from the words of the old fox.[15] It is something that did not exist prior to this. Hence, we have to say it is something rarely heard.

[68:4]

大修行を摸得するに、これ大因果なり。この因果、かならず圓因滿果なるがゆえに、いまだかつて落・不落の論あらず、昧・不昧の道あらず。不落因果、もしあやまりならば、不昧因果もあやまりなるべし。將錯就錯すといへども、墮野狐身あり、脱野狐身あり。不落因果、たとひ迦葉佛時にはあやまりなりとも、釋迦佛時はあやまりにあらざる道理もあり。不昧因果、たとひ現在釋迦佛のときは脱野狐身すとも、迦葉佛時、しかあらざる道理も現成すべきなり。

---

13 **His saying something for the student** (*i gakunin dō* 爲學人道): A fixed expression in Chinese for a word of teaching from the master, repeated below, in section 20. The point here is, presumably, that the old man's having answered the student in the past corresponds to Baizhang's answering the old man in the present. Similarly, in the next sentence, the student's past questioning corresponds to the old man's present questioning.

14 **"If you take up one, you can't take up a second; if you let the first move go, you fall into the second"** (*ko ichi futoku ko ni, hōka ichijaku, raku zai dai ni* 擧一不得擧二、放過一著、落在第二): A saying appearing with some frequency in Chan texts, attributed to the Tang-dynasty monk Qianfeng 乾峰 (dates unknown), a follower of Dongshan 洞山. (See, e.g., *Biyan lu* 碧巖錄, T.2003.48:165b4.) The reference to "moves" is to a board game: "if you pass on your turn, play goes to the other." The exact meaning in this context is subject to interpretation; it is most often taken to mean that, since the two answers in the story are equivalent, whichever one considers, it obviates the other. (See, e.g., SZ.22:392-393.)

15 **the Yongping [era] of the Later Han** (*Gokan Eihei* 後漢永平): 58-75 CE, the date traditionally given for the transmission of Buddhism to China.

the Putong [era] of the Liang dynasty (*Ryōdai Futsū* 梁代普通): 520-527 CE, a date traditionally given for the arrival in China of the "Ancestral Master," Bodhidharma.

When we get hold of the "great practice," it is great "cause and effect." Since this cause and effect is always the perfect cause and the complete effect, there has never been an issue of "falling" or "not falling," nor words about "in the dark" or "not in the dark."[16] If "*not falling into cause and effect*" is a mistake, "*not being in the dark about cause and effect*" should also be a mistake. Though it may be *making a mistake of a mistake*, there is *descending into the body of a fox*, there is *shedding the body of a fox*.[17] There is also the reasoning that, while "*not falling into cause and effect*" may be a mistake at the time of Kāśyapa, it is not a mistake at the time of Buddha Śākyamuni. And there should also occur the reasoning that, while "*not being in the dark about cause and effect*" may "*shed the body of a fox*" in the present time of Buddha Śākyamuni, it does not at the time of Buddha Kāśyapa.

[68:5] {2:188}
老人道の後五百生墮野狐身は、作麼生是墮野狐身。さきより野狐ありて、先百丈をまねきおとさしむるにあらず、先百丈、もとより野狐なるべからず。先百丈の精魂いでて野狐皮袋に撞入す、といふは外道なり。野狐きたりて先百丈を呑却すべからず。もし、先百丈さらに野狐となる、といはば、まづ脱先百丈身あるべし、のちに墮野狐身すべきなり。以百丈山換野狐身なるべからず、因果の、いかでかしかあらん。因果の、本有にあらず、始起にあらず。因果のいたづらなるありて、人をまつことなし。

The old man said, "*Thereafter, for five hundred lives, I have descended into the body of a fox.*" *How did he descend into the body of a fox?* It is not the case that there was a previously existing fox that attracted the former Baizhang to fall [into its body]; nor could the former Baizhang have originally been a fox.[18] To say that the spirit of the former Baizhang emerged from him and forced its way into the skin bag of a fox would be non-Buddhist. The fox could not have come up and swallowed the former Baizhang. If we say the former Baizhang became a fox, he must first have shed the body of the former Baizhang and then descended into the body of the fox. One cannot exchange Mount Baizhang for the body of a fox.[19] How could cause and effect be like this? Cause and effect is

16 **the perfect cause and the complete effect** (*en'in manka* 圓因滿果): An expression presumably rearranging the phrase "perfect and complete cause and effect" (*enman inga* 圓滿因果); generally understood as affirming the absolute value of both cause and effect, or the non-differentiation of spiritual training and its fruit.

17 **making a mistake of a mistake** (*shōshaku jushaku* 將錯就錯): An idiom, found in Zen texts, meaning "to recognize one's mistake as such," "to turn a mistake to one's advantage," or "to make one mistake after another"; see Supplementary Notes, s.v. "Make a mistake of a mistake."

18 **the former Baizhang** (*sen Hyakujō* 先百丈): I.e., the monk formerly living on Mount Baizhang.

19 **Mount Baizhang** (*Hyakujōzan* 百丈山): I.e., again, the monk formerly on Mount Baizhang.

neither originally existent nor newly arisen.[20] Cause and effect does not waste time waiting for the person.

[68:6]
たとひ不落因果の祇對、たとひあやまれりとも、かならず野狐身に墮すべからず。學人の問著を錯對する業因によりて、野狐身に墮すること必然ならば、近來ある臨濟・德山、およびかの門人等、いく千萬枚の野狐にか墮在せん。そのほか二三百年來の杜撰長老等、そこばくの野狐ならん。しかあれども、墮野狐せりときこえず。おほからば、見聞にもあまるべきなり。あやまらずもあるらんといふつべしといへども、不落因果よりもはなはだしき胡亂答話のみおほし。佛法の邊におくべからざるも、おほきなり。參學眼ありてしるべきなり、未具眼はわきまふべからず。しかあればしりぬ、あしく祇對するによりて野狐身となり、よく祇對するによりて野狐身とならず、といふべからず。この因緣のなかに、脫野狐身ののちいかなりといはず、さだめて皮袋につつめる眞珠あるべきなり。

Even if the answer, "he does not fall into cause and effect," were a mistake, one would not necessarily descend into the body of a fox. If it were inevitable that one descended into the body of a fox by the karmic cause of giving a mistaken answer to a student's question, how many thousand or myriad times more recently would Linji, Deshan, and their followers have descended into a fox?[21] In addition, how many of the illiterate elders of the past two or three hundred years would be foxes?[22] Yet one does not hear that they have descended into foxes. If there were many of them, there would be more than enough to hear of them. Though we may grant that there are some who are not mistaken, there are many more confused answers worse than "*he does not fall into cause and effect.*" There are many not to be placed in the proximity of the buddha dharma. We know them when we have the eye of study; those unendowed with the eye will not distinguish them. Thus, we know that we cannot say either that one becomes a fox body by giving a bad answer or that one does

20 **Cause and effect is neither originally existent nor newly arisen** (*inga no hon'u ni arazu, shiki ni arazu* 因果の、本有にあらず、始起にあらず): A reference, presumably, to the relationship between the effect (the fox) and its cause (the monk): the effect neither inheres in the cause nor is wholly independent of it.

21 **Linji, Deshan, and their followers** (*Rinzai Tokusan oyobi kano monjin tō* 臨濟・德山およびかの門人等): I.e., Linji Yixuan 臨濟義玄 (d. 866), founder of the Linji lineage; and his contemporary Deshan Xuanjian 德山宣鑑 (780-865). These two figures are singled out for criticism elsewhere in the *Shōbōgenzō*.

22 **illiterate elders** (*zusan chōrō tō* 杜撰長老等): "Illiterate" is a loose translation for *zusan* 杜撰, more literally, "Du composition," used in pejorative reference to a literary work that, like those of Du, is ignorant of classical precedents. (Du is most often identified as the Song-dynasty poet Du Mo 杜默; for alternative theories, see M.14477.122.) Dōgen regularly uses the term to refer to those in the Chan tradition who are ignorant of the tradition. "Elders" (*chōrō* 長老) here likely refers to the abbots of Chinese monasteries.

not become a fox body by giving a good answer. In this episode, nothing is said of what happens after he "sheds the body of the fox." Surely, there is a true pearl wrapped in a skin bag.

[68:7] {2:189}

しかあるに、すべていまだ佛法を見聞せざるともがらいはく、野狐を脱しをはりぬれば、本覺の性海に歸するなり、迷妄によりて、しばらく野狐に墮生すといへども、大悟すれば、野狐身はすてて本性に歸するなり。これは、外道の本我にかへる、といふ義なり、さらに佛法にあらず。もし、野狐は本性にあらず、野狐に本覺なし、といふは、佛法にあらず、大悟すれば野狐身は、はなれぬ、すてつる、といはば、野狐の大悟にあらず、閑野狐なるべし。しかいふべからざるなり。

Yet those who have not yet heard the buddha dharma all say that when he had shed the fox he returned to the ocean of the nature of original awakening.[23] Although by delusion he temporarily descended to birth as a fox, when he had his great awakening, he discarded the fox body and returned to his original nature. This is the theory of other paths, that one returns to an original self; it is not at all the buddha dharma.[24] To say that the fox is not the original nature, that the fox lacks original awakening, this is not the buddha dharma. If we say that, when he had his great awakening, he left the fox body and cast it off, this is not the great awakening of the fox, it is just a useless fox. We should not say this.

[68:8]

今百丈の一轉語によりて、先百丈五百生の野狐、たちまちに脱野狐すといふ、この道理あきらむべし。もし、傍觀の、一轉語すれば傍觀脱野狐身す、といはば、從來のあひだ、山河大地、いく一轉語となくおほくの一轉語しきりなるべし。しかあれども、從來いまだ脱野狐身せず、いまの百丈の一轉語に脱野狐身す。これ疑殺古先なり。山河大地いまだ一轉語せず、といはば、今百丈、つひに開口のところなからん。

Now, we should clarify the reasoning whereby, through Baizhang's "turning word," the fox of the former Baizhang's five hundred lives suddenly "shed the fox." If we say that, because an onlooker gives a turning word, the onlooker sheds the body of a fox, the mountains, rivers, and the whole earth up till now have been giving, not a single turning word,

23 **ocean of the nature of original awakening** (*hongaku no shōkai* 本覺の性海): "The ocean of the nature" (*shōkai* 性海) is a common term in East Asian Buddhist texts, perhaps especially popular in Huayan literature, for the ultimate realm of suchness. "Original awakening" (*hongaku* 本覺) is widely used in East Asian Buddhism to designate the bodhi inherent in the buddha nature, in contrast to the "initial awakening" (*shikaku* 始覺) attained at the culmination of the bodhisattva path.

24 **theory of other paths, that one returns to an original self** (*gedō no honga ni kaeru to iu gi* 外道の本我にかへるといふ義): Likely a reference to Hindu theories of a universal ātman.

but so many turning words. Yet he did not shed the body of a fox up till now and sheds the body of the fox only now by Baizhang's turning word. This raises doubts about our old forebears.[25] If we say that the mountains, rivers, and the whole earth have not given a turning word, Baizhang would never have opened his mouth.

[68:9]

また往往の古德、おほく、不落・不昧の道、おなじく道是なる、といふを競頭道とせり。しかあれども、いまだ不落・不昧の語脈に體達せず。かるがゆえに、堕野狐身の皮肉骨髓を參ぜず、脱野狐身の皮肉骨髓を參ぜず、頭正あらざれば尾正いまだし。老人道の後五百生堕野狐身、なにかこれ能堕、なにかこれ所堕なる。正當堕野狐身のとき、從來の盡界、いまいかなる形段かある。不落因果の語脈、なにとしてか五百枚なる。いま山後巖下の一條皮、那裏得來なりとかせん。不落因果の道は、堕野狐身なり、不昧因果の聞は、脱野狐身なり。堕・脱ありといへども、なほこれ野狐の因果なり。

Again, the virtuous of old have frequently competed in saying that the words "not falling" and "not being in the dark" are equally words that are right. Yet they have not personally realized the stream of the words "not falling" and "not being in the dark."[26] For this reason, they do not study the skin, flesh, bones, and marrow of "*descending into the body of a fox*," they do not study the skin, flesh, bones, and marrow of "*shedding the body of the fox*"; since the head is not true, the tail is not true.[27] The old man said, "*Thereafter, for five hundred lives, I have descended into*

25 **This raises doubts about our old forebears** (*kore gisatsu kosen nari* これ疑殺古先なり): Perhaps meaning that this raises the question of how the turning words of the mountains, rivers, and the whole earth differ from those of the old forebears.

26 **have not personally realized the stream of the words** (*gomyaku ni taitatsu sezu* 語脈に體達せず): I.e., "have not understood the sense of the words." "Personally realize" translates a term, *taitatsu* 體達, that is variously interpreted: some take the element *tai* 體 here in its basic sense of "body"; others, in its more abstract sense of essence; still others treat it as a verb meaning "to penetrate" (*tsū* 通). "The stream of words" (*gomyaku* 語脈) refers to the reasoning, or logic, of a statement; the term occurs often in Zen texts in the expression "to turn round in the stream of words" (*gomyaku ri tenkyaku* 語脈裏轉却).

27 **the skin, flesh, bones, and marrow** (*hi niku kotsu zui* 皮肉骨髓): An expression, occurring very often throughout the *Shōbōgenzō*, indicating the essence or truth or entirety of something or someone. From the famous story, known as *Daruma hi niku kotsu zui* 達摩皮肉骨髓, of Bodhidharma's testing of four disciples, to whom he said of each in turn that he (or, in one case, she) had gotten his skin, flesh, bones, and marrow; recorded in the *shinji Shōbōgenzō* 眞字正法眼藏 (DZZ.5:230, case 201) and alluded to often in Dōgen's writings. See Supplementary Notes, s.v. "Skin, flesh, bones, and marrow."

since the head is not true, the tail is not true (*zushin arazareba bishin imadashi* 頭正あらざれば尾正いまだし): From the idiom, "true from head to tail." Here, perhaps, "the head" refers to "descending," "the tail" to "shedding." Alternatively, "the head" may refer to the failure to understand "not falling" and "not being in the dark"; the tail, to not studying "descending" and "shedding."

the body of a fox." What is the one that "descended"? What is the one into which it "descended"? At the very time that he "descended into the body of a fox," what shape did all the previous worlds have now?[28] Why did the stream of the words, "*does not fall into cause and effect,*" amount to five hundred times?[29] Where did the single pelt "beneath a cliff behind the mountain" come from? The saying, "*does not fall into cause and effect*" is "*descending into the body of a fox*"; the hearing of "*not in the dark about cause and effect*" is "*shedding the body of the fox.*" Though we may say there is "descending" and "shedding," they are still the "cause and effect" of the fox.

[68:10] {2:190}

しかあるに、古來いはく、不落因果は撥無因果に相似の道なるがゆえに墜堕す、といふ。この道、その宗旨なし、くらき人のいふところなり。たとひ、先百丈ちなみありて、不落因果、と道取すとも、大修行の瞞他不得なるあり、撥無因果なるべからず。またいはく、不昧因果は因果にくらからずといふは、大修行は超脱の因果なるがゆえに脱野狐身す、といふ。まことにこれ八九成の參學眼なり。しかありといへども、迦葉佛時曾住此山、釋迦佛時今住此山。曾身今身、日面月面、遮野狐精、現野狐精するなり。

Nevertheless, from ancient times it has been said that he descended because "*he doesn't fall into cause and effect*" are words that seem to eliminate cause and effect. These words are meaningless, something said by the blind. Even if the former Baizhang did have occasion to say, "*he doesn't fall into cause and effect,*" he has "the great practice" that cannot deceive; he is not eliminating cause and effect.[30] It is also said that he "*sheds the body of the fox*" because "*he is not in the dark about cause and effect*" — i.e., he is not blind to cause and effect — means that "great practice" is a transcendent cause and effect.[31] This is truly an eye of study eight or nine tenths complete.[32] While this may be so,

28 **what shape did all the previous worlds have now?** (*jūrai no jinkai, ima ikanaru gyōdan ka aru* 從來の盡界、いまいかなる形段かある): I.e., "how was the universe affected by the former Baizhang's rebirth as a fox."

29 **Why did the stream of the words "does not fall into cause and effect" amount to five hundred times?** (*furaku inga no gomyaku, nani toshite ka gohyaku mai naru* 不落因果の語脈、なにとしてか五百枚なる): I.e., "why did the former Baizhang's words result in five hundred rebirths as a fox?"

30 **he has "the great practice" that cannot deceive** (*dai shugyō no manta futoku naru ari* 大修行の瞞他不得なるあり): The expression "cannot deceive" (*manta futoku* 瞞他不得) is a fixed idiom; the sense here is likely "the one of great practice does not deceive."

31 **he is not blind to cause and effect** (*inga ni kurakarazu* 因果にくらからず): Or "he is not ignorant about (or oblivious of) cause and effect." Dōgen is giving a Japanese reading of the Chinese verb *bumei* 不昧 (translated here as "not in the dark about").

32 **an eye of study eight or nine tenths complete** (*hakku jō no sangaku gen* 八九成の

"At the time of Buddha Kāśyapa,
He once lived on this mountain";
At the time of Buddha Śākyamuni,
He now lives on this mountain.[33]
His body "once" and his body "now,"
The sun face and the moon face,
Concealing the fox spirit,
Revealing the fox spirit.

[68:11]

野狐、いかにしてか五百生の生をしらん。もし、野狐の知をもちいて五百生をしる、といはば、野狐の知、いまだ一生の事を盡知せず、一生いまだ野狐皮に撞入するにあらず。野狐は、かならず五百生の墮を知取する、公案現成するなり。一生の生を盡知せず、しることあり、しらざることあり。もし身知ともに生滅せずば、五百生を算數すべからず。算數することあたはずば、五百生の言、それ虚設なるべし。もし、野狐の知にあらざる知をもちいてしる、といわば、野狐のしるにあらず。たれ人か野狐のためにこれを代知せん。知・不知の通路、すべてなくば、墮野狐身といふべからず。墮野狐身せずば、脱野狐身あるべからず。墮・脱ともになくば、先百丈あるべからず、先百丈なくば、今百丈あるべからず。みだりにゆるすべからず、かくのごとく參詳すべきなり。この宗旨を擧拈して、梁・陳・隋・唐・宋のあひだに、ままにきこゆる謬説、ともに勘破すべきなり。

How could the fox know the lives of its "five hundred lives"? If we say it uses the knowledge of a fox to know the five hundred lives, the knowledge of a fox does not thoroughly know even the things of a single life; a single life does not push its way into the skin of the fox.[34] That the fox knows invariably about its descent over five hundred lives is the realizing of a kōan.[35] It does not thoroughly know the life of a single life: it knows [some]; it does not know [some]. If both its body and its knowledge are not born and extinguished together, it could not calculate five hundred lives; and, if its calculations are off, the words, "five hundred lives," would be empty conjecture. If we say that it knows using knowledge that is not

參學眼): "Eight or nine tenths" (*hakku jō* 八九成) is a fixed idiom used to express both praise and criticism; see Supplementary Notes, s.v. "Eight or nine tenths complete."

33 **"At the time of Buddha Kāśyapa, he once lived on this mountain"** (*Kashō butsu ji sō jū shi san* 迦葉佛時曾住此山): Dōgen here shifts into a set of four-character Chinese lines, beginning with the fox's report of his origins. The grammatical subject is unexpressed and might also be taken as "I."

34 **a single life does not push its way into the skin of the fox** (*isshō imada yako hi ni tōnyū suru ni arazu* 一生いまだ野狐皮に撞入するにあらず): An odd locution playing on a common Zen expression, "to push one's way into" (*tonyū* 撞入) a womb or skin bag.

35 **the realizing of the kōan** (*kōan genjō suru* 公案現成する): The sense is uncertain; possibly, meaning here something like, "settles the case." Dōgen uses a verbal form of one of his favorite expressions; see Supplementary Notes, s.v. "Realized kōan."

the knowledge of a fox, then it is not the fox that knows. So, who knows in place of the fox? If there is no passage [to resolve this issue] of knowing or not knowing, we cannot say that he descended into the body of a fox. If he did not descend into the body of a fox, he could not shed the body of the fox. If there is neither descent nor shedding, there is no former Baizhang. If there is no former Baizhang, there is no present Baizhang. Do not rashly accept [this story]; we should investigate it in detail in this way. Taking up its meaning, we should see through all the absurd theories that we occasionally hear from the Liang, Chen, Sui, Tang, and Song.[36]

[68:12] {2:191}
老非人、また今百丈に告していはく、乞依亡僧事例。この道、しかあるべからず。百丈よりこのかた、そこばくの善知識、この道を疑著せず、おどろかず。その宗趣は、死野狐いかにしてか亡僧ならん、得戒なし、夏臘なし、威儀なし、僧宗なし。かくのごとくなる物類、みだりに亡僧の事例に依行せば、未出家の何人死、ともに亡僧の例に準ずべきならん。死優婆塞、死優婆夷、もし請することあらば、死野狐のごとく亡僧の事例に依準すべし。依例をもとむるに、あらず、きかず、佛道にその事例を正傳せず。おこなはんとおもふとも、かなふべからず。いま百丈の、依法火葬す、といふ、これあきらかならず、おそらくはあやまりなり。しるべし、亡僧の事例は、入涅槃堂の功夫より、到菩提園の辦道におよぶまで、みな事例ありて、みだりならず。巖下の死野狐、たとひ先百丈の自稱すとも、いかでか大僧の行李あらん、佛祖の骨髓あらん、たれか先百丈なることを證據する。いたづらに野狐精の變怪をまことなりとして、佛祖の法儀を輕慢すべからず。佛祖の兒孫としては、佛祖の法儀をおもくすべきなり。百丈のごとく、請するにまかすることなかれ。一事・一法もあひがたきなり。世俗にひかれ、人情にひかれざるべし。

The old "non-human" now addresses Baizhang, saying, "*I beg the rites for a deceased monk.*" These words cannot be right. Ever since Baizhang, so many wise friends have failed to doubt or be surprised by these words.[37] The issue here is how a dead fox could be a deceased monk. It lacks the precepts; it lacks tenure; it lacks deportment; it lacks the essentials of a monk.[38] If we rashly perform the rites for a deceased monk for such a creature, we should follow the precedents for a deceased monk at all the deaths of anyone who has not left home. If it were requested for the dead *upāsaka* and dead *upāsikā*, as with the dead fox, we should follow the rites for a deceased monk. If we look for such precedents, there are not any, we hear of none; this precedent is not correctly transmitted in the way of the buddhas. Even if we thought to do

36 **Liang, Chen, Sui, Tang, and Song** (*Ryō Chin Zui Tō Sō* 梁・陳・隋・唐・宋): The major Chinese dynasties from the time of Bodhidharma to Dōgen's day.

37 **wise friends** (*zen chishiki* 善知識): I.e., Buddhist teachers.

38 **tenure** (*gerō* 夏臘): I.e., years of summer retreats, by which a monk's seniority is reckoned.

it, we could not accomplish it. It says here that Baizhang "*cremated it in accordance with the dharma.*" This is not clear and is likely a mistake. We should realize that the procedures for a deceased monk, from the exertions on entering the nirvāṇa hall to pursuing the way on reaching the bodhi grounds, all have their procedures and are not random.[39] Even if it called itself the former Baizhang, how could the dead fox beneath the cliff have the observances of a fully ordained monk, have the bones and marrow of the buddhas and ancestors? Who verified that it was the former Baizhang? We should not demean the rites of the buddhas and ancestors, foolishly taking as true the apparitions of a fox spirit. As descendants of the buddhas and ancestors, we should take seriously the rites of the buddhas and ancestors. Do not go along with requests as Baizhang did. Each procedure, each dharma is hard to encounter; we should not be tempted by the worldly or tempted by human emotion.

[68:13] {2:192}
この日本國のごとくは、佛儀祖儀あひがたく、ききがたかりしなり。而今、まれにもきくことあり、みることあらば、ふかく髻珠よりもおもく崇重すべきなり。無福のともがら、尊崇の信心あつからず。あはれむべし、それ、事の輕重を、かつていまだしらざるによりてなり。五百歳の智なし、一千年の智なきによりてなり。しかありといふとも、自己をはげますべし、他己をすすむべし。一禮拜なりとも、一端坐なりとも、佛祖より正傳することあらば、ふかくあひがたきにあふ、大慶快をなすべし、大福德を懽喜すべし。このこころなからんともがら、千佛の出世にあふとも、一功德あるべからず、一得益あるへからず、いたづらに附佛法の外道なるべし。くちに佛法をまなぶに相似なりとも、くちに佛法をとくに證實あるべからず。

In a place like this Land of Japan, it has been difficult to encounter, difficult to hear, the rites of the buddha and the rites of the ancestors. Now, if we do rarely hear and see them, we should seriously respect them more deeply than the jewel in the topknot.[40] The unfortunate types have a limited sense of reverence. What a pity. It is because they have never understood how to evaluate things. It is because they lack the wisdom of five hundred years, the wisdom of one thousand years.[41] Nevertheless, we should brace ourselves, we should encourage others. Even a single bow, even a single upright sitting, if it is correctly transmitted from the buddhas and ancestors, we should feel deeply as a great felicity, difficult to encounter, and rejoice at our great good fortune. Those who lack this

39 **bodhi grounds** (*bodai on* 菩提園): I.e., the monastic cemetery.

40 **jewel in the topknot** (*keiju* 髻珠): I.e., the king's most precious possession.

41 **the wisdom of five hundred years** (*gohyaku sai no chi* 五百歳の智); **the wisdom of one thousand years** (*issen nen no chi* 一千年の智): Presumably, "wisdom lasting five hundred or a thousand years."

attitude, though they encounter the appearance in the world of a thousand buddhas, will not have a single merit, will not have a single benefit. They are followers of other paths vainly appended to the buddha dharma. Though they have the appearance of learning the buddha dharma with their mouths, they lack the authenticity to speak the buddha dharma with their mouths.

[68:14]

しかあればすなはち、たとひ國王·大臣なりとも、たとひ梵天・釋天なりとも、未作僧のともがら、きたりて亡僧の事例を請せんに、さらに聽許することなかれ。出家受戒し大僧となりてきたるべし、と答すべし。三界の業報を愛惜して、三寶の尊位を願求せざらんともがら、たとひ千枚の死皮袋を拈來して亡僧の事例をけがし、やぶるとも、さらにこれ、をかしのはなはだしきなり、功德となるべからず。もし佛法の功德を結良緣せんとおもはば、すみやかに佛法によりて出家受戒し、大僧となるべし。

Therefore, if those who have not yet become monks — even if it be the king of the land or a great minister, even if it be the Deva Śakra of the Heaven of Brahmā — should come to you requesting the rites of a deceased monk, do not listen to them. We should respond by saying they should come back to us when they have left home, received the precepts, and become fully ordained monks. Although those who are attached to the karmic rewards of the three realms and do not aspire to the exalted state of the three treasures were to bring a thousand dead skin bags and [try to] defile and destroy the rites of the deceased monk, this is just ludicrous and would not result in merit. If they would form good conditions for merit in the buddha dharma, then in accordance with the buddha dharma, they should quickly leave home, receive the precepts, and become fully ordained monks.

[68:15]

今百丈至晩上堂、擧前因緣。この擧底の道理、もとも未審なり、作麼生擧ならん。老人すでに五百生來のをはり、脱從來身といふがことし。いまいふ五百生、そのかず人間のごとく算取すべきか、野狐道のごとく算數すべきか、佛道のごとく算數するか。いはんや老野狐の眼睛、いかでか百丈を覰見することあらん。野狐に覰見せらるるは、野狐精なるべし、百丈に覰見せらるるは、佛祖なり。

Now, regarding this, "*In a convocation that evening,*" Baizhang "*raised the above incident*": the rationale of this "raising" is very unclear. How did he raise it? It seems that the old man had ended his five hundred lives and shed the body he had up till then. These "five hundred lives" — should we calculate their number according to humans? Should we calculate according to the way of the fox? Calculate according to the way of the buddha? Moreover, how could the eye of the old fox see Baizhang? What is seen by the fox must be a fox spirit; what is seen by Baizhang is the buddhas and ancestors.

[68:16] {2:192}

このゆえに、枯木禪師法成和尚、頌曰、百丈親曾見野狐、爲渠參請太心麤、而今敢問諸參學、吐得狐涎盡也無。

Therefore, Chan Master Kumu, Reverend Facheng, says in a verse,[42]
Baizhang once personally encountered a fox;
Consulted by it, he got really rough.
Now, I take the liberty of asking you students,
Have you finished vomiting up the fox slaver?

[68:17]

しかあれば、野狐は百丈親曾眼睛なり。吐得狐涎、たとひ半分なりとも、出廣長舌、代一轉語なり。正當恁麼時、脱野狐身、脱百丈身、脱老非人身、脱盡界身なり。

So, the fox is the eye of "*Baizhang once personally.*"[43] In "*vomiting up the fox slaver,*" even if it is half, he "*sticks out his long broad tongue,*" and it is "*a turning word in my stead.*"[44] *At this very time, "he sheds the body of the fox"; he sheds the body of Baizhang; he sheds the body of the old non-human; he sheds the body of all the worlds.*

[68:18]

黄檗便問、古人錯對一轉語、堕五百生野狐身、轉轉不錯、合作箇什麼。

Huangbo asked, "The man of old, with the single turning word of a mistaken response, fell for five hundred lives into the body of a fox. What would happen if he turned and turned without a mistake?"

[68:19]

いまこの問、これ佛祖道現成なり。南嶽下の尊宿のなかに、黄檗のごとくなるは、さきにもいまだあらず、のちにもなし。しかあれども、老人もいまだいはず、錯對學人、と。百丈もいまだいはず、錯對せりける、と。なにとしてかいま黄檗みだりにいふ、古人錯對一轉語、と。もし、錯によれりといふならん、といはば、黄檗、いまだ百丈の大意をえたるにあらず。佛祖道の錯對・不錯對は、黄檗いまだ參究せざるかごとし。この一段の因縁に、先百丈も錯對といはず、今百丈も錯對といはず、と參學すべきなり。

42 **Chan Master Kumu, Reverend Facheng** (*Koboku zenji Hōjō oshō* 枯木禪師法成和尚): I.e., Kumu Facheng 枯木法成 (1071-1128). His verse can be found at *Chanzong songgu lianzhu tonji* 禪宗頌古聯珠通集, ZZ.115:113a4-5.

43 **the fox is the eye of "Baizhang once personally"** (*yako wa Hyakujō shinzō ganzei nari* 野狐は百丈親曾眼睛なり): Presumably, meaning something like, "the fox is what Baizhang personally saw."

44 **"sticks out his long broad tongue"** (*shutsu kōchō zetsu* 出廣長舌): A fixed expression for the tongue (or, by extension, the speech) of a buddha.

This question here is a statement of the buddhas and ancestors. Among the worthies under Nanyue, there were none like Huangbo before him or after him. Nevertheless, the old man did not say that he gave a mistaken response to the student; Baizhang also did not say that he gave a mistaken response. Why then does Huangbo rashly say, "*the old man, with the single turning word of a mistaken response*"? If we say that he said it because [he thought] it was mistaken, then Huangbo has not got Baizhang's larger intention. It seems Huangbo has not yet investigated the mistaken response and unmistaken response of the way of the buddhas and ancestors. We should study that, in this episode, the former Baizhang has not said it was a mistaken response, the present Baizhang has not said it was a mistaken response.

[68:20] {2:194}

しかありといへども、野狐皮五百枚、あつさ三寸なるをもて、曾住此山し、爲學人道するなり。野狐皮に脱落の尖毛あるによりて、今百丈一枚の臭皮袋あり。度量するに、半野狐皮の脱來なり、轉轉不錯の墮・脱あり、轉轉代語の因果あり、歴然の大修行なり。

Nevertheless, with five hundred fox skins three inches thick, he "*once lived on this mountain*," "*saying something for his students.*"[45] Since the fox skins have their fur sloughed off, the present Baizhang has his one stinking skin bag.[46] If you gauge it, it is half the fox skin shedding.[47] There is the "descending" and the "shedding" of his "*turning and turning without a mistake*"; there is the "cause and effect" of his *turning and turning a word in his stead*: it is "the great practice" of "the distinct."[48]

---

45 **with five hundred fox skins three inches thick** (*yako hi gohyaku mai, atsusa sansun naru o mote* 野狐皮五百枚、あつさ三寸なるをもて): I.e., wearing a fox skin five hundred times. The thickness here suggests the common idiom "facial skin three inches thick" (*menpi kō sanzun* 面皮厚三寸) — i.e., "thick skinned," normally used in the sense of "shameless" or "impudent."

46 **Since the fox skins have their fur sloughed off, the present Baizhang has his one stinking skin bag** (*yako hi ni datsuraku no senmō aru ni yorite, kon Hyakujō ichimai no shū hitai ari* 野狐皮に脱落の尖毛あるによりて、今百丈一枚の臭皮袋あり): Presumably meaning that Baizhang's human skin is the pelt of the fox devoid of its fur. See Supplementary Notes, s.v. "Slough off," and "Bag of skin."

47 **half the fox skin shedding** (*han yako hi no datsurai* 半野狐皮の脱來): Perhaps meaning that Baizhang is still half a fox — i.e., that the fox and Baizhang are inseparable.

48 **"the great practice" of "the distinct"** (*rekinen no dai shugyō* 歴然の大修行): Or "the distinct great practice." The translation assumes that Dōgen has in mind here the fixed expression "cause and effect are distinct" (*inga rekinen* 因果歴然). If this assumption is correct, the sense of this difficult passage would seem to be that the great practice is the distinct cause and effect of the present Baizhang repeatedly speaking for the former Baizhang.

[68:21]

いま黄檗きたりて、轉轉不錯、合作箇什麼、と問著せんに、いふべし、也堕作野狐身と。黄檗もし、なにとしてか恁麼なる、といはば、さらにいふべし、這野狐精。かくのごとくなりとも、錯・不錯にあらず。黄檗の問を、問得是なり、とゆるすことなかれ。また黄檗、合作箇什麼、と問著せんとき、摸索得面皮也未、といふべし、また、儞脱野狐身也未、といふべし、また、儞答他學人不落因果也未、といふべし。

If Huangbo were now to come and ask, "*What would happen if he turned and turned without a mistake?*" we should say, "*He'd still fall into the fox body.*" If Huangbo asked why, we should say, "This fox spirit!"[49] Still, this is not a matter of "mistaken" or "not mistaken." Do not excuse Huangbo's question, saying that his question got it right. Again, when Huangbo asks, "*What would happen?*" we should say, "*Have you felt the skin of your face or not?*" Or we should say, "*Have you been released yet from the body of a fox or not?*" Or we should say, "*Do you answer to the student so that he doesn't fall into cause and effect or not?*"

[68:22]

しかあれども、百丈道の、近前來與儞道、すでに、合作箇這箇の道處あり。黄檗、近前す、亡前失後なり。與百丈一掌する、そこばくの野狐變なり。

Nevertheless, Baizhang's saying, "*Come forward and I'll tell you,*" already has the saying "*this is what would happen.*" Huangbo comes forward, forgetting himself.[50] His giving Baizhang a blow is so many transformations of the fox.

[68:23] {2:195}

百丈拍手笑云、將爲胡鬚赤、更有赤鬚胡。

The Master clapped his hands and laughed, saying, "Here, I thought the foreigner's beard is red, but now here's a red bearded foreigner."[51]

[68:24]

この道取、いまだ十成の志氣にあらず、わづかに八九成なり。たとひ八九成をゆるすとも、いまだ八九成あらず。十成をゆるすとも、八九成なきものなり。しかあれどもいふべし、百丈道處通方、雖然未出野狐窟、黄檗脚跟點地、雖然猶滞蟷螂徑、與掌拍手、一有二無、赤鬚胡胡鬚赤。

---

49 **"This fox spirit!"** (*sha yako zei* 這野狐精): A fixed expression of opprobrium for one pretending to be what one is not.

50 **forgetting himself** (*bōzen shitsugo* 亡前失後): An idiomatic expression (more often written 忘前失後; literally "forgetting before and losing after") meaning "to lose sight of who one is."

51 **The Master clapped his hands** (*Hakujō hakushu* 百丈拍手): Dōgen merely repeats here the Chinese of his text in section 1.

This saying is not a spirit ten tenths complete; it is barely eight or nine tenths complete. Even if we accept eight or nine tenths complete, it still lacks eight or nine tenths complete. Even if we accept ten tenths complete, it is something lacking eight or nine tenths complete. Be this as it may, we should say,

Baizhang's words penetrate the quarters;
Yet he hasn't got out of the fox's den.
Huangbo's feet touch the earth;
Yet he's still stuck on the mantis track.
They give a blow; they clap their hands.
One exists; two do not.
The red-bearded foreigner; the foreigner's beard is red.

正法眼藏大修行第六十八
Treasury of the True Dharma Eye
Great Practice
Number 68

[Ryūmonji MS:]
爾時寬元二年甲辰三月九日、在越宇吉峰古精舍示衆
Presented to the assembly at the old vihāra at Kippō, Etsuu; ninth day, third month of the senior wood year of the dragon, the second year of Kangen [17 April 1244][52]

[*Himitsu* MS:]
同三月十三日、在同精舍侍者寮書寫之。惠弉
Copied at the acolyte's quarters of the same vihara; thirteenth day, third month of the same year [April 21, 1244]. Ejō[53]

52 The *Himitsu* 秘密 MS shares an identical colophon.

53 **Ejō** 惠弉: Written with a homonym for Ejō 懷奘.

TREASURY OF THE TRUE DHARMA EYE

NUMBER 69

The Samādhi of Self-Verification

Jishō zanmai

自證三昧

The Samādhi of Self-Verification

Jishō zanmai

Introduction

This work was composed in the spring of 1244, at Kippōji in Echizen. It represents number 69 of the seventy-five-chapter *Shōbōgenzō* and number 74 of the Honzan edition (or 75 in the Iwanami and Shūmuchō versions). It is not included in the sixty-chapter *Shōbōgenzō* compilation but is found as the sixth text in fascicle 2 of the *Himitsu* collection.

The title of the work, *jishō zanmai* 自證三昧, is not a common expression: while it occurs occasionally in the East Asian tantric literature, it is not favored in Zen texts and is not used by Dōgen elsewhere. Like the English "self-verification," the term *jishō* 自證 is slightly ambiguous and could be understood as indicating a validating experience "of oneself," "by oneself," or "for oneself." Dōgen emphasizes here that the Buddhist study of the self is not done on one's own but always guided by scripture and the instruction of teachers. Moreover, it is not done solely for one's own edification but also in order to share that study with others.

These remarks occupy the first half of his essay. For the remainder of the piece, Dōgen engages in an *ad hominem* attack on the influential twelfth-century Chan figure Dahui Zonggao 大慧宗杲, who liked to use the expression "self-verification and self-awakening" (*jishō jigo* 自證自悟). Dōgen dismisses this monk as an ambitious lightweight, never certified by his teachers. Dahui was the most prominent representative of the Linji lineage in his day and the teacher of Zhuoan Deguang 拙菴德光, some of whose Japanese dharma descendants made up the leadership of Dōgen's community. Hence, the comments on Dahui here are often read as a contribution to those descendants' re-education. Dōgen ends his essay with the claim that only his own Caodong lineage represents the line of direct descent of the buddhas and ancestors.

正法眼藏第六十九
Treasury of the True Dharma Eye
Number 69
自證三昧
The Samādhi of Self-Verification

[69:1] {2:196}

諸佛・七佛より、佛佛祖祖の正傳するところ、すなはち修證三昧なり。いはゆる或從知識・或從經卷なり、これはこれ佛祖の眼睛なり。

From the buddhas, from the seven buddhas, what buddha after buddha and ancestor after ancestor has correctly transmitted is the samādhi of practice and verification.[1] It is what is called *whether from a wise friend, whether from a sūtra scroll*; this is the eye of the buddhas and ancestors.[2]

[69:2]

このゆえに、曹溪古佛、問僧云、還假修證也無。僧云、修證不無、染汚即不得。

Therefore,

The Old Buddha of Caoxi asked the monk, "Does it nevertheless depend on practice and verification?"[3]

The monk answered, "It's not that it lacks practice and verification, but it can't be defiled by them."

1 **samādhi of practice and verification** (*shushō zanmai* 修證三昧): Some MS witnesses read here *jishō zanmai* 自證三昧 ("the samādhi of self-verification"). While the term *samādhi* has the narrow sense of a paranormal psychological state of extreme concentration, it is likely used here in the broader sense, found often in the literature, of a spiritual practice. The unusual expression "samādhi of practice and verification" is often understood here as a spiritual practice in which the practice and its fruit are coterminous. See Supplementary Notes, s.v. "Practice and verification."

2 **whether from a wise friend, whether from a sūtra scroll** (*waku jū chishiki waku jū kyōkan* 或從知識・或從經卷): I.e., whether [one's understanding of Buddhism derives] from a teacher or from a text. Fixed expressions occurring together several times in the *Shōbōgenzō*; see Supplementary Notes. Below (sections 4-8), Dōgen will discuss each in turn.

3 **The Old Buddha of Caoxi** (*Sōkei kobutsu* 曹溪古佛): I.e., the Sixth Ancestor, Huineng 慧能. "The monk" here is the Ancestor's disciple Nanyue Huairang 南嶽懷讓 (677-744); the topic is the Ancestor's question to Nanyue, "What thing is it that comes like this?" Their famous exchange is recorded in Dōgen's *shinji Shōbōgenzō* 眞字正法眼藏 (DZZ.5:178, case 101) and quoted often in his writings.

[69:3]

しかあればしるべし、不染汚の修證、これ佛祖なり、佛祖三昧の霹靂風雷なり。

Thus, we know that nondefiling practice and verification are the buddhas and ancestors, are the thunder and lightning of the samādhi of the buddha and ancestors.[4]

[69:4]

或從知識の正當恁麼時、あるひは半面を相見す、あるひは半身を相見す、あるひは全面を相見す、あるひは全身を相見す、半自を相見することあり、半他を相見することあり。神頭の披毛せるを相證し、鬼面の戴角せるを相修す。異類行の隨他來あり、同條生の變異去あり。かくのごとくのところに爲法捨身すること、いく千萬廻といふことをしらず。爲身求法すること、いく億百劫といふことをしらず。これ或從知識の活計なり、參自從自の消息なり。瞬目に相見するとき破顔あり、得髓を禮拜するちなみに斷臂す。

At the very moment of *whether from a wise friend,* we may see half the face; we may see half the body; we may see the whole face; we may see the whole body. There is seeing half oneself; there is seeing half the other. We verify that the spirit's head is clad in fur; we practice that the demon's face is crowned by horns.[5] There is the coming along with it of the moving of different types; there is the going on transforming of those born together.[6] In such circumstances, we do not know how many

4 **samādhi of the buddha and ancestors** (*busso zanmai* 佛祖三昧): Another unusual expression not found in the literature or elsewhere in the *Shōbōgenzō*.

5 **We verify that the spirit's head is clad in fur; we practice that the demon's face is crowned by horns** (*jinzu no himō seru o sōshō shi, kimen no taikaku seru o sōshu su* 神頭の披毛せるを相證し、鬼面の戴角せるを相修す): Perhaps meaning something like, "we realize what we really are." Dōgen is playing here with two fixed expressions sometimes used in self-deprecating reference to monks: "spirit heads and demon faces" (*jinzu kimen* 神頭鬼面; i.e., "weird things"), and "clad in fur and crowned by horns" (*himō taikaku* 披毛戴角; i.e., "beastly").

6 **There is the coming along with it of the moving of different types; there is the going on transforming of those born together** (*irui gyō no zui ta rai ari, dōjō shō no hen'i ko ari* 異類行の隨他來あり、同條生の變異去あり): Perhaps meaning something like, "[practice and verification involve] 'coming back' to help others and 'going on' transforming oneself." The awkward translation struggles to retain Dōgen's continued play with familiar idioms. "Coming along with it" (*zui ta rai* 隨他來) would seem to be a variation on the recommendation, seen elsewhere in the *Shōbōgenzō*, of Dasui Fazhen 大隋法眞 (834-919) to "go along" (*zui ta ko* 隨他去) with "this" (*shako* 這箇) when it is destroyed with the chiliocosm at the end of a kalpa. See Supplementary Notes, s.v. "Goes along with it."

"The moving of different types" (*irui gyō* 異類行) derives from the expression, "moving among different types" (*irui chū gyō* 異類中行), generally taken to indicate the salvific activities of the buddhas and bodhisattvas among the various forms of living beings;

thousands of myriads of times we *discard the body for the sake of the dharma*; we do not know how many millions of hundreds of kalpas we *seek the dharma for the sake of our bodies*.[7] This is the way of life of *whether from a wise friend*, the circumstances of attending the self and following the self.[8] It has breaking into a smile upon seeing the blink; it cuts off an arm when making a bow to get the marrow.[9]

[69:5] {2:197}
おほよそ七佛の前後より、六祖の左右にあまれる見自の知識、ひとりにあらず、ふたりにあらず。見他の知識、むかしにあらず、いまにあらず。

In sum, from before and after the seven buddhas, to beyond the left and right of the Sixth Ancestor, the wise friends who have seen themselves are not one, are not two; the wise friends who have seen the other are not past, are not present.[10]

[69:6]
或從經卷のとき、自己の皮肉骨髓を參究し、自己の皮肉骨髓を脱落するとき、桃華眼睛づから突出來相見せらる、竹聲耳根づから霹靂相聞せらる。おほよそ經卷に從學するとき、まことに經卷出來す。その經卷といふは、盡十方界・山河大地・草木自他なり、喫飯著衣・造次動容なり。この一一の經典にしたがひ學道するに、さらに未曾有の經卷、いく千萬卷となく出現在前するなり。是字の句ありて宛然なり、非字の偈あらたに歷然なり。これらにあふことをえて、拈身心して參學するに、長劫を消盡し、長劫を擧起すといふとも、かならず通利の到處あり。放身心して參學するに、朕兆を抉出し、朕兆を趯飛すといふとも、かならず受持の功、成ずるなり。

---

especially associated with Nanchuan Puyuan 南泉普願 (748-835) and occurring often in Dōgen's writings; see Supplementary Notes, s.v. "Move among different types."

7 **discard the body for the sake of the dharma** (*i hō sha shin* 爲法捨身): A fixed expression for Buddhist ascesis. The following "seek the dharma for the sake of the body" (*i shin gu hō* 爲身求法) is Dōgen's variation. Elsewhere in the *Shōbōgenzō*, we find the variant "discard the dharma for the sake of the body" (*ishin shahō* 爲身捨法).

8 **attending the self and following the self** (*san ji jū ji* 參自從自): An unusual phrase, perhaps playing off the glyph *jū* 從 in the expression "whether from a wise friend" (*waku jū chishiki* 或從知識).

9 **breaking into a smile** (*hagan* 破顏); **cuts off an arm** (*danpi* 斷臂): Reference to two famous tales of dharma transmission: 1) the story of the first transmission on Vulture Peak, when the Buddha held up a flower and (in Dōgen's version) blinked, and Mahākāśyapa smiled (see Supplementary Notes, s.v. "Break into a smile"); and 2) the legend of the Second Ancestor, Huike 慧可, who cut off his arm as an offering to Bodhidharma and subsequently succeeded the latter when he expressed his understanding with a wordless bow and was praised as having gotten Bodhidharma's marrow (see Supplementary Notes, s.v. "Cut off an arm").

10 **are not past, are not present** (*mukashi ni arazu, ima ni arazu* むかしにあらず、いまにあらず): Likely in the sense "beyond past and present" (*chōkokon* 超古今), "timeless" or "for all time."

At the time of *whether from a sūtra scroll*, when we investigate our own skin, flesh, bones, and marrow and slough off our own skin, flesh, bones, and marrow, the peach blossoms and the eye themselves are seen to pop out; the bamboo sound and the ear themselves are heard to thunder.[11] In general, when we study from a sūtra scroll, the sūtra scroll truly emerges. This "sūtra scroll" means the entire world in the ten directions; the mountains, rivers, and the whole earth; grass and trees, self and other; it is our having meals and wearing clothes, our hasty acts and demeanor.[12]

In studying the way from each one of these scriptures, so many thousands of myriads of previously non-existent sūtra scrolls appear before us. They have lines in positive terms, exactly so; they have gāthās in negative terms, distinctly so.[13] Having been able to encounter them, when we take up body and mind and study them, though we may exhaust long kalpas and take up long kalpas, we will inevitably be well versed in them everywhere. When we cast aside body and mind and study them, though we may gouge out any portent and jump free from any portent, the merit of receiving and upholding them will invariably be attained.[14]

[69:7]

いま西天の梵文を、東土の法本に飜譯せる、わづかに半萬軸にたらず。これに三乘・五乘・九部・十二部あり。これらみな、したがひ學すべき經卷なり。したがはざらんと迴避せんとすとも、うべからざるなり。かるがゆえに、あるひは眼睛となり、あるひは吾髓となりきたれり。頭角正なり、尾條正なり。他よりこれをうけ、これを他にさづくといへども、ただ眼睛の活出なり、自他を脱落す。ただ吾髓の附囑なり、自他を透脱せり。眼睛・吾髓、それ自にあらず、他にあらざるがゆえに、佛祖、むかしよりむかしに正傳しきたり、而今より而今に附囑するなり。拄杖經あり、横説

11 **peach blossoms and the eye** (*tōka ganzei* 桃華眼睛): Allusion to the story, cited several times in the *Shōbōgenzō*, of Lingyun Zhiqin 靈雲志勤 (dates unknown), who was awakened upon seeing peach trees in bloom. See Supplementary Notes, s.v. "Peach blossoms" and "Eye."

bamboo sound and the ear (*chikusei nikon* 竹聲耳根): Allusion to the story, cited several times in the *Shōbōgenzō*, of Xiangyan Zhixian 香嚴智閑 (d. 898), who gained an understanding upon hearing the sound of a bit of debris striking a bamboo stalk; see Supplementary Notes, s.v. "A painted cake can't satisfy hunger." Dōgen recounts the episode in his "Shōbōgenzō keisei sanshoku" 正法眼藏溪聲山色.

12 **mountains, rivers, and the whole earth** (*senga daichi* 山河大地): A standard expression for the natural world.

13 **lines in positive terms** (*zeji no ku* 是字の句); **gāthās in negative terms** (*hiji no ge* 非字の偈): Unusual expressions, perhaps meaning texts that use what we would call cataphatic and apophatic language respectively.

14 **gouge out any portent and jump free from any portent** (*chinchō o kesshutsu shi, chinchō o tekihi su* 朕兆を抉出し、朕兆を趯飛す): Probably meaning "gone beyond all being"; from the stock expression "before the germination of any portent" (*chinchō mibō* 朕兆未萠), used to describe what precedes being.

縦説、おのれづから空を破し、有を破す。拂子經あり、雪を澡し、霜を澡す。坐禪經の一會・兩會あり、袈裟經一巻十袠あり。これら、諸佛祖の護持するところなり。かくのごとくの經卷にしたがひて、修證得道するなり。あるひは天面・人面、あるひは日面月面あらしめて、從經卷の功夫現成するなり。

At present, the translations of the Sanskrit texts of Sindh in the West into the dharma books of the Land of the East do not amount to half a myriad spindles.[15] There are the three vehicles, the five vehicles, the nine sections, the twelve sections.[16] They are all sūtra scrolls we should follow and study; even if we try to avoid following them, we cannot. Hence, they have become the eye, or become "my marrow"; they are right at the horns and right at the tail.[17] Though we may receive them from another or confer them on another, it is just the vital emergence of the eye, sloughing off self and other; it is just the bequest of "my marrow," transcending self and other. Because the eye and "my marrow" are not self and are not other, the buddhas and ancestors have directly transmitted them from the past to the past and bequeath them from the present to the present. There are staff scriptures; preaching horizontally and preaching vertically, they themselves break up emptiness and break up being. There are whisk scriptures; they clean off the snow and clean off the frost.[18] There are one or two collections of seated meditation scrip-

---

15 **half a myriad spindles** (*hanman jiku* 半萬軸): I.e., five thousand scrolls. The imperially sponsored catalog of the Buddhist canon, the *Kaiyuan shijiao lu* 開元釋教錄, compiled in 730 by Zhisheng 智昇, is said to record a total of 5,048 fascicles; but, of course, many of these titles were not translations from Sanskrit.

16 **the three vehicles, the five vehicles, the nine sections, the twelve sections** (*sanjō gojō kubu jūnibu* 三乘・五乘・九部・十二部): Various divisions of the Buddhist teachings. "The three vehicles" (*sanjō* 三乘) refers to the *śrāvaka*, *pratyeka-buddha*, and bodhisattva vehicles; "the five vehicles" (*gojō* 五乘) is an East Asian innovation that adds to the three vehicles the teachings for humans and for devas; "the nine sections" and "the twelve sections" are venerable lists (the latter including all the former) of sacred genres. For Dōgen's understanding of these, see "Shōbōgenzō bukkyō" 正法眼藏佛教.

17 **they have become the eye, or become "my marrow"** (*arui wa ganzei to nari, arui wa gozui to narikitareri* あるひは眼睛となり、あるひは吾髓となりきたれり): "My marrow" (*gozui* 吾髓) alludes to Bodhidharma's words to his dharma heir, Huike 慧可, "You've gotten my marrow" (*nyo toku go zui* 汝得吾髓); see Supplementary Notes, s.v. "Skin, flesh, bones, and marrow." Though less certain, given the context of transmission here, "the eye" (*ganzei* 眼睛) may evoke the "eye" in the "treasury of the true dharma eye" (*shōbōgenzō* 正法眼藏) transmitted on Vulture Peak. See above, Note 9.

they are right at the horns and right at the tail (*zukaku shin nari, bijō shin nari* 頭角正なり、尾條正なり): I.e., true from head to tail; variant of the more common *zushin bishin* 頭正尾正.

18 **staff scriptures** (*shujō kyō* 拄杖經); **whisk scriptures** (*hossu kyō* 拂子經): I.e., the master's ceremonial staff and fly whisk as scriptures. See Supplementary Notes, s.v. "Staff," "Whisk."

tures; there is one roll in ten spindles of *kāṣāya* scriptures. These are what the buddhas and ancestors protect and maintain. From such sūtra scrolls, they practice and verify and gain the way. Causing a deva face or a human face, or a sun face or moon face, the work of "*from a sūtra scroll*" is realized.[19]

[69:8] {2:198}
しかあるに、たとひ知識にもしたがひ、たとひ經卷にもしたがふ、みなこれ自己にしたがふなり。經卷おのれづから自經卷なり、知識おのれづから自知識なり。しかあれば、遍參知識は遍參自己なり、拈百草は拈自己なり、拈萬木は拈自己なり、自己はかならず恁麼の功夫なりと參學するなり。この參學に、自己を脱落し、自己を契證するなり。

Nevertheless, whether one follows a wise friend or follows a sūtra scroll, they are both following oneself. Sūtra scrolls are themselves sūtra scrolls of oneself; wise friends are themselves wise friends of oneself. Therefore, to study widely with a wise friend is to study widely with oneself; to take up the hundred grasses is to take up oneself; to take up the myriad trees is to take up oneself.[20] We study that one's self is always such concentrated effort. In this study, we slough off ourselves, we accord with and verify ourselves.

[69:9]
これによりて、佛祖の大道に、自證自悟の調度あり、正嫡の佛祖にあらざれば正傳せず、嫡嫡相承する調度あり、佛祖の骨髓にあらざれば正傳せず。かくのごとく參學するゆえに、人のために傳授するときは、汝得吾髓の附囑有在なり、吾有正法眼藏附囑摩訶迦葉なり。爲説は、かならずしも自他にかかはれず。他のための説著、すなはちみづからのための説著なり、自と自と同參の聞・説なり。一耳はきき、一耳はとく、一舌はとき、一舌はきく、乃至、眼・耳・鼻・舌・身・意・根・識・塵等もかくのごとし。さらに一身一心ありて、證するあり、修するあり。みみづからの聞・説なり、舌づからの聞・説なり。昨日は他のために不定法をとくといへども、今日はみづからのために定法をとかるるなり。かくのごとくの日面あひつらなり、月面あひつらなれり。他のために法をとき、法を修するは、生生のところに法をきき、法をあきらめ、法を證するなり。今生にも法を他のためにとく。誠心あれば、自己の得法やすきなり。あるひは、他人の法をきくをもたすけすすむれば、みづからが學法、よきたよりをうるなり。身中にたよりをえ、心中にたよりをうるなり。聞法を障礙するがごときは、みづからが聞法を障礙せらるるなり。生生の身身に法をとき、法をきくは、世世に聞法するなり。前來わが正傳せし法を、さらに今世にもき

19 **sun face or moon face** (*nichimen gachimen* 日面月面): Likely an allusion to two buddhas named in the *Foming jing* 佛名經, or to a famous saying by Mazu Daoyi 馬祖道一 (709-788); see Supplementary Notes, s.v. "Sun face, moon face."

20 **hundred grasses** (*hyakusō* 百草); **myriad trees** (*manboku* 萬木): I.e., the natural world as a scripture. In his "Shōbōgenzō bukkyō" 正法眼藏佛經, Dōgen writes that there are scriptures written "using the script of the hundred grasses or using the script of the myriad trees."

くなり。法のなかに生じ、法のなかに滅するがゆえに、盡十方界のなかに法を正傳しつれば、生生にきき、身身に修するなり。生生を法に現成せしめ、身身を法ならしむるゆえに、一塵・法界ともに拈來して、法を證せしむるなり。

Based on this, in the great way of the buddhas and ancestors, there is an implement for self-verification and self-awakening that is not directly transmitted by those who are not buddhas and ancestors of direct succession; there is an implement inherited by successor after successor that is not directly transmitted to those who are not the bones and marrow of the buddhas and ancestors. Because we study in this way, when we transmit it to someone, there is a bequest of "you've gotten my marrow"; it is "*I have a treasury of the true dharma eye, which I bequeath to Mahākāśyapa.*"[21] Preaching for someone's sake does not necessarily have to do with self or other: preaching for the sake of the other is preaching for one's own sake; it is a hearing and preaching in which self and self study together.[22] One ear hears, and one ear preaches; one tongue preaches and one tongue hears; and so on in the same way for eye, ear, nose, tongue, body, and mind; for organ, consciousness, and object.[23] Further, they have one body and one mind, have verifying and practicing: the ear itself hears and preaches; the tongue itself hears and preaches.[24] Yesterday, we may preach an indeterminate dharma for another's sake; but today, a determinate dharma is preached for our sake.[25]

21 **"I have a treasury of the true dharma eye, which I bequeath to Mahākāśyapa"** (*go u shōbōgenzō fuzoku Makakashō* 吾有正法眼藏附囑摩訶迦葉): The Buddha's words upon transmitting the dharma on Vulture Peak; see Supplementary Notes, s.v. "Treasury of the true dharma eye."

22 **it is a hearing and preaching in which self and self study together** (*ji to ji to dōsan no mon setsu nari* 自と自と同參の聞・説なり): I.e., the self as speaker and self as listener study together.

23 **eye, ear, nose, tongue, body, and mind; for organ, consciousness, and object** (*gen ni bi zetsu shin i kon shiki jin* 眼・耳・鼻・舌・身・意・根・識・塵): I.e., the six senses and the sense organ, sense consciousness, and sense object.

24 **they have one body and one mind** (*isshin isshin arite* 一身一心ありて): Or "there is one body and one mind"; the translation assumes this refers to each of the items listed in the previous sentence — i.e., each has its own identity, with its own practice and verification.

25 **Yesterday, we may preach an indeterminate dharma for another's sake** (*sakujitsu wa ta no tame ni fujō hō o toku to iedomo* 昨日は他のために不定法をとくといへども): After words (also cited in "Shōbōgenzō ikka myōju" 正法眼藏一顆明珠) attributed to Buddha Śākyamuni in the *Liandeng huiyao* 聯燈會要 (ZZ.136:443b9-11):

> 世尊因外道問、昨日説何法。云説定法。外道云、今日説何法、云説不定法。外道云、昨日説定法。 今日何故説不定法。云昨日定。今日不定。
>
> The World-Honored One was once asked by a non-Buddhist, "What dharma did you preach yesterday?"

Such sun faces are lined up, and moon faces are lined up.[26]

To preach the dharma, to practice the dharma, for the sake of another is to hear the dharma, to clarify the dharma, to verify the dharma, in lifetime after lifetime. In this life as well, we are preaching for the sake of others; yet, when we do it with a sincere mind, we ourselves easily attain the dharma. Or, when we help and encourage others to hear the dharma, our own study of the dharma gains good advantage; it gains an advantage in our bodies, and it gains an advantage in our minds. Those who obstruct [others from] hearing the dharma are themselves obstructed from hearing the dharma. To preach the dharma, to hear the dharma, in body after body of life after life is to hear the dharma in generation after generation: the dharma that we directly transmitted previously, we now hear again in this generation.[27] Since we are born in the dharma and expire in the dharma, when we have directly transmitted the dharma in the entire world in the ten directions, we hear it in life after life, we practice it in body after body.[28] Since we manifest life after life in the dharma and make body after body into the dharma, we take up both a single dust mote and the dharma realm and cause the dharma to be verified.

[69:10] {2:199}

しかあれば、東邊にして一句をききて、西邊にきたりて、一人のためにとくべし。これ、一自己をもて、聞著・説著を一等に功夫するなり、東自・西自を一齊に修證するなり。なにとしても、ただ佛法祖道を自己の身心にあひちかづけ、あひいとなむを、よろこび、のぞみ、こころざすべし。一時より一日におよび、乃至一年より一生までのいとなみとすべし。佛法を精魂として弄すべきなり。これを、生生をむなしくすごさざるとす。

He said, "I preached a determinate dharma."
The non-Buddhist said, "What dharma do you preach today?"
He said, "I'm preaching an indeterminate dharma."
The non-Buddhist said, "Yesterday, you preached a determinate dharma. Why are you preaching an indeterminate dharma today?"
He said, "Yesterday was determinate. Today is indeterminate."

26 **Such sun faces are lined up, and moon faces are lined up** (*kaku no gotoku no nichimen aitsuranari, gachimen aitsuranareri* かくのことくの日面あひつらなり、月面あひつらなれり): Perhaps meaning no more than that such days pass one after another; but, given the allusion just above to the Buddhas Sun Face and Moon Face, the sense may also be that there is a new buddha with a new teaching each day.

27 **hear the dharma in generation after generation** (*sese ni monpō suru* 世世に聞法する): I.e., our preaching of the dharma in our past lives enables us to hear the dharma in our future lives. "Generation" (or "age"; *se* 世) here refers to the individual's rebirth.

28 **Since we are born in the dharma and expire in the dharma** (*hō no naka ni shōji, hō no naka ni messuru ga yue ni* 法のなかに生じ、法のなかに滅するがゆえに): The translation follows Kawamura's punctuation here. This clause could also be read with the preceding sentence: "The dharma that we directly transmitted previously, we now hear again in this generation; for we are born in the dharma and expire in the dharma."

Thus, hearing a phrase in the east, we should come to the west and teach it to someone. This is by a single self, working equally at hearing and preaching, practicing and verifying equally our eastern self and western self. Whatever we do, we should rejoice in, hope for, and aspire to bringing near to our bodies and minds, and living by, the dharma of the buddhas and the way of the ancestors. We should live by them from one hour to one day, from one year to one lifetime. We should play with the buddha dharma as the spirit.[29] This is what it means not to pass life after life in vain.

[69:11] {2:200}

しかあるを、いまだあきらめざればひとのためにとくべからず、とおもふことなかれ。あきらめんことをまたんは、無量劫にもかなふべからず。たとひ人佛をあきらむとも、さらに天佛あきらむべし。たとひ山のこころをあきらむとも、さらに水のこころをあきらむべし。たとひ因緣生法をあきらむとも、さらに非因緣生法をあきらむべし。たとひ佛祖邊をあきらむとも、さらに佛祖向上をあきらむべし。これらを一世にあきらめをはりて、のちに他のためにせんと擬せんは、不功夫なり、不丈夫なり、不參學なり。

However, do not think that we should not teach others when we have not yet got clear ourselves. If we wait to be clear, we will not be able to do it for innumerable kalpas. Even should we clarify human buddhas, we must still clarify deva buddhas.[30] Even should we clarify the mind of mountains, we must still clarify the mind of waters. Even should we clarify dharmas arising from causes and conditions, we must still clarify dharmas not arising from causes and conditions.[31] Even should we clarify the vicinity of the buddhas and ancestors, we must still clarify what is beyond the buddhas and ancestors. To imagine that we will clarify these in one lifetime and then teach them to others is not making concentrated effort, is not being resolute, is not studying.

---

29 **We should play with the buddha dharma as the spirit** (*buppō o seikon toshite rō su beki nari* 佛法を精魂として弄すべきなり): From the common expression "playing with the spirit" (*rō zeikon* 弄精魂), occurring often in Chan literature; it can indicate a distracted, or "possessed," state of mind but is sometimes used in ironic reference to spiritual practice.

30 **human buddhas** (*ninbutsu* 人佛); **deva buddhas** (*tenbutsu* 天佛): Unusual terms; as used in "Shōbōgenzō gyōbutsu iigi" 正法眼藏行佛威儀, they indicate buddhas appearing in the human and deva realms respectively.

31 **dharmas arising from causes and conditions** (*innen shō hō* 因緣生法); **dharmas not arising from causes and conditions** (*hi innen shō hō* 非因緣生法): Presumably, "conditioned (*ui* 有爲; S. *saṃskṛta*) dharmas" and "unconditioned (*mui* 無爲; S. *asaṃskṛta*) dharmas," respectively.

[69:12]
おほよそ學佛祖道は、一法一儀を參學するより、すなはち爲他の志氣を衝天せしむるなり。しかあるによりて、自他を脱落するなり。さらに自己を參徹すれば、さきより參徹他己なり。よく他己を參徹すれば、自己參徹なり。この佛儀は、たとひ生知といふとも、師承にあらざれば、體達すべからず。生知、いまだ師にあはざれば、不生知をしらず、不生不知をしらず。たとひ生知といふとも、佛祖の大道はしるべきにあらず、學してしるべきなり。自己を體達し、他己を體達す、佛祖の大道なり。ただまさに自初心の參學をめぐらして、他初心の參學を同參すべし。初心より自他ともに同參しもてゆくに、究竟同參に得到するなり。自功夫のごとく、他功夫をもすすむべし。

In general, in studying the way of the buddhas and ancestors, once we have studied a single dharma or a single behavior, we let our determination to help others assault the heavens.[32] Through this, we slough off self and other. Going further, when we study and master ourselves, it is our previous study and mastery of the other; when we study and master the other, it is study and mastery of ourselves. This buddha behavior, even those of innate knowledge cannot personally realize if it is not received from a teacher.[33] Those of innate knowledge, if they have not encountered a teacher, do not know non-innate knowledge, they do not know non-innate non-knowledge.[34] They may have innate knowledge, but they cannot know the great way of the buddhas and ancestors; they must study it to know it. Personally to realize oneself and personally to realize the other, is the great way of the buddhas and ancestors. Reflecting on our own study as beginners, we should study together the study of others' study as beginners. When self and other go on studying together from their time as beginners, they reach an ultimate study together. Like our own concentrated effort, we should encourage the concentrated effort of others.

---

32 **assault the heavens** (*shōten* 衝天): A fixed phrase for vaulting ambition or high aspiration; occurs several times in Dōgen's writings.

33 **innate knowledge** (*shōchi* 生知): See Supplementary Notes, s.v. "Knowledge at birth."

34 **do not know non-innate knowledge, they do not know non-innate non-knowledge** (*fushōchi o shirazu, fushō fuchi o shirazu* 不生知をしらず、不生不知をしらず): Or perhaps the latter clause should be read, "they do not know what is neither innate nor knowledge." The English "innate" here masks Dōgen's play with the glyph *shō* 生 ("birth") in *shōchi* 生知 ("knowledge at birth"), used for those innately wise; and *fushō* 不生 ("unborn"), used in reference to the emptiness, or "non-arising," of phenomena. Hence, this sentence could be read, "They do not know the knowledge of the unborn; they do not know the non-knowledge of the unborn."

[69:13] {2:201}

しかあるに、自證自悟等の道をききて、麤人おもはくは、師に傳受すべからず、自學すべし。これは、おほきなるあやまりなり。自解の思量分別を邪計して師承なきは、西天の天然外道なり。これをわきまへざらんともがら、いかでか佛道人ならん。いはんや自證の言をききて、積聚の五蘊ならんと計せば、小乘の自調に同ぜん。大乘・小乘をわきまへざるともがら、おほく佛祖の兒孫と自稱するおほし。しかあれども、明眼人、だれか瞞ぜられん。

However, upon hearing the words "self-verification," "self-awakening," and the like, crude people think that one should not receive transmission from a teacher but should study on one's own. This is a big mistake. To be without instruction from a teacher, reckoning mistakenly with the discriminations of the thinking of one's own understanding, is an other path of natural occurrence in Sindh in the West.[35] How could those types who do not discern this be people of the way of the buddhas? Not to mention that, upon hearing the term "self-verification," if we reckon it to be the accumulated five aggregates, it will be the same as the self-control of the Small Vehicle.[36] There are many of the types unable to distinguish between the Great Vehicle and the Small Vehicle who call themselves descendants of the buddhas and ancestors. However, among those with clear eyes, who would be deceived by them?

* * * * *

35 **other path of natural occurrence in Sindh in the West** (*Saiten no tennen gedō* 西天の天然外道): I.e., non-Buddhist religious teaching of India that denies the laws of cause and effect.

36 **if we reckon it to be the accumulated five aggregates** (*shakujū no goon naran to keiseba* 積聚の五蘊ならんと計せば): Presumably meaning that, "if we take the self of 'self-verification' to be the self of the five *skandhas*," then, like the followers of the Small Vehicle, we think this is a matter of disciplining oneself. See Supplementary Notes, s.v. "Four elements and five aggregates."

[69:14]
大宋國紹興のなかに、徑山の大慧禪師宗杲といふあり。もとはこれ經論の學生なり。遊方のちなみに、宣州の理禪師にしたがひて、雲門の拈古、および雪竇の頌古・拈古を學す、參學のはじめなり。雲門の風を會せずして、つひに洞山の微和尚に參學すといへども、微、つひに堂奥をゆるさず。微和尚は、芙蓉和尚の法子なり、いたづらなる席末人に齊肩すべからず。杲禪師、ややひさしく參學すといへども、微の皮肉骨髓を摸著することあたはず、いはんや、塵中の眼睛ありとだにもしらず。

In the Land of the Great Song, during the Shaoxing, there was a certain Zonggao, Chan Master Dahui of Mount Jing.[37] Originally a student of the sūtras and treatises, during his wanderings, he became a follower of Chan Master Chen of Xuanzhou, under whom he studied the comments on old cases by Yunmen, as well as the verses and comments on old cases by Xuedou; this was the beginning of his study.[38]

Failing to understand the style of Yunmen, he eventually studied with Reverend Wei of Dongshan; but, in the end, Wei did not admit him into the interior of the hall.[39] Reverend Wei was a dharma child of Reverend Furong; he should not be of equal stature to some insignificant person in the last seat.[40] Though Chan Master Gao may have studied with him for quite some time, he was unable touch Wei's skin, flesh, bones, and marrow, much less know that the eye in the dust even exists.[41]

---

37 **Shaoxing** (*Jokō* 紹興): The era covering 1131-1162, in the reign of the Song-dynasty Emperor Gaozong 高宗.

Zonggao, Chan Master Dahui of Mount Jing (*Kinzan no Daie zenji Sōkō* 徑山の大慧禪師宗杲): I.e., Dahui Zonggao 大慧宗杲 (1089–1163), who twice served as abbot of the Xingsheng Wanshou Chan Monastery 興聖萬壽禪寺 on Jingshan 徑山 in Hangzhou 杭州. Dōgen's account here of Dahui's studies is loosely derived (though quite different) from the *Dahui Puzue chanshi zongmen wuku* 大慧普覺禪師宗門武庫, T.1998B.47:953a25ff.

38 **Chan master Chen of Xuanzhou** (*Senshū no Tei zenji* 宣州の理禪師): I.e., Mingjiao Shaochen 明教紹珵 (dates unknown).

Yunmen (*Unmon* 雲門); **Xuedou** (*Seppō* 雪竇): I.e., Yunmen Wenyen 雲門文偃 (864-949); Xuedou Zhongxian 雪竇重顯 (980-1052).

39 **Reverend Wei of Dongshan** (*Tōzan no Bi oshō* 洞山の微和尚): I.e., Dongshan Daowei 洞山道微 (dates unknown).

did not admit him into the interior of the hall (*dōō o yurusazu* 堂奥をゆるさず): I.e., did not grant him private interviews in the abbot's quarters.

40 **Reverend Furong** (*Fuyō oshō* 芙蓉和尚): I.e., the important Caodong master Furong Daokai 芙蓉道楷 (1043-1118).

some insignificant person in the last seat (*itazura naru sekimatsu nin* いたづらなる席末人): The "end of the seats" (*sekimatsu* 席末) refers to the lowest ranking place in a seating arrangement.

41 **touch Wei's skin, flesh, bones, and marrow** (*Bi no hi niku kotsu zui o mojaku suru*

[69:15]
あるとき、佛祖の道に、臂香嗣書の法あり、とばかりききて、しきりに嗣書を微和尚に請す。しかあれども、微和尚ゆるさず。つひにいはく、なんぢ、嗣法を要せば、倉卒なることなかれ。直須功夫勤學すべし。佛祖受授不妄付授也、吾不惜付授、只是儞未具眼在。ときに宗杲いはく、本具正眼、自證自悟、豈有不妄付授也。微和尚、笑而休矣。のちに湛堂準和尚に參ず。

Once, upon hearing that, in the way of the buddhas and ancestors, there is a procedure of forearm incense and inheritance certificate, he repeatedly begged an inheritance certificate of Reverend Wei.[42]

Reverend Wei, however, did not approve, finally saying, "If you want to inherit the dharma, do not be hasty. You should make effort and pursue your study. *The conferral of the buddhas and ancestors is not transferred indiscriminately. I do not begrudge conferring it; it is just that you still do not possess the eye.*"

At this point, Zonggao replied, "*The true eye originally possessed is self-verified and self-awakened. How could it be conferred indiscriminately?*"[43]

Reverend Wei laughed and retired.

Thereafter, [Zonggao] studied with Reverend Zhantang Zhun.[44]

微の皮肉骨髓を摸著する): I.e., "understand Wei's teaching." "Touch" here loosely renders *mojaku* 摸著 ("to grope"), from the common expression, "to grope but not touch it" (*mo fujaku* 摸不著) — i.e., "look for it without finding it."

eye in the dust (*jinchū no ganzei* 塵中の眼睛): An unusual expression, likely meaning "the eye of the buddhas and ancestors within the world of the six senses" — "dust" (*jin* 塵) being a common term for the objects of the senses; no doubt the same eye discussed by Daowei and Dahui in the following section. See Supplementary Notes, s.v. "Eye," and "Dust."

42 **Once** (*aru toki* あるとき): Dōgen's account here continues loosely to reflect the *Dahui Puzue chanshi zongmen wuku* 大慧普覺禪師宗門武庫 (T.1998B.47:953b4-6). The exchange between Daowei and Dahui, however, does not occur here, and Dōgen's source (if any) is unclear.

forearm incense and inheritance certicate (*hikō shisho* 臂香嗣書): A rite of burning incense on the forearm and receiving a document of succession from a master.

43 **"The true eye originally possessed is self-verified and self-awakened"** (*hon gu shōgen, jishō jigo* 本具正眼、自證自悟): Though Dahui's words are given in Chinese, as if quoting a text, the *Zongmen wuku* 宗門武庫 (T.1998B.47:953b5-6) has a rather different version here: Dahui is dismissive of the ceremony of burning incense and transmitting the dharma, thinking to himself,

> 豈佛祖自證自悟之法。
> How can it be the dharma of the self-verification and self-awakening of the buddhas and ancestors?

44 **Reverend Zhantang Zhun** (*Tandō Jun oshō* 湛堂準和尚): I.e., Zhantang Wenzhun 湛堂文準 (1061-1115).

[69:16] {2:202}

湛堂一日問宗杲云、儞鼻孔、因什麼今日無半邊。杲云、寶峰門下。湛堂云、杜撰禪和。杲看經次、湛堂問、看什麼經。杲曰、金剛經。湛堂云、是法平等、無有高下、爲什麼、雲居山高、寶峰山低。杲曰、是法平等、無有高下。湛堂云、儞作得箇座主。使下。又一日、湛堂見於粧十王處、問宗杲上座曰、此官人、姓什麼。杲曰、姓梁。湛堂以手自摸頭曰、爭奈姓梁底、少箇幞頭。杲曰、雖無幞頭、鼻孔髣髴。湛堂曰、杜撰禪和。

One day, Zhantang asked Zonggao, "Why is your nose half missing today?"[45]

Gao said, "In the tradition of Baofeng."[46]

Zhantang said, "Illiterate Chan monk."

Once when Gao was looking at a sūtra, Zhantang asked him, "What sūtra are you looking at?"

Gao said, "The Diamond Sūtra*."*

Zhantang said, "This dharma is equal, without high or low. Why is Mount Yunju high and Mount Baofeng low?"

Gao said, "This dharma is equal, without high or low."

Zhantang said, "You've become quite the prelate," and sent him away.[47]

Again, one day, Zhantang, looking at depictions of the ten kings, asked Senior Seat Zonggao, "What's this official's name?"[48]

Gao said, "His name is Liang."[49]

Zhangtang felt his own head and said, "Why is the one named Liang missing his headdress?"

Gao said, "He may not have the headdress, but the nose looks just the same."

Zhantang said, "Illiterate Chan monk."

---

45 **One day** (*ichinichi* 一日): Though their order differs, the following three dialogues are in the Chinese of the *Zongmen wuku* 宗門武庫 (T.1998B.47:953b6-14).

46 **"In the tradition of Baofeng"** (*Hōhō monka* 寶峰門下): Or "A follower of Baofeng." I.e., "I'm your student." "Baofeng" 寶峰 refers to Zhantang's monastery, the Baofengsi 寶峰寺 at Letan 泐潭 in modern Jiangxi prefecture.

47 **"prelate"** (*zasu* 座主): The abbot of a Teachings monastery (*kyōji* 教寺 or *kyōin* 教院) — an institution where the abbacy is restricted to members of the Tiantai school; likely used here sarcastically, in the sense "know it all" or "smart ass." See Supplementary Notes, s.v. "Prelate Liang."

48 **the ten kings** (*jūō* 十王): The ten kings of the underworld.

49 **"His name is Liang"** (*Shō Ryō tei* 姓梁底): Zhangtang's lay surname was Liang 梁.

[69:17]

湛堂一日問宗杲云、杲上座、我這裏禪、儞一時理會得。教儞說也說得、教儞參也參得、教儞做頌古・拈古・小參・普說・請益、儞也做得。祇是儞有一件事未在、儞還知否。杲曰、甚麼事未在。湛堂曰、儞祇缺這一解在、囮。若作不得這一解、我方丈與儞說時、便有禪、儞纔出方丈、便無了也。惺惺思量時、便有禪、纔睡著、便無了也。若如此、如何敵得生死。杲曰、正是宗杲疑處。

One day, Zhangtang asked Zonggao, "Senior Seat Gao, you understood my Chan here at once.[50] *I have you teach it, and you can teach it. I have you study it, and you can study it. I have you do verses on the old cases, comments on the old cases, small convocations, public sermons, requests for instruction, and you can do them. There's just one thing still missing. Do you know what it is?"*

Gao said, "What thing is missing?"

Zhangtang said, "You just lack this one understanding: Ha! So long as you don't get this one understanding, when I'm talking with you in the abbot's quarters, you have Chan, but, as soon as you leave the abbot's quarters, you don't; when you're wide awake and thinking, you have Chan, but, as soon as you go to sleep, you don't. If you're like this, how can you confront life and death?

Gao said, "This is exactly what Zonggao has doubts about."

[69:18] {2:203}

後稍經載、湛堂示疾。宗杲問曰、和尚百年後、宗杲依附阿誰、可以了此大事。湛堂囑曰、有箇勤巴子、我亦不識他。雖然、儞若見他、必能成就此事。儞若見他了、不可更他遊、後世出來參禪也。

Some years later, Zhangtang became ill. Zonggao asked him, "After the Reverend's hundredth year, on whom should Zonggao rely to comprehend this great matter?"[51]

Zhangtang advised him, "There is a certain Qin Bazi.[52] *I don't know him, but if you happen to meet him, you will definitely be able to achieve this matter. Once you've met him, don't wander off to others. Study Chan when you come back in the next life."*

50 **One day** (*ichinichi* 一日): Continuing to quote the Chinese of the *Zongmen wuku* 宗門武庫 (T.1998B.47:953b14-22).

51 **Some years later** (*go shō kei sai* 後稍經載): Continuing to quote (with slight variation) the *Zongmen wuku* 宗門武庫 (T.1998B.47:953b22-25).

52 **"Qin Bazi"** (*Gon Hasu* 勤巴子): I.e., Yuanwu Keqin 圜悟克勤 (1063–1135). The name Bazi 巴子 refers to Yuanwu's origins in Sichuan.

[69:19] {2:204}

この一段の因緣を檢點するに、湛堂、なほ宗杲をゆるさず。たびたび開發を擬すといへども、つひに缺一件事なり。補一件事あらず、脱落一件事せず。微和尚、そのかみ嗣書をゆるさず、なんぢいまだしきことあり、と勸勵する、微和尚の觀機あきらかなること、信仰すべし。正是宗杲疑處、を究參せず、脱落せず、打破せず、大疑せず、被疑礙なし。そのかみ、みだりに嗣書を請する、參學の倉卒なり、無道心のいたりなり、無稽古のはなはだしきなり、無遠慮なりといふべし、道機ならずといふべし、疏學のいたりなり。貪名愛利によって、佛祖の堂奧を、をかさんとす。あはれむべし、佛祖の語句をしらざることを。稽古はこれ自證と會せず、萬代を渉獵するは自悟ときかず、學せざるによりて、かくのごとく不是あり、かくのごとくの自錯あり。かくのごとくなるによりて、宗杲禪師の門下に、一箇半箇の眞巴鼻あらず、おほくこれ假低なり。佛法を會せず、佛法を不會せざるは、かくのごとくなり。而今の雲水、かならず審細の參學すべし、疏慢なることなかれ。

When we examine this episode, Zhangtang did not accept Zonggao. While he sought repeatedly to discover it, he was still *lacking the "one thing.*" He did not *fill in the "one thing"*; he did not *slough off the "one thing.*" Previously, Reverend Wei denied him an inheritance certicate, urging him on by saying, "You're not ready." We should trust the clarity of Reverend Wei's insight into his abilities. "*This is exactly what Zonggao has doubts about*": he did not investigate this; he did not slough it off; he did not break through it; he did not have the great doubt about it; he was not obstructed by the doubt. Previously, his recklessly begging a document of succession was precipitate, was an extreme case of one lacking the mind of the way, was a flagrant case of lacking learning from the ancients. We have to say he was thoughtless; we have to say he was not fit for the way; he was an extreme case of neglect of study. From his lust for fame and love of profit, he would violate the interior of the hall of the buddhas and ancestors. How pitiful that he did not know the words of the buddhas and ancestors. Because he did not understand that learning from the ancients is self-verification, and had not heard, had not studied, that perusing the myriad generations is self-awakening, he had this kind of error, he had this kind of self-mistake.[53] Because he was like this, among the followers of Chan Master Zonggao, there is not one or one half with a real nose grip; most of them are fakes and inferiors.[54]

---

53 **perusing the myriad generations** (*bandai o shōryō suru* 萬代を渉獵する): I.e., reading through the classical literature.

self-mistake (*jisaku* 自錯): Playing on "self-verification" (*jishō* 自證) and "self-awakening" (*jigo* 自悟).

54 **a real nose grip** (*shin habi* 眞巴鼻): I.e., a real grasp; a common metaphor, from the nose ring used to lead cattle. See Supplementary Notes, s.v. "Nose."

fakes and inferiors (*ketei* 假低): A tentative translation of an unusual compound expres-

Failure to understand the buddha dharma, and failure not to understand the buddha dharma, are like this.[55] Monks of the present should study in detail; do not be neglectful.

[69:20] {2:205}

宗杲因湛堂之囑、而湛堂順寂後、參圜悟禪師於京師之天寧。圜悟一日陞堂、宗杲有神悟、以悟告呈圜悟。悟云、未也、子雖如是、而大法故未明。

> *On Zhangtang's advice, following Zhangtang's quiesence, Zonggao studied with Chan Master Yuanwu at Tianning in the capital.*[56] *One day, when Yuanwu ascended to the hall, Zonggao had a spiritual awakening.*[57] *He reported his awakening to Yuanwu.*
>
> *Wu said, "Not yet. You may be like this, but the great dharma is not yet clarified."*

[69:21]

又一日、圜悟上堂、擧五祖演和尚、有句無句語。宗杲聞、而言下得大安樂法。又呈解圜悟。圜悟笑曰、吾不欺汝耶。

> *Again, one day, in a convocation, Yuanwu took up the words of Reverend Yan of Wuzu on "affirmative statements and negative statements."*[58] *Upon hearing it, Zonggao attained the dharma of great bliss. Again, he expressed his understanding to Yuanwu. Yuanwu laughed and said, "I didn't trick you?"*

[69:22]

これ宗杲禪師、のちに圜悟に參ずる因緣なり。圜悟の會にして、書記に充す。しかあれども、前後いまだあらたなる得處みえず、みづから普説・陞堂のときも、得處を擧せず。しるべし、記錄者は神悟せるといひ、得大安樂法と記せりといへども、させることなきなり。おもくおもふことなかれ、ただ參學の生なり。

---

sion. Some MS witnesses read *ketei* 假底, perhaps meaning "frauds."

55 **failure not to understand the buddha dharma** (*buppō o fue sezaru* 佛法を不會せざる): Perhaps meaning "failure to avoid misunderstandings of the buddha dharma."

56 **Chan Master Yuanwu at Tianning in the capital** (*Engo zenji o kyōshi shi tennei* 圜悟禪師於京師之天寧): I.e., Yuanwu Keqin 圜悟克勤, at the Tianningsi 天寧寺 in the Northern Song capital of Bianjing 汴京 (modern Kaifeng). This and the following dialogue are based on the "Dahui Pujue chansi taming" 大慧普覺禪師塔銘 (at *Dahui Pujue chansi yulu* 大慧普覺禪師語錄, T.1998A.47:836b19-24).

57 **ascended to the hall** (*shindō* 陞堂): I.e., held a formal convocation in the dharma hall; synonymous with *jōdō* 上堂 ("convocation"), used in the next section.

58 **the words of Reverend Yan of Wuzu on "affirmative statements and negative statements"** (*Goso En oshō uku muku go* 五祖演和尚有句無句語): I.e., Yuanwu's teacher, Wuzu Fayan 五祖法演 (d. 1104). The words in question are likely comments on the popular saying attributed to Weishan Lingyou 潙山靈祐 (771-853) found at *shinji Shōbōgenzō* 眞字正法眼藏, DZZ.5:208, case 157; see Supplementary Notes, s.v. "Like vines relying on a tree."

This is an episode of Chan Master Zonggao's later studying with Yuanwu. He served as secretary in Yuanwu's community.[59] Nevertheless, we do not see that he had any new attainments before or after; and, in his own public sermons and formal convocations, he does not bring up any attainments. We should recognize that, while his biographer wrote that he had a "spiritual awakening" and "attained the dharma of great bliss," we need not make anything of this.[60] Do not take it seriously: he was just an ordinary student.

[69:23]

圜悟禪師は古佛なり、十方中の至尊なり。黄檗よりのちは、圜悟のごとくなる尊宿、いまだあらざるなり、他界にも、まれなるべき古佛なり。しかあれども、これをしれる人天まれなり、あはれむべき娑婆國土なり。いま圜悟古佛の説法を擧して、宗杲上座を檢點するに、師におよべる智、いまだあらず、師にひとしき智、いまだあらず、いかにいはんや、師よりもすぐれたる智、ゆめにもいまだみざるがごとし。

Chan Master Yuanwu was an old buddha, most honored in the ten directions. After Huangbo, there is no venerable like Yuanwu; he was an old buddha who must be rare even in the other world.[61] Nevertheless, there are few humans or devas who recognize this; ours is a sad Sahā land. If we examine Senior Seat Zonggao by holding up the teachings of Old Buddha Yuanwu, it seems he lacked wisdom approaching his master's, lacked wisdom equaling his master's; how much less did he ever see, even in his dreams, wisdom exceeding his master's.

[69:24] {2:206}

しかあればしるべし、宗杲禪師は減師半徳の才におよばざるなり。ただわづかに華嚴・楞嚴等の文句を諳誦して傳説するのみなり、いまだ佛祖の骨髓あらず。宗杲おもはくは、大小の隠倫わづかに依草附木の精靈にひかれて保任せるところの見解、これを佛法とおもへり。これを佛法と許せるをもて、はかりしりぬ、佛祖の大道いまだ參究せずといふことを。圜悟よりのち、さらに他遊せず、智識をとぶらはず。みだりに大刹の主として、雲水の參頭なり。のこれる語句、いまだ大法のほとりにおよばず。しかあるを、しらざるともがらおもはくは、宗杲禪師、むかしにもはぢざるとおもふ。み、しれるものは、あきらめざると決定せり。つひに大法をあきらめず、いたづらに口吧吧地のみなり。

59 **secretary** (*shoki* 書記): One of the six monastic offices, in charge of records and correspondence.

60 **his biographer** (*kirokusha* 記錄者): I.e., the official Zhang Jun 張浚, author of the "Dahui Pujue chansi taming" 大慧普覺禪師塔銘 passages Dōgen has just quoted.

61 **Huangbo** (*Ōbaku* 黄檗): I.e., the famous ninth-century figure Huangbo Xiyun 黄檗希運.

Thus, we should realize that the talents of Chan Master Zonggao did not amount to *reducing the teacher's merits by half*.[62] He just memorized and conveyed a few passages of the *Huayan*, *Laṅka*, and the like; he still lacked the bones and marrow of the buddhas and ancestors.[63] Zonggao thought that the view maintained by major and minor hermits simply taken by the spirits that *adhere to the grasses and attach to the trees* — that this was the buddha dharma.[64] Given that he accepted this as the buddha dharma, it is clear that he never investigated the great way of the buddhas and ancestors. After Yuanwu, he did not travel to others or consult wise friends; he brazenly headed up the monks as the master of great monasteries. The words he has left us do not reach the vicinity of the great dharma. Those who do not know, however, think that Chan Master Zonggao owes no apologies even to the ancients; those who see and know are certain that he did not understand. In the end, he did not understand the great dharma but just meaninglessly ran his mouth, blah, blah.[65]

[69:25]

しかあればしりぬ、洞山の微和尚、まことに後鑑あきらかにあやまらざりけりといふことを。宗杲禪師に參學せるともがらは、それすゑまでも、微和尚をそねみ、ねたむこと、いまにたえざるなり。微和尚はただゆるさざるのみなり。準和尚のゆるさざることは、微よりもはなはだし、まみゆるごとには、勘過するのみなり。しかあれども、準和尚をねたまず。而今およびこしかたのねたむともがら、いくばくの懡㦬なりとかせん。

Thus, we know that Reverend Wei of Dongshan was truly a clear mirror on the future and was not mistaken. The resentment of and hostility toward Reverend Wei among those, to the last, who studied with Chan Master Zonggao remains unabated even now. Reverend Wei simply failed to acknowledge him; Reverend Zhang's failure to acknowledge

62 **reducing the teacher's merits by half** (*gen shi han toku* 減師半德): From the Zen saying, "A view equal to the master's reduces the master's virtue by half" (*ken yo shi sai gen shi han toku* 見與師齊減師半德).

63 **the *Huayan*, *Laṅka*, and the like** (*Kegon Ryōgon tō* 華嚴・楞嚴等): I.e., the *Avatamsaka*, *Laṅkāvatāra*, and other sūtras.

64 **major and minor hermits** (*daishō no inrin* 大小の隱倫): From the common trope expressed in the well-known verse by the Jin-dynasty poet Wang Kangju 王康琚:

小隱隱林薮、大隱隱朝市。

The minor hermit secludes himself in woods and marshes;
The major hermit secludes himself in court and market.

the spirits that adhere to the grasses and attach to the trees (*esō fuboku no shōryō* 依草附木の精靈): A fixed idiom for spirits of the dead that cling to the world; used in Chan texts for those who cling to words.

65 **just meaninglessly ran his mouth, blah, blah** (*itazura ni ku haha chi nomi* いたづらに口吧吧地のみ): From the Chinese onomatopoeia *baba* 吧吧 for blathering on.

him was even more severe than Wei's: at every encounter, he did nothing but point out his mistakes. Yet, they do not resent Reverend Zhang. How shameful are those in present and past who resent [Reverend Wei].

[69:26]
おほよそ大宋國に佛祖の兒孫と自稱するおほかれども、まことを學せるすくなきゆえに、まことををしふるすくなし。そのむね、この因緣にてもはかりしりぬべし。紹興のころ、なほかくのごとし。いまはそのころよりもおとれり、たとふるにもおよばず。いまは佛祖の大道、なにとあるべしとだにもしらざるともがら、雲水の主人となれり。

Generally speaking, although there are many in the Land of the Great Song who call themselves descendants of the buddhas and ancestors, since there are few who have studied the real thing, there are few who teach the real thing. That point can be clearly seen in this episode as well. It was like this even in the Shaoxing period; now things are even worse than then, beyond compare. Nowadays, those who do not even know what the great way of the buddhas and ancestors is supposed to be have become the leaders of the monks.

[69:27] {2:207}
しるべし、佛佛祖祖、西天東土、嗣書正傳は、青原山下これ正傳なり。青原山下よりのち、洞山おのづから正傳せり。自餘の十方、かつてしらざるところなり。しるものはみなこれ洞山の兒孫なり、雲水に聲名をほどこす。宗杲禪師、なほ生前に自證自悟の言句をしらず、いはんや自餘の公案を參徹せんや。いはんや宗杲禪老よりも晩進、たれか自證の言をしらん。

We should understand that, in the direct transmission of the inheritance certificates of buddha after buddha and ancestor after ancestor in Sindh in the West and the Land of the East, it is the line under Mount Qingyuan that is the direct transmission.[66] From the line under Mount Qingyuan, naturally it was directly transmitted by Dongshan.[67] This is something unknown to others in the ten directions; those who know it are all descendants of Dongshan, who spread his name among the clouds and water.[68] Chan Master Zonggao throughout his life did not understand the words "self-verification" and "self-awakening," much less did he master any other kōan. How much less, then, among the latecomers after Chan Elder Zonggao could anyone understand the words "self-verification."

66 **it is the line under Mount Qingyuan that is the direct transmission** (*Seigenzanka kore shōden nari* 青原山下これ正傳なり): I.e., the lineage of the Sixth Ancestor's disciple Qingyuan Xingsi 青原行思 (d. 740) is the main line of descent.

67 **Dongshan** (*Tōzan* 洞山): I.e., Dongshan Liangjie 洞山良价 (807-869), in the fourth generation after Qingyuan; founder of Dōgen's Caodong 曹洞 (J. Sōtō) lineage.

68 **clouds and water** (*unsui* 雲水): I.e., the monastic community.

[69:28]

しかあればすなはち、佛祖道の道自道他、かならず佛祖の身心あり、佛祖の眼睛あり。佛祖の骨髓なるがゆえに、庸者の得皮にあらず。

Thus, speaking of the self and speaking of the other in the way of the buddhas and ancestors always has the body and mind of the buddhas and ancestors, the eye of the buddhas and ancestors. Since it is the bones and marrow of the buddhas and ancestors, it is not the skin got by the mediocre.

正法眼藏自證三昧第六十九
Treasury of the True Dharma Eye
The Samādhi of Self-Verification
Number 69

[Ryūmonji MS:]

爾時寬元二年甲辰二月二十九日、在越宇吉峰精舍示衆
Presented to the assembly at Kippō Vihāra, Etsuu; twenty-ninth day, second month of the senior wood year of the dragon, the second year of Kangen [8 April 1244][69]

[*Himitsu* MS:]

同四月十二日、越州在吉峰下侍者寮書寫之。懷奘
Copied this in the acolyte's quarters beneath Kippō, Esshū; twelfth day, fourth month, of the same year [21 May 1244]. Ejō

69 The *Himitsu* 秘密 MS shares an identical colophon.

TREASURY OF THE TRUE DHARMA EYE

NUMBER 70

Empty Space

Kokū

虚空

Empty Space

Kokū

Introduction

This short chapter was composed in the spring of 1245, at Dōgen's new Daibutsu Monastery in Echizen. Number 70 in the seventy-five-chapter *Shōbōgenzō*, it occurs as number 56 in the sixty-chapter compilation and number 76 in the Honzan edition (or 77 in the Iwanami and Shūmuchō versions).

True to its title, the essay discusses several passages from Zen literature on the topic of space. Most of the piece is devoted to a line-by-line commentary on the story of the Tang-dynasty monks Shigong Huizang 石鞏慧藏 and Xitang Zhizang 西堂智藏 in conversation on how to grab hold of space. Following this, Dōgen adds some rather cursory remarks on three additional passages and ends with the advice that space be understood as "the treasury of the true dharma eye, the wondrous mind of nirvāṇa" transmitted by the buddhas and ancestors.

正法眼藏第七十
Treasury of the True Dharma Eye
Number 70

虚空
Empty Space

[70:1] {2:208}

這裏是什麼處在のゆえに、道現成をして佛祖ならしむ。佛祖の道現成、おのづから嫡嫡するゆえに、皮肉骨髓の渾身せる、掛虚空なり。虚空は、二十空等の群にあらず。おほよそ、空ただ二十空のみならんや、八萬四千空あり、およびそこばくあるべし。

Due to "*where are we here?*" the buddhas and ancestors are made from their statements.[1] Because the statements of the buddhas and ancestors themselves pass from successor to successor, their skin, flesh, bones, and marrow form "the whole body" that "hangs in empy space."[2] "Empty

1 **Due to "where are we here?" the buddhas and ancestors are made from their statements** (*shari ze jūmo sho zai no yue ni, dōgenjō o shite busso narashimu* 這裏是什麼處在のゆえに、道現成をして佛祖ならしむ): A tentative translation of a difficult sentence variously interpreted. Perhaps the most interesting reading might be that it is the sacred space they inhabit ("where are we here") that makes the statements of the masters the words of buddhas and ancestors. "Where are we here?" (*shari ze jūmo sho zai* 這裏是什麼處在) is a fixed rhetorical question warning the interlocutor to keep the conversation at the highest level of truth, beyond dualities. It is best known, perhaps, from the retort of the monk Puhua 普化 (dates unknown), when charged with being rough by Linji Yixuan 臨濟義玄 (d. 866) (*Linji lu* 臨濟錄, T.1985.47:503b5-6; recorded also at *shinji Shōbōgenzō* 眞字正法眼藏, DZZ.5:174, case 96):

> 這裏是什麼所在、説麤説細。
>
> Where are we here, that we're talking of rough and talking of fine?

An identical remark is attributed to Huangbo Xiyun 黄檗希運 (dates unknown) in the *Biyan lu* 碧巖錄 (T.2003.48:152c9-10; quoted by Dōgen in the first part of his "Shōbōgenzō gyōji" 正法眼藏行持).

2 **their skin, flesh, bones, and marrow form "the whole body" that "hangs in empty space"** (*hi niku kotsu zui no konjin seru, ka kokū nari* 皮肉骨髓の渾身せる、掛虚空なり): Another difficult sentence, perhaps meaning that the teachings passed down from successor to successor in the lineage (the "skin, flesh, bones, and marrow" of Bodhidharma) reverberate throughout space (like the wind chime speaking of wisdom to the winds). The expression "skin, flesh, bones, and marrow" (*hi niku kotsu zui* 皮肉骨髓) is commonly used by Dōgen for the essence or truth or entirety of something or someone, as handed down in the ancestral tradition of Zen; see Supplementary Notes, s.v. "Skin, flesh, bones, and marrow." "The whole body hanging in space" evokes a verse on the wind chime by Dōgen's teacher, Tiantong Rujing 天童如淨 (1162-1227), the first

space" does not belong among the twenty aspects of emptiness, and the like.[3] More generally, how could emptiness be of only twenty types? There must be eighty-four thousand types of emptiness and so many more.[4]

* * * * *

[70:2]

撫州石鞏慧藏禪師、問西堂智藏禪師、汝還解捉得虚空麼。西堂曰、解捉得。師曰、儞作麼生捉。西堂以手撮虚空。師曰、儞不解捉虚空。西堂曰、師兄作麼生捉。師把西堂鼻孔拽。西堂作忍痛聲曰、太殺人、拽人鼻孔直得脱去。師曰、直得恁地捉始得。

Chan Master Huizang of Shigong in Fuzhou asked Chan Master Xitang Zhizang, "Can you grab hold of empty space?"[5]

Xitang said, "I can."

The Master said, "How do you do it?"

Xitang pinched empty space with his hand. The Master said, "You can't grab hold of empty space."

Xitang said, "How does my elder brother grab it?"

The Master grabbed Xitang's nose and pulled it. Xitang cried out in pain and said, "What a brute. You could pull a person's nose right off!"

The Master said, "That's how you have to grab hold of it."

---

line of which Dōgen will quote below, section 13 (from *Rujing heshang yulu* 如淨和尚語錄, T.2002A.48:132b15-16):

渾身似口掛虚空、不問東西南北風、一等爲他談般若、滴丁東了滴丁東。

Its whole body, like a mouth, hanging in empty space,
Without asking if the winds are from east, west, south, or north,
Equally, for them, it talks of prajñā:
Di dingdong liao di dingdong.

3 **the twenty aspects of emptiness, and the like** (*nijū kū tō* 二十空等): A list of empty categories found in Xuanzang's translation of the *Mahā-prajñā-pāramitā sūtra* (*Da bore poluomiduo jing* 大般若波羅蜜多經, T.220.5:13b22-26). "And the like" (*tō* 等) here likely indicates other such lists of emptiness, of eighteen, sixteen, etc.

4 **eighty-four thousand** (*hachiman shisen kū* 八萬四千空): A standard figure for an enormous number, as in "eighty-four thousand afflictions," "eighty-four thousand teachings," etc.

5 **Chan Master Huizang of Shigong in Fuzhou** (*Bushū Shakukyō Ezō zenji* 撫州石鞏慧藏禪師); **Chan Master Xitang Zhizang** (*Seidō Chizō zenji* 西堂智藏禪師): I.e., Shigong Huizang 石鞏慧藏 (dates unknown) and Xitang Zhizang 西堂智藏 (735-814), two disciples of Mazu Daoyi 馬祖道一 (709-788). Their dialogue, referred to several times in the *Shōbōgenzō*, can be found at *Jingde chuandeng lu* 景德傳燈錄 (T.2076.51:248b24-29), and at *shinji Shōbōgenzō* 眞字正法眼藏 (DZZ.5:256, case 248).

[70:3] {2:209}
石鞏道の、汝還解捉得虚空麽。なんぢまた通身是手眼なりや、と問著するなり。

Shigong's words, "*Can you grab hold of empty space?*" are asking, "*Is your body throughout hands and eyes?*"[6]

[70:4]
西堂道の、解捉得。虚空一塊触而染汚なり。染汚よりこのかた、虚空落地しきたれり。

Xitang's words, "*I can*," are *empty space is a single lump; touch it, and it's defiled.*[7] After it is defiled, "*empty space has fallen on the ground.*"[8]

[70:5]
石鞏道の、儞作麽生捉、喚作如如、早是變了也なり。しかもかくのごとくなりといへども、隨變而如去也なり。

Shigong's words, "*How do you do it?*" are "*As soon as you call it such and such, it's already changed.*"[9] Nevertheless, while this may be so, *following along with change, it goes thus.*[10]

[70:6]
西堂以手撮虚空。只會騎虎頭、未會把虎尾なり。

"*Xitang pinched empty space with his hand.*" He "*only knew how to ride on the tiger's head but not how to pull the tiger's tail.*"[11]

---

6 **"Is your body throughout hands and eyes?"** (*nanji mata tsūshin ze shugen nari ya* なんぢまた通身是手眼なりや): After the words of Daowu Yuanzhi 道吾圓智 (769-835), describing how the Bodhisattva Avalokiteśvara uses his thousand hands, each with an eye in the palm. The dialogue in which the line occurs is recorded in Dōgen's *shinji Shōbōgenzō* 眞字正法眼藏 (DZZ.5:182, case 105) and discussed in "Shōbōgenzō Kannon" 正法眼藏觀音. See Supplementary Notes, s.v. "His body throughout is hands and eyes."

7 **"empty space is a single lump; touch it, and it's defiled"** (*kokū ikkai soku ni zenna* 虚空一塊触而染汚): Given in Chinese, as if quoting a text, but no source is known.

8 **"empty space has fallen on the ground"** (*kokū raku chi* 虚空落地): Recalling the words of Zhaozhou Congshen 趙州從諗 (778-897) describing the time when the cypress tree becomes a buddha; in a dialogue found, for example, in the *Zhaozhou lu* 趙州錄 (ZZ.118:321b14-16) and discussed in "Shōbōgenzō hakujushi" 正法眼藏柏樹子.

9 **"As soon as you call it such and such, it's already changed"** (*kan sa nyonyo, sō ze henryō ya* 喚作如如、早是變了也): An oft-quoted saying attributed to Nanchan Puyuan 南泉普願 (748-835) (see, e.g., *Biyan lu* 碧巖錄, T.2003.48:199a6-7).

10 **following along with change, it goes thus** (*zui hen ni nyo ko ya* 隨變而如去也): In Chinese, as if a quotation, but no source is known. "It goes thus" translates *nyoko* 如去, a term used for a tathāgata ("one gone thus").

11 **He "only knew how to ride on the tiger's head but not how to pull the tiger's tail"** (*shi e ki kotō, mie ha kobi* 只會騎虎頭、未會把虎尾): A saying attributed to Yang-

[70:7]

石鞏道、儞不解捉虛空。ただ不解捉のみにあらず、虛空也未夢見在なり。しかもかくのごとくなりといへども、年代深遠、不欲爲伊擧似なり。

Shigong said, "You can't grab hold of empty space." It is not just that he cannot grab hold of it; *he has never seen empty space even in his dreams.* Nevertheless, while this may be so, "*the age is so remote, I wouldn't want to bring it up with him.*"[12]

[70:8]

西堂道、師兄作麼生。和尚也道取一半、莫全靠某甲なり。

Xitang said, "How does my elder brother grab it?" This is, "*Reverend, say half; don't rely entirely on me.*"[13]

[70:9]

石鞏把西堂鼻孔拽。しばらく參學すべし、西堂の鼻孔に石鞏藏身せり、あるいは鼻孔拽石鞏の道現成あり。しかもかくのごとくなりといへども、虛空一團、磕著築著なり。

---

shan Huiji 仰山慧寂 (803-887) (see, e.g., *Yangshan Huiji chanshi yulu* 仰山慧寂禪師語錄, T.1990.47:587c3).

12 **"the age is so remote, I wouldn't want to bring it up with him"** (*nendai jin'on, fuyoku i i koji* 年代深遠、不欲爲伊擧似): After another remark by Yangshan Huiji 仰山慧寂, when asked whether anyone else besides Linji received transmission from Huangbo (see, e.g., *Linji yulu* 臨濟語錄, T.1985.47:505a10-12; *Tiansheng guangdeng lu* 天聖廣燈錄, ZZ.135:684b6-8):

> 仰云、有。秖是年代深遠、不欲擧似和尚。
>
> Yang said, "There was. But the age is so remote that I wouldn't want to bring it up with the Reverend."

13 **"Reverend, say half; don't rely entirely on me"** (*oshō ya dōshu ippan, mo zen kō bōkō* 和尚也道取一半、莫全靠某甲): The words of Shitou Qixian 石頭希遷 (700-790) to his master Qingyuan Xingsi 青原行思, found in various texts; here is the version recorded in *shinji Shōbōgenzō* 眞字正法眼藏 (DZZ.5:126, case 1):

> 吉州青原山弘濟禪師〈嗣大鑑、諱行思〉曾問石頭、儞從甚處來。石頭曰、曹溪來。師乃拈拂子曰、曹溪還有這箇麼。頭曰、非但曹溪、西天亦無。師曰、子莫曾到西天否。頭曰、若到即有也。師曰、未在更道。頭曰、和尚也須道取一半。莫全靠希遷。師云、不辭向汝道。恐已後無人承當。
>
> Chan Master Hongji of Mount Qingyuan in Jizhou (succeeded Dajian, called Xingsi) once asked Shitou, "Where did you come from."
> Shitou said, "From Caoxi."
> The Master held up his whisk and said, "In Caoxi, do they have this?"
> Tou said, "Not just Caoxi; they don't even have it in Sindh in the West."
> The Master said, "Have you actually been to Sindh in the West?"
> Tou said, "If I'd been there, they'd have it."
> The Master said, "Not yet. Say more."
> Tou said, "Reverend, you should also say half; don't rely entirely on Qixian."
> The Master said, "I don't refuse to say something for you, but I'm afraid that afterwards, no one will accept it."

"Shigong grabbed Xitang's nose and pulled it." We should study this a bit. Shigong hid himself in Xitang's nose; or perhaps there is a statement "the nose pulled Shigong."[14] Nevertheless, while this may be so, *the single ball of empty space bangs and hits.*[15]

[70:10] {2:210}

西堂作忍痛聲曰、太殺人、拽人鼻孔、直得脱去。從來は人にあふとおもへども、たちまちに自己にあふことをえたり。しかあれども、染汚自己即不得なり、修己すべし。

"Xitang cried out in pain and said, 'What a brute. You could pull a person's nose right off!'" Up till now he had thought to meet another, but suddenly he was able to meet himself. Nevertheless, *he cannot defile the self*; he should practice the self.[16]

[70:11]

石鞏道、直得恁地捉始得。恁地捉始得は、なきにあらず。ただし、石鞏と石鞏と、共出一隻手の捉得なし、虛空と虛空と共出一隻手の捉得あらざるがゆえに、いまだみづからの費力をからず。

Shigong said, "That's how you have to grab hold of it." It is not that it is not "*how you have to grab hold of it*"; but, because he does not have a "grabbing hold" in which Shigong and Shigong "each extends a single hand," or a "grabbing hold" in which empty space and empty space "each extends a single hand," he has not made use of his own efforts.[17]

---

14 **Shigong hid himself in Xitang's nose** (*Seidō no bikū ni Shakukyō zōshin seri* 西堂の鼻孔に石鞏藏身せり): From the stock phrase "to hide oneself in the nostrils" (*bikū ri zōshin* 鼻孔裏藏身). The term *bikū* 鼻孔 ("nose" or "nostrils") is regularly used to indicate the true person, what one really is; see Supplementary Notes, s.v. "Nose."

15 **bangs and hits** (*katsujaku chikujaku* 磕著築著): Variant of the fixed expression *chikujaku katsujaku* 築著磕著 ("hits and bangs"; said to express the sound of stones hitting together), best known from a remark (quoted in "Shōbōgenzō ten hōrin" 正法眼藏轉法輪) of Wuzu Fayan 五祖法演 (d. 1104); see Supplementary Notes, s.v. "Hitting and banging."

16 **he cannot defile the self; he should practice the self** (*zenna jiko soku futoku nari, shu ko su beshi* 染汚自己即不得なり、修己すべし): Reminiscent of the famous exchange, so often cited by Dōgen, between the Sixth Ancestor and his student Nanyue Huairang 南嶽懷讓 (e.g., at *shinji Shōbōgenzō* 眞字正法眼藏 (DZZ.5:178, case 101):

> 祖曰、還假修證否。師曰、修證即不無、染汚即不得。
>
> The Ancestor said, "Then does it ['the thing that comes like this'] depend on practice and verification?"
>
> The Master [Huairang] answered, "It's not that it lacks practice and verification, but it can't be defiled by them."

For the full context, see Supplementary Notes, s.v. "Not defiled."

17 **"each extends a single hand"** (*gu shutsu isseki shu* 共出一隻手): Words, alluded to elsewhere in the *Shōbōgenzō*, of Luoshan Daoxian 羅山道閑 (dates unknown), in a story recorded in Dōgen's *shinji Shōbōgenzō* 眞字正法眼藏 (DZZ.5:175-176, case 97):

[70:12]
おほよそ盡界には、容虚空の間隙なしといへども、この一段の因縁、ひさしく虚空の霹靂をなせり。石鞏・西堂よりのち、五家の宗匠と稱する參學おほしといへども、虚空を見聞測度せるまれなり、石鞏・西堂より前後に、弄虚空を擬するともがら面面なれども、著手せるすくなし。石鞏は虚空をとれり、西堂は虚空を覷見せず。大佛、まさに石鞏に爲道すべし、いはゆる、そのかみ西堂の鼻孔をとる、捉虚空なるべくば、みづから石鞏の鼻孔をとるべし。指頭をもて指頭をとることを會取すべし。しかあれども、石鞏、いささか捉虚空の威儀をしれり。たとひ捉虚空の好手なりとも、虚空の内外を參學すべし、虚空の殺活を參學すべし、虚空の輕重をしるべし。佛佛祖祖の功夫辦道・發心修證・道取聞聲、すなはち捉虚空なると保任すべし。

In sum, while there may be no interstices in all the worlds to accommodate empty space, this one episode has long been a thunderbolt in empty space. Ever since Shigong and Xitang, while the students of it calling themselves masters of the five houses may have been many, the ones who saw and heard, fathomed and measured empty space have been rare; although before and after Shigong and Xitang various types have thought to play with empty space, few have laid their hands on it.[18]

Shigong took hold of empty space; Xitang did not see empty space. Daibutsu should say this to Shigong: if taking hold of Xitang's nose before was "*grabbing hold of empty space*," you should have taken hold of Shigong's nose; you should understand taking hold of your finger with your finger.[19] Still, Shigong did understand something of the deportment of "*grabbing hold of empty space.*" Yet, even if we are skilled at "*grabbing hold of empty space*," we should study the interior and exterior of empty space; we should study how to kill and give life to space; we should know the weight of space. We should maintain the understanding that the concentrated effort and pursuit of the way, the bringing forth of the mind [of bodhi], the practice and verification, the speech and the hearing, of buddha after buddha and ancestor after ancestor — this is "*grabbing hold of empty space.*"

A monk asked Luoshan how much he should pay to have a stūpa built. Luoshan said,

> 若將三文錢與匠人、和尚此生決定不得塔。若將兩文錢與匠人、和尚與匠人共出一隻手。若將一文錢與匠人、帶累匠人眉鬚墮落。
>
> If you offer the artisan three cash, the Reverend will definitely not get a stūpa in this lifetime. If you offer the artisan two cash, the Reverend and the artisan will each put out one hand. If you offer the artisan one cash, you'll so perplex him that the artisan's eyebrows and beard will fall off.

18 **the students of it calling themselves masters of the five houses** (*goke no shūshō to shō suru sangaku* 五家の宗匠と稱する參學): I.e., teachers in the five lineages into which Chan was organized by the Song historians who took up this topic for study.

19 **Daibutsu** 大佛: I.e., Dōgen, speaking of himself as abbot of the Daibutsu Monastery.

* * * * *

[70:13] {2:211}
先師天童古佛道、渾身似口掛虚空。あきらかにしりぬ、虚空の渾身は虚空にかかれり。

My former master, the Old Buddha of Tiantong, said, "The whole body, like a mouth, hanging in empty space."[20]

Clearly, "the whole body" of empty space is "hanging in empty space."

* * * * *

[70:14]
洪州西山亮座主、因參馬祖。祖問、講什麼經。師曰、心經。祖曰、將什麼講。師曰、將心講。祖曰、心如工伎兒、意如和伎者、六識爲伴侶、爭解講得經。師曰、心既講不得、莫是虚空講得麼。祖曰、却是虚空講得。師拂袖而退。祖召云、座主。師回首。祖曰、從生至老、只是這箇。師因而有省。遂隱西山、更無消息。

Prelate Liang of Xishan in Hongzhou once consulted with Mazu.[21] *Mazu asked him, "What sūtra are you lecturing on?"*

The Master said, "The Heart Sūtra."[22]

Mazu said, "With what do you lecture?"

The Master said, "I lecture with the mind."

Mazu said, "'The mind is like the lead actor; the intellect, like a supporting actor; the six consciousnesses make up the cast.'[23] *How can they lecture on the sūtra?"*

---

20 **My former master, the Old Buddha of Tiantong** (*senshi Tendō kobutsu* 先師天童古佛): I.e., Tiantong Rujing 天童如淨. See above, Note 2.

21 **Prelate Liang of Xishan in Hongzhou** (*Kōshū Seizan Ryō zasu* 洪州西山亮座主): Xishan Liang 西山亮 (dates unknown), a student of Mazu Daoyi 馬祖道一. "Prelate" (*zasu* 座主) refers to the abbot of a Teachings monastery (*kyōji* 教寺 or *kyōin* 教院) — an institution where the abbacy is restricted to members of the Tiantai school; a title implying a mastery of Buddhist learning that could invite the sarcasm of Chan masters. "Xishan" 西山 is the mountain in present-day Jiangxi province. This dialogue is found in various Chan sources, as well as Dōgen's *shinji Shōbōgenzō* 眞字正法眼藏 (DZZ.5:126, case 4); see Supplementary Notes, s.v. "Prelate Liang."

22 **"The *Heart Sūtra*"** (*Shingyō* 心經): I.e., the popular *Bore boluomiduo xin jing* 般若波羅蜜多心經 (T.251). The subsequent discussion of "the mind" here plays on the two meanings ("heart" and "mind") of the glyph *shin* 心 in the sūtra title.

23 **"'The mind is like the lead actor'"** (*shin nyo kōgiji* 心如工伎兒): Mazu quotes here a verse in the *Laṅkāvatāra-sūtra* (*Dasheng ru lengqie jing* 大乘入楞伽經, T.672.16:620a17-18):

The Master said, "Since the mind can't lecture, isn't it empty space that can lecture?"

Mazu said, "In fact, it's empty space that can lecture."

The Master shook out his sleeves and withdrew. Mazu called after him, "Prelate."[24]

The Master turned. Mazu said, "From birth to old age, it's just this."[25]

The Master thereupon had an insight. He subsequently hid himself in Mount Xi and was not heard of again.

[70:15]

しかあればすなはち、佛祖はともに講經者なり。講經はかならず虛空なり、虛空にあらざれば、一經をも講ずることをえざるなり。心經を講ずるにも、身經を講ずるにも、ともに虛空をもて講ずるなり。虛空をもて思量を現成し、不思量を現成せり。有師智をなし、無師智をなす、生知をなし、學而知をなす、ともに虛空なり。作佛作祖、おなじく虛空なるべし。

Thus, the buddhas and ancestors are all lecturers on the sūtras. Lecturing on the sūtras is invariably empty space; were it not empty space, there could be no lecturing on a single sūtra. Whether we lecture on a "mind sūtra" or we lecture on a "body sūtra," we use empty space to lecture.[26] We use empty space to realize thinking and to realize not thinking.[27] Producing the wisdom gained with a teacher, producing wisdom gained without a teacher, producing innate knowledge, producing knowledge gained from study — all these are empty space. Becoming a buddha and becoming an ancestor must similarly be empty space.

心如工伎兒、意如和伎者、五識爲伴侶、妄想觀伎衆。

The mind is like the lead actor;
The intellect, like a supporting actor;
The six consciousnesses make up the cast;
Deluded thoughts, the audience.

24 **shook out his sleeves** (*hosshū* 拂袖): A stock gesture of annoyance or dismissal.

25 **"From birth to old age, it's just this"** (*jū shō shi rō shi ze shako* 從生至老只是這箇): An identical saying is attributed to Shitou Xiqian 石頭希遷 in conversation with Wuxie Lingmo 五洩靈黙 (747-818) (*Jingde chuandeng lu* 景德傳燈錄 (T.2076.51:254b10-11): Having failed to understand Shitou's teaching, Wuxie was leaving.

石頭呼之云、闍梨。師迴顧。石頭云、從生至老只是遮箇。漢更莫別求。

Shitou called to him, "Ācārya."
The Master [Wuxie] turned and looked back. Shitou said, "From birth to old age, it's just this. A man shouldn't look for anything else."

26 **"mind sūtra"** (*shingyō* 心經); **"body sūtra"** (*shingyō* 身經): Further play with the glyph *shin* 心 in the title of the *Heart Sūtra*.

27 **to realize thinking and to realize not thinking** (*shiryō o genjō shi, fushiryō o genjō seri* 思量を現成し、不思量を現成せり): Likely an allusion to the famous saying on meditation, much treasured by Dōgen, by Yaoshan Weiyan 藥山惟儼 (751-834); see Supplementary Notes, s.v. "Yaoshan's not thinking."

* * * * *

[70:16] {2:212}
第二十一祖婆修盤頭尊者道、心同虚空界、示等虚空法、證得虚空時、無是無非法。

The Twenty-first Ancestor, Venerable Vasubandhu, said,[28]
The mind is the same as the realm of empty space;
It reveals the dharmas equivalent to empty space.
When we are able to verify empty space,
There are no dharmas, right or wrong.

[70:17]
いま壁面人と人面壁と、相逢相見する墻壁心・枯木心、これはこれ虚空界なり。應以此身得度者、即現此身、而爲說法、これ、示等虚空法なり。應以他身得度者、即現他身而爲說法、これ、示等虚空法なり。被十二時使、および使得十二時、これ、證得虚空時なり。石頭大底大、石頭小底小、これ、無是無非法なり。

Here, the person facing the wall and the wall facing the person encounter each other, see each other; and this wall mind, the mind of the dried-up tree — this is "the realm of empty space."[29] "*For those who ought to attain deliverance by this body, I appear in this body and preach the dharma to them*" — this is "*revealing the dharmas equivalent to empty space.*"[30] "*For those who ought to attain deliverance by that body, I appear in that body and preach the dharma to them*" — this is "*revealing the dharmas equivalent to empty space.*" "*To be employed by the twelve times*" and "*to employ the twelve times*" — this is "*when we are able to*

---

28 **The Twenty-first Ancestor, Venerable Vasubandhu** (*dainijūichi so Bashubanzu sonja* 第二十一祖婆修盤頭尊者): The verse, found at *Jingde chuandeng lu* 景德傳燈錄 (T.2076.51:208b21-22), is attributed not to Vasubandhu but to the Seventh Ancestor, Vasumitra (*Bashumitsu* 婆須蜜).

29 **the person facing the wall and the wall facing the person** (*heki men nin to nin men heki to* 壁面人と人面壁と): From the famous legend that Bodhidharma sat facing a wall for nine years.

the mind of the dried-up tree (*koboku shin* 枯木心): Suggesting the mind in meditation, from the idiom "dried-up trees and dead ashes" (*koboku shikai* 枯木死灰); see Supplementary Notes, s.v. "Dried-up tree."

30 **"For those who ought to attain deliverance by this body"** (*ō i shi shin tokudo sha* 應以此身得度者): From the Avalokiteśvara chapter of the *Lotus Sūtra* (*Miaofa lianhua jing* 妙法蓮華經, T.262.9:57a23ff.), in which it is said that, to those who can attain deliverance through contact with a particular body (a buddha, a *pratyeka-buddha*, a *śrāvaka*, etc.), the Bodhisattva Avalokiteśvara appears as that body and preaches the dharma for them.

verify empty space."[31] "*The bigness of the stones is big; the smallness of the stones is small*" — this is "*there are no dharmas, right or wrong.*"[32]

[70:18]
かくのごとく、虚空、しばらくこれを、正法眼藏涅槃妙心、と參究するのみなり。

In this way, for a while, we only investigate empty space as "the treasury of the true dharma eye, the wondrous mind of nirvāṇa."[33]

正法眼藏虚空第七十
Treasury of the True Dharma Eye
Empty Space
Number 70

[Ryūmonji MS:]
爾時寛元三年乙巳三月六日、在越宇大佛寺示衆
Presented to the assembly at Daibutsu Monstery, Etsuu; sixth day, third month of the junior wood year of the snake, the third year of Kangen [4 April 1245][34]

---

31 **"To be employed by the twelve times" and "to employ the twelve times"** (*hi jūniji shi, oyobi shitoku jūni ji* 被十二時使、および使得十二時): From a popular saying attributed to Zhaozhou Congshen 趙州從諗 (778-897); see Supplementary Notes, s.v. "Employ the twelve times."

32 **"The bigness of the stones is big; the smallness of the stones is small"** (*sekitō dai tei dai, sekitō shō tei shō* 石頭大底大、石頭小底小): A saying attributed to Guizong Daoquan 歸宗道詮 (930-985); see, e.g., *Jingde chuandeng lu* 景德傳燈錄 (T.2076.51:403b10-12):

問、九峯山中還有佛法也無。師曰、有。曰、如何是九峯山中佛法。師曰、山中石頭大底大小底小。

[A monk] asked, "Does the buddha dharma exist on Mount Jiufeng?"
The Master [Daoquan] said, "It does."
He asked, "What is the buddha dharma on Mount Jiufeng?"
The Master said, "The bigness of the stones on the mountain is big, the smallness small."

33 **In this way** (*kaku no gotoku* かくのごとく): Some MS witnesses add the genetive *no* の here, yielding, "For a while, we only investigate such empty space . . . ."

34 The Tōunji 洞雲寺 MS shares an identical colophon.

[Tōunji MS:]

弘安二年己卯五月十七日、在同國中浜新善光寺書寫之。義雲
Copied this at the new Zenkō Monastery, at Nakahama, in the same province; seventeenth day, fifth month of the junior earth year of the rabbit, the second year of Kōan [27 June 1279]. Giun[35]

于時文明十二庚子年三月十一日、於于越州吉祥山永平寺承陽庵書寫之。比丘光周
Copied this in the Jōyō Hermitage, Eihei Monastery, Mount Kichijō, Esshū; eleventh day, third month, senior metal year of the rat, the twelfth year of Bunmei [1480]. Bhikṣu Kōshū[36]

35 **Giun** 義雲: Fifth abbot of Eiheiji (1253–1333).

36 **Bhikṣu Kōshū** (*biku Kōshū* 比丘光周): Fifteenth abbot of Eiheiji (1434–1492?).

[Tōunji MS:]

[illegible]

Copied this at the new Zenkō Monastery, in [illegible] in the same province, seventeenth day, fifth month of the junior earth year of the rabbit, the second year of Kōan [1279]. Gien[35]

[illegible]

Copied this in the [illegible] Hermitage, Eihei Monastery, Mount Kichijō, Esshū, eleventh day, third month, senior metal year of the rat, the twelfth year of Bunmei [1480]. Bikku Kōshū[36]

35. Gien [illegible], fifth abbot of Eiheiji [illegible]

36. Bikku Kōshū [illegible]

Treasury of the True Dharma Eye

Number 71

The Pātra Bowl

Hou

鉢盂

The Pātra Bowl

Hou

Introduction

This short chapter was presented to the assembly in the spring of 1245, at Daibutsuji, in Echizen. Number 71 in the seventy-five-chapter *Shōbōgenzō*, it is number 42 in the sixty-chapter compilation and number 77 in the ninety-five-chapter Honzan edition (or 78 in the Iwanami and Shūmuchō versions).

The compound term *hou* 鉢盂 (also read *hatsuu*), used for the alms bowl of the Buddhist mendicant, combines the transliteration of a Sanskrit word for "bowl" or "vessel" (*pātra*) with a Chinese word for "bowl" or "basin." Along with the robe (*kāṣāya*), the alms bowl was one of the few possessions permitted the bhikṣu and *bhikṣuṇī* and, therefore, was emblematic of the renunciant status. In Zen tradition, the legend developed that, along with the *kāṣāya*, the ancestors passed on their *pātra* to their disciples. Here, Dōgen expands on that tradition, to invest the *pātra* with meanings that transcend the physical bowl itself and its historical understandings.

正法眼藏第七十一
Treasury of the True Dharma Eye Number 71

鉢盂
The Pātra Bowl

[71:1] {2:213}

七佛向上より七佛に正傳し、七佛裏より七佛に正傳し、渾七佛より渾七佛に正傳し、七佛より二十八代正傳しきたり、第二十八代の祖師、菩提達磨高祖、みづから神丹國にいりて、二祖大祖正宗普覺大師に正傳し、六代つたはれて曹溪にいたる。傳東西、都盧五十一傳、すなはち正法眼藏涅槃妙心なり、袈裟・鉢盂なり。ともに先佛は先佛の正傳を保任せり。かくのごとくして佛佛祖祖正傳せり。

Directly transmitted from beyond the seven buddhas to the seven buddhas, directly transmitted from within the seven buddhas to the seven buddhas, directly transmitted from the whole of the seven buddhas to the whole of the seven buddhas, it was directly transmitted from the seven buddhas through the twenty-eight generations; the ancestral master of the twenty-eighth generation, the Eminent Ancestor Bodhidharma, personally entering the Land of Cīnasthāna, directly transmitted it to the Second Ancestor, Great Master Pujue, the Great Ancestor Zhengzong; passed down through six generations, it reached Caoxi. What was transmitted east and west, through fifty-one transmissions in all, was the treasury of the true dharma eye, the wondrous mind of nirvāṇa, was the *kāṣāya* and the *pātra* bowl.[1] Each of the prior buddhas maintained the direct transmission of the prior buddhas. In this way, they were directly transmitted by buddha after buddha and ancestor after ancestor.

1 **fifty-one transmissions in all** (*toro gojūichi den* 都盧五十一傳): Some versions read "fifty-one generations" (*gojūichi dai* 五十一代). This figure represents the twenty-eight ancestors in India plus the twenty-three generations of ancestors from Bodhidharma's disciple Huike 慧可 — here identified by his title, Great Master Pujue (*Fukaku daishi* 普覺大師) — through Dōgen's master, Tiantong Rujing 天童如淨 (1162-1227). "Caoxi" (*Sōkei* 曹溪) is Huineng of Caoxi 曹溪慧能, the famous Sixth Ancestor. See Supplementary Notes, s.v. "Buddhas and ancestors."

[71:2]
しかあるに、佛祖を參學する、皮肉骨髓・拳頭眼睛、おのおの道取あり。いはゆる、あるいは、鉢盂はこれ佛祖の身心なり、と參學するあり、あるいは、鉢盂はこれ佛祖の飯椀なり、と參學するあり、あるいは、鉢盂はこれ佛祖の眼睛なり、と參學するあり、あるいは、鉢盂はこれ佛祖の光明なり、と參學するあり、あるいは、鉢盂はこれ佛祖の眞實體なり、と參學するあり、あるいは鉢盂はこれ佛祖の正法眼藏涅槃妙心なり、と參學するあり、あるいは、鉢盂はこれ佛祖の轉身處なり、と參學するあり、あるいは、佛祖はこれ鉢盂の縁底なり、と參學するあり。かくのごとくのともがらの參學の宗旨、おのおの道得の處分ありといへども、さらに向上の參學あり。

Thus, the skin, flesh, bones, and marrow, the fists and eyes, who study the buddhas and ancestors each has their own saying: there are those who understand that the *pātra* bowl is the body and mind of the buddhas and ancestors; there are those who understand that the *pātra* bowl is the meal bowl of the buddhas and ancestors; there are those who understand that the *pātra* bowl is the eye of the buddhas and ancestors; there are those who study that the *pātra* bowl is the radiance of the buddhas and ancestors; there are those who study that the *pātra* bowl is the true body of the buddhas and ancestors; there are those who study that the *pātra* bowl is the treasury of the true dharma eye, the wondrous mind of nirvāṇa, of the buddhas and ancestors; there are those who study the *pātra* bowl as the place where the buddhas and ancestors turn around; there are those who study the buddhas and ancestors as the rim and bottom of the *pātra* bowl.[2] While the essential points understood by such people may each have the status of a saying, there is a further understanding beyond them.[3]

---

2 **the skin, flesh, bones, and marrow, the fists and eyes** (*hi niku kotsu zui kotō ganzei* 皮肉骨髓・拳頭眼睛): I.e., the Chan masters. See Supplementary Notes, s.v. "Skin, flesh, bones, and marrow," "Fist," "Eye."

the radiance of the buddhas and ancestors (*busso no kōmyō* 佛祖の光明): Reference to the aureola surrounding the body, one of the thirty-two marks of a buddha's body.

the place where the buddhas and ancestors turn around (*busso no tenshin sho* 佛祖の轉身處): The term *tenshin sho* 轉身處 (also read *tenjin sho*; "where one turns oneself" or "turns one's body") occurs frequently in Chan texts for an occasion of spiritual transformation; the only instance of its use in the *Shōbōgenzō*.

3 **have the status of a saying** (*dōtoku no shobun ari* 道得の處分あり): I.e., qualify as a significant utterance. The sense of *shobun* 處分 (rendered here "status") is open to interpretation: it could be read as "disposition" or "judgment" but also simply as "allotment" or "portion."

[71:3] {2:214}

先師天童古佛、大宋寶慶元年、住天童日、上堂云、記得、僧問百丈、如何是奇特事。百丈云、獨坐大雄峰。大衆不得動著、且教坐殺者漢。今日忽有人、問淨上座如何是奇特事、只向他道、有甚奇特。畢竟如何。淨慈鉢盂、移過天童喫飯。

My former master, the Old Buddha of Tiantong, in the first year of Baoqing of the Great Song, on the day he took up residence at Tiantong, ascended the hall and said,[4]

We may recall,

A monk asked Baizhang, "What is the extraordinary matter?"[5]

Baizhang said, "Sitting alone on Daxiong Peak."[6]

Members of the great assembly, don't be moved. Just let the fellow sit there. If today someone were to ask Senior Seat Jing, "What is the extraordinary matter?" I would just say to him, "What extraordinary matter is there?"[7] *In the end, what is it?*[8] *The Jingci pātra bowl has moved to Tiantong for its meals.*[9]

[71:4]

しるべし、奇特事は、まさに奇特人のためにすべし、奇特事には、奇特の調度をもちいるべきなり、これすなはち奇特の時節なり。しかあればすなはち、奇特事の現成せるところ、奇特鉢盂なり。これをもて、四天王をして護持せしめ、諸龍王をして擁護せしむる、佛道の玄軌なり。このゆえに、佛祖に奉獻し、佛祖より付屬せらる。

We should recognize that extraordinary matters are due to extraordinary people; and, for extraordinary matters, extraordinary implements

---

4 **My former master, the Old Buddha of Tiantong** (*senshi Tendō kobutsu* 先師天童古佛): I.e., Tiantong Rujing 天童如淨, who became abbot of the Jingdesi 景德寺 on Mount Tiantong 天童山 in 1225, during Dōgen's sojurn in China. Quoted from the *Rujing heshang yulu* 如淨和尚語錄 (T.2002A.48:127b1-5). The same passage is quoted in "Shōbōgenzō kajō" 正法眼藏家常.

5 **Baizhang** (*Hyakujō* 百丈): I.e., Baizhang Huaihai 百丈懷海 (749-814); his conversation occurs in several sources (see, e.g., *Biyan lu* 碧巖錄, T.2003.48:166c26-27). Dōgen cites Baizhang's words several times in his *Eihei kōroku* 永平廣錄 (DZZ.3:92, no. 147; 3:242, no. 378; 4:30, no. 443).

6 **"Daxiong Peak"** (*Daiyū hō* 大雄峰): Another name for the location of Baizhang's monastery, Mount Baizhang 百丈山, in present-day Jiangxi province.

7 **Senior Seat Jing** (*Jō jōza* 淨上座): A self-reference as abbot.

8 **"In the end, what is it?"** (*hikkyō ikan* 畢竟如何): Though this and the following sentence are treated here as Rujing's final comment on the subject, they could as well be read as part of his answer to the question.

9 **The Jinci *pātra* bowl has moved to Tiantong** (*Jinzu hou ika Tendō* 淨慈鉢盂移過天童): A reference to Rujing's relocation from his former post at the Jingcisi 淨慈寺 to Mount Tiantong 天童山.

should be used.[10] This is an extraordinary occasion. Thus, where extraordinary matters occur, the extraordinary is the *pātra* bowl.[11] Consequently, to have the four deva kings protect it and to have the dragon kings support it are the profound standards of the way of the buddhas.[12] Therefore, it is offered up to the buddhas and ancestors and handed down from the buddhas and ancestors.[13]

[71:5] {2:215}

佛祖の堂奥に參學せざるともがらいはく、佛袈裟は、絹なり、布なり、化糸のおりなせるところなり、といふ、佛鉢盂は、石なり、瓦なり、鐵なり、といふ。かくのごとくいふは、未具參學眼のゆえなり。佛袈裟は佛袈裟なり、さらに、絹・布の見あるべからず、絹・布等の見は、舊見なり。佛鉢盂は佛鉢盂なり、さらに、石・瓦といふべからず、　鐵・木といふべからず。

The types that do not study in the interior of the halls of the buddhas and ancestors say the *kāṣāya* of the Buddha is silk, or is linen, or is woven of transformation thread; they say the *pātra* bowl of the Buddha is stone, or is earthenware, or is iron.[14] That they say this is because they

10 **extraordinary matters are due to extraordinary people** (*kitokuji wa, masa ni kitokunin no tame ni su beshi* 奇特事は、まさに奇特人のためにすべし): Some readers take *tame ni* here, not as "due to," but as "for the sake of, " and thus read, "extraordinary matters should be done for extraordinary people." More likely, here and in the next clause, Dōgen is praising Rujing and his bowl as "extraordinary." In the subsequent sentence, "This is an extraordinary occasion" (*kore sunawachi kitoku no jisetsu nari* これすなはち奇特の時節なり), the antecedent of "this" is unclear: perhaps, the combination of an extraordinary person and extraordinary implement; or perhaps, the arrival of Rujing as abbot of Tiantong.

11 **the extraordinary is the *pātra* bowl** (*kitoku hou nari* 奇特鉢盂なり): Or, perhaps, "it [i.e., where extraordinary matters occur] is the *pātra* bowl."

12 **to have the four deva kings protect it and to have the dragon kings support it** (*shitennō o shite goji seshime, sho ryūō o shite yōgo seshimuru* 四天王をして護持せしめ、諸龍王をして擁護せしむる): Perhaps reflecting the Buddha's prediction, found in the *Lianhuamian jing* 蓮華面經 (T.386.12:1075b16ff) that, when his alms bowl was broken and the Buddha dharma was threatened in Jambudvīpa, the bowl would travel to the palace of the dragon king and thence to the palace of the four deva kings, there to be protected and venerated.

13 **offered up to the buddhas and ancestors** (*busso ni bugon shi* 佛祖に奉獻し): Likely reflecting the tradition that the four deva kings give alms bowls to the buddhas (see, e.g., *Mohe bore boluomi jing* 摩訶般若波羅蜜經, T.223.8:221a22-25; *Fo benxing ji jing* 佛本行集經, T.190.3:801c23ff).

14 **transformation thread** (*keshi* 化絲): Likely a reference to the notion that the silk thread of the Buddha's *kāṣāya* does not involve injury because it does not come from the mouth of the silkworm, but rather emerges as a "transformation," or "manifestation" (*ke* 化), or from the mouths of "transformation girls" (*kenyo* 化女; presumably, females born spontaneously, rather than from the womb) on another continent. (See *Fayuan zhulin* 法苑珠林, T.2122.53:561a16-23; b22-c8.) In his "Shōbōgenzō den'e" 正法眼藏傳

are not yet equipped with the eye of study. The *kāṣāya* of the Buddha is the *kāṣāya* of the Buddha; there should be no further views about silk or linen; views about silk, linen, and the like, are old views.[15] The *pātra* bowl of the Buddha is the *pātra* bowl of the Buddha; we should not say further it is stone or earthenware; we should not say it is iron or wood.

[71:6]

おほよそ佛鉢盂、これ造作にあらず、生滅にあらず、去來せず、得失なし。新舊にわたらず、古今にかかはれず。佛祖の衣・盂は、たとひ雲水を採集して現成せしむとも、雲水の籮籠にあらず、たとひ草木を採集して現成せしむとも、草木の籮籠にあらず。その宗旨は、水は衆法を合成して水なり、雲は衆法を合成して雲なり。雲を合成して雲なり、水を合成して水なり。鉢盂は、但以衆法合成鉢盂なり、但以鉢盂合成衆法なり、但以渾心合成鉢盂なり、但以虛空合成鉢盂なり、但以鉢盂合成鉢盂なり。鉢盂は鉢盂に罣礙せられ、鉢盂に染汚せらる。

In sum, the *pātra* bowl of the Buddha is not manufactured, is not subject to arising and ceasing, does not come and go, has no gain or loss. It does not extend to new or old; it has nothing to do with past or present. The robes and bowls of the buddhas and ancestors, even if made to appear by gathering together clouds and water, are not the nets and cages of clouds and water; even if made to appear by gathering together grasses and trees, are not the nets and cages of grasses and trees.[16] The essential point is that water is water by the combination of dharmas; clouds are clouds by the combination of dharmas. Clouds are clouds combined; water is water combined. The *pātra* bowl is just *the dharmas combine to form the pātra bowl*, are *just the pātra bowl combines to form the dharmas*, are just *the whole mind combines to form the pātra bowl*, are just *empty space combines to form the pātra bowl*, are just *the pātra bowl*

衣, Dōgen is highly critical of those who concern themselves with the material used for the *kāṣāya*.

15 **old views** (*kyūken* 舊見): A term, repeated below, not encountered elsewhere in the *Shōbōgenzō*; probably indicating "prior views" — i.e., views of the sort held before one has studied the buddha dharma.

16 **made to appear by gathering together clouds and water** (*unsui o saishū shite genjō seshimu* 雲水を採集して現成せしむ): Likely playing with the common use of "clouds and water" (*unsui* 雲水) in reference to the peripatetic monk; hence, robes and bowls appear where monks gather.

are not the nets and cages of clouds and water (*unsui no rarō ni arazu* 雲水の籮籠にあらず): "Nets and cages" (*rarō* 籮籠) is a common expression for the categories of understanding that trap the mind; see Supplementary Notes. The phrase may be understood either as "[the robes and bowls] are not trapped by the clouds and water," or as "[the robes and bowls] do not trap the clouds and water." Similarly, with the "grasses and trees" of the next clause.

combines to form the pātra bowl.[17] The *pātra* bowl is obstructed by the *pātra* bowl, is defiled by the *pātra* bowl.[18]

[71:7]
いま雲水の傳持せる鉢盂、すなはち四天王奉獻の鉢盂なり。鉢盂、もし四天王奉獻せざれば、現前せず。いま諸方に傳佛正法眼藏の佛祖の正傳せる鉢盂、これ透脱古今底の鉢盂なり。しかあれば、いまこの鉢盂は、鐵漢の舊見を覰破せり、木橛の商量に拘牽せられず。瓦・礫の聲色を超越せり、石・玉の活計を罣礙せざるなり。碌甎といふことなかれ、木橛といふことなかれ。かくのごとく承當しきたれり。

The *pātra* bowl transmitted and kept by the clouds and water now is precisely the *pātra* bowl offered up by the four deva kings.[19] Had the four deva kings not offered up the *pātra* bowl, it would not appear before us. The *pātra* bowl now directly transmitted by the buddhas and ancestors in all quarters who transmit the treasury of the true dharma eye — this is a *pātra* bowl transcending past and present. Thus, this present *pātra* bowl has seen through the old views of the man of iron and is not constrained by deliberations over wooden stakes.[20] It has transcended the sights and sounds of tiles and pebbles; it is not obstructed by the business of stones or jewels. Do not call it a brick; do not call it a stake.[21] This is how it has been understood.

---

17 **The *pātra* bowl is just the dharmas combine to form the *pātra* bowl** (*hou wa, tan i shuhō gō jō hou nari* 鉢盂は、但以衆法合成鉢盂なり): Variation on a passage, discussed in the "Shōbōgenzō kaiin zanmai" 正法眼藏海印三昧, from the *Vimalakīrti Sūtra*, in which Vimalakīrti is instructing the Bodhisattva Mañjuśrī on how a sick bodhisattva should regard his body (*Weimo jing* 維摩經, T.475.14:545a3-4):

> 但以衆法合成此身。起唯法起滅唯法滅。
> It is just the dharmas that combine to form this body. When it arises, it is simply the dharmas arising; when it ceases, it is simply the dharmas ceasing.

18 **The *pātra* bowl is obstructed by the *pātra* bowl, is defiled by the *pātra* bowl** (*hou wa hou ni keige serare, hou ni zenna seraru* 鉢盂は鉢盂に罣礙せられ、鉢盂に染汚せらる): Likely meaning something like, "the *pātra* bowl is just completely itself." The verb "obstruct" (*keige* 罣礙) here exemplifies Dōgen's habit of using the word in the sense "to identify with," "to be defined by."

19 **clouds and water** (*unsui* 雲水): I.e., monks.

20 **the old views of the man of iron** (*tekkan no kyūken* 鐵漢の舊見); **deliberations over wooden stakes** (*bokuketsu no shōryō* 木橛の商量): Dōgen is playing here with two terms suggestive of the opinions that the *pātra* was originally made from iron or wood. "Man of iron" (*tekkan* 鐵漢) normally indicates a stalwart practitioner; see Supplementary Notes, s.v. "Man of iron." For "wooden stake" (*bokuketsu* 木橛; also read *mokketsu*), see Supplementary Notes, s.v. "Wooden stake."

21 **Do not call it a brick; do not call it a stake** (*rokusen to iu koto nakare, bokuketsu to iu koto nakare* 碌甎といふことなかれ、木橛といふことなかれ): Readers disagree on the meaning of the term *rokusen* 碌甎 (also written 碌塼 or 碌磚), often understood here as "stones and tiles"; the translation takes it as equivalent to the homophonous *rokusen*

{2:216}

正法眼藏鉢盂第七十一
Treasury of the True Dharma Eye
The Pātra Bowl
Number 71

[Ryūmonji MS:]
爾時寬元三年三月十二日、在越宇大佛精舍示衆
Presented to the assembly at Daibutsu Vihāra, Etsuu; twelfth day, third month of the third year of Kangen [10 April 1245][22]

[Tōunji MS:]

寬元乙巳七月二十七日、在大佛寺侍司書写。懷奘
Copied in the acolyte's office, Daibutsu Monastery; twenty-seventh day, seventh month of the junior wood year of the snake, Kangen [20 August 1245]. Ejō

于時文明十一己亥年臘月十三日、於永平寺承陽庵書寫之。比丘光周
Copied this in the Jōyō Hermitage, Eihei Monastery; thirteenth day, month of offerings, junior earth year of the pig, the eleventh year of Bunmei [24 January 1480]. Bhikṣu Kōshū[23]

甋甎 ("brick"). Dōgen is playing again with terms involving two materials, clay and wood, from which the alms bowl might be made — terms that may also be read as figures of speech for stupidity; their juxtaposition here may reflect words attributed to Shitou Xiqian 石頭希遷 (700-791) (*Jingde chuandeng lu* 景德傳燈錄, T.2076.51:309b5-6):

> 問如何是禪。師曰、碌塼。又問、如何是道。師曰、木頭。
>
> [Daowu] asked, "What is Chan?"
> The Master [Shitou], said, "A brick."
> He asked again, "What is the way?"
> The Master said, "A piece of wood."

22 The Tōunji 洞雲寺 MS shares an identical colophon.

23 **month of offerings** (*rōgetsu* 臘月): The twelfth lunar month.

Bhikṣu Kōshū (*biku Kōshū* 比丘光周): Fifteenth abbot of Eiheiji (1434–1492?).

[236]

[illegible]

Treasury of the True Dharma Eye

[illegible]

Number 20

[illegible MS:]

[illegible]

Presented to the assembly at [illegible], [illegible] month of the [illegible] year of [illegible] April 124[illegible]

[Eiheiji MS:]

[illegible]

Copied this at the [illegible] Monastery, twenty-seventh day, seventh month of the junior wood year of the snake, Kangen [illegible] [illegible] 1245]. Ejō

[illegible]

Copied this at the [illegible] Monastery, [illegible] day, [illegible] month of [illegible], the eleventh year of [illegible] [illegible] January [illegible]. [illegible]

[illegible] playing [illegible] involving [illegible] and wood, from which [illegible] of speech for [illegible] [illegible]

[illegible] asked, "What is [illegible]?"

The Master [illegible] said, "[illegible]"

[illegible] asked again, "What is [illegible]?"

The Master said, "[illegible]"

22 [illegible] MS [illegible]

23 [illegible] month of [illegible] [illegible]

[illegible] 1902 [illegible]

Treasury of the True Dharma Eye

Number 72

The Retreat

Ango

安居

The Retreat

Ango

Introduction

This chapter, one of the longest in the *Shōbōgenzō*, was composed during the summer retreat of 1245, at Daibutsuji, Dōgen's new monastery in Echizen province. Number 72 in the seventy-five-chapter compilation, it is number 57 in the sixty-chapter version and number 78 in the Honzan edition (or 79 in the Iwanami and Shūmuchō versions).

As its title indicates, the text deals with the summer rain retreat, the three-month period (typically, from the mid-fourth to the mid-seventh months of the lunar calendar) during which monastics were expected to remain cloistered for an uninterrupted period of intensive training. While the retreat was, as Dōgen emphasizes, an ancient and widespread practice in the Buddhist saṃgha, in this essay, the focus is on the particular version of the retreat that the author experienced in the Chan monasteries of Song-dynasty China.

The text is divided quite clearly into three parts. The first part opens with a verse by Dōgen's teacher, Tiantong Rujing 天童如淨, and continues with several other citations on the retreat, used to make the points that the retreat is the authentic tradition of Buddhism, that the meaning of the retreat is much more than simply ninety days of ascetic practice, and that joining the retreat is by no means a withdrawal into a private silence. The long second part, beginning in our section 12, takes the reader passage by passage through the instructions on the summer retreat in the *Chanyuan qinggui* 禪苑清規 (*Rules of Purity for the Chan Park*), the Song-dynasty Chan monastic code most influential in Dōgen's day. Here, Dōgen's comments are largely limited to amplification of the details of the rituals described. Finally, beginning in section 58, Dōgen returns to more general remarks on the retreat, in which, in addition to introducing several more quotations on the institution, he reiterates the significance of its observance for the tradition of the buddhas and ancestors and assures his disciples in the 1245 retreat that they are now, by their participation in the observance, members of that tradition.

正法眼藏第七十二

Treasury of the True Dharma Eye Number 72

安居

The Retreat

[72:1] {2:217}

先師天童古佛、結夏小參云、平地起骨堆、虛空剜窟籠。驀透兩重關、拈却黑漆桶。

In a small convocation upon binding the retreat, my former master, the Old Buddha of Tiantong, said,[1]

Building a mound on level ground;
Digging a hole in empty space.[2]
When we quickly pass the twofold barrier,
We take away the black lacquer bucket.[3]

[72:2]

しかあれば、得遮巴鼻子了、未免喫飯伸脚睡、在這裏三十年なり。すでにかくのごとくなるゆえに、打併調度、いとまゆるくせず。その調度に、九夏安居あり、これ佛佛祖祖の頂𩕳面目なり、皮肉骨髓に親曾しきたれり。

---

1 **my former master, the Old Buddha of Tiantong** (*senshi Tendō kobutsu* 先師天童古佛): I.e., Dōgen's teacher, Tiantong Rujing 天童如淨 (1162-1227). His saying is from the *Rujing heshang yulu* 如淨和尚語錄 (T.2002A.48:129a28-29), under the heading "small convocation upon binding the retreat" (*ketsuge shōsan* 結夏小參) — i.e., an informal talk by the abbot at the opening of the summer retreat.

2 **Building a mound on level ground; digging a hole in empty space** (*heichi ki kottai, kokū wan kutsurō* 平地起骨堆、虛空剜窟籠): Two idioms, occurring several times in Chan literature, that suggest the deluded tendency to create features on an otherwise featureless landscape — the former, by addition, or assertion; the latter, by subtraction, or negation. The term *kottai* 骨堆, referring to a mound or hillock (*kotai* 孤堆), is sometimes taken more literally here as a "bone (or ash) heap," while *kutsurō* 窟籠 ("hole") is sometimes taken as "pit and cage" (i.e., "traps"); whether Dōgen read them in this way is uncertain.

3 **the twofold barrier** (*ryōju kan* 兩重關): A common expression for the spiritual issue of dualistic thinking; here, perhaps, the preceding two tendencies.

take away the black lacquer bucket (*nenkyaku kokushittsū* 拈却黑漆桶): I.e., rid oneself of ignorance, "black lacquer bucket" (*kokushittsū* 黑漆桶) being a common metaphor for the darkness of ignorance; see Supplementary Notes, s.v. "Lacquer bucket." The term *nenkyaku* 拈却, understood here in a common usage as "to take out," "to remove," is sometimes interpreted as "to twirl" or "to fiddle with."

佛祖の眼睛・頂額を拈來して、九夏の日月とせり、安居一枚、すなはち佛佛祖祖と喚作せるものなり。安居の頭尾、これ佛祖なり、このほかさらに寸土なし、大地なし。

So, "*Once we've got this nose grip,*" *we can't help* "*having a meal and stretching out to sleep,*" *right here for thirty years.*[4] Since this is the case, we do not relax from arranging our implements. Among these implements, we have the ninety-day summer retreat. It is the crown of the head and the face of buddha after buddha and ancestor after ancestor, personally experienced in their skin, flesh, bones, and marrow. Taking up the eye and the crown of the head of the buddhas and ancestors, we regard them as the days and months of the ninety-day summer retreat; one retreat is precisely the thing we call "buddha after buddha and ancestor after ancestor." The retreat from head to tail — this is the buddhas and ancestors; apart from this, there is not "an inch of ground," there is not "the whole earth."[5]

---

4 **"Once we've got this nose grip"** (*toku sha habisu ryō* 得遮巴鼻子了): This sentence is given in Chinese. The "nose grip" (*habisu* 把鼻子), or nose ring or rope by which one leads livestock, is a common metaphor for "getting a hold, or handle, on something"; see Supplementary Notes, s.v. "Nose." The phrasing here perhaps reflects the words of Fuyan Wenyan 福嚴文演 of Tanzhou 潭州:

> 得這些巴鼻子了、便乃應用無窮。
>
> Once we've got this nose grip, then we should use it forever.

"having a meal and stretching out to sleep" (*kippan shinkyaku sui* 喫飯伸脚睡): Likely reflecting Rujing's 如淨 use of the phrase in his small convocation talk cited above (*Rujing heshang yulu* 如淨和尚語錄, T.2002A.48:129b2). The phrase is suggestive of "the four universal vows" of Haihui Shouduan 海會守端 (1025-1072) (e.g., at *Liandeng huiyao* 聯燈會要, ZZ.136:671a18-b3):

> 示衆云、釋迦老子有四弘誓願。煩惱無邊誓願斷。法門無邊誓願學衆生無邊誓願度。無上菩提誓願成。法華亦有四弘誓願。飢來要喫飯。寒來要添衣。困來伸脚睡。熱處要風吹。
>
> Addressing the assembly, he said, "Old man Śākyamuni had four universal vows. The afflictions are limitless; I vow to sever them. The dharma gates are limitless; I vow to study them. Living beings are limitless; I vow to deliver them. Unsurpassed bodhi, I vow to attain it. Fahua [i.e., Shouduan] also has four universal vows. When I'm hungry, I want a meal. When it's cold, I want warm robes. When I'm tired, I stretch out and sleep. When the place is hot, I want a breeze."

right here for thirty years (*zai shari sanjū nen* 在這裏三十年): Based on a conventional number of years of practice that it takes to master Chan. "Right here" (*zai shari* 這裏) likely indicates the monastery, but may also suggest the spiritual state of having "got this nose grip."

5 **there is not "an inch of ground," there is not "the whole earth"** (*sundo nashi, daichi nashi* 寸土なし、大地なし): From the saying, quoted in "Shōbōgenzō soku shin ze butsu" 正法眼藏即心是佛, of Changling Shouzhou 長靈守卓 (1065-1123) (*Jingde chuandeng lu* 景德傳燈錄, T.2076.51:464a26):

> 若人識得心、大地無寸土。
>
> If a person knows the mind, there isn't an inch of ground on the whole earth.

[72:3] {2:218}

夏安居の一橛、これ新にあらず、舊にあらず、來にあらず、去にあらず。その量は、拳頭量なり、その様は、巴鼻様なり。しかあれども、結夏のゆえにきたる、虚空塞破せり、あまれる十方あらず。解夏のゆえにさる、帀地を裂破す、のこれる寸土あらず。このゆえに、結夏の公案現成する、きたるに相似なり。解夏の籮籠打破する、さるに相似なり。かくのごとくなれども、親曾の面面、ともに結・解を罣礙するのみなり。萬里無寸草なり、還吾九十日飯錢來なり。

The single term of the summer retreat — it is not new, and it is not old; it does not come, and it does not go.[6] Its measure is the measure of the fist; its mode is the mode of the nose hold. Nevertheless, because we bind the retreat, it comes, and empty space is completely clogged by it, with nothing left in the ten directions; because we unbind the retreat, it goes, rending asunder the entire earth, without an inch of ground remaining.[7] Therefore, the kōan of binding the retreat appears, and it seems to come; the nets and cages of unbinding the retreat are broken, and it seems to go. While this is so, those with personal experience all just obstruct the binding and unbinding.[8] It is "*not an inch of grass for ten thousand miles*"; it is "*give me back the money for the ninety days of meals.*"[9]

6 **The single term of the summer retreat** (*ge ango no ikketsu* 夏安居の一橛): Taking *ketsu* 橛 ("stake") here as a symbol of "binding the retreat" (*ketsuge* 結夏), which in ancient India entailed "staking out boundaries" (S. *sīmābandha*) to create a ritually pure place — a "monastery" (S. *vihāra*) — for the duration of the rainy season retreat. See Supplementary Notes, s.v. "Wooden stake."

7 **bind the retreat** (*ketsuge* 結夏); **unbind the retreat** (*kaige* 解夏): Technical terms for the opening and closing of the retreat. In East Asia, the metaphor of "binding" and "unbinding" refers to the tightening and loosening of the rule (*sei* 制) under which monks live during the period. In Indian vinaya texs translated into Chinese, the terms refer to the ritual binding and dissolution of the physical "boundaries" (S. *sīmā*) that define a monastery, within which the three-month-long rainy season (*ge* 夏, S. *varṣa*) retreat is to be held.

empty space is completely clogged (*kokū sokuha seri* 虚空塞破せり): I.e., it is everywhere. A fairly common expression, more often in the reverse order: "to clog up empty space" (*sokuha kokū* 塞破虚空).

rending asunder the entire earth (*sōchi o reppa su* 帀地を裂破す): Not a particularly common expression, a variant appears in "Shōbōgenzō soku shin ze butsu" 正法眼藏即心是佛 in the phrase "the entire earth is rent asunder" (*sōchi reppa su* 帀地裂破す).

8 **those with personal experience all just obstruct the binding and unbinding** (*shinzō no menmen, tomo ni ketsu ge o keige suru nomi nari* 親曾の面面、ともに結・解を罣礙するのみなり): Perhaps meaning something like, "those intimately acquainted with the coming and going of the retreat simply come and go with it." "Personal experience" is a loose rendering of the adverbial expression *shinzō* 親曾 ("personally once"); an unusual usage found often in Dōgen's writing. The verb "obstruct" (*keige* 罣礙) here exemplifies Dōgen's habit of using the word in the sense "to identify with," "to be defined by."

9 **"not an inch of grass for ten thousand miles"** (*banri musun sō* 萬里無寸草): A

[72:4]

黄龍死心和尚云、山僧行脚三十餘年、以九十日爲一夏。增一日也不得、減一日也不得。

Reverend Huanglong Sixin said, "In this mountain monk's thirty-odd years of pilgrimage, ninety days make a single summer retreat.[10] *It wouldn't do to add one day; it wouldn't do to subtract one day."*

[72:5]

しかあれば、三十餘年の行脚眼、わづかに見徹するところ、九十日爲一夏安居のみなり。たとひ增一日せんとすとも、九十日かへりきたりて競頭參すべし、たとひ減一日せんとすといふとも、九十日かへりきたりて競頭參するものなり。さらに九十日の窟籠を跳脱すべからず。この跳脱は、九十日の窟籠を手脚として跨跳するのみなり。

Thus, all that the eye of "thirty-odd years of pilgrimage" discerns is just that "*ninety days make a single summer retreat.*" Even if we tried to add a day, the ninety days would come back, racing with each other; even if we tried to subtract a day, the ninety days would come back, racing with each other. We could never jump out of the ninety-day hole. To jump out of it is just to spring up with the ninety-day hole as our hands and feet.

[72:6]

九十日爲一夏は、我箇裏の調度なりといへども、佛祖のみづからはじめてなせるにあらざるがゆえに、佛佛祖祖嫡嫡正稟して今日にいたれり。しかあれば、夏安居にあふは、諸佛諸祖にあふなり、夏安居にあふは、見佛見祖なり、夏安居、ひさしく作佛祖せるなり。この九十日爲一夏、その時量、たとひ頂𩕳量なりといへども、一劫・十劫のみにあらず、百千無量劫のみにあらざるなり。餘時は、百千無量等の劫波に使得せらる、九十日は百千無量等の劫波を使得するゆえに、無量劫波たとひ九十日にあうて見

well-known saying found in many Zen texts, from an anecdote involving Dongshan Liangjie 洞山良价 (807-869) and Shishuang Qingzhu 石霜慶諸 (807-888), a version of which is recorded in Dōgen's *shinji Shōbōgenzō* 眞字正法眼藏 (DZZ.5:166); see Supplementary Notes, s.v. "Not an inch of grass for ten thousand miles."

"give me back the money for the ninety days of meals" (*gen go kujū nichi hansen rai* 還吾九十日飯錢來): Words of Chan master Yunmen Wenyan 雲門文偃 (864-949) (*Yunmen Kuangzhen chanshi guanglu* 雲門匡眞禪師廣錄, T.1988.47:550c4-6):

> 問、初秋夏末、前程忽有人問、如何祇對。師云、大衆退後。進云、過在什麼處。師云。還我九十日飯錢來。
>
> Someone asked, "It's the beginning of autumn, and the summer retreat is over. On my journey, if someone suddenly asks me about it, how should I answer?"
> The Master said," The great assembly is dismissed."
> He pursued it, saying, "Where's the fault?"
> The Master said, "Give me back the money for the ninety days of meals."

10 **Reverend Huanglong Sixin** (*Ōryō Shishin oshō* 黄龍死心和尚): I.e., Sixin Wuxin 死心悟新 (1043-1114). His words are cited in a lecture by Xueting Yuanling 雪庭元淨, in the *Jiatai pudeng lu* 嘉泰普燈錄 (ZZ.137:222b10-11).

佛すとも、九十日かならずしも劫波にかかはれず。しかあれば、參學すべし、九十日爲一夏は、眼睛量なるのみなり。身心安居者、それまたかくのごとし。

While [the convention] "*ninety days make a single retreat*" may be an implement of our place here, since it is not something that any of the buddhas and ancestors originated on their own, it has come down to the present day through buddha after buddha and ancestor after ancestor directly instructed in generation after generation of legitimate succession. Thus, to meet the summer retreat is to meet the buddhas and the ancestors; to meet the summer retreat is to see the buddhas and see the ancestors. The summer retreat has long made buddhas and ancestors. While the amount of time in this "*ninety days make a single retreat*" may be the dimensions of the crown of the head, it is not one kalpa or ten kalpas; it is not merely hundreds of thousands of innumerable kalpas.[11] Other times are employed by the hundreds of thousands of innumerable kalpas, while the ninety days employ the hundreds of thousands of innumerable kalpas; hence, although the hundreds of thousands of innumerable kalpas meet the ninety days and see the buddhas, the ninety days do not necessarily involve the kalpas.[12] Thus, we should understand that "ninety days make a single retreat" is just the measure of the eye.[13] The "retreat of body and mind" is also like this.[14]

[72:7] {2:219}

夏安居の活鱍鱍地を使得し、夏安居の活鱍鱍地を跳脱せる、來處あり、職由ありといへども、他方・他時よりきたり、うつれるにあらず、當處・當時より起興するにあらず。來處を把定すれば、九十日たちまちにきたる、職由を摸索すれば、九十日たちまちにきたる。凡・聖これを窟宅とせり、命根とせりといへども、はるかに凡・聖の境界を超越せり。思量分別のおよぶところにあらず、不思量分別のおよぶところにあらず、思量・不思量の不及のみにあらず。

Making use of the brisk liveliness of the summer retreat and jumping out of the brisk liveliness of the summer retreat may have their origins

11 **the dimensions of the crown of the head** (*chōnei ryō* 頂顴量): Perhaps to be understood, "equal to the dimensions of the buddhas and ancestors themselves." See Supplementary Notes, s.v. "Crown of the head."

12 **Other times are employed by the hundreds of thousands of innumerable kalpas** (*yoji wa, hyakusen muryōtō no kōha ni shitoku seraru* 餘時は、百千無量等の劫波に使得せらる): The notion of "employing" time here may reflect a saying, appearing frequently in Dōgen's writing, attributed to Zhaozhou Congshen 趙州從諗 (778-897); see Supplementary Notes, s.v. "Employ the twelve times."

13 **the measure of the eye** (*ganzei ryō* 眼睛量): Presumably, meaning that the length of the retreat corresponds to the dimensions of the eye that sees the buddhas and ancestors.

14 **The "retreat of body and mind"** (*shinjin ango* 身心安居): Reference to a passage in the *Yuanjue jing* 圓覺經 that Dōgen will quote below, section 62.

and have their reasons, but they have not moved, coming from another quarter or another time, and they do not arise from this place and this time. When we hold fast to their origins, the ninety days suddenly come; when we grope for their reasons, the ninety days suddenly come. While both the common person and the sage may make them their den, make them their lives, they far transcend the realms of the commoner and the sage.[15] They are not something reached by thinking or discrimination; they are not something reached by not thinking or discrimination; they are not merely unreached by thinking or not thinking.[16]

[72:8]

世尊在摩竭陀國、爲衆説法。是時將欲白夏、乃謂阿難曰、諸大弟子・人天四衆、我常説法、不生敬仰。我今入因沙臼室中、坐夏九旬。忽有人來問法之時、汝代爲我説、一切法不生、一切法不滅。言訖掩室而坐。

> *The World-Honored One was in the Land of Magadha, preaching the dharma to the saṃgha.*[17] *At that time, wishing to call the summer retreat, he spoke to Ānanda, saying,*
>
> > *Though I constantly preach the dharma, the great disciples, and the humans and devas of the fourfold saṃgha do not respect it.*[18] *I shall now enter the Indra-śaila-guhā chamber for the ninety-day summer retreat.*[19] *Should anyone come asking about the dharma, you should preach in my stead that all dharmas do not arise, all dharmas do not pass away.*
>
> *So saying, he shut the chamber and sat.*

---

15 **the commoner and the sage** (*bonshō* 凡聖): Standard terms for the ordinary person (S. *pṛthagjana*; "commoner") and the advanced Buddhist adept (S. *ārya*; "noble").

their den (*kuttaku* 窟宅): Literally, "cave dwelling," used for the "lair" or "haunt" of wild animals, spirits, bandits, etc.; resonating with the "the ninety-day hole" (*kujūnichi no kutsurō* 九十日の窟籠) in section 5, above.

16 **They are not something reached by thinking or discrimination** (*shiryō funbetsu no oyobu tokoro ni arazu* 思量分別のおよぶところにあらず): Suggestive of the famous line from the *Lotus Sūtra* (*Miaofa lianhua jing* 妙法蓮華經, T.262.9:7a20):

> 是法非思量分別之所能解。
>
> This dharma is not something that can be understood by thinking and discrimination.

17 **The World-Honored One** (*seson* 世尊): From a lecture by Chan Master Shengyin Xianjing 勝因咸靜 of Chuzhou 楚州 (*Jiatai pudeng lu* 嘉泰普燈錄, ZZ.137:158b11-15). There is no known source in a sūtra.

18 **fourfold saṃgha** (*shishu* 四衆): A term that can refer to (a) bhikṣu, *bhikṣuṇī*, *upāsaka* and *upāsikā* (monks, nuns, lay men and women); or to (b) bhikṣu, *bhikṣuṇī*, *śrāmaṇera* and *śrāmaṇerikā* (fully ordained monks, fully ordained nuns, novice monks, and novice nuns).

19 ***Indra-śaila-guhā* chamber** (*Inshakyū shitsu* 因沙臼室): An abbreviated transliteration of the Sanskrit name meaning "rock cave of Indra"; said to have been located at Mount Veda (*Bidasan* 毗陀山) outside the city of Magadha.

[72:9] {2:220}

しかありしよりこのかた、すでに二千一百九十四年＜當日本寛元三年乙巳歳＞なり。堂奥にいらざる兒孫、おほく摩竭掩室を無言説の證據とせり。いま邪黨おもはくは、掩室坐夏の佛意は、それ言説をもちいるはことごとく實にあらず、善巧方便なり、至理は言語道斷し、心行處滅なり、このゆえに、無言・無心は至理にかなふべし、有言有念は非理なり、このゆえに、掩室坐夏九旬のあひだ、人跡を斷絕せるなり、とのみいひ、いふなり。これらのともがらのいふところ、おほきに世尊の佛意に孤負せり。いはゆる、もし言語道斷、心行處滅を論ぜば、一切の治生產業、みな言語道斷し、心行處滅なり。言語道斷とは、一切の言語をいふ、心行處滅とは、一切の心行をいふ。いはんや、この因緣、もとより無言をたふとびんためにはあらず。通身ひとへに泥水し入草して、説法度人、いまだのがれず、轉法拯物、いまだのがれざるのみなり。もし兒孫と稱するともがら、坐夏九旬を、無言説なり、といはば、還吾九旬坐夏來、といふべし。

Since then, it has already been two thousand one hundred ninety-four years (to the present junior wood year of the snake, the third year of Kangen in Japan).[20] Descendants that have not entered the interior of the hall have often taken shutting the chamber at Magadha as evidence of ineffability.[21] Misguided groups today think that the Buddha's intention in shutting the chamber for the summer retreat was that all use of language is untrue, a skillful means; that the ultimate truth is *the way of words cut off, the locus of mentation extinguished*; and that, therefore, no words and no mind must accord with the ultimate truth, while words and thought are not the truth.[22] Therefore, they say only that during the ninety days of shutting the chamber for summer retreat, he cut off human traces.

What this bunch says is completely contrary to the buddha intention of the World-Honored One. That is, if we argue for "the way of words cut off; the locus of mentation extinguished," all life-sustaining work is "the way of words cut off; the locus of mentation extinguished": "the way of words cut off" refers to all language; "the locus of mentation extinguished" refers to all mental activities. Not to mention that basically this episode is not for the purpose of exalting wordlessness. His body

---

20 **two thousand one hundred ninety-four years** (*nisen ippyaku kujūshi nen* 二千一百九十四年): Parenthetical date in the original; reflecting the traditional East Asian Buddhist reckoning of the date of the *parinirvāṇa* of the Buddha as 949 BCE, figured here from 1245, the third year of the Japanese Kangen era.

21 **Descendants that have not entered the interior of the hall** (*dōō ni irazaru jison* 堂奥にいらざる兒孫): I.e., Buddhist followers without deep study of the teachings.

ineffability (*mugonsetsu* 無言説): Sometimes parsed here as "wordless preaching."

22 **the way of words cut off, the locus of mentation extinguished** (*gongodō dan, shingyōsho metsu* 言語道斷、心行處滅): The two phrases represent a single common expression, occurring often in East Asian Buddhist texts, for a truth beyond language and thinking.

throughout entirely in the mud and water, in the grass, he never shirks preaching the dharma and delivering people, never shirks turning the dharma and saving beings.[23] If those that call themselves his descendants say that the ninety days of the summer retreat are "ineffable," we should say, "*Give me back my ninety-day summer retreat.*"[24]

[72:10]

阿難に勅令していはく、汝代爲我説、一切法不生、一切法不滅、と代説せしむ。この佛儀、いたづらにすごすべからず。おほよそ掩室坐夏、いかでか無言無説なりとせん。しばらくもし阿難として、當時すなはち世尊に白すべし、一切法不生、一切法不滅、作麼生説、縱説恁麼、要作什麼。かくのごとく白して、世尊の道を聽取すべし。おほよそ而今の一段の佛儀、これ説法・轉法の第一義諦、第一無諦なり、さらに無言説の證據とすべからず。もしこれを無言説とせば、可憐三尺龍泉劍、徒掛陶家壁上梭ならん。

He commanded Ānanda to preach on his behalf, saying, "*You should preach in my stead that all dharmas do not arise, all dharmas do not pass away.*" We should not casually pass over this behavior of the Buddha. In general, how could we take his shutting the chamber for summer retreat as being without words and without preaching? If, for the moment, we were Ānanda, at this point we would say to the World-Honored One, "*All dharmas do not arise, all dharmas do not pass away. How should I preach of them? And, even if I did preach of them like this, what's the use?*" Saying this, we would listen to the World-Honored One's words. In general, the Buddha's behavior in the present passage is the prime truth and the prime non-truth; we should certainly not take it as ineffability.[25] If we took it as ineffability, it would be, "*How sad the three-foot*

23 **His body throughout entirely in the mud and water, in the grass** (*tsūshin hitoe ni deisui shi nissō shite* 通身ひとへに泥水し入草して): I.e., the Buddha always fully engaged in his role as a teacher. "Mud and water" (*deisui* 泥水), here put in verbal form, is doubtless shorthand for "entering the mud and entering the water" (*nyūdei nyūsui* 入泥入水; also read *nyūdei nissui*) or "dragged through the mud and drenched with water" (*dadei taisui* 拕泥帯水), common idioms referring to the Chan master's "getting his hands dirty," as we might say, in the teaching of his students. See Supplementary Notes, s.v. "Dragged through the mud and drenched with water." "In the grass" (*nissō* 入草) suggests entering into the mundane world of things. Dōgen seems to be combining allusions here to (a) the expression "his whole body in the grass" (*zenshin nissō* 全身入草) with (b) the saying (discussed in "Shōbōgenzō Kannon" 正法眼藏觀音) "his body throughout is hands and eyes" (*tsūshin ze shugen* 通身是手眼), in reference to the salvific activities of the bodhisattva Avalokiteśvara (for which, see Supplementary Notes).

24 **"Give me back my ninety-day summer retreat"** (*kan go kujun zage rai* 還吾九旬坐夏來): Variation on Yunmen's words (section 3, above), "Give me back the money for the ninety days of food."

25 **the prime truth and the prime non-truth** (*daiichi gi tai, daiichi mu tai* 第一義諦、第一無諦): The former expression is a standard term for the ultimate truth (S. *paramārtha-satya*), as opposed to the conventional truth (S. *saṃvṛti-satya*); the latter is

Longquan sword; a shuttle hanging useless on the Tao family's wall."[26]

[72:11] {2:221}

しかあればすなはち、九旬坐夏は古轉法輪なり、古佛祖なり。而今の因縁のなかに、時將欲白夏とあり。しるべし、のがれずおこなはるる九旬坐夏安居なり、これをのがるるは外道なり。おほよそ世尊在世には、あるひは忉利天にして九旬安居し、あるひは耆闍窟山靜室中にして、五百比丘、ともに安居す。五天竺國のあひだ、ところを論ぜず、ときいたれば白夏安居し、九夏安居おこなはれき。いま現在せる佛祖、もとも一大事としておこなはるるところなり、これ修證の無上道なり。梵網經中に、冬安居あれども、その法つたはれず、九夏安居の法のみつたはれり。正傳、まのあたり五十一世なり。

Thus, the ninety-day summer retreat is the old turning of the dharma wheel, is the old buddhas and ancestors. It is said in the present episode, "*at the time, he wished to call the summer retreat.*" We should recognize that this is the summer retreat of ninety days that he carried out without shirking; those that shirk it are followers of other paths. Generally, when the World-Honored One was in the world, he sometimes held the ninety-day retreat in the Trāyatriṃśa heaven, or he held the retreat together with five hundred bhikṣus in quiet quarters on Mount Gṛdhrakūṭa.[27] Throughout the Land of the Fivefold Sindhu, no matter where, when the time came, the summer retreat was called and the ninety-day summer retreat carried out.[28] It is something still carried out as "the one great matter" by the buddhas and ancestors who have come down to the present; it is the unsurpassed path of practice and verification.[29] Although, in

---

Dōgen's play with the word *mutai* 無諦 ("truth of nothingness"), used as a synonym for *kūtai* 空諦 ("truth of emptiness").

26 **"How sad the three-foot Longquan sword; a shuttle hanging useless on the Tao family's wall"** (*karen sanjaku Ryūsen ken, to ka Tōke hekijō sa* 可憐三尺龍泉劍、徒掛陶家壁上梭): Presumably, cited as an example of seriously underestimating what one is dealing with. Variant of lines by Foxing Fatai 佛性法泰 (dates unknown), commenting on an old case involving Weishan Lingyou 潙山靈祐 (771-853); See Supplementary Notes, s.v. "Like vines relying on a tree."

27 **Trāyatriṃśa heaven** (*tōriten* 忉利天): Heaven of the Thirty-three Devas, located atop Mount Sumeru. Reference to the legend that the Buddha held a ninety-day summer retreat in this heaven for the sake of his mother; see, e.g., *Mohemoye jing* 摩訶摩耶經, T.383.12:1005a6-8; *Fo sheng daolitian wei mu shuo fa jing* 佛昇忉利天爲母說法經, T.815.17:787b6-8.

Mount Gṛdhrakūṭa (*Gijakussen* 耆闍窟山): More often written 耆闍崛山; "Vulture Peak" (*Ryōjusen* 靈鷲山).

28 **Land of the Fivefold Sindhu** (*Go tenjiku koku* 五天竺國): The Indian subcontinent, as traditionally divided into the four cardinal points and the center. The name *Tenjiku* 天竺 represents a transliteration of "Sindhu" (from the Indus).

29 **"the one great matter"** (*ichidaiji* 一大事): A fixed idiom for the work of leading beings to supreme bodhi; best known from the famous passage in the *Lotus Sūtra*, in which

the *Brahmā*'s *Net Sūtra*, there is a winter retreat, its procedure has not been transmitted; only the procedure of the ninety-day summer retreat has been transmitted.[30] Its direct transmission is right before us in the fifty-first generation.[31]

* * * * *

[72:12]

清規云、行脚人欲就處所結夏、須於半月前掛搭。所貴茶湯人事、不倉卒。

In the Rules of Purity, it is said,[32]

An itinerant who wishes to go somewhere for a binding of the retreat, should register there one-half month in advance.[33] *It is a desideratum that the tea salutations not be rushed.*[34]

[72:13] {2:222}

いはゆる半月前とは、三月下旬をいふ。しかあれば、三月内にきたり掛搭すべきなり。すでに四月一日よりは、比丘僧、ありきせず、諸方の接待、

Buddha Śākyamuni reveals that the buddhas come into this world only to lead beings to buddhahood. See Supplementary Notes, s.v. "Buddhas, the world-honored ones, appear in the world for the reason of one great matter alone."

30 ***Brahmā's Net Sūtra*** (*Bonmō kyō* 梵網經): A Chinese aprochrypon that is the *locus classicus* for the bodhisattva precepts (*bosatsu kai* 菩薩戒) used in East Asian Buddhism, the *Fanwang jing* 梵網經 is the oldest source to recommend summer and winter retreats, a system that may have begun in Central Asia or China (T.1484.24:1008a13):

佛子常應二時頭陀冬夏坐禪結夏安居。

Disciples of the Buddha should twice engage in *dhūta*, winter and summer, sitting in meditation and binding the retreat.

31 **fifty-first generation** (*gojūisse* 五十一世): Typically taken to be Dōgen's reference to himself as the fifty-first in the lineage of ancestors descended from the Buddha. Elsewhere, however, he speaks of his teacher, Rujing, as representing the fifty-first generation — a discrepancy that arises from the custom of counting Bodhidharma twice, as both the twenty-eighth Indian and the first Chinese ancestor.

32 ***Rules of Purity*** (*Shingi* 清規): I.e., the *Chanyuan qinggui* 禪苑清規, the Chan monastic code by Changlu Zongze 長蘆宗賾 (d. 1107?). The quotation is from the opening lines of the section of the text dealing with the summer retreat (ZZ.111:887a17-888b4). From this point in our text through section 57, below, Dōgen will cite and comment on virtually all of this section of the *Chanyuan qinggui*, sometimes quoting the original Chinese, sometimes translating it into Japanese.

33 **register** (*kata* 掛搭): Literally, "to hang up on a hook" — i.e., to hang one's walking staff and other travel gear on a hook in the monks' quarters of a monastery, thereby taking up residence; by extension, to register as a resident of the monastery.

34 **It is a desideratum that the tea salutations not be rushed** (*shoki satō ninji, fusōsotsu* 所貴茶湯人事、不倉卒): Or, perhaps, "The valued tea salutations should not be rushed." "The tea salutations" (*satō ninji* 茶湯人事) refers to the formal tea held at the beginning of retreats to welcome the participants.

および諸寺の旦過、みな門を鎖せり。しかあれば、四月一日よりは、雲衲みな、寺院に安居せり、菴裏に掛搭せり。あるひは白衣舍に安居せる、先例なり。これ、佛祖の儀なり、慕古し、修行すべし。拳頭・鼻孔、みな面面に寺院をしめて、安居のところに掛搭せり。

"One-half month in advance" refers to the final ten-day period of the third month; thus, one should arrive and register during the third month. From the first day of the fourth month, the bhikṣu saṃgha does not go about, and the gates are closed at the reception offices in all quarters and the overnight lodgings of the monasteries. Thus, from the first day of the fourth month, all those robed in clouds are in retreat at a monastery or registered at a cloister.[35] Or there is precedent for holding the retreat at the residence of a lay follower.[36] These are observances of the buddhas and ancestors; we should admire the ancients and practice them. All the fists and noses, each and every one, claiming a monastery, is registered at a place of retreat.[37]

[72:14]

しかあるを、魔黨いはく、大乘の見解、それ要樞なるべし。夏安居は、聲聞の行儀なり、あながちに修習すべからず。かくのごとくいふともがらは、かつて佛法を見聞せざるなり。阿耨多羅三藐三菩提、これ九旬安居坐夏なり。たとひ大乘・小乘の至極ありとも、九旬安居の枝葉華果なり。

However, the minions of Māra say the essential pivot must be the understanding of the Great Vehicle; the summer retreat is a procedure of the *śrāvaka*; we need not necessarily practice it. Those that talk like this have never seen or heard the buddha dharma. *Anuttara-samyak-saṃbodhi* — this is the ninety-day retreat of summer. While there may be the extremes of Great Vehicle and Small Vehicle, they are the branches, leaves, flowers, and fruit of the ninety-day retreat.

---

35 **those robed in clouds** (*unnō* 雲衲): I.e., itinerant monks; synonymous with the more common *unsui* 雲水 ("clouds and water").

in retreat at a monastery or registered at a cloister (*jiin ni ango seri, anri ni kata seri* 寺院に安居せり、菴裏に掛搭せり): Or, possibly, "in retreat at a monastery and registered at a cloister [within that institution]."

36 **residence of a lay follower** (*byakue sha* 白衣舍): Literally, " dwelling of a white-robed," the designation of the traditional garb of the Buddhist laity participating in ceremonies at a monastery.

37 **All the fists and noses, each and every one, claiming a monastery, is registered at a place of retreat** (*kentō bikū, mina menmen ni jiin o shimete, ango no tokoro ni kata seri* 拳頭・鼻孔、みな面面に寺院をしめて、安居のところに掛搭せり): "Fists" (*kentō* 拳頭) and "noses" (*bikū* 鼻孔) refer to accomplished teachers and students; see Supplementary Notes, s.v. "Fist," "Nose." The translation of "each and every one" loses the continued play with body parts in *menmen* 面面 ("face after face"). The verb *shimete* しめて here likely represents 占める ("to occupy," "to claim as one's own").

[72:15]
四月三日の粥罷より、はじめてことをおこなふといへども、堂司、あらかじめ四月一日より戒臘の榜を理會す。すでに四月三日の粥罷に、戒臘牓を衆寮前にかく、いはゆる前門の下間の窓外にかく。寮窓みな櫺子なり。粥罷にこれをかけ、放參鐘ののち、これををさむ。三日より五日にいたるまで、これをかく。ををさむる時節、かくる時節、おなじ。

Although it is only put into practice from the end of gruel on the third day of the fourth month, the hall manager prepares the ordination seniority notice in advance, from the first day of the fourth month.[38] Then, at the end of gruel on the third day of the fourth month, he hangs the ordination seniority notice in front of the common quarters; that is, it is hung outside the window in the space to the left of the front door. The windows of these quarters are all latticed. It is hung at the end of gruel and taken down after the bell for release from convocation.[39] It is hung out from the third day through the fifth day; the times [each day] for taking it in and the times for hanging it up are the same.

[72:16] {2:223}
かの榜、かく式あり。知事・頭首によらず、戒臘のままにかくなり。諸方にして頭首・知事をへたらんは、おのおの首座・監寺とかくなり。數職をつとめたらんなかには、そのちにつとめておほきならん職をかくべし。かつて住持をへたらんは、某甲西堂とかく。小院の住持をつとめたりといへども、雲水にしられざるは、しばしばこれをかくして稱せず。もし師の會裏にしては、西堂なるもの、西堂の儀なし、某甲上座とかく例もあり。おほくは衣鉢侍者寮に歇息する、勝躅なり。さらに衣鉢侍者に充し、あるいは燒香侍者に充する、舊例なり。いはんやその餘の職、いづれも師命にしたがふなり。他人の弟子のきたれるが、小院の住持をつとめたるといへども、おほきなる寺院にては、なほ首座・書記・都寺・監寺等に請するは、依例なり、芳躅なり。小院の小職をつとめたるを稱するをば、叢林わらふなり。よき人は、住持をへたる、なほ小院をば、かくして稱せざるなり。

There is a standard form for writing the notice. It is written strictly according to ordination seniority, without consideration for stewards or prefects. Those who have served somewhere as prefects or stewards are

38 **end of gruel** (*shukuha* 粥罷): I.e., the conclusion of breakfast, gruel (*shuku* 粥) being the standard fare at the morning meal.

hall manager (*dōsu* 堂司): I.e., the rector (*inō* 維那), the monastic officer in charge of the assembly of monks.

ordination seniority notice (*kairō no bō* 戒臘の榜): I.e., the signboard listing the monks in the retreat according to their seniority, by years since their ordination; to be described in the following sections.

39 **bell for release from convocation** (*hōsan shō* 放參鐘): The bell announcing that no informal convocation with the abbot will be held; here, taken to indicate the close of evening meditation (*bansan* 晩參).

listed accordingly as "head seat" or "comptroller."[40] For those having served in multiple postions, the highest, later position held should be listed. Those who have served as abbots should be listed as "West Hall (Name)."[41] Those who, though having served as abbot of a small cloister, are unknown by the monks in training, are often listed without such identification. Those who are west halls while being members of the master's community do not play the role of a west hall; there are instances of their being listed as "Senior Seat (Name)."[42] The many who stay in the quarters of the robe and bowl acolyte are fine precedents.[43] In addition, there are old instances of their actually filling the role of robe and bowl acolyte or filling the role of incense acolyte, not to mention other positions, all of which are in keeping with the master's orders.[44] When others' disciples have come, even though they have served as abbots of small cloisters, in the large monasteries, it is a customary practice and a refined example to request only [the titles of] head seat, secretary, prior, comptroller, and the like.[45] Those boasting that they have served in a minor position at a small cloister will be laughed at by the monastic community. Good people who have served as abbot, when it is just a small cloister, will keep it

40 **Those who have served somewhere as prefects or stewards are listed accordingly as "head seat" or "comptroller"** (*shohō ni shite chōshu chiji o hetaran wa, onoono shuso kansu to kaku nari* 諸方にして頭首・知事をへたらんは、おのおの首座・監寺とかくなり): I.e., those who have ever held monastic offices are given the titles of those offices. "Prefects" (*chōshu* 頭首) and "stewards" (*chiji* 知事) are the two sets of six major monastic offices: the prefect offices are (1) head seat (*shuso* 首座), (2) secretary (*shoki* 書記), (3) canon prefect (*chizō* 知藏), (4) guest prefect (*shika* 知客), (5) hall prefect (*chiden* 知殿), and (6) bath prefect (*chiyoku* 知浴); the steward offices are (1) prior (*tsūsu* 都寺), (2) comptroller (*kansu* 監寺), (3) assistant comptroller (*fūsu* 副寺), (4) rector (*inō* 維那), (5) head cook (*tenzo* 典座), and (6) labor steward (*shissui* 直歲).

41 **"West Hall"** (*seidō* 西堂): The title used for a retired abbot in residence, from the name of the quarters in which such monks were housed.

42 **Those who are west halls while being members of the master's community** (*shi no eri ni shite wa, seidō naru mono* 師の會裏にしては、西堂なるもの): I.e., those among the immediate disciples of the abbot who have themselves previously served as abbots. Such monks will not play the senior advisory role assigned to the west hall monks.

"Senior Seat" (*jōza* 上座): An honorific for a senior monk, used variously for an abbot, a head monk, an elder, a monk of over twenty years standing, etc.

43 **quarters of the robe and bowl acolyte** (*ehatsu jisha ryō* 衣鉢侍者寮): I.e., the residence of the acolyte who serves as the abbot's personal valet.

44 **incense acolyte** (*shōkō jisha* 燒香侍者): I.e., the acolyte assisting the abbot at rituals.

45 **head seat, secretary, prior, comptroller, and the like** (*shuso shoki tsūsu kansu tō* 首座・書記・都寺・監寺等): I.e., the various monastic offices, of lesser status than west hall. The former two here are prefect offices; the latter two, steward offices. Though the agent of this request is unstated, presumably, it is the individual in question who requests that they be listed under one or another such title, rather than as a west hall.

to themselves and not identify themselves as such.

[72:17]
榜式かくのごとし、

The form for the notice is as follows:

[72:18]
某國某州某山寺、今夏、結夏海衆、戒臘如後。
陳如尊者
堂頭和尚
建保元戒
某甲上座 某甲藏主
某甲上座 某甲上座
建保二戒
某甲西堂 某甲維那
某甲首座 某甲知客
某甲上座 某甲浴主
建暦元戒
某甲直歳 某甲侍者
某甲首座 某甲首座
某甲化主 某甲上座
某甲典座 某甲堂主
建暦三戒
某甲書記 某甲上座
某甲西堂 某甲首座
某甲上座 某甲上座
右謹具呈、若有誤錯、各請指揮、謹狀。
某年四月三日 堂司比丘某甲謹狀

(Name) Mountain monastery, (Name) prefecture, (Name) country.

This summer, upon binding the retreat, the ordination seniority of the oceanic assembly is as follows:[46]

46 **oceanic assembly** (*kaishu* 海衆): I.e., the entire monastic saṃgha, likened to an ocean.

Venerable Kauṇḍinya

The Reverend Head of Hall [47]

Ordained first year of Kenpō [1213]:

Senior Seat (Name)	*Canon Prefect (Name)*
Senior Seat (Name)	*Senior Seat (Name)*

Ordained second year of Kenpō [1214]:

West Hall (Name)	*Rector (Name)*
Head Seat (Name)	*Guest Prefect (Name)*
Senior Seat (Name)	*Bath Manager (Name)*

Ordained first year of Kenryaku [1211]:

Labor Steward (Name)	*Acolyte (Name)*
Head Seat (Name)	*Head Seat (Name)*
Chief Fundraiser (Name)	*Senior Seat (Name)*
Head Cook (Name)	*Hall Chief (Name)*

Ordained third year of Kenryaku [1213]:

Secretary (Name)	*Senior Seat (Name)*
West Hall (Name)	*Head Seat (Name)*
Senior Seat (Name)	*Senior Seat (Name)*

The above is respectfully submitted. Instruction on any errors requested. Respectfully.

Respectfully, Hall Manager Bhikṣu (Name)

Third day, fourth month, (Name) year.

[72:19] {2:225}

かくのごとくかく。しろきかみにかく。眞書にかく、草書・隷書等をもちいず。かくるには、布線のふとさ兩米粒許なるを、その紙榜頭につけてかくるなり。たとへば、簾・額の、すぐならんがごとし。四月五日の放參罷に、をさめをはりぬ。

It is written like this. It is written on white paper, in regular script, not in cursive script, clerical script, or the like. When hanging it, it is hung from a string, about as thick as two grains of rice, attached to the top of the paper notice. It hangs straight down, like a curtain or a plaque. It is finally taken down following release from convocation on the fifth day of the fourth month.

---

47 **Venerable Kauṇḍinya** (*Jinnyo sonja* 陳如尊者): One of the five ascetics to whom the Buddha delivered his first sermon at Sarnath, said to have been first to realize the truth of the teachings; a ceremonial presence in the monks' hall.

The Reverend Head of Hall (*dōchō oshō* 堂頭和尚): I.e., the abbot.

[72:20]
四月八日は佛生會なり。

The eighth day of the fourth month is the Buddha's birthday assembly.

[72:21]
四月十三日の齋罷に、衆寮の僧衆、すなはち本寮につきて煎點諷經す。寮主、ことをおこなふ。點湯燒香、みな寮主これをつとむ。寮主は、衆寮の堂奥に、その位を安排せり。寮首座は、寮の聖僧の左邊に安排せり。しかあれども、寮主、いでて燒香行事するなり。首座・知事等、この諷經におもむかず、ただ本寮の僧衆のみ、おこなふなり。維那、あらかじめ一枚の戒臘牌を修理して、十五日の粥罷に、僧堂前の東壁にかく、前架のうへにあたりてかく、正面のつぎのみなみの間なり。清規云、堂司預設戒臘牌、香華供養。(在僧堂前設之)

On the thirteenth day of the fourth month, following the midday meal, the assembly of monks of the common quarters holds a tea and sūtra chanting session in their quarters. The quarters chief conducts it: the preparation of the tea and the burning of the incense are both performed by the quarters chief. The quarters chief is positioned at the interior of the hall of the common quarters; the quarters head seat is positioned to the left of the Sacred Monk of the quarters.[48] Nevertheless, it is the quarters chief who comes forward and performs the rite of burning incense. The head seat, stewards, and the like, do not attend this sūtra chanting; it is performed only by the assembly of monks of these quarters.

After gruel on the fifteenth day, the rector, having prepared in advance a single ordination seniority placard, hangs it on the east wall in front of the saṃgha hall; it is hung above the front shelving, in the space just to the south of the center.[49] *In the Rules of Purity, it is said,*[50]

The hall manager sets up the ordination seniority placard, with offerings of incense and flowers. (This is set up in front of the saṃgha hall.)

[72:22]
四月十四日の齋後に、念誦牌を僧堂前にかく。諸堂、おなじく念誦牌をかく。至晩に、知事、あらかじめ土地堂に香華をまうく、額のまへにまうくるなり。集衆念誦す。

"On the fourteenth day of the fourth month, following the midday meal, the recitations placard is hung" in front of the saṃgha hall.[51] Sim-

---

48 **Sacred Monk** (*shōsō* 聖僧): The tutelary deity of the common quarters, whose image is enshrined there; often the Bodhisattva Avalokiteśvara.

49 **the front shelving** (*zenka* 前架): Shelves at the east end of the saṃgha hall used for food service.

50 ***Rules of Purity*** (*Shingi* 清規): *Chanyuan qinggui* 禪苑清規, ZZ.111:887b7.

51 **"On the fourteenth day of the fourth month"** (*shigatsu jūshi nichi* 四月十四日):

ilarly, the recitations placard is hung in the various halls. "At evening, the stewards prepare in advance incense and flowers at the local deities hall"; they are arranged in front of the plaque.[52] "The assembly is gathered and performs the recitation."

[72:23] {2:226}

念誦の法は、大衆集定ののち、住持人、まづ燒香す、つぎに、知事・頭首、燒香す。浴佛のときの、燒香の法のごとし。つぎに、維那、くらいより正面にいでて、まづ住持人を問訊して、つぎに土地堂にむかうて問訊して、おもてをきたにして、土地堂にむかうて念誦す。詞云、

The procedure for the recitation: After the great assembly has gathered, first the abbot burns incense; next, the stewards and prefects burn incense. It is like the procedure for burning incense when bathing the Buddha. Next, the rector, coming to the front from their place, first bows to the abbot, then bows facing the local deities hall. Facing north, toward the local deities hall, they recite. "*The words are*":[53]

[72:24]

竊以薫風扇野、炎帝司方、當法王禁足之辰、是釋子護生之日。躬裒大衆、肅詣靈祠、誦持萬德洪名、廻向合堂眞宰。所祈、加護得遂安居。仰憑尊衆念。

We privately consider:

A fragrant breeze fans the plains;
The flaming emperor rules his quarter.[54]
At a time that the King of the Dharma banned our travel,
On a day that the children of Śākya guard their lives,
Personally, we gather the great assembly,

A Japanese reworking of the *Chanyuan qinggui* 禪苑清規 (ZZ.111:887b1-2):

四月十四日齋後、掛念誦牌。至晩、知事豫備香華法事、於土地前集衆念誦。

On the fourteenth day of the fourth month, following the midday meal, the recitations placard is hung out. At evening, the stewards prepare in advance for the incense and flower dharma rite. In front of the hall of the local deity, the assembly is gathered and performs the recitation.

52 **"the local deities hall"** (*doji dō* 土地堂): The shrine dedicated to the autochthonous tutelary spirits.

in front of the plaque (*gaku no mae* 額のまへ): I.e., the plaque identifying the shrine as the "Local Deities Hall."

53 **"The words are"** (*shi un* 詞云): Beginning here through the following section, Dōgen quotes the Chinese text of the *Chanyuan qinggui* 禪苑清規 (ZZ.111:887b2-4).

54 **A fragrant breeze** (*kunpū* 薫風); **The flaming emperor** (*entei* 炎帝): I.e, the summer season has arrived, with a southern wind and the sun high in the south.

Reverently, we visit the sacred shrine.[55]
Reciting the great names with their myriad virtues,
We dedicate to the true rulers of all the halls.[56]
We pray that their protection may enable a successful retreat. We respectfully invite the venerable assembly to recite:

[72:25]
清淨法身毘盧舍那佛 金打
圓滿報身盧舍那佛 金打
千百億化身釋迦牟尼佛 金打
當來下生彌勒尊佛 金打
十方三世一切諸佛 金打
大聖文殊師利菩薩 金打
大聖普賢菩薩 金打
大悲觀世音菩薩 金打
諸尊菩薩摩訶薩 金打
摩訶般若波羅蜜 金打

Buddha Vairocana, pure dharma body (bell)[57]
Buddha Rocana, complete reward body (bell)
Buddha Śākyamuni, of thousands of hundreds of koṭis *of transformation bodies (bell)*
The Buddha Maitreya, of future birth (bell)
All buddhas of the ten directions and three times (bell)
Bodhisattva Mañjuśrī, great sage (bell)
Bodhisattva Samantabhadra, great sage (bell)
Bodhisattva Avalokiteśvara, of great compassion (bell)
All the honored bodhisattvas-mahāsattvas *(bell)*
The Mahā-prajñā-pāramitā *(bell)*

---

55 **the King of the Dharma banned our travel** (*hōō kinsoku* 法王禁足); **the children of Śākya guard their lives** (*Shakashi goshō* 釋子護生): I.e., at this time, when we followers of Śākyamuni are not to travel but to nurture ourselves in the summer retreat.

56 **the great names with their myriad virtues** (*mantoku kōmei* 萬德洪名); **the true rulers of all the halls** (*gattō shinsai* 合堂眞宰): I.e., the auspicious names to be chanted and the tutelary spirits of the entire monastery to whom the merit from the recitation will be offered.

57 **The Buddha Vairocana** (*Birushano fu* 毘盧舍那佛): Beginning the so-called "ten buddha names" (*jūbutsumyō* 十佛名), recited at mealtimes and other ritual occasions. The *Chanyuan qinggui* 禪苑清規 at this point (ZZ.111:887b4) says merely, "and so on" (*yunyun* 云云), without giving the content of the recitation.

[72:26] {2:227}
念誦功德、竝用廻向護持正法土地龍神。伏願、神光協贊、發揮有利之勳、梵樂興隆、亦錫無私之慶。再憑尊衆念。十方三世一切諸佛、諸尊菩薩摩訶薩、摩訶般若波羅蜜。

All the merit from the recitation is dedicated to the local dragon spirits who protect the true dharma.[58] *We humbly pray that their spiritual radiance may aid us and foster beneficial accomplishments, that our pure bliss may prosper, and that they may confer selfless blessings.*[59] *Again, I invite the venerable assembly to recite:*

All buddhas of the ten directions and three times
All the honored bodhisattvas-mahāsattvas,
The Mahā-prajñā-pāramitā.[60]

[72:27]
ときに鼓響すれば、大衆、すなはち雲堂の點湯の座に赴す。點湯は庫司の所辦なり。大衆赴堂し、次第巡堂し、被位につきて正面而坐す。知事一人、行法事す、いはゆる燒香等をつとむるなり。清規云、本合監院行事、有故維那代之。

At this point, when the drum sounds, the members of the great assembly proceed to their seats for the tea service in the cloud hall.[61] The tea service is carried out by the administrators.[62] Members of the great assembly proceed to the hall, "circumambulate the hall, assume their assigned places, and sit" facing forward.[63] "One of the stewards performs the dharma rites" — i.e., takes charge of burning incense, etc. *In the Rules of Purity, it is said,*

58 **the merit from the recitation** (*nenju kudoku* 念誦功德): Slightly variant version of the *Chanyuan qinggui* 禪苑清規, ZZ.111:887b4-5.

59 **that our pure bliss may prosper** (*bonraku kōryū* 梵樂興隆): An odd entreaty, and in fact the original gives the more likely "that our pure park [i.e., monastery] may prosper" (*bon'en kōryū* 梵苑興隆).

60 **All buddhas of the ten directions and three times** (*jihō sanshi ishi shifu* 十方三世一切諸佛): The three lines recited here are a standard chant now known as the "the great verse" (*makabon* 摩訶梵). The *Chanyuan qinggui* 禪苑清規 (ZZ.111:887b5) abbreviates it with the simple prompt "The ten directions, etc." (*shifeng deng* 十方等).

61 **the cloud hall** (*undō* 雲堂): I.e., the saṃgha hall.

62 **the administrators** (*kusu* 庫司): I.e., the steward offices of prior (*tsūsu* 都寺), comptroller (*kansu* 監寺), and assistant comptroller (*fūsu* 副寺).

63 **"circumambulate the hall"** (*shidai jundō shi* 次第巡堂し): Text in quotation marks here represents Dōgen's Japanese version of the *Chanyuan qinggui* 禪苑清規 at ZZ.111:887b7-8.

Fundamentally, the comptroller is to perform the ceremony; if there is reason, the rector may substitute for him.[64]

[72:28]

すべからく念誦已前に寫牓して、首座に呈す。知事、搭袈裟・帶坐具して、首座に相見するとき、あるいは兩展三拜しをはりて、牓を首座に呈す。首座答拜す、知事の拜とおなじかるべし。牓は、箱に複[ネ+秋]子をしきて、行者にもたせゆく。首座、知事をおくりむかふ。

"An invitation should always be written prior to the recitation service and presented to the head seat."[65] When the stewards, wearing their *kāṣāya* and carrying their sitting cloths, meet the head seat, they may perform the two spreadings and three prostrations, after which they present the invitation to the head seat.[66] The head seat makes prostrations in reply; these should be the same as the prostrations of the stewards. The invitation, in a box draped with a folded covering cloth, is given to a postulant to carry. The head seat welcomes and sends off the stewards.

[72:29] {2:228}

牓式
庫司、今晩 就
雲堂煎點、特爲
首座
大衆、聊表結制之儀。伏冀
衆慈同垂
光降。
寛元三年四月十四 庫司比丘某甲等謹白

Form for invitation:[67]

The administrators, this evening,
shall serve a tea refeshment in the cloud hall, especially for the head seat
and great assembly, as a rite to mark the binding of the rule. We humbly wish

64 ***Rules of Purity*** (*Shingi* 清規): *Chanyuan qinggui* 禪苑清規, ZZ.111:887b8.

65 **"An invitation should always be written prior to the recitation service"** (*subekaraku nenju izen ni shabō shite* すべからく念誦已前に寫牓して): The sentence is a Japanese translation of the *Chanyuan qinggui* 禪苑清規 at ZZ.111:887b8.

66 **the two spreadings and three prostrations** (*ryōten sanpai* 兩展三拜): A standard ritual practice, in which three sets of three bows are abbreviated by simply spreading the sitting cloth (on which the bows would have been made) for the first two sets.

67 **Form for invitation** (*bōshiki* 牓式): The form quotes *Chanyuan qinggui* 禪苑清規, ZZ.111:887b8-9. (The source does not include any date; the Japanese date given here [corresponding to 1245] is for the retreat during which the "Shōbōgenzō ango" was composed.)

that members of the assembly will all kindly favor us with their presence.
Fourteenth day, fourth month, third year of Kangen,
Respectfully, Administration Hall bhikṣu (Names)

[72:30]
知事の第一の名字をかくなり。牓を首座に呈してのち、行者をして、雲堂前に貼せしむ、堂前の下間に貼するなり。前門の南頰の外面に、牓を貼する板あり。このいた、ぬれり。殼漏子あり。殼漏子は、牓の初にならべて、竹釘にてうちつけたり。しかあれば、殼漏子もかたはらに押貼せり。この牓は、如法につくれり。五分許の字にかく、おほきにかかず。殼漏子の表書は、かくのごとくかく、狀請 首座 大衆 庫司比丘 某甲 等 謹封

The name of the top steward is written. After the invitation is presented to the head seat, a postulant is asked to post it in front of the cloud hall; it is posted on the south section of the front of the hall. On the outer surface of the wall to the south of the front entrance, there is a board for posting notices; the board is lacquered. There is an envelope; the envelope is aligned with the beginning of the invitation and affixed to it with a bamboo pin. Thus, the envelope is also pinned up alongside. This invitation is produced according to proper procedure; it is written in glyphs of about a half inch, not written large. The writing on the front of the envelope is as follows:

Invitation to the Head Seat and the Great Assembly.

Respectfully enclosed, Administration Hall bhikṣu (Name).

[72:31] {2:229}
煎點、をはりぬれば、牓ををさむ。

When the tea refreshment is over, the invitation is taken down.

[72:32]
十五日の粥前に、知事・頭首・小師・法眷、まづ方丈内にまうでて人事す。住持人、もし隔宿より免人事せば、さらに方丈にまうづべからず。免人事といふは、十四日より、住持人、あるいは頌子、あるいは法語をかける牓を、方丈門の東頰に貼せり、あるいは雲堂前にも貼す。

On the fifteenth day, before gruel, the stewards, prefects, disciples, and dharma relatives first go inside the abbot's quarters and perform salutations.[68] If, from the previous day, the abbot has excused himself from salutations, then they should not go to the abbot's quarters.

---

68 **On the fifteenth day** (*jūgo nichi* 十五日): The first two sentences here represent a Japanese rendering of *Chanyuan qinggui* 禪苑清規, ZZ.111:887b10-11.

disciples, and dharma relatives (*shōshi hakken* 小師・法眷): I.e., the disciples of the abbot and others in his lineage.

"To excuse himself from salutations" means that, from the fourteenth day, the abbot has posted a notice with a verse or dharma phrase on the east side of the entrance to the abbot's quarters, or they may also post it in front of the cloud hall.

[72:33]

十五日の陞座罷、住持人、法座よりおりて、堦のまへにたつ。拜席の北頭をふみて、面南してたつ。知事、近前して兩展三禮す。一展云、

On the fifteenth day, "following the mounting the seat presentation," the abbot descends from the dharma seat and stands before the stairs.[69] Stepping on the northern edge of the prostration mat, they stand facing south. "The stewards, coming forward, perform the two spreadings and three prostrations."

On the first spreading, they say,[70]

[72:34]

此際、安居禁足獲奉巾瓶。唯仗和尚法力資持願無難事。一展叙寒暄、觸禮三拜。＜叙寒暄云者、展坐具三拜了、収坐具、進云、即辰孟夏漸熱、法王結夏之辰、伏惟堂頭和尚、法候動止萬福、下情不勝感激之至。＞

> *On this occasion, in retreat and forbidden to travel, we have been given the opportunity to serve the cloth and flask.*[71] *We only rely on Your Reverence's dharma power to help sustain us and pray there will be no difficulties.*

On the second spreading, they offer seasonal greetings and then make three abbreviated prostrations.[72]

(On "offering season's greetings": when spreading the sitting cloth and making three prostrations is finished, gather up the sitting cloth, advance, and say,[73]

---

69 **"following the mounting the seat presentation"** (*shinzo ha* 陞座罷): I.e., after the abbot's formal talk from the altar in the dharma hall. Passages in quotations marks here are Japanese renderings of *Chanyuan qinggui* 禪苑清規, ZZ.111:887b11-12.

70 **On the first spreading, they say** (*itten un* 一展云): From here through "three abbreviated prostrations," Dōgen quotes directly the Chinese at *Chanyuan qinggui* 禪苑清規, ZZ.111:887b11-12.

71 **serve the cloth and flask** (*hō kinbyō* 奉巾瓶): A fixed expression meaning "to attend upon" a master; from the hand towel and water jug used in his ablutions.

72 **three abbreviated prostrations** (*sokurei sanpai* 觸禮三拜): Literally, three "touch prostrations" (*sokurei* 觸禮), in which the sitting cloth is simply placed on the floor but not opened out.

73 **On "offering season's greetings"** (*jo kanken un sha* 叙寒暄云者): These parenthetical instructions on the greetings, given here in Chinese, do not appear in the *Chanyuan qinggui* and are not included in some versions of the "Shōbōgenzō ango." Moreover, the instructions conflict with those of the *Chanyuan qinggui* just quoted, which say that the

On this day, at the first of summer, it is gradually becoming hotter. On the occasion of binding the retreat of the Dharma King, we humbly hope that the condition and activities of the Reverend Head of Hall may enjoy myriad blessings; we are overcome with extreme gratitude.)[74]

[72:35]

かくのごとくして、その次に觸禮三拜、ことばなし、住持人みな答拜す。

In this way, next, they make the three abbreviated prostrations; without speaking, the abbot makes a prostration in reply to all.[75]

[72:36]

住持人念、此者、多幸得同安居、亦冀某<首座、監寺>人等、法力相資、無諸難事。首座・大衆、同此式也。

The abbot recites,[76]

Here, we are most fortunate to be able to spend the same retreat together; and it is my hope that, thanks to the dharma power of (Names) (head seat, comptroller, etc.), there will be no difficulties.

The head seat and the great assembly follow this same form.

[72:37] {2:230}

このとき、首座・大衆・知事等、みな面北して禮拜するなり。住持人ひとり面南にして、法座の堦前に立せり。住持人の坐具は、拜席のうへに展ずるなり。

At this time, the head seat, great assembly, stewards, and the rest, all pay obeisance facing north; the abbot alone faces south, standing before the stairs to the dharma seat. The abbot's sitting cloth is spread over the prostration mat.

---

greetings are to be offered after the second spreading of the sitting cloth and before the three abbreviated prostrations.

74 **we humbly hope that the condition and activities of the Reverend Head of Hall may enjoy myriad blessings** (*fukui dōchō oshō, hōkō dōshi banpuku* 伏惟堂頭和尚、法候動止萬福): Though not, it seems, a fixed form of salutation in Chan texts, Dōgen uses almost identical expressions in the "Shōbōgenzō gyōji" 正法眼藏行持 (part 2) and *Eihei kōroku* 永平廣錄 (DZZ.3:134, no. 196).

75 **In this way** (*kaku no gotoku shite* かくのごとくして): The text switches back to Dōgen's Japanese comment, which reasserts the order given in the *Chanyuan qinggui* quotation, rather than that of the parenthetical instructions.

76 **The abbot recites** (*jūjinin nen* 住持人念): Quoting the Chinese at *Chanyuan qinggui* 禪苑清規, ZZ.111:887b13.

[72:38]

つぎに首座・大衆、於住持人前、兩展三禮。このとき、小師・侍者・法眷・沙彌、在一邊立、未得與大衆雷同人事。いはゆる、一邊にありてたつ、とは、法堂の東壁のかたはらにありてたつなり。もし東壁邊に施主の垂箔のことあらば、法鼓のほとりにたつべし、また西壁邊にも立すべきなり。

Next, the head seat and great assembly do two spreadings and three prostrations in front of the abbot.[77] At this time, the disciples, acolytes, dharma relatives, and *śrāmanera* stand to one side; they are not to offer salutations in unison with the great assembly.

To say that they "stand to one side" means that they stand beside the east wall of the dharma hall. Should there be donors' screens by the east wall, they should stand near the dharma drum, or they should stand by the west wall.[78]

[72:39]

大衆、禮拜、をはりて、知事、まづ庫堂にかへりて主位に立す。つぎに首座、すなはち大衆を領して庫司にいたりて人事す、いはゆる知事と觸禮三拜するなり。このとき小師・侍者・法眷等は、法堂上にて住持人を禮拜す。法眷は、兩展三拜すべし、住持人の答拜あり。小師・侍者、おのおの九拜す、答拜なし。沙彌、九拜、あるいは十二拜なり、住持人、合掌してうくるのみなり。

Once the great assembly has finished its prostrations, the stewards first return to the administration hall and stand in the host postion.[79] Next, the head seat, leading the great assembly, goes to the administration hall and performs salutations — i.e., performs three abbreviated prostrations to the stewards. During this time, the disciples, acolytes, dharma relatives, and the like, pay obeisance to the abbot in the dharma hall.

Dharma relatives should do the two spreadings and three prostrations, with the abbot making prostrations in reply. Disciples and acolytes each make nine prostrations, with no prostrations in reply. For *śrāmanera*, it is nine prostrations or twelve prostrations, with the abbot merely accepting them with joined palms.

---

77 **Next** (*tsugi ni* つぎに): The first two sentences here represent a Japanese rendering of *Chanyuan qinggui* 禪苑清規, ZZ.111:887b14-15.

78 **donors' screens** (*seshu no suihaku* 施主の垂箔): I.e., hanging screens behind which donors could attend the ceremony.

79 **Once the great assembly has finished its prostrations** (*daishu, raihai, owarite* 大衆、禮拜、をはりて): The first three sentences here represent a Japanese rendering (with minor interpolation) of *Chanyuan qinggui* 禪苑清規, ZZ.111:887b16-17.

the host postion (*shui* 主位): I.e., toward the rear of the hall, facing the entrance.

[72:40]
つぎに首座、僧堂前にいたりて、上間の知事床のみなみのはしにあたりて、雲堂の正面にあたりて、面南にして大衆にむかうてたつ。大衆面北して、首座にむかうて觸禮三拜す。首座、大衆をひきて入堂し、戒臘によりて巡堂、立定す。知事、入堂し、聖僧前にて大展禮三拜しておく。つぎに首座前にて觸禮三拜す、大衆答拜す。知事、巡堂一帀していで、くらいによりて叉手してたつ。

"Next, the head seat, going in front of the saṃgha hall," next to the southern end of the steward's platform to the right of the entrance, at the front of the cloud hall, stands "facing south" across from the great assembly.[80] "The great assembly, facing north, makes three abbreviated prostrations" to the head seat. The head seat, leading the members of the great assembly, enters the hall; "in order of ordination seniority, they circumambulate the hall and stand at their assigned places. The stewards enter the hall, make three prostrations with sitting cloth fully spread before the Sacred Monk, then rise. Next, they make three abbreviated prostrations before the head seat; the great assembly makes prostrations in reply." The stewards "circumambulate the hall once and exit," standing with hands folded at their places.

[72:41] {2:231}
住持人入堂、聖僧前にして燒香、大展三拜起。このとき、小師於聖僧後避立。法眷随大衆。つぎに住持人、於首座觸禮三拜。いはく、住持人、ただくらいによりてたち、面西にて觸禮す。首座・大衆、答拜、さきのごとし。

"The abbot enters the hall, burns incense" in front of the Sacred Monk, "makes three prostrations with sitting cloth fully spread, then rises.[81] During this time, *the disciples stand apart, behind the Sacred Monk; dharma relatives stay with the great assembly.*" Next, "*the abbot makes three abbreviated prostrations to the head seat.*" That is, the abbot, simply standing in his place, faces west and makes the abbreviated prostrations. "The prostrations in reply" by the head seat and great assembly are "as before."

80 **"Next, the head seat, going in front of the saṃgha hall"** (*tsugi ni shuso, sōdō zen ni itarite* つぎに首座、僧堂前にいたりて): This paragraph mixes Japanese translation of the *Chanyuan qinggui* 禪苑清規 (ZZ.111:887b18-888a2), given here inside quotation marks, with Dōgen's interpolations.

81 **"The abbot enters the hall"** (*jūjinin nyūdō* 住持人入堂): Again, the paragraph mixes direct quotation and Japanese translation of the *Chanyuan qinggui* 禪苑清規 (ZZ.111:888a2-4), given here inside quotation marks, with Dōgen's interpolations.

[72:42]

住持人、巡堂していづ。首座、前門の南頰よりいでて、住持人をおくる。住持人出堂ののち、首座已下、對禮三拜していはく、此際、幸同安居、恐三業不善、且望慈悲。この拜は、展坐具拜、三拜なり。かくのごとくして、首座・書記・藏主等、おのおのその寮にかへる。もしそれ衆寮僧は、寮主・寮首座已下、おのおの觸禮三拜す。致語は、堂中の法におなじ。

The abbot "circumambulates the hall" and exits.[82] The head seat, exiting from the south side of the front entrance, sees off the abbot. "After the abbot has exited the hall, *everyone from the head seat on down makes three prostrations to each other* and says, '*On this occasion, we are fortunate to spend the retreat together. We fear our threefold karma might not be good and beg compassion.*'" These prostrations are three prostrations with sitting cloth spread. Having done this, "the head seat," secretary, canon prefect, and the others, all "return to their own quarters. If they are monks of the common quarters, from the quarters chief and quarters head seat on down, each makes three abbreviated prostrations. Their greetings are the same as those in the ceremony in the hall."

[72:43]

住持人、こののち、庫堂よりはじめて巡寮す。次第に大衆相隨送至方丈、大衆乃退。いはゆる住持人、まづ庫堂にいたる。知事と人事しをはりて、住持人いでて巡寮すれば、知事、しりへにあゆめり。知事のつぎに、東廊のほとりにある人、あゆめり。住持人、このとき延壽院にいらず。東廊より西におりて、山門をとほりて巡寮すれば、山門の邊の寮にある人、あゆみつらなる。みなみより西の廊下、および諸寮にめぐる。このとき、西をゆくときは北にむかふ。このときより、安老・勤舊・前資・頤堂・單寮のともがら、淨頭等、あゆみつらなれり。維那・首座等、あゆみつらなる。つぎに衆寮の僧衆、あゆみつらなる。巡寮は、寮の便宜によりてあゆみくははる。これを大衆相送とはいふ。

The abbot, thereafter, makes the rounds of the quarters, beginning with the administrative hall.[83] *In this sequence, the great assembly accompanies him, escorting him as far as the abbot's quarters, whereupon the great assembly withdraws.*

This means that the abbot first goes to the administration hall.[84] After their salutions with the stewards are finished, when the abbot leaves on

82 **The abbot "circumambulates the hall" and exits** (*jūjinin, jundō shite izu* 住持人、巡堂していづ): Again, the paragraph mixes direct quotation and Japanese translation of the *Chanyuan qinggui* 禪苑清規 (ZZ.111:888a4-6), given here inside quotation marks, with Dōgen's interpolations.

83 **The abbot, thereafter, makes the rounds of the quarters** (*jūjinin, kono nochi, kudō yori hajimete junryō su* 住持人、こののち、庫堂よりはじめて巡寮す): A Japanese translation of *Chanyuan qinggui* 禪苑清規, ZZ.111:888a7-8.

84 **This means that the abbot first goes to the administration hall** (*iwayuru jūjinin, mazu kudō ni itaru* いはゆる住持人、まづ庫堂にいたる): From here, Dōgen departs

their rounds of the quarters, the stewards walk behind them. Following the stewards, walk those who are located along the east corridor. The abbot does not enter the life-prolonging cloister at this time.[85] They proceed on their rounds, descending west from the east corridor and passing the mountain gate, where those in quarters near the mountain gate fall into the line.[86] From the south, they circle through the west corridor and the various quarters there. At this point, when they are going up the west side, they are heading north. From here, those in [quarters for] elderly practitioners, retired senior officers and retired junior officers, the elderly care hall, and individual quarters, as well as the toilet manager, and so on, fall into the line. The rector, head seat, and the others, fall in. Next, the monks of the common quarters fall in. The rounds of the quarters is joined according to the convenience of the quarters. This is what is meant by "escorted by the great assembly."

[72:44] {2:232}
かくのごとくして、方丈の西階よりのぼりて、住持人は、方丈の正面のもやの住持人のくらいによりて、面南にて叉手してたつ。大衆は、知事已下、みな面北にて住持人を問訊す。この問訊、ことにふかかるべし。住持人、答問訊あり。大衆、退す。

In this way, the abbot, having climbed the west stairs of the abbot's quarters, stands at the abbot's place in the main room in front of the abbot's quarters, with folded hands, facing south. The great assembly, from the stewards on down, all face north and bow with joined palms. This bow should be especially deep. The abbot makes a bow with joined palms in reply. The great assembly withdraws.

[72:45]
先師は、方丈に大衆をひかず、法堂にいたりて、法座の堦前にして面南、叉手してたつ。大衆、問訊して退す、これ古往の儀なり。

My former master did not lead the great assembly to the abbot's quarters but went to the dharma hall, where he stood with folded hands, facing south in front of the stairs to the dharma seat. The great assembly bowed with joined palms and withdrew. This is a rite from ages past.

---

from the *Chanyuan qinggui* to provide his own comments. He will return briefly to his Chinese source in section 46, below.

85 **the life-prolonging cloister** (*enju in* 延壽院): I.e., the infirmary; also called the "nirvāṇa cloister" (*nehan in* 涅槃院) because it served as a hospice for dying monks.

86 **mountain gate** (*sanmon* 山門): I.e., the main gate of the monastery, located at the center of the south corridor.

[72:46]
しかうしてのち、衆僧、おのおのこころにしたがひて人事す。人事とは、あひ禮拜するなり。たとへば、おなじ鄉間のともがら、あるいは照堂、あるひは廊下の便宜のところにして、幾十人もあひ拜して、同安居の理致を賀す。しかあれども、致語は、堂中の法になずらふ、人にしたがひて今案のことばも存す。あるいは小師をひきいたる本師あり、これ小師かならず本師を拜すべし、九拜をもちいる。法眷の、住持人を拜する、兩展三拜なり、あるいはただ大展三拜す。法眷の、ともに衆にあるは、拜、おなじかるべし。師叔・師伯、またかならず拜あり。隣單・隣肩、みな拜す、相識・道舊ともに拜あり。單寮にあるともがらと、首座・書記・藏主・知客・浴主等と、到寮拜賀すべし。單寮にあるともがらと、都寺・監寺・維那・典座・直歳・西堂・尼師・道士等とも、到寮、到位して拜賀すべし。到寮せんとするに、人しげくて入寮門にひまをえざれば、牓をかきてその寮門におす。その牓は、ひろさ一寸餘、ながさ二寸ばかりなる白紙にかくなり。かく式は、

"Thereafter, the monks of the assembly make salutations as they please."[87] "Salutations" refers to paying obeisance to each other. For example, those from the same home district, even some tens of people, in the illuminated hall or a convenient place in a corridor, may make prostrations to each other, expressing felicitations on their spending the retreat together.[88] Even in this case, the greetings are patterned after the ceremonies in the hall, though there are also extemporaneous words according to the individual. There may be masters who have brought along disciples; these disciples should always make prostrations to their masters, using nine prostrations. When dharma relatives make prostrations to the abbot, it is two spreadings and three prostrations or just three prostrations with sitting cloth fully spread; when dharma relatives are together with the assembly, their prostrations should be the same.[89] There are always prostrations for one's master's younger dharma brothers and older dharma brothers. Neighbors on the platform and those in adjacent positions all make prostrations; there are prostrations for all acquaintances and old associates. Those in individual quarters, and the head seat, secretary, canon prefect, guest prefect, bath manager, and the like, must be visited in their quarters and given congratulatory prostrations;

---

87 **"Thereafter, the monks of the assembly make salutations as they please"** (*shikōshite nochi, shusō, onoono kokoro ni shitagaite ninji su* しかうしてのち、衆僧、おのおのこころにしたがひて人事す): A Japanese translation of *Chanyuan qinggui* 禪苑清規, ZZ.111:888a8.

88 **illuminated hall** (*shōdō* 照堂): A covered corridor behind the saṃgha hall, so called because it was provided with skylights, windows, or open sides to let in light.

89 **when dharma relatives are together with the assembly, their prostrations should be the same** (*hakken no, tomo ni shu ni aru wa, hai, onajikaru beshi* 法眷の、ともに衆にあるは、拜、おなじかるべし): Could be understood, "the same as above" or "the same as everyone else."

those in individual quarters, and the prior, comptroller, rector, cook, labor steward, west halls, nuns, Daoists, and the like, must also be visited in the quarters or visited in their places and given congratulatory prostrations. Should one seek to visit some quarter where the entrance way is so crowded with people that there is no space, a notice is written and stuck on the quarters entrance. The notice is written on white paper about one inch wide and two inches long. The form for writing it:

[72:47] {2:233}

巣雲 懐昭等
　拜賀
又ノ式
某甲
　禮賀
又ハ式
某寮某甲
　拜賀
又ノ式
　某甲拜
　賀
又ノ式
　某甲
　禮賀
又ノ式
　某甲
　禮拜

Sōun, Eshō, et al.
Congratulatory Prostrations
Alternative form:
(Name)
Obeisance
Alternative form:
(Name) of (name) quarters
Congratulatory Prostrations
Alternative form:
Prostrations by (Name)
Congratulations
Alternative form:
(Name)
Congratulatory Obeisance

Alternative form:
(Name)
Prostrations

[72:48]
かくしき、おほけれど、大旨かくのごとし。しかあれば、門側には、この牓あまたみゆるなり。門側には、左邊におさず、門の右におすなり。この牓は、齋罷に、本寮主、をさめとる。今日は、大小諸堂・諸寮、みな門簾をあげたり。

There are many forms for writing, but this is the general idea. Thus, many of these notices can be seen on the side of doorways. With regard to the side of doorways, they are attached to the right side of the doorway, not to the left side. These notices are taken down by the chief of the quarter after the midday meal. On this day, all the halls and quarters, large and small, have their doorway screens open.

[72:49] {2:234}
堂頭・庫司・首座、次第に煎點といふことあり。しかあれども、遠島・深山のあひだには、省略すべし、ただこれ禮數なり。退院の長老、および立僧の首座、おのおの本寮につきて、知事・頭首のために特爲煎點するなり。

There is a practice whereby, "in order, the head of hall, administrators, and head seat serve tea refreshments."[90] However, deep in the mountains on a remote island, we should omit them; they are just formalities.[91] "Elders retired from an abbacy, as well as additional head seats, hold special tea refreshments in their own quarters for the stewards and prefects."[92]

[72:50]
かくのごとく結夏してより、功夫辦道するなり。衆行を辦肯せりといへども、いまだ夏安居せざるは、佛祖の兒孫にあらず、また佛祖にあらず。孤獨園、靈鷲山、みな安居によりて現成せり。安居の道場、これ佛祖の心印なり、諸佛の住世なり。

After thus binding the retreat, we pursue the way with concentrated effort. While they may have confirmed many practices, those who have

---

90 **"in order, the head of hall, administrators, and head seat serve tea refreshments"** (*dōchō kusu shuso shidai ni senten* 堂頭・庫司・首座・次第に煎點): A Japanese translation of *Chanyuan qinggui* 禪苑清規, ZZ.111:888a9.

91 **deep in the mountains on a remote island** (*entō shinzan* 遠島深山): I.e., at our Daibutsuji 大佛寺, deep in the mountains of Japan.

92 **"Elders retired from an abbacy"** (*taiin no chōrō, oyobi rissō no shuso* 退院の長老、および立僧の首座): A Japanese translation of *Chanyuan qinggui* 禪苑清規, ZZ.111:888a12-13. "Additional head seats" (*rissō shuso* 立僧首座) refers to learned monks asked to lecture to the assembly.

yet to participate in a summer retreat are not the descendants of the buddhas and ancestors, are not buddhas and ancestors. Both the Garden of Anāthapiṇḍada and Vulture Peak appeared due to retreats.[93] The practice place of the retreat — this is the mind seal of the buddhas and ancestors, the presence in the world of the buddhas.

[72:51]

解夏。七月十三日、衆寮煎點諷經、またその月の寮主、これをつとむ。

Unbinding the retreat.[94]

On the thirteenth day of the seventh month, a tea refreshment and sūtra chanting in the common quarters.[95] Again, it is the quarters chief of that month who serves.

[72:52]

十四日晩念誦、來日陞堂・人事・巡寮・煎點、竝同結夏。唯牓狀詞語、不同而已。庫司湯牓云、庫司今晩、就雲堂煎點、特爲首座・大衆、聊表解制之儀、伏冀、衆慈同垂光降。庫司比丘某甲白。土地堂念誦詞云、切以金風扇野、白帝司方。當覺皇解制之時、是法歲周圓之日。九旬無難、一衆咸安。誦持諸佛洪名、仰報合堂眞宰、仰憑大衆念。

On the evening of the fourteenth day, recitations.[96] *On the following day, the mountain seat presentation, salutations, rounds of the quarters, and tea refreshment are all the same as for the binding of the retreat. Only the wording of the notices is not the same. The administrators' tea invitation says:*[97]

The administrators, this evening, shall serve a tea refreshment in the cloud hall, especially for the head seat and great assembly, as a rite to mark the unbinding of the retreat. We humbly wish that members

93 **the Garden of Anāthapiṇḍada and Vulture Peak** (*Kodokuon, Ryōjusen* 孤獨園、靈鷲山): Two spots where Buddha Śākyamuni is often depicted as residing. The name *Kodokuon* 孤獨園 (literally, "Orphan Park") represents an abbreviated translation of the name Anāthapiṇḍada ("donor to orphans"), the owner of the property.

94 **Unbinding the retreat** (*kaige* 解夏): The title of the section of the *Chanyuan qinggui* 禪苑清規 (ZZ.111:888a14), immediately following the section on binding the retreat that Dōgen has just finished discussing.

95 **On the thirteenth day of the seventh month, a tea refreshment and sūtra chanting in the common quarters** (*shichi gatsu jūsan nichi, shuryō senten fugin* 七月十三日、衆寮煎點諷經): Given in Chinese, as if citing a source, but this ceremony does not occur in the *Chanyuan qinggui* 禪苑清規.

96 **On the evening of the fourteenth day, recitations** (*jūshi nichi ban nenju* 十四日晩念誦): This entire section is a quotation of the Chinese (with slight variation) of *Chanyuan qinggui* 禪苑清規, ZZ.111:888a15-18.

97 **The administrators' tea invitation says** (*kusu tō bō un* 庫司湯牓云): Dōgen supplies the complete wording here, where the *Chanyuan qinggui* (ZZ.111:888a16-17) has abbreviated it.

of the assembly all kindly favor us with their presence. Announced by Administration Hall bhikṣu (Names).

The phrasing for the recitation at the local deities hall says,

We are keenly aware:
A golden breeze fans the plains;
The white emperor rules his quarter.
At the time when the King of Awakening's rule is unbound,
On the day that the dharma year's cycle is full,
Ninety days without hardships;
The entire assembly safe and sound.
Reciting the great names of the buddhas,
We repay the true rulers of all the halls.
We respectfully invite the great assembly to recite.

[72:53] {2:235}

これよりのちは、結夏の念誦におなじ。

What follows is the same as the recitation at binding the retreat.[98]

[72:54]

陞堂罷、知事等謝詞。いはく、伏喜法歳周圓、無諸難事、此蓋和尚法力廕林、下情無任感激之至。

Following the mountain seat presentation, the steward's words of thanks:[99]

We are humbly delighted that the dharma year has come full cycle, with no difficulties. Surely this is the sheltering grove of Your Reverence's dharma power.[100] *We are overcome with extreme gratitude.*

[72:55]

住持人謝詞。いはく、此者法歳周圓、皆謝某＜首座・鑑寺＞人等法力相資、不任感激之至。

The abbot's words of thanks:[101]

---

98 **What follows is the same as the recitation at binding the retreat** (*kore yori nochi wa, ketsuge no nenju ni onaji* これよりのちは、結夏の念誦におなじ): Japanese translation of the note at *Chanyuan qinggui* 禪苑清規, ZZ.111:888a18.

99 **The steward's words of thanks** (*chiji tō jaji* 知事等謝詞): From *Chanyuan qinggui* 禪苑清規, ZZ.111:888b1.

100 **the sheltering grove** (*onrin* 廕林): I.e., protection. The *Chanyuan qinggui* 禪苑清規 has here "sheltering eves" (*onbi* 廕庇).

101 **The abbot's words of thanks** (*jūjinin jashi* 住持人謝詞): From *Chanyuan qinggui* 禪苑清規, ZZ.111:888b2.

Here, the dharma year has come full cycle. We are all thankful for the assistance of the dharma power of (head seat, comptroller) (Names). We are overcome with extreme gratitude.

[72:56]
堂中首座已下・寮中寮主已下謝詞。いはく、九夏相依、三業不善、惱亂大衆、伏望慈悲。

In the hall, from the head seat on down, and in the quarters, from the quarters chief on down, words of thanks:[102]

Relying on each other for the ninety-day retreat, if our threefold karma has not been good and has vexed the great assembly, we beg compassion.[103]

[72:57]
知事・頭首告云、衆中兄弟行脚、須俟茶湯罷、方可隨意。(如有緊急緣事不在此限。)

The stewards and prefects make announcements, saying, "Brethren in the assembly departing on pilgrimage should wait until after the tea, at which time they may do as they wish."[104] *(If there are urgent circumstances, they do not fall under this restriction.)*

* * * * *

[72:58]
この儀は、これ威音空王の前際後際よりも頂𩕳量なり。佛祖のおもくすること、ただこれのみなり。外道・天魔の、いまだ惑亂せざる、ただこれのみなり。三國のあひだ、佛祖の兒孫たるもの、いまだひとりもこれをおこなはざるなし。外道は、いまだまなびず。佛祖一大事の本懷なるがゆえに、得道のあしたより涅槃のゆふべにいたるまで、開演するところ、ただ安居の宗旨のみなり。西天の五部の僧衆ことなれども、おなじく九夏安居を護持して、かならず修證す。震旦の九宗の僧衆、ひとりも破夏せず。生前にすべて九夏安居せざらんをば、佛弟子・比丘僧と稱すべからず。ただ因地に修習するのみにあらず、果位の修證なり。大覺世尊、すでに一代のあひだ、一夏も欠如なく修證しましませり。しるべし、果上の佛證なりといふこと。

102 **In the hall** (*dōchū* 堂中): From *Chanyuan qinggui* 禪苑清規, ZZ.111:888b2-3.

103 **threefold karma** (*sangō* 三業): I.e., acts of body, speech, and mind.

104 **The stewards and prefects make announcements** (*chiji chōshu koku* 知事・頭首告): From *Chanyuan qinggui* 禪苑清規, ZZ.111:888b3-4. The final parenthetical qualification is in the original; it is not clear whether it is part of the announcement itself. These lines end the section on unbinding the retreat in the *Chanyuan qinggui*.

These rites are the dimensions of the crown of the head, greater than the times before and after Majestic Voice, King of Emptiness.[105] What the buddhas and ancestors take seriously is nothing but these; what the other paths and the Deva Māra have never confused and disrupted is nothing but these. Throughout the three countries, there is not a single person among those who are the descendants of the buddhas and ancestors who has ever failed to carry these out; the other paths have never learned them.[106] Because they are the original intention of "the one great matter" of the buddhas and ancestors, from the morning of their gaining the way to the evening of their nirvāṇa, what they proclaim is nothing but the essential point of the retreat.[107] The saṃghas of the five denominations in Sindh in the West may have differed, but they equally upheld, and always practiced and verified, the ninety-day summer retreat; not one of the saṃghas of the nine schools in Cīnasthāna rejected the summer retreat.[108] Those who never in their lives practice the ninety-day summer retreat should not be called disciples of the Buddha or members of the bhikṣu saṃgha. It is practiced and learned not only at the stage of cause; it is the practice and verification of the level of effect.[109] The Greatly Awakened World-Honored One, throughout his entire career, practiced

---

105 **the dimensions of the crown of the head, greater than the times before and after Majestic Voice, King of Emptiness** (*kore Ion Kūō no zensai gosai yori mo chōnei ryō* これ威音空王の前際後際よりも頂顊量): An unusual image, probably meaning something like, "the true dimensions of the summer retreat are greater than the entire universe." "Crown of the head" (*chōnei* 頂顊) occurs often in Dōgen's writing in the sense "what something really is"; see Supplementary Notes, s.v. "Crown of the head." "Before and after Majestic Voice" alludes to a passage in the *Liuzu danjing* 六祖壇經, in which the necessity of having one's awakening approved by a Zen master is said to be different "before" and "after." Dōgen's apparent identification of the buddha "King Majestic Voice" with the buddha "King of Emptiness" is idiosyncratic; see Supplementary Notes s.v. "Before King Majestic Voice" and "Before King of Emptiness."

106 **the three countries** (*sangoku* 三國): I.e., India, China, and Japan.

107 **"the one great matter"** (*ichi daiji* 一大事): See Note 29, above.

108 **the five denominations in Sindh in the West** (*Saiten no gobu* 西天の五部): Reference to the tradition that, some one hundred years after the time of Buddha Śākyamuni, there arose among the followers of Upagupta, separate vinaya collections in the five schools of Dharmaguptaka, Sarvāstivāda, Mahīśāsaka, Kāśyapīya, and Vātsīputrīya (sometimes replaced by Mahāsāṃghika).

the nine schools in Cīnasthāna (*Shintan no kushū* 震旦の九宗): Nine traditions into which the Japanese of Dōgen's day classified Chinese Buddhism: (1) Kośa (*Kusha* 俱舍), (2) Satyasiddhi (*Jōjitsu* 成實), (3) Vinaya (*Ritsu* 律), (4) Dharma Marks (*Hossō* 法相), (5) Three Treatises (*Sanron* 三論), (6) Flower Garland (*Kegon* 華嚴), (7) Tiantai (*Tendai* 天台), (8) Mantra (*Shingon* 眞言), and (9) Chan (*Zen* 禪); Pure Land (*Jōdo* 淨土) was sometimes added to this list.

109 **the stage of cause** (*inji* 因地); **the level of effect** (*kai* 果位): I.e., the path leading to bodhi and the attainment of bodhi.

and verified it without missing a single retreat. We should realize that it is the Buddha's verification of the effect.[110]

[72:59] {2:236}

しかあるを、九夏安居は修證せざれども、われは佛祖の兒孫なるべし、といふはわらふべし、わらふにたらざるおろかなるものなり。かくのごとくいはんともがらのことばをば、きくべからず、共語すべからず、同坐すべからず、ひとつみちをあゆむべからず。佛法には、梵壇の法をもて惡人を治するがゆえに。

Those who say, nevertheless, "Though I don't practice and verify the ninety-day summer retreat, I can be a descendant of the buddhas and ancestors," are laughable, are so stupid they are not worth laughing at. We should not listen to the words of those who talk like this. We should not converse with them; we should not sit with them; we should not walk the same path with them. For, in the buddha dharma, evildoers are dealt with by the practice of *brahmadaṇḍa*.[111]

[72:60]

ただまさに九夏安居、これ佛祖と會取すべし、保任すべし。その正傳しきたれること、七佛より摩訶迦葉におよぶ。西天二十八祖、嫡嫡正傳せり。第二十八祖みづから震旦にいでて、二祖大祖正宗普覺大師をして正傳せしむ。二祖よりこのかた、嫡嫡正傳して、而今に正傳せり。震旦にいりて、まのあたり佛祖の會下にして正傳し、日本國に正傳す。すでに正傳せる會にして、九旬坐夏しつれば、すでに夏法を正傳するなり。この人と共住して安居せんは、まことの安居なるべし。まさしく佛在世の安居より、嫡嫡面授しきたれるがゆえに、佛面祖面、まのあたり正傳しきたれり、佛祖身心、したしく證契しきたれり。かるがゆえにいふ、安居をみるは、佛をみるなり、安居を證するは、佛を證するなり、安居を行ずるは、佛を行ずるなり、安居をきくは、佛をきくなり、安居をならふは、佛を學するなり。

We should understand, we should maintain, the ninety-day summer retreat as itself the buddhas and ancestors. Its direct transmission reached Mahākāśyapa from the seven buddhas. The twenty-eight ancestors of Sindh in the West transmitted it directly from successor to successor; the Twenty-eighth Ancestor himself, departing for Cīnasthāna, caused the Second Ancestor, the Eminent Ancestor Zhengzong, Great Master Pujue, to receive the direct transmission. Ever since the Second Ancestor, directly transmitted by successor after successor, it has been directly transmitted to the present.

---

110 **the Buddha's verification of the effect** (*kajō no busshō* 果上の佛證): I.e., what the Buddha realized as a buddha.

111 **the practice of *brahmadaṇḍa*** (*bondan no hō* 梵壇の法): The silent treatment; the punishment of exclusion by silence (*mokuhin* 默擯). Dōgen uses the transliteration of the Sanskrit (meaning "brahma staff").

Entering Cīnasthāna, I personally received the direct transmission in an assembly of the buddhas and ancestors and am directly transmitting it to the Land of Japan. Since you have kept a ninety-day summer retreat in an assembly where it has been directly transmitted, we have directly transmitted the dharma of the retreat. When you keep a retreat with this person, it is an authentic retreat. Because it has truly been conferred face-to-face by successor after successor since the retreats during the lifetime of the Buddha, the faces of the buddhas and faces of the ancestors have been directly transmitted firsthand, and the bodies and minds of the buddhas and ancestors have been intimately verified. For this reason, we say that to see the retreat is to see the Buddha; to verify the retreat is to verify the Buddha; to practice the retreat is to practice the Buddha; to hear of the retreat is to hear the Buddha; to study the retreat is to study the Buddha.

[72:61] {2:237}

おほよそ九旬安居を、諸佛諸祖いまだ違越しましまさざる法なり。しかあればすなはち、人王・釋王・梵王等、比丘僧となりて、たとひ一夏なりといふとも、安居すべし、それ見佛ならん。人衆・天衆・龍衆、たとひ一九旬なりとも、比丘・比丘尼となりて安居すべし、すなはち見佛ならん。佛祖の會にまじはりて、九旬安居しきたれるは、見佛來なり。われらさいはひに、いま露命のおちざるさきに、あるいは天上にもあれ、あるいは人間にもあれ、すでに一夏安居するは、佛祖の皮肉骨髓をもて、みづからが皮肉骨髓に換却せられぬるものなり。佛祖きたりてわれらを安居するがゆえに、面面人人の、安居を行ずるは、安居の、人人を行ずるなり。恁麼なるがゆえに、安居あるを千佛萬祖といふのみなり。ゆえいかんとなれば、安居、これ佛祖の皮肉骨髓・心識・身體なり。頂𩕳・眼睛なり、拳頭・鼻孔なり、圓相・佛性なり、拂子・拄杖なり、竹篦・蒲團なり。安居は、あたらしきをつくりいだすにあらざれども、ふるきをさらにもちいるにはあらざるなり。

In sum, the ninety-day retreat is a dharma from which the buddhas and the ancestors have never deviated. This being the case, human kings, King Śakra, King Brahmā, and the like, becoming members of the bhikṣu saṃgha, if only for one summer, should keep the retreat; that would be seeing the Buddha. Humans, devas, and dragons, if only for one ninety-day period, should become bhikṣu or *bhikṣuṇī* and keep the retreat; this in itself would be seeing the Buddha. To have joined an assembly of the buddhas and ancestors and kept the ninety-day retreat is to have seen the Buddha. Fortunately, now, before our dewdrop lives have been lost, those of us who have already kept a summer retreat, whether in the heavens above or among humans, have had our own skin, flesh, bones, and marrow exchanged for the skin, flesh, bones, and marrow of the buddhas and ancestors. Because the buddhas and ancestors come and keep the retreat through us, each and every person's practice of the retreat is the retreat's practice of each person.[112] This being so, those with a retreat can only be called "a thousand buddhas and ten thousand ancestors."[113] Why is this? The retreat is the skin, flesh, bones, and marrow, the mind and consciousness, the physical body, of the buddhas and ancestors; it is their crown of the head and eyes, it is their fist and nose; it is their round form and buddha nature; it is their whisk and staff; it is their bamboo staff and reed cushion.[114] Though the retreat is not the creating of something new, it is not the re-implementing of something old.

* * * * *

[72:62]

世尊告圓覺菩薩、及諸大衆、一切衆生言、若經夏首三月安居、當爲清淨菩薩止住。心離聲聞不假徒衆。至安居日、即於佛前作如是言、我比丘・比丘尼・優婆塞・優婆夷、某甲、踞菩薩乘、修寂滅行、同入清淨實相住持、以大圓覺爲我伽藍、心身安居。平等性智、涅槃自性、無繫屬故。今我敬請、不依聲聞、當與十方如來及大菩薩三月安居。爲修菩薩無上妙覺大因緣故、不繫徒衆。善男子、此名菩薩示現安居。

The World-Honored One addressed Bodhisattva Complete Awakening, along with various great assemblies and all living beings, saying,[115]

> *If you pass the three-month retreat at the start of summer, you should stay with pure bodhisattvas, with your mind apart from the śrāvakas, not relying on the community of followers. When the day of the retreat arrives, speak the following words before the Buddha:*
>
> > *I, the bhikṣu or bhikṣuṇī or upāsaka or upāsikā (Name), seated on the bodhisattva vehicle, cultivate the practice of peaceful extinction, entering purity together with others and abiding in the mark of reality. Taking great complete awakening as my monastery, mind and body keep the retreat; for the*

112 **the buddhas and ancestors come and keep the retreat through us** (*busso kitarite warera o ango suru* 佛祖きたりてわれらを安居する): Attempt to render an odd locution, in which "we" (*warera* われら) is the object of the verb "to retreat" (*ango suru* 安居する); perhaps intended to convey the image of the buddhas and ancestors "residing peacefully" (*ango* 安居) in us.

113 **"a thousand buddhas and ten thousand ancestors"** (*senbutsu manso* 千佛萬祖): A fixed expression suggesting buddhas and ancestors everywhere, or in everyone.

114 **their round form and buddha nature** (*ensō busshō* 圓相佛性): The term *ensō* 圓相 could be taken here as the "circular shape" often drawn by the Chan master as a sign of perfection; but its combination with "buddha nature" (*busshō* 佛性) suggests the "full moon form" (*engetsusō* 圓月相) used to represent the buddha nature (see "Shōbōgenzō busshō" 正法眼藏佛性).

115 **The World-Honored One** (*Seson* 世尊): From the *Yuanjue jing* 圓覺經, T.842.17:921a19-28.

> *cognition of essential identity and the nature of nirvāṇa are without bonds.*[116] *Now, I respectifully request not to follow the śrāvakas but to keep the three-month retreat together with the tathāgatas of the ten directions and the great bodhisattvas. In order to practice the great causes and conditions of the unsurpassed wondrous awakening of the bodhisattva, I am not bound to the community of followers.*
>
> *Good son, this is called the bodhisattva's manifestation of the retreat.*

[72:63] {2:238}

しかあればすなはち、比丘・比丘尼・優婆塞・優婆夷等、かならず安居三月にいたるごとには、十方如來、および大菩薩とともに、無上妙覺大因縁を修するなり。しるべし、優婆塞・優婆夷も安居すべきなり。この安居のところは、大圓覺なり。しかあればすなはち、鷲峰山・孤獨園、おなじく如來の大圓覺伽藍なり。十方如來及大菩薩、ともに安居三月の修行あること、世尊のをしへを聽受すべし。

Thus, whenever they reach the three months of retreat, "bhikṣus, *bhikṣuṇīs*, *upāsakas*, and *upāsikās*" "practice the great causes and conditions of the unsurpassed wondrous awakening" "together with tathāgatas of the ten directions and the great bodhisattvas." We should recognize that *upāsakas* and *upāsikās* should also keep the retreat. The location of this retreat is "great complete awakening"; so Vulture Peak and the Garden of Anāthapiṇḍada are similarly "monasteries" of "great complete awakening." We should heed the World-Honored One's teaching that the "tathāgatas of the ten directions and the great bodhisattvas" all practice during the three months of the retreat.

[72:64]

世尊、於一處九旬安居。至自恣日、文殊倐來在會。迦葉問文殊、今夏何處安居。文殊云、今夏在三處安居。迦葉於是集衆、白槌欲擯文殊。纔擧犍稚、即見無量佛刹顯現、一一佛所有一一文殊、有一一迦葉、擧槌欲擯文殊。世尊、於是告迦葉云、汝今欲擯阿那箇文殊。于時迦葉茫然。

The World-Honored One spent the ninety-day retreat in one place.[117] *When the day of unburdening oneself arrived, Mañjuśrī came into the*

---

116 **mind and body keep the retreat** (*shinjin ango* 心身安居): Or, perhaps, "mind and body reside in peace." The clause following could be read with the next sentence: "Because the cognition of essential identity and the nature of nirvāṇa are without bonds, now, I respectfully request . . . ."

117 **The World-Honored One** (*Seson* 世尊): Quoting the *Yuanwu Foguo chanshi yulu* 圓悟佛果禪師語錄, which recounts the story twice (at T.1997.47:792a11-16, and T.1997.47:805a10-15). The original source is the *Da fangguang baoqie jing* 大方廣寶篋經 (T.462.14:474a17-b14).

assembly.[118] *Kāśyapa asked Mañjuśrī, "Where did you keep the retreat this summer?"*

Mañjuśrī said, "I kept the retreat in three places this summer."[119]

Kāśyapa thereupon gathered the assembly and announced with a blow of the mallet that he wished to expel Mañjuśrī. No sooner had he raised the ghaṇṭa *mallet than he saw incalculable buddha* kṣetras *appear, and in each place where there was a buddha, there was a Mañjuśrī, and there was a Kāśyapa raising the mallet and wishing to expel Mañjuśrī.*[120] *The Word-Honored One addressed Kāśyapa, saying, "Now, which Mañjuśrī did you wish to expel?"*

At this point, Kāśyapa was at a loss.[121]

[72:65] {2:239}

圜悟禪師拈古云、鐘不擊不響、鼓不打不鳴。迦葉既把定要津、文殊乃十方坐斷。當時好一場佛事、可惜放過一著。待釋迦老子道欲擯阿那箇文殊、便與擊一槌看、他作什麼合殺。

Chan Master Yuanwu's comment on this case says:[122]

If the bell is not struck, it does not ring;
If the drum is not beat, it does not sound.
Kāśyapa had seized the key port;
So Mañjuśrī occupied the ten directions.
To that point, a splendid Buddhist rite;
A pity they let one move slip by.[123]

118 **the day of unburdening oneself** (*jishi nichi* 自恣日): The last day of the summer retreat (S. *pravaraṇa*), on which participants may express their thoughts and repent of their transgressions.

119 **"I kept the retreat in three places this summer"** (*konge zai sansho ango* 今夏在三處安居): Moving about during the summer retreat is, of course, an infraction. In the original sūtra story (*Da fangguang baoqie jing* 大方廣寶篋經, T.462.14:474a22-24), Mañjuśrī reports that he spent one month in the palace of the queen of Śrāvastī, the wife of king Prasenajit; one month in the young men's study hall; and one month in a house of prostitutes.

120 ***ghaṇṭa* mallet** (*kensui* 犍稚): Also written 犍槌; a gong, bell, or other percussion instrument.

121 **At this point, Kāśyapa was at a loss** (*uji Kashō bōzen* 于時迦葉茫然): This line does not occur in the version ending at T.1997.47:805a15. The original sūtra story has the Buddha at this point explain to Kāśyapa that Mañjuśrī spent the summer retreat leading five hundred courtesans of the palace, five hundred young men, and five hundred prostitutes to the stage of non-regression on the bodhisattva path.

122 **Chan Master Yuanwu** (*Engo zenji* 圜悟禪師): I.e., Yuanwu Keqin 圜悟克勤 (1063–1135). His comment occurs at *Yuanwu Foguo chanshi yulu* 圓悟佛果禪師語錄, T.1997.47:792a16-20.

123 **To that point, a splendid Buddhist rite; A pity they let one move slip by** (*tōji*

Wait till old man Śākya says, "Which Mañjuśrī did you wish to expel?" Then try striking with the mallet. How will he end it?

[72:66]

圜悟禪師頌古云、大象不遊兎徑、燕雀安知鴻鵠、據令宛若成風、破的渾如嚙鏃、遍界是文殊、遍界是迦葉、相對各儼然。擧椎何處罰。好一劄、金色曾落却。

Chan Master Yuanwu's verse on this case says:[124]

Great elephants do not follow rabbit tracks;
How could swallows and sparrows know the swan?[125]
He keeps the command, just like "raising a breeze";
He hits the mark, like "biting the arrowhead."[126]
In the realms everywhere, it is Mañjuśrī;
In the realms everywhere, it is Kāśyapa.
Facing each other, they are each so serious;
He raises the mallet; where is the punishment?
One good jab, and the golden dhūta has already dropped it.[127]

[72:67] {2:240}

しかあればすなはち、世尊一處安居、文殊三處安居なりといへども、いまだ不安居あらず。もし不安居は、佛及菩薩にあらず。佛祖の兒孫なるもの、安居せざるはなし、安居せんは、佛祖の兒孫としるべし。安居するは、佛祖の身心なり、佛祖の眼睛なり、佛祖の命根なり。安居せざらんは、佛祖の兒孫にあらず、佛祖にあらざるなり。いま泥木・素金・七寶の佛菩薩、みなともに安居三月の夏坐おこなはるべし。これすなはち、住持

---

kō ichijō butsuji, kaseki hōka itchaku 當時好一場佛事、可惜放過一著): I.e., a good story, but Kāśyapa failed to make the next move (by striking with the mallet, as Yuanwu suggests).

124 **Chan Master Yuanwu's verse on this case** (*Engo zenji juko* 圜悟禪師頌古): From *Yuanwu Foguo chanshi yulu* 圓悟佛果禪師語錄, T.1997.47:805a16-19.

125 **Great elephants** (*daizō* 大象); **swallows and sparrows** (*enjaku* 燕雀): Often taken as references to Mañjuśrī and Kāśyapa, respectively.

126 **He keeps the command, just like "raising a breeze"** (*kyorei enjaku seifū* 據令宛若成風): Thought to reflect the story in the *Zhuangzi* 莊子 (Xu Wugui 徐無鬼; KR.5c0126.024.13a), in which Carpenter Shi 匠石 "produced a wind" (*jō fū* 成風) by whirling his axe, thereby removing a piece of mud from the nose of the man of Ying without disturbing him. "Keeping the command" (*kyōrei* 據令) here is usually taken to mean obeying the rules of the summer retreat.

He hits the mark, like "biting the arrowhead" (*hateki konnyo ketsuzoku* 破的渾如嚙鏃): Thought to be a reference to the story, in the *Taiping guangji* 太平廣記 (Jiqiao 伎巧, KR3l0118.227.5a), of Du Jun Mo 督君謨, who could catch arrows with his teeth.

127 **One good jab, and the golden *dhūta* has already dropped it** (*kō issatsu, konjiki zuda sō rakukyaku* 好一劄、金色頭陀曾落却): Likely meaning that, as soon as the Buddha challenged him, Kāśyapa ("the golden-hued ascetic") dropped his mallet.

佛法僧寶の故實なり、佛訓なり。おほよそ佛祖の屋裏人、さだめて坐夏安居三月つとむべし。

Thus, though the World-Honored One may have spent the retreat in one place, while Mañjuśrī spent the retreat in three places, they never failed to keep the retreat. Those who fail to keep the retreat are neither buddhas nor bodhisattvas. Among the descendants of the buddhas and ancestors, there are none who fail to keep the retreat; those who do keep the retreat should be recognized as descendants of the buddhas and ancestors. To keep the retreat is the body and mind of the buddhas and ancestors, is the eye of the buddhas and ancestors, is the life source of the buddhas and ancestors. Those who do not keep the retreat are not the descendants of the buddhas and ancestors, are not buddhas and ancestors. The present buddhas and bodhisattvas of clay or wood, silk or gold, or the seven treasures must all be undertaking a summer of sitting for the three months of the retreat.[128] This is the ancient precedent, the buddha instruction, of abiding in the treasures of buddha, dharma, and saṃgha. In sum, residents within the house of the buddhas and ancestors should definitely engage in the three months of sitting in the summer retreat.

正法眼藏安居第七十二
Treasury of the True Dharma Eye
The Retreat
Number 72

[Ryūmonji MS:]

爾時寬元三年乙巳夏安居六月十三日、在越宇大佛寺示衆
Presented to the assembly at Daibutsu Monastery, Etsuu; thirteenth day, sixth month, summer retreat of the junior wood year of the snake, the third year of Kangen [8 July 1245][129]

[Tōunji MS:]

弘安二年夏安居五月二十日、在同國中浜新善光寺書寫之。義雲
Copied this at the new Zenkō Monastery, Nakahama, in the same province; twentieth day, fifth month, summer retreat of the second year of Kōan [30 June 1279]. Giun[130]

---

128 **The present buddhas and bodhisattvas of clay or wood, silk or gold, or the seven treasures** (*ima deiboku sokin shippō no butsu bosatsu* いま泥木・素金・七寶の佛菩薩): Likely referring to the Buddhist icons in the monastery. The glyphs *sokin* 素金 are variously interpreted: as "undyed silk and gold," as "silver and gold," or as "pure gold"; the translation takes *so* 素 as the silk background of painted images.

129 The Tōunji 洞雲寺 MS shares an identical colophon.

130 **Giun** 義雲: Fifth abbot of Eiheiji (1253–1333).

于時文明十二庚子年卯月十二日、於于越州吉祥山永平寺承陽庵書寫之。比丘光周

Copied this in the Jōyō Hermitage, Eihei Monastery, Mount Kichijō, Esshū; twelfth day, month of deutzia blossoms, senior metal year of the rat, the twelfth year of Bunmei [21 May 1480]. Bhikṣu Kōshū[131]

131 **month of deutzia blossoms** (*bōgetsu* 卯月): The fourth lunar month (*uzuki* 卯月). **Bhikṣu Kōshū** (*biku Kōshū* 比丘光周): Fifteenth abbot of Eiheiji (1434–1492?).

Treasury of the True Dharma Eye

Number 73

Reading Other Minds

Tashin tsū

他心通

Reading Other Minds

Tashin tsū

Introduction

According to its colophon, this chapter was composed at Dōgen's Daibutsuji in Echizen during the summer retreat of 1245. It occurs as number 73 in the seventy-five-chapter *Shōbōgenzō* and as number 79 in the ninety-five-chapter Honzan edition (or 80 in the Iwanami and Shūmuchō versions). The origin of the text, however, is complicated by the fact that it repeats material found in a version of the "Shin fukatoku" 心不可得 chapter preserved in the twenty-eight-text *Himitsu Shōbōgenzō* collection, where it is listed as number 4 of fascicle 1. This latter work (number 19 in the Honzan edition of the *Shōbōgenzō* and translated below, in Volume 7, as Supplementary Text 4) is quite similar in its first half to the "Shin fukatoku" chapter appearing as number 8 of the seventy-five-chapter *Shōbōgenzō*, while in its second half introduces the material from our text here; it bears a colophon, similar to that of number 8, dated during the summer retreat of 1241 at Kōshōji.

The "Tashin tsū" deals with a single anecdote in Zen literature, the famous story of the eighth-century Chan master Nanyang Huizhong's 南陽慧忠 test of the mind-reading powers of an Indian monk. Dōgen quotes the story verbatim from the Chinese, along with half a dozen comments on it by Chinese masters; he then proceeds sharply to criticize previous understandings of the story, for assuming that the monk might actually have read the master's mind, and for failing to see that the test was really about the monk's understanding of Buddhism.

正法眼藏第七十三
Treasury of the True Dharma Eye
Number 73
他心通
Reading Other Minds

[73:1] {2:241}

西京光宅寺慧忠國師者、越州諸暨人也。姓冉氏。自受心印、居南陽白崖山黨子谷、四十餘祀、不下山門、道行聞于帝里。唐肅宗上元二年、勅中使孫朝進賫詔徴赴京。待以師禮。勅居千福寺西禪院。及代宗臨御、復迎止光宅精藍十有六載、随機説法。時有西天大耳三藏、到京、云得他心慧眼。帝勅令與國師試驗。三藏才見師便禮拜立于右邊。師問曰、汝得他心通耶。對云、不敢。師曰、汝道、老僧即今在什麼處。三藏云、和尚是一國之師、何得却去西川看競渡。師再問、汝道、老僧即今在什麼處。三藏云、和尚是一國之師、何得却在天津橋上看弄猢猻。師第三問、汝道、老僧即今在什麼處。三藏良久、罔知去處。師叱曰、這野狐精、他心通在什麼處。三藏無對。

National Teacher Huizhong, of the Guangzhai Monastery in the Western Capital, was a native of Zhuji in Yuezhou; his family name was Ran.[1] *After receiving the mind seal, he stayed at Dangzi Valley, Mount Baiya, in Nanyang, where for more than forty years he never descended from his monastery.*[2] *Word of his practice of the way reached the*

---

1 **Reading Other Minds** (*tashin tsū* 他心通): Or "the knowledge of others' thoughts"; S. *para-citta-jñāna*, one of the five or six paranormal knowledges (*jinzū* 神通; S. *abhijñā*). Traditionally held to be available to spiritual adepts, whether Buddhist or otherwise, who have mastered the four levels of dhyāna. While not a prerequisite for nirvāṇa, this knowledge was considered one of the attainments of the perfectly awakened buddhas, and, therefore, its cultivation was a part of the traditional bodhisattva path. See Supplementary Notes, s.v. "Spiritual powers."

National Teacher Huizhong (*Echū kokushi* 慧忠國師): I.e., Nanyang Huizhong 南陽慧忠 (d. 775), disciple of the Sixth Ancestor. The Guangzhaisi 光宅寺, established 677, was one of the great monastic centers of Chang'an during the Tang; Zhuji 諸暨 was in the present-day Shaoxing 紹興 district of Zhejiang Province. The story Dōgen tells here was well known and appears in several sources; the version here seems to be from the *Jingde chuandeng lu* 景德傳燈錄 (T.2076.51:244a7-21); see also, e.g., the *Liandeng huiyao* 聯燈會要, ZZ.136:483a6-b1. Dōgen also cites the story in his "Shōbōgenzō shin fukatoku" 正法眼藏心不可得 (Supplementary Texts version) and *Eihei kōroku* 永平廣錄 (DZZ.3:132, no. 196; DZZ.4:198, no. 27).

2 **Dangzi Valley, Mount Baiya, in Nanyang** (*Nanyō Hakugaisan Tōshikoku* 南陽白崖山黨子谷): In present-day Henan province.

imperial seat, and in the second year of Shangyuan, the Tang Emperor Suzong dispatched an imperial commissioner, Sun Chaojin, to summon him to the capital.[3] *There, he was received with the etiquette due a teacher and installed in the Xichan Cloister of Qianfu Monastery.*[4] *Upon the ascension of the Emperor Daizong, he was reinstalled in the Guangzhai Monastic Complex, where for sixteen years he taught the dharma in accord with the abilities of his audiences.*[5]

During this time, a certain Tripiṭaka Master Daer from Sindh in the West arrived in the capital, saying that he had achieved the wisdom eye that knows the minds of others.[6] *The Emperor ordered the National Teacher to test him. As soon as the Tripiṭaka Master saw the Teacher, he bowed and stood respectfully off to his right side.*

The Teacher asked him, "You have the knowledge of other minds?"

"I wouldn't presume," he replied.[7]

"Tell me," said the Teacher, "where's this old monk right now?"

The Tripiṭaka Master said, "Reverend, you are the teacher to a nation; how could you go off to Xichuan to watch the boat races?"[8]

The Teacher asked again, "Tell me, where's this old monk right now?"

The Tripiṭaka Master said, "Reverend, you are the teacher to a nation; how could you be on the Tianjin bridge watching the playing monkeys?"[9]

---

3 **the second year of Shangyuan** (*Jōgen ninen* 上元二年): 761. The Emperor Suzong 肅宗 reigned 756-762.

4 **installed in the Xichan Cloister of Qianfu Monastery** (*choku ko Senpukuji Saizenin* 勅居千福寺西禪院): I.e., was given an imperial order to reside at this important monastery in Chang'an. The *Jingde chuandeng lu* 景德傳燈錄 (T.2076.51:244a11) has here "initially resided" (*sho ko* 初居).

5 **the ascension of the Emperor Daizong** (*Daisō ringyo* 代宗臨御): Reigned 762-779.

6 **a certain Tripiṭaka Master Daer from Sindh in the West** (*u Saiten Daini sanzō* 有西天大耳三藏): A figure unknown from other sources, whose name is literally "Big Ears." "Tripiṭaka" (*sanzō* 三藏) is an honorific title expressing mastery of the Buddhist canon.

the wisdom eye that knows the minds of others (*tashin egen* 他心慧眼): I.e., *tashin tsū* 他心通, the paranormal power to read others' minds.

7 **I wouldn't presume** (*fukan* 不敢): "I dare not [claim such a thing]"; a colloquial expression of modest acknowledgement of a compliment.

8 **"go off to Xichuan to watch the boat races"** (*kyo Shisen kan keito* 去西川看競渡): Presumably, the dragon boat festival, held on the fifth day of the fifth month, commemorating the legend of the suicide by drowning of the poet Chu Yuan 屈原 (ca. 340-278 BCE).

9 **"on the Tianjin bridge watching the playing monkeys"** (*zai Tenshinkyō jō kan rō koson* 在天津橋上看弄猢猻): Probably a performance of trained monkeys. The Tianjin bridge 天津橋 was located in Luoyang.

The Teacher asked a third time, "Tell me, where's this old monk right now?"

The Tripiṭaka Master said nothing for a while, not knowing where the Teacher had gone.

The Teacher said, "This fox spirit! Where's his knowledge of other minds?"

The Tripiṭaka Master had no response.

[73:2]

僧問趙州曰、大耳三藏、第三度、不見國師在處、未審、國師在什麼處。趙州云、在三藏鼻孔上。僧問玄沙、既在鼻孔上、爲什麼不見。玄沙曰、只爲太近。僧問仰山曰、大耳三藏、第三度、爲什麼不見國師。仰山曰、前兩度是涉境心、後入自受用三昧、所以不見。海會端曰、國師若在三藏鼻孔上、有什麼難見。殊不知、國師在三藏眼睛裏。玄沙徵三藏曰、汝道、前兩度還見麼。雪竇明覺重顯禪師曰、敗也敗也。

A monk asked Zhaozhou, "I don't understand why the Tripiṭaka Master Daer didn't see where the National Teacher was the third time.[10] *Where was the National Teacher?"*

Zhaozhou said, "He was on the Tripiṭaka Master's nose."

A monk asked Xuansha, "If he was on his nose, why didn't he see him?"[11]

Xuansha said, "Because he was too close."

A monk asked Yangshan, "Why didn't the Tripiṭaka Master Daer see the National Teacher the third time?"[12]

Yangshan said, "The first two times were the mind that plays across objects. After that, he entered the samādhi of personal enjoyment; that's why he didn't see him."[13]

---

10 **A monk asked Zhaozhou** (*sō mon Jōshū* 僧問趙州): I.e., Zhaozhou Congshen 趙州從諗 (778-897). The exchange occurs at *Jingde chuandeng lu* 景德傳燈錄, T.2076.51:244a23-24.

11 **A monk asked Xuansha** (*sō mon Gensha* 僧問玄沙): I.e., Xuansha Shibei 玄沙師備 (835-908). The exchange occurs at *Jingde chuandeng lu* 景德傳燈錄, T.2076.51:244a24.

12 **A monk asked Yangshan** (*sō mon Kyōzan* 僧問仰山): I.e., Yangshan Huiji 仰山慧寂 (803-887). The exchange occurs at *Jingde chuandeng lu* 景德傳燈錄, T.2076.51:244a21-22.

13 **mind that plays across objects** (*shōkyō shin* 涉境心): i.e., ordinary consciousness. **samādhi of personal enjoyment** (*jijuyū zanmai* 自受用三昧): A technical term for the state in which a buddha experiences his awakening.

Duan of Haihui said, "If the National Teacher was on the Tripiṭaka Master's nose, why would it be hard to see him?[14] *He's completely unaware that the National Teacher was in the Tripiṭaka Master's eye."*

Xuansha summoned the Tripiṭaka Master, saying, "Tell me, did you in fact see the first two times?"[15]

Chan Master Mingjue Zhongxian of Xuedou said, "Defeated! Defeated!"[16]

[73:3] {2:243}

大證國師の、大耳三藏を試驗せし因緣、ふるくより下語し道著する臭拳頭おほしといへども、ことに五位の老拳頭あり。しかあれども、この五位の尊宿、おのおの諦當甚諦當はなきにあらず、國師の行履を覷見せざるところおほし。ゆえいかんとなれば、古今の諸員みなおもはく、前兩度は、三藏あやまらず國師の在處をしれり、とおもへり。これすははち、古先のおほきなる不是なり、晚進しらずばあるべからず。

From long ago there have been many stinking fists who offered comments and sayings on the episode of the National Teacher Dazheng's testing the Tripiṭaka Master Daer, but in particular we have these five old fists.[17] Nevertheless, while it is not the case that each of these five venerables is not "*on the mark, right on the mark*," there is much in the conduct of the National Teacher that they do not see.[18] The reason is that until now everyone has thought that the Tripiṭaka Master correctly knew the whereabouts of the National Teacher the first two times. This is a major error by our old forebears – one that latecomers should not fail to recognize.

---

14 **Duan of Haihui** (*Kaie Tan* 海會端): I.e., Haihui Shouduan 海會守端 (1025-1072). This exchange is not found in the *Jingde chuandeng lu* 景德傳燈錄 notice; rather, it can be found at *Liandeng huiyao* 聯燈會要, ZZ.136:483a18-b1. The grammatical subject of "unaware" is unstated; presumably, Zhaozhou.

15 **Xuansha summoned the Tripiṭaka Master** (*Gensha chō Sanzō* 玄沙徵三藏): Xuansha's remark appears at *Jingde chuandeng lu* 景德傳燈錄, T.2076.51:244a23 — though not as a direct challenge to the Tripiṭaka Master but as a question to a monk who raised the issue with Xuansha.

16 **Chan Master Mingjue Zhongxian of Xuedou** (*Setchō Myōkaku Jūken zenji* 雪竇明覺重顯禪師): I.e., Xuedou Zhongxian 雪竇重顯 (980-1052). His comment occurs in the *Mingjue chanshi yulu* 明覺禪師語錄 (T.1996.47:671c21-22). It is unclear who has been defeated; some commentators take it to be the Tripiṭaka Master; others, Xuansha.

17 **the National Teacher Dazheng** (*Daishō kokushi* 大證國師): Title awarded Huizhong 慧忠 by the Tang Emperor Daizong 代宗. "Fist" (*kentō* 拳頭) is a common reference to the Chan teacher; see Supplementary Notes, s.v. "Fist."

18 **"on the mark, right on the mark"** (*taitō jin taitō* 諦當甚諦當): A fixed expression of approval.

[73:4]
いま、五位の尊宿を疑著すること兩般あり。一者いはく、國師の、三藏を試驗する本意をしらず。二者いはく、國師の身心をしらず。

My doubts about these five venerables are of two sorts: first, that they do not know the National Teacher's basic intention in testing the Tripiṭaka Master; second, that they do not know the National Teacher's body and mind.

[73:5]
しばらく、國師の三藏を試驗する本意をしらず、といふは、第一番に國師いはく、汝道老僧即今在什麼處、といふ本意は、三藏、もし佛法を見聞する眼睛なりや、と試問するなり、三藏、おのづから佛法の他心通ありや、と試問するなり。當時、もし三藏に佛法あらば、老僧即今在什麼處、としめされんとき、出身のみちあるべし、親曾の便宜あらしめん。いはゆる國師道の、老僧即今在什麼處は、作麼生是老僧、と問著せんがことし。老僧即今在什麼處は、即今是什麼時節と問著するなり。在什麼處は、這裏是什麼處在と道著するなり。喚什麼作老僧の道理あり。國師かならずしも老僧にあらず、老僧かならず拳頭なり。大耳三藏、はるかに西天よりきたれりといへども、このこころをしらざることは、佛道を學せざるによりてなり、いたづらに外道・二乘のみちをのみまなべるによりてなり。

Now, when I say that they do not know the National Teacher's basic intention in testing the Tripiṭaka Master, I mean this: that his basic intention in initially saying, "*Tell me, where's this old monk right now?*" is to test whether the Tripiṭaka Master is an eye to see the buddha dharma – to test whether the Tripiṭaka Master has the knowledge of others' minds according to the buddha dharma.[19] If at that point the Tripiṭaka Master had the buddha dharma, when he goes to express "*Where this old monk is right now*" he would have some way out of the body, would bring about some personal advantage.[20] The National Teacher's saying, "Where's this old monk right now?" is like his asking, "*What is 'this old monk'?*" "*Where's this old monk right now?*" is asking, "*What time is 'right now'?*" "Where's?" is saying, "*Where are we here?*"[21] There is reason [to say it is also asking,] "*What is it we are calling an 'old monk'?*" A national teacher is not always an "old monk"; an "old monk"

19 **is an eye to see the buddha dharma** (*buppō o kenmon suru ganzei nari* 佛法を見聞する眼睛なり): Some modern editions revise this to "has the eye" (*ganzei ari* 眼睛あり).

20 **way out of the body** (*shusshin no michi* 出身のみち); **personal advantage** (*shinzō no bengi* 親曽の便宜): Probably meaning something like "[a response that demonstrates] a higher perspective and a personal mastery." The term *shusshin* 出身, while having the colloquial sense "advance one's status," is regularly used in Chan texts for "liberation."

21 **"Where are we here?"** (*shari ze jūmo sho zai* 這裏是什麼處在): A fixed rhetorical question, occurring several times in the *Shōbōgenzō*, that warns the interlocutor to keep the conversation at the highest level of truth, beyond dualities.

is always a "fist." That the Tripiṭaka Master Daer, though he came all the way from Sindh in the West, does not understand this intention is because he has not studied the way of the buddhas, because he has only learned in vain the other paths and the paths of the two vehicles.[22]

[73:6] {2:244}

國師かさねてとふ、汝道老僧即今在什麼處。ここに、三藏、さらにいたづらのことばをたてまつる。國師かさねてとふ、汝道老僧即今什麼處。ときに、三藏、ややひさしくあれども、茫然として祇對なし。國師、ときに三藏を叱していはく、這野狐精他心通在什麼處。かくのごとく叱せらるといへども、三藏、なほいふことなし、祇對せず、通路なし。

The National Teacher asks again, "*Tell me, where's this old monk right now?*" Here again, the Tripiṭaka Master offers worthless words.

Again, the National Teacher asks, "*Tell me, where's this old monk right now?*" This time, the Tripiṭaka Master is silent for a while but is at a loss and has no reply. Then, the National Teacher rebukes him, saying, "*This fox spirit! Where's his knowledge of other minds?*" Yet, though he is thus rebuked, the Tripiṭaka Master still has nothing to say, no reply, no passage.[23]

[73:7]

しかあるを、古先みなおもはくは、國師の、三藏を叱すること、前兩度は國師の所在をしれり、第三度のみしらず、みざるがゆえに、國師に叱せらる、とおもふ。これ、おほきなるあやまりなり。國師の、三藏を叱することは、おほよそ三藏、はじめより佛法也未夢見在なるを叱するなり。前兩度はしれりといへども、第三度をしらざる、と叱するにあらざるなり。おほよそ、他心通をえたりと自稱しながら、他心通をしらざることを叱するなり。

Still, our old forebears all think that the National Teacher's rebuke of the Tripiṭaka Master is only because, although he knows the National Teacher's whereabouts the first two times, he does not know and cannot see this the third time. This is a big mistake. The National Teacher rebukes the Tripiṭaka Master because from the beginning the Tripiṭaka Master has *never seen the buddha dharma even in his dreams*; he does not rebuke him because, although he knows the first two times, he does not know the third time. In short, he rebukes him because, while claiming to have attained the knowledge of other minds, he does not know knowledge of other minds.

---

22 **the other paths and the paths of the two vehicles** (*gedō nijō no michi* 外道二乘のみち): I.e., non-Buddhist religions and non-Mahāyāna Buddhism.

23 **passage** (*tsūro* 通路): Perhaps playing on the word *tsū* ("to pass through" or "to penetrate") in *tashin tsū* 他心通 ("knowing [or 'penetrating'] other minds").

[73:8] {2:245}

國師まづ、佛法に他心通ありや、と問著し、試驗するなり。すでに、不敢、といひて、あり、ときこゆ。そののち、國師おもはく、たとひ佛法に他心通ありといひて、他心通を佛法にあらしめば、恁麼なるべし、道處もし擧處なくば、佛法なるべからず、とおもへり。三藏、たとひ第三度わづかにいふところありとも、前兩度のごとくあらば、道處あるにあらず、總じて叱すべきなり。いま國師、三度こころみに問著することは、三藏、もし國師の問著をきくことをうるやと、たびたびかさねて三番の問著あるなり。

First, the National Teacher tests him by asking whether there is the knowledge of other minds in the buddha dharma; since he answers, "I wouldn't presume," it seems there is.[24]

Thereafter, the National Teacher thought, "If we say there is the knowledge of other minds in the buddha dharma, if we attribute this knowledge to the buddha dharma, it would be like this.[25] If a statement has nothing it brings up, it is not the buddha dharma."[26] Even if the Tripiṭaka Master had something to say the third time, if he had anything like the first two times, it would not be a statement, and he would be rebuked for all [three answers]. The National Teacher questions him three times in order to ask again and again whether the Tripiṭaka Master has really heard the National Teacher's question.

[73:9]

二者いはく、國師の身心をしれる古先なし。いはゆる國師の身心は、三藏法師のたやすく見及すべきにあらず、知及すべきにあらず、十聖三賢およばず、補處・等覺のあきらむるところにあらず。三藏學者の凡夫なる、いかでか國師の渾身をしらん。この道理、かならず一定すべし。國師の身心は、三藏の學者しるべし、みるべし、といはば、謗佛法なり。經論師と齊肩なるべし、と認ずるは、狂顚のはなはだしきなり。他心通をえたらんともがら、國師の在處しるべし、と學することなかれ。

---

24 **whether there is the knowledge of other minds in the buddha dharma** (*buppō ni tashin tsū ari ya* 佛法に他心通ありや): This sentence might more naturally be read, "whether he has the knowledge of other minds in the buddha dharma; since he answers, 'I wouldn't presume,' it seems he does." The sentence following, however, suggests that, for Dōgen, the question is not about the Tripiṭaka.

25 **it would be like this** (*inmo naru beshi* 恁麼なるべし): The subject is unexpressed here; likely, the Tripiṭaka Master's answer (that has "nothing to bring up"). Alternatively, some readers take *inmo* 恁麼 ("like this") as the ultimate truth of "suchness" and the subject as "knowledge of other minds."

26 **If a statement has nothing it brings up** (*dōsho moshi kosho nakuba* 道處もし擧處なくば): I.e., "if there is no significant point to what is said." This sentence, treated here as a continuation of what the National Teacher thought, might well be read as Dōgen's comment. The "statement" (*dōsho* 道處) in the following sentence should be taken as one that does have a significant point.

My second point is that none of our old forebears has known the body and mind of the National Teacher. The body and mind of the National Teacher is not something that a Tripiṭaka dharma master can easily discern, can easily recognize; not something reached by the ten sages and three worthies; not something understood by the virtually awakened, the heir apparent.[27] How could a scholar of the Tripiṭaka who is a common person know the full body of the National Teacher?[28] We should be certain about this principle. To say that the body and mind of the National Teacher could be known by a scholar of the Tripiṭaka is to slander the buddha dharma; to consider that he is of equal stature as the masters of the sūtras and commentaries is the extreme of madness. Do not think that those who have got the knowledge of other minds can know the whereabouts of the National Teacher.

[73:10]

他心通は、西天竺國の土俗として、これを修得するともがら、ままにあり。發菩提心によらず、大乘の正見によらず、他心通をえたるともがら、他心通のちからにて佛法を證究せる勝躅、いまだかつてきかざるところなり。他心通を修得してのちにも、さらに凡夫のごとく發心し修行せば、おのづから佛道に證入すべし。ただ他心通のちからをもて佛道を知見することをえば、先聖みなまづ他心通を修得して、そのちからをもて佛果をしるべきなり。しかあること、千佛萬祖の出世にも、いまだあらざるなり。すでに佛祖の道をしることあたはざらんは、なににかはせん、佛道に不中用なりといふべし。他心通をえたるも、他心通をえざる凡夫も、ただひとしかるべし。佛性を保任せんことは、他心通も凡夫もおなじかるべきなり。

As a local custom of the Land of Sindhu in the West, there are occasionally types there who have cultivated the knowledge of other minds.[29] We have never yet heard of precedents in which, without bringing forth the mind of bodhi, without the right view of the Great Vehicle, those who have got the knowledge of other minds fully verified the buddha dharma

---

27 **the ten sages and three worthies** (*jisshō sanken* 十聖三賢): I.e., those on the ten advanced stages (S. *bhūmi*) of the bodhisattva path and the three preliminary (S. *bhadra*) stages preceding these.

the virtually awakened, the heir apparent (*fusho tōgaku* 補處・等覺): I.e., a bodhisattva destined to become the next buddha, a bodhisattva on the penultimate stage of the path, just prior to buddhahood.

28 **common person** (*bonbu* 凡夫): An ordinary person (S. *pṛthagjana*), yet to have advanced to the level of the spiritual "noble" (S. *ārya*).

29 **As a local custom of the Land of Sindhu in the West** (*Sai Tenjiku koku no dozoku toshite* 西天竺國の土俗として): Dōgen's dismissal of the knowledge of other minds as merely Indian cultural practice, while fully in keeping with the spirit of the story he is explicating here, is of course in conflict with traditional claims that all buddhas have this paranormal power. His further point in this section, that having such power does not in itself significantly change one's spiritual status is in keeping with traditional Buddhist understanding.

on the strength of their knowledge of other minds. Even after cultivating the knowledge of other minds, they must, like common people, go on to bring forth the mind [of bodhi] and engage in the practice, and thereby themselves enter verification of the way of the buddhas.

If one could know the way of the buddhas simply on the strength of the knowledge of other minds, all the prior sages would have first cultivated the knowledge of other minds and used it to know the fruit of buddhahood; yet this has never happened in all the appearances in the world of a thousand buddhas and ten thousand ancestors. Since it cannot know the way of the buddhas and ancestors, what good is it? It is of no use to the way of the buddhas. Those who have got the knowledge of other minds and common people who have not got the knowledge of other minds are equal; in their maintaining the buddha nature, those with the knowledge of other minds and common people are the same.

[73:11] {2:246}

學佛のともがら、外道・二乘の五通・六通を、凡夫よりもすぐれたりとおもふことなかれ。ただ道心あり、佛法を學せんものは、五通・六通よりもすぐれたるべし。頻伽の、卵にある、聲まさに衆鳥にすぐれたるがごとし。いはんやいま西天に他心通といふは、他念通といひぬべし。念起はいささか緣ずといへども、未念は茫然なり、わらふべし。いかにいはんや、心かならずしも念にあらず、念かならずしも心にあらず。心の、念ならんとき、他心通しるべからず、念の、心ならんとき、他心通しるべからず。

Those who study Buddhism, do not think that those with the five powers or six powers of the other paths and two vehicles are superior to the common person.[30] Those who simply have the mind of the way and who would study the buddha dharma are superior to those with the five or six powers. They are like the *kalaviṅka*, whose voice even inside the shell is superior to that of other birds.[31] Not to mention that what is called in Sindh in the West the knowledge of other minds ought rather to be called the knowledge of others' thoughts: while it may be somewhat aware when a thought has arisen, it is quite at a loss when a thought has not arisen. This is laughable. It goes without saying that the mind is not necessarily thought; thought is not necessarily the mind. When the mind

30 **those with the five powers or six powers of the other paths and two vehicles** (*gedō nijō no gozū rokutsū* 外道・二乘の五通・六通): The standard set of the five powers (*gozū* or *gotsū* 五通; also *gojinzū* 五神通) includes (1) the ability to transform the body and move about by psychic travel, (2) paranormal vision, (3) paranormal hearing, (4) knowledge of other minds, and (5) knowledge of past lives. While, in traditional exegesis, these are understood to be attainable by non-Buddhist yogis, a sixth power, the knowledge of the exhaustion of the *āsraya* (*ro* 漏), or spiritual "contaminants," is reserved for those with personal insight (*ken* 見; S. *darśana*) into the truth of Buddhism.

31 **the *kalaviṅka*** (*binga* 頻伽): Variously identified as the sparrow or the Indian cuckoo, a Himalayan bird of melodious voice, said to sing while still in the shell.

is thought, the knowledge of other minds cannot know it; when thought is the mind, the knowledge of other minds cannot know it.[32]

[73:12]

しかあればすなはち、西天の五通・六通、このくにの薙草修田もおよぶべからず、都無所用なり。かるがゆえに、震旦國より東には、先徳みな五通六通をこのみ修せず、その要、なきによりてなり。尺璧は、なほ要なるべし、五通・六通は要にあらず。尺璧、なほ寶にあらず、寸陰、これ要樞なり。五、六通、たれの、寸陰をおもくせん人か、これを修習せん。おほよそ他心通のちから、佛智の邊際におよぶべからざる道理、よくよく決定すべし。

Thus, the five powers or six powers of Sindh in the West are all quite useless, not the equal of cutting the weeds and cultivating the paddies in our land. Therefore, the fact that, from the Land of Cīnasthāna eastward, none of the prior worthies has cared to cultivate the five powers or six powers is because they are worthless.[33] Even a one-foot jewel has worth, but the five powers or six powers are worthless. A one-foot jewel is still not a treasure, but an inch of shadow is pivotal.[34] For those who take seriously that inch of shadow, who would cultivate the five or six powers? In sum, we should be very firmly convinced of the principle that the power of the knowledge of other minds cannot reach the borders of the buddha wisdom.

[73:13] {2:247}

しかあるを、五位の尊宿、ともに、三藏さきの兩度は國師の所在をしれり、とおもへる、もともあやまれるなり。國師は佛祖なり、三藏は凡夫なり、いかでか相見の論にもおよばん。

To think, nevertheless, as do our five venerables, that the Tripiṭaka Master knew the whereabouts of the National Teacher the first two times he was asked is greatly mistaken. The National Teacher is a buddha and ancestor; the Tripiṭaka Master is a common person. How could there be any question of their seeing each other?

---

32 **When the mind is thought** (*shin no nen naran toki* 心の念ならんとき): A sentence subject to varied interpretation. Perhaps, the argument here is that, if (a) mind (*shin* 心) and its thoughts (*nen* 念) are not the same, and (b) the knowledge in question is of the thoughts and not of the mind, then (c) we cannot know the mind that thinks and we cannot know the thoughts in that mind.

33 **from the Land of Cīnasthāna eastward** (*Shintan koku yori higashi ni* 震旦國より東に): Dōgen uses the transliteration of the Sanskrit name for China ("Land of the Qin"). His claim here is odd, since Chinese Buddhism had its fair share of monks famed for their paranormal powers.

34 **A one-foot jewel** (*sekiheki* 尺璧); **an inch of shadow** (*sun'in* 寸陰): From the old Chinese saying, "The sage does not value a one-foot jewel but gives weight to an inch of shadow [i.e., a moment of time]."

[73:14]

國師、まづいはく、汝道老僧即今在什麼處。この問、かくれたるところなし、あらはれたる道處あり。三藏のしらざらんは、とがにあらず、五位の尊宿のきかず、みざるは、あやまりなり。すでに國師いはく、老僧即令在什麼處、となり。さらに汝道老僧心即今在什麼處、といはず、老僧念即今在什麼處、といはず。もとも、きき、しり、みとがむべき道處なり。しかあるを、しらず、みず、國師の道處をきかず、みず。かるがゆえに、國師の身心をしらざるなり。道處あるを國師とせるがゆえに、もし道處なきは國師なるべからざるがゆえに。いはんや國師の身心は、大小にあらず、自他にあらざること、しるべからず。頂顙あること、鼻孔あること、わすれたるがごとし。國師、たとひ行李ひまなくとも、いかでか作佛を圖せん。かるがゆえに、佛を拈じて相待すべからず。

First, the National Teacher asks, "*Tell me, where's this old monk right now?*" There is nothing hidden in this question; it makes an obvious statement. That the Tripiṭaka Master might not understand it is not his fault; that the five venerables do not hear it or see it is a mistake. It says that the National Teacher clearly asked, "*Where is this old monk right now?*" He never says, "*Tell me, where is this old monk's mind right now?*" He does not say, "*Where are this old monk's thoughts right now?*" This is a statement that we should definitely hear and know, see and take to heart.

Nevertheless, they do not know or see it; they do not hear or see the National Teacher's statement. And for this reason, they do not know the body and mind of the National Teacher. For it is having a statement that makes a national teacher; for without a statement one would not be a national teacher. How much less, then, can they understand that the body and mind of the National Teacher are not big or small, self or other. It is as if they have forgotten that he has a crown of the head or a nose. Though the National Teacher may never take time from his practice, how could he figure to make a buddha?[35] For this reason, he should not be treated relative to "buddha."

[73:15] {2:248}

國師、すでに佛法の身心あり、神通修證をもて測度すべからず、絕慮忘緣を擧して擬議すべからず、商量・不商量のあたれるところにあらざるべし。國師は、有佛性にあらず、無佛性にあらず、虛空身にあらず。かくのごとくの國師の身心、すべてしらざるところなり。いま曹溪の會下には、青原・南嶽のほかは、わづかに大證國師、その佛祖なり。

---

35 **how could he figure to make a buddha?** (*ikadeka sabutsu o zusen* いかでか作佛を圖せん): From the famous dialogue, much cited by Dōgen, in which Nanyue Huairang 南嶽懷讓 (677-744) likens "figuring to make a buddha" (*zu sabutsu* 圖作佛) by sitting in meditation to trying to make a mirror by rubbing a tile. See Supplementary Notes, s.v. "Nanyue polishes a tile"; for Dōgen's comments on the dialogue, see "Shōbōgenzō zazen shin" 正法眼藏坐禪箴.

Since the National Teacher has the body and mind of the buddha dharma, we should not measure him by the practice and verification of the spiritual powers, we should not consider him in terms of cutting off considerations and forgetting objects.[36] He is not something that can be determined by deliberating or not deliberating. The National Teacher is not one who has the buddha nature nor one who lacks the buddha nature; he is not the body of empty space.[37] This kind of body and mind of the National Teacher is something entirely unknown [to any of the five venerables]. In the community of Caoxi, apart from Chingyuan and Nanyue, only this National Teacher Dazheng was a buddha and ancestor.[38]

[73:16]

いま五位の尊宿、おなじく勘破すべし。

Now we need to see through each of our five venerables.

[73:17]

趙州いはく、國師は三藏の鼻孔上にあるがゆえにみず、といふ。この道處、そのいひなし。國師なにとしてか三藏の鼻孔上にあらん、三藏いまだ鼻孔あらず。もし三藏に鼻孔ありとゆるさば、國師かへりて三藏をみるべし。國師の、三藏をみること、たとひゆるすとも、ただこれ鼻孔對鼻孔なるべし、三藏さらに國師と相見すべからず。

Zhaozhou says that he did not see him because the National Teacher was "*on his nose*." This statement does not make sense. How could the National Teacher be on the Tripiṭaka Master's nose? The Tripiṭaka Master does not yet have a nose.[39] If we admit that the Tripiṭaka Master does have a nose, then on the contrary the National Teacher should see the Tripiṭaka master. Even if we admit that the National Teacher does see the Tripiṭaka Master, this would only mean that they are nose to nose; it would not mean that the Tripiṭaka Master actually saw the National Teacher.

---

36 **cutting off considerations and forgetting objects** (*zetsuryo bōen* 絕慮忘緣): Two standard expressions for contemplative practice, often used in a pejorative sense in Chan texts.

37 **body of empty space** (*kokū shin* 虛空身): The highest of the ten buddha bodies listed in the *Avataṃsaka-sūtra* (e.g., at *Huayan jing* 華嚴經, T.278.9:565b19). A term not used elsewhere in the *Shōbōgenzō*.

38 **community of Caoxi** (*Sōkei no eka* 曹溪の會下): I.e., the disciples of the Sixth Ancestor, Huineng 慧能 of Caoxi 曹溪, among whom Qingyuan Xingsi 青原行思 (d. 740) and Nanyue Huairang 南嶽懷讓 were the two most prominent.

39 **The Tripiṭaka Master does not yet have a nose** (*Sanzō imada bikū arazu* 三藏いまだ鼻孔あらず): I.e., the Tripiṭaka Master still lacks real substance; reflecting a common use of the term "nose" (*bikū* 鼻孔) for what defines a person. See Supplementary Notes, s.v. "Nose."

[73:18]
玄沙いはく、只爲太近。まことに太近は、さもあらばあれ、あたりにはいまだあたらず。いかならんかこれ太近。おもひやる、玄沙いまだ太近をしらず、太近を參ぜず。ゆえいかんとなれば、太近に相見なしとのみしりて、相見の、太近なることをしらず。いふべし、佛法におきて遠之遠なりと。もし第三度のみを太近といはば、前兩度は太遠在なるべし。しばらく玄沙にとふ、なんぢなにをよんでか太近とする。拳頭をいふか、眼睛をいふか。いまよりのち、太近にみるところなし、といふことなかれ。

Xuansha says, "*Because he was too close.*" To be sure, this may be "too close"; but as for hitting it, it still has not hit it. What is this "too close"? I suspect that Xuansha still does not understand "too close," has not studied "too close." I say this because he understands only that there is no seeing in "too close"; he does not understand that seeing is "too close." We have to say that, in terms of the buddha dharma, he is the farthest of the far. If we say it was "too close" only the third time, then it must have been "too far" the first two times. Now, I want to ask Xuansha, "What is it that you call 'too close'? Is it a fist ? Is it an eye? From now on, don't say there's nothing seen 'too close.'"

[73:19] {2:249}
仰山いはく、前兩度是涉境心、後入自受用三昧所以不見。仰山、なんぢ東土にありながら、小釋迦のほまれを西天にほどこすといへども、いまの道取、おほきなる不是あり。涉境心と自受用三昧と、ことなるにあらず。かるがゆえに、涉境心と自受用とのことなるゆえにみず、といふべからず。しかあれば、自受用と涉境心とのゆえを立すとも、その道取、いまだ道取にあらず。自受用三昧にいれば他人われをみるべからず、といはば、自受用さらに自受用を證すべからず、修證あるべからず。

Yangshan says, "*The first two times were the mind that plays across objects. After that, he entered the samādhi of personal enjoyment; that's why he didn't see him.*" Yangshan, while being from the Eastern Earth, you have a reputation in Sindh in the West as a little Śākya; but your saying here has a big error.[40] The mind that plays across objects and the samādhi of the personal enjoyment are not different; for this reason, we cannot say that he does not see him by reason of some difference between the mind that plays across objects and personal enjoyment. Therefore, though you set up the mind that plays across objects and personal

40 **you have a reputation in Sindh in the West as a little Śākya** (*shō Shaka no homare o Saiten ni hodokosu* 小釋迦のほまれを西天にほどこす): From the tradition (e.g., at *Yangshan Huiji chanshi yulu* 仰山慧寂禪師語錄, T.1990.47:582a10-72) that an Indian monk who had used his paranormal powers to fly to China to worship Mañjuśrī was so impressed by Yangshan that he said,

特來東土禮文殊。卻遇小釋迦。

I came to the Land of the East especially to make obeisance to Mañjuśrī, and instead I met a little Śākyamuni.

enjoyment as the reasons, your saying is not yet a saying. If you say that when I enter the samādhi of personal enjoyment, others cannot see me, then personal enjoyment would not be able to verify personal enjoyment, and there could be no cultivation and verification of it.

[73:20]

仰山、なんぢ、前兩度は實に國師の所在を三藏みるとおもひ、しれりと學せば、いまだ學佛の漢にあらず。おほよそ大耳三藏は、第三度のみにあらず、前兩度も國師の所在はしらず、みざるなり。この道取のごとくならば、三藏の、國師の所在をしらざるのみにあらず、仰山も、いまだ國師の所在をしらずといふべし。しばらく仰山にとふ、國師即今在什麼處。このとき、仰山もし開口を擬せば、まさに一喝をあたふべし。

Yangshan, if you think that the Tripiṭaka Master really saw the National Teacher's whereabouts the first two times, if you study that he really knew, you are not yet a man who studies Buddhism. The Tripiṭaka Master Daer does not know or see the whereabouts of the National Teacher not only the third time but the first two times as well. From a saying like this, we have to say that it is not just the Tripiṭaka Master who does not know the National Teacher's whereabouts; Yangshan does not yet know either. Let us ask Yangshan, "*Where is the National Teacher right now?*" If he thinks to open his mouth, we should give him a shout.

[73:21]

玄沙の徴にいはく、前兩度還見麼。いまこの前兩度還見麼の一言、いふべきをいふときこゆ。玄沙みづから、自己の言句を學すべし。この一句、よきことはすなはちよし、しかあれどもただこれ見如不見といはんがごとし。ゆえに是にあらず。これをききて、

Xuansha summoned him, saying, "*Did you in fact see the first two times?*" These words, "*Did you in fact see the first two times?*" sound as if they are saying what needs to be said. Xuansha should learn from his own words. But granted that this line has its value, it seems to be saying only that "his seeing is like not seeing." Hence, it is not right. Hearing this,

[73:22] {2:250}

雪竇山明覺禪師重顯いはく、敗也敗也。これ、玄沙のいふところを道とせるとき、しかいふとも、玄沙の道は道にあらずとせんとき、しかいふべからず。

Zhongxian, Chan Master Mingjue of Mount Xuedou, said, "*Defeated! Defeated!*" Though we may say this when we have taken what Xuansha says as saying something; when we take Xuansha's saying as not saying anything, we cannot say it.

[73:23]

海會の端いはく、國師若在三藏鼻孔上、有什麼難見、殊不知國師在三藏眼睛裏。これまた第三度を論ずるのみなり。前兩度もかつていまだみざることを、呵すべきを呵せず、いかでか國師を三藏の鼻孔上にあり、眼睛裏にあるともしらん。もし恁麼いはば、國師の言句、いまだきかずといふべし。三藏、いまだ鼻孔なし、眼睛なし。たとひ、三藏おのれが眼睛・鼻孔を保任せんとすとも、もし國師きたりて鼻孔・眼睛裏にいらば、三藏の鼻孔・眼睛、ともに當時裂破すべし。すでに裂破せば、國師の窟籠にあらず。

Duan of Haihui said, "*If the National Teacher was on the Tripiṭaka Master's nose, why would it be hard to see him? He's completely unaware that the National Teacher was in the Tripiṭaka Master's eye.*" This also only discusses the third time. It does not scoff, as it should scoff, at the fact that he never sees the first two times. How can he know whether the National Teacher is on his nose or in his eye? If this is what he says, we have to say that he has not heard the words of the National Teacher. The Tripiṭaka Master does not yet have a nose or eye. Even if we were to say that he does maintain eye and nose, if the National Teacher were to enter them, the Tripiṭaka Master's nose and eye would burst on the spot. Since they would burst, they are no hole for the National Teacher.

[73:24]

五位の尊宿、ともに國師をしらざるなり。國師は、これ一代の古佛なり、一世界の如來なり、佛正法眼藏、あきらめ正傳せり、木槵子眼、たしかに保任せり、自佛に正傳し、他佛に正傳す、釋迦牟尼佛と同參しきたれりといへども、七佛と同時參究す、かたはらに三世諸佛と同參しきたれり、空王のさきに成道せり、空王ののちに成道せり、正當空王佛に同參成道せり。國師、もとより娑婆世界を國土とせりといへども、娑婆かならずしも法界のうちにあらず、盡十方界のうちにあらず。釋迦牟尼佛の、娑婆國の主なる、國師の、國土をうばはず、罣礙せず。たとえば、前後の佛祖おのおのそこばくの成道あれど、あひうばはず、罣礙せざるがごとし。前後の佛祖の成道、ともに成道に罣礙せらるるがゆえに、かくのごとし。

None of the five venerables knows the National Teacher. The National Teacher is the old buddha of his age, the tathāgata of his world. He clarified and directly transmitted the treasury of the true dharma eye of the Buddha; he surely maintained the eye of the soapberry seed.[41] He directly transmitted it to his own buddha; he transmitted it to others' buddhas.[42] Though we may say that he has studied together with Buddha

---

41 **the eye of the soapberry seed** (*mokukansu gen* 木槵子眼): From the image of replacing the eye with a soapberry seed (i.e., gaining a Buddhist way of seeing); from the use of the seed (S. *ariṣṭa*) in the Buddhist rosary (*juzu* 珠數; S. *mālā*).

42 **his own buddha** (*jibutsu* 自佛); **others' buddhas** (*tabutsu* 他佛): Unusual expressions appearing elsewhere in the *Shōbōgenzō*; perhaps meaning "the buddha in himself" and "the buddha in others."

Śākyamuni, he studied at the same time as the seven buddhas and, in addition, has studied together with all the buddhas of the three times.[43] He attained the way before King of Emptiness; he attained the way after King of Emptiness; he practiced together and attained the way precisely with Buddha King of Emptiness.[44] Though we may say that of course the National Teacher took this Sahā world as his domain, Sahā is not necessarily within the dharma realm; it is not within the entire world of the ten directions.[45] The rulership of Buddha Śākyamuni over the Sahā domain does not usurp or obstruct the National Teacher's domain. Similarly, for example, however many times the way is attained by each of the earlier and later buddhas and ancestors, they do not usurp or obstruct each other. This is the case because the attainments of the way by the earlier and later buddhas and ancestors are all obstructed by the attainment of the way.[46]

[73:25] {2:251}

大耳三藏の、國師をしらざるを證據として、聲聞・緣覺人・小乘のともがら、佛祖の邊際をしらざる道理、あきらかに決定すべし。國師の、三藏を叱する宗旨、あきらめ學すべし。いはゆる、たとひ國師なりとも、前兩度は所在をしられ、第三度はわづかにしられざらんを叱せんは、そのいひなし。三分に兩分しられんは、全分をしれるなり。かくのごとくならん、叱すべきにあらず。たとひ叱すとも、全分の不知にあらず。三藏のおもはんところ、國師の懡㦬なり。わづかに第三度しられずとて叱せんには、たれか國師を信ぜん。三藏の前兩度をしりぬるちからをもて、國師をも叱しつべし。

From the evidence that the Tripiṭaka Master Daer does not know the National Teacher, clearly we should be firmly convinced of the principle that the *śrāvaka*s and *pratyeka-buddhas*, the Small Vehicle types, do not

43 **the seven buddhas** (*shichi butsu* 七佛); **all the buddhas of the three times** (*sanze shobutsu* 三世諸佛): I.e., the line of ancient buddhas culminating in Buddha Śākyamuni and the various buddhas of past, present, and future; see Supplementary Notes, s.v. "Seven buddhas."

44 **King of Emptiness** (*Kūō* 空王): Here, as elsewhere in the *Shōbōgenzō*, Dōgen seems to be identifying a buddha mentioned in Chapter 9 of the *Lotus Sūtra* with Buddha Majestic Voice (*Ion'ō butsu* 威音王佛), often considered the first buddha to appear at the beginning of our kalpa; see Supplementary Notes, s.v. "Before King of Emptiness" and "Before King Majestic Voice."

45 **the National Teacher took this Sahā world as his domain** (*shaba sekai o kokudo to seri* 娑婆世界を國土とせり): I.e., the National Teacher was a buddha in the buddha Land of Sahā, ruled by Buddha Śākyamuni. At issue here is the traditional question of how there could be more than one buddha in a single buddha land.

46 **are all obstructed by the attainment of the way** (*jōdō ni keige seraruru* 成道に罣礙せらるる): Perhaps meaning something like, "are all the complete attainment of the way." The verb "obstruct" (*keige* 罣礙) here exemplifies Dōgen's habit of using the word in the sense "to identify with," "to be defined by."

know the borders of the buddhas and ancestors. We should clarify and study the essential point of the National Teacher's rebuke of the Tripiṭaka Master. It does not make sense that, although being the National Teacher, he would rebuke him for knowing his whereabouts the first two times and merely failing to know the third time: knowing two parts out of three is knowing it all, in which case he should not rebuke him.[47] Even if he does rebuke him, it would not be for failing to know at all; hence, from the Tripiṭaka Master's perspective, it would be the National Teacher who is humiliated. Who would trust the National Teacher if he rebuked him for failing to know only the third time? The Tripiṭaka Master could have rebuked the National Teacher, on the grounds that the Tripiṭaka Master did have the power to know the first two times.

[73:26]

國師の、三藏を叱せし宗旨は、三度ながら、はじめよりすべて國師の所在・所念・身心をしらざるゆえに叱するなり、かつて佛法を見聞・習學せざりけることを叱するなり。この宗旨あるゆえに、第一度より第三度にいたるまで、おなじことばにて問著するなり。第一番に三藏まうす、和尚是一國之師、何得却去西川看競渡。しかいふに、國師いまだいはず、なんぢ三藏、まことに老僧所在をしれり、とゆるさず、ただかさねざまに三度、しきりに問するのみなり。この道理をしらず、あきらめずして、國師よりのち數百歳のあひだ、諸方の長老、みだりに下語、説道理するなり。前來の箇箇、いふことすべて國師の本意にあらず、佛法の宗旨にかなはず。あはれむべし、前後の老古錐、おのおの蹉過せること。

The essential point of the National Teacher's rebuke of the Tripiṭaka Master is this: he rebukes him because from the beginning, throughout all three times, he does not know the National Teacher's whereabouts, thoughts, or body and mind; he rebukes him because he has never seen, heard, learned, or studied the buddha dharma. It is because of this essential point that, from the first time to the third time, he questions him with exactly the same words. The first time, the Tripiṭaka Master says, "*Reverend, you are the teacher to a nation; how could you go off to Xichuan to watch the boat races?*" Thus addressed, the National Teacher never acknowledges it, saying, "Indeed you did know where this old monk was." He simply repeats himself, asking the same question three times. Without understanding or clarifying the reason behind this, for several hundred years since the time of the National Teacher, the elders in all quarters have been arbitrarily giving their comments and explanations. Nothing that any has said so far has been the original intention of the National Teacher or in accord with the essential point of the buddha

47 **knowing two parts out of three is knowing it all** (*sanbun ni ryōbun shiraren wa, zenbun o shireru nari* 三分に兩分しられんは、全分をしれるなり): Perhaps meaning that, for the purposes of testing his mind-reading abilities, he had fully proven himself.

dharma. What a pity that each of these venerable old awls, one after the next, has missed it.

[73:27] {2:252}
いま佛法のなかに、もし他心通ありといはば、まさに他身通あるべし、他拳頭通あるべし、他眼睛通あるべし。すでに恁麼ならば、まさに自心通あるべし、自身通あるべし。すでにかくのごとくならんには、自心の自拈、いまし自心通なるべし。かくのごとく道取現成せん、おのれづから心づからの他心通ならん。

In the buddha dharma, if we are going to say that there is the knowledge of other minds, there should be the knowledge of other bodies, the knowledge of other fists, the knowledge of other eyes. Since this is so, there should also be the knowledge of one's own mind, the knowledge of one's own body. And once it is like this, one's own mind taking up itself is at once the knowledge of one's own mind. The expression of words like this is the knowledge of other minds of the self itself and mind itself.

[73:28]
しばらく問著すべし、拈他心通也是、拈自心通也是、速道速道。是則且置、汝得吾髓、是他心通也。

Let me just ask, "*Should we take up the knowledge of other minds, or should we take up the knowledge of our own mind? Speak up! Speak up!*"[48]

Leaving that for the moment, "you've gotten my marrow" is the knowledge of other minds.[49]

正法眼藏他心通第七十三
Treasury of the True Dharma Eye
Reading Other Minds
Number 73

[Ryūmonji MS:]
爾時寛元三年乙巳七月四日、在越宇大佛寺示衆
Presented to the assembly at Daibutsu Monastery, Etsuu; fourth day, seventh month of the junior wood year of the snake, the third year of Kangen [28 July 1245]

48 **Let me just ask** (*shibaraku monjaku su beshi* しばらく問著すべし): What follows here is given in Chinese, suggesting that Dōgen is concluding his remarks here with a formal comment on the story.

49 **"you've gotten my marrow"** (*nyo toku go zui* 汝得吾髓): From the famous comment of Bodhidharma acknowledging his disciple Huike's understanding; see Supplementary Notes, s.v. "Skin, flesh, bones, and marrow."

于時天文十六天丁未六月三日、在能州興慂精舎寫旃了。喆囟賢拙衲

Copied this at Kōtoku Vihāra, Nōshū; third day, sixth month, junior fire year of the sheep, sixteenth year of Tenbun [20 June 1547]. Patch-robed Tessō Ken[50]

50 **Tessō Ken** 喆囟賢: I.e., Tessō Hōken 喆囟芳賢 (d. 1551), copyist of the Ryūmonji 龍門寺 MS.

Treasury of the True Dharma Eye

Number 74

The King Requests Saindhava

Ō saku sendaba

王索仙陀婆

The King Requests Saindhava

Ō saku sendaba

Introduction

This relatively short work was presented in the late autumn of 1245, at Dōgen's Daibutsuji, in Echizen. Number 74 of the seventy-five-chapter *Shōbōgenzō*, it represents number 80 in the Honzan edition (or 81 in the Iwanami and Shūmuchō versions).

The work deals with a passage in the *Nirvāṇa Sūtra*, in which the Buddha points out that his followers should interpret his words according to context. So, for example, when a king requests *saindhava* (something "of Sindh"), the wise minister knows that the word can have various referents and offers the correct one depending on the context of the request.

The sūtra passage was well-known in Chan circles, and thus the term *saindhava* could function as marker for what the Buddha's words really mean. Here, Dōgen cites and comments on several passages from Chan literature in which the term appears. This chapter represents one of several in which we see Dōgen exploring the nature of language, reference, and meaning.

正法眼藏第七十四
Treasury of the True Dharma Eye Number 74
王索仙陀婆
The King Requests Saindhava

[74:1] {2:253}

有句無句、如藤如樹、餧驢餧馬、透水透雲。すでに恁麼なるゆえに、

Affirmative statements, negative statements,
Like the vines, like the tree.[1]
Feeding the donkey, feeding the horse;
Passing through water, passing through clouds.[2]

Since it is like this,

[74:2]

大般涅槃經中、世尊道、譬如大王告諸群臣仙陀婆來。仙陀婆者、一名四實。一者鹽、二者器、三者水、四者馬。如是四物、共同一名。有智之臣、善知此名。若王洗時、索仙陀婆、即便奉水。若王食時、索仙陀婆、即便奉鹽。若王食已欲飲漿時、索仙陀婆、即便奉器。若王欲遊、索仙陀婆、即便奉馬。如是智臣、善解大王四種密語。

In the Mahāparinirvāṇa-sūtra, the World-Honored One said,[3]

---

1 **Affirmative statements, negative statements** (*uku muku* 有句無句): Or "with words, without words." Sometimes taken as representing the first two of the famous four propositions (*shiku* 四句; S. *catuṣkoṭi*) used in Buddhist rhetoric and argument: affirmation, denial, both, neither; sometimes taken as speech and silence. This line and the next here reflect the common Zen expression, "affirmative statements and negative statements, like vines relying on a tree" (*uku muku nyo tō ki ju* 有句無句如藤倚樹); see Supplementary Notes, s.v. "Like vines relying on a tree."

2 **Feeding the donkey, feeding the horse** (*i ro i ba* 餧驢餧馬): A fixed expression, typically in sarcastic reference to the Buddhist teachings as fodder. Dōgen's lines here likely reflect the words of Xuedou Zhongxian 雪竇重顯 (980-1052) (*Mingjue chanshi yulu* 明覺禪師語錄, T.1996.47:685a24-25; *Liandeng huiyao* 聯燈會要, ZZ.136:897a4-5):

> 云黑豆未生芽時如何。師云、餧驢餧馬。云生芽後如何。師云、透水透沙。
>
> [A monk] asked, "How about when the black beans have not yet sprouted?"
> The Master said, "Feeding the donkey, feeding the horse."
> He asked, "How about after they're sprouted?"
> The Master said, "Passing through water, passing through sand."

3 **the *Mahāparinirvāṇa-sūtra*** (*Daihatsu nehan gyō* 大般涅槃經): A passage occurring in both the so-called "northern" and "southern" versions of the *Da banniepan jing* 大般涅槃經 (T.374.12:421a29-b7; T.375.12:662b17-24).

It is like the case of a great king ordering his ministers to bring him saindhava.[4] *"Saindhava" is a single name for four things: (1) salt, (2) a vessel, (3) water, and (4) a horse. These four things all have the same name. The wise minister well understands this name: when it is time for the king to bathe, and he requests* saindhava, *he immediately offers him water; when it is time for the king to eat, and he requests* saindhava, *he immediately offers him salt; when the king has finished eating and wishes to drink his broth, and he requests* saindhava, *he immediately offers him a vessel; when the king wishes to travel, and he requests* saindhava, *he immediately offers him a horse. In this way, the wise minister, well understands the fourfold cryptic word of the great king.*

[74:3] {2:254}

この王索仙陀婆、ならびに臣奉仙陀婆、きたれることひさし、法服とおなじくつたはれり。世尊、すでにまぬかれず擧拈したまふゆえに、兒孫、しげく擧拈せり。疑著すらくは、世尊と同參しきたれるは、仙陀婆を履踐とせり。世尊と不同參ならば、更買草鞋行脚、進一歩始得。すでに佛祖屋裏の仙陀婆、ひそかに漏泄して、大王家裏に仙陀婆あり。

This "*king requesting saindhava*" and "*minister offering saindhava*" have come to us from long ago, have been transmitted the same as the dharma robe. Since the World-Honored One could not avoid taking them up, his descendants repeatedly took them up. We can surmise that those who have had the same practice as the World-Honored One have taken *saindhava* as something to be emulated. If we lack the same practice as the World-Honored One, we should "*buy another pair of sandals and set out on pilgrimage*"; "*we only get it when we take a step forward.*"[5] The *saindhava* within the house of the buddhas and ancestors has already quietly leaked out, and there is *saindhava* in the houses of great kings.

* * * * *

4 ***saindhava*** (*sendaba* 仙陀婆): "Of Sindh"; i.e., a product of the Indus River region.

5 **"buy another pair of sandals and set out on pilgrimage"; "we only get it when we take a step forward"** (*kō bai sōai angya, shin ippo shi toku* 更買草鞋行脚、進一歩始得): A sentence in Chinese. The expression "buy another pair of sandals and set out on pilgrimage" (i.e., undertake further study) is found fairly often in Zen literature. Dōgen's version here seems to be a variant of the words, again, of Xuedou Zhongxian 雪竇重顯 (*Liandeng huiyao* 聯燈會要, ZZ.136:895b11):

和尚更買草鞋行脚始得。

Only when the Reverend buys another pair of sandals and sets out on pilgrimage will he get it.

[74:4]

大宋慶元府天童山宏智古佛上堂、示衆云、擧、僧問趙州、王索仙陀婆時如何。趙州曲躬叉手。雪竇拈云、索鹽奉馬。師云、雪竇一百年前作家、趙州百二十歳古佛。趙州若是、雪竇不是、雪竇若是、趙州不是。且道畢竟如何。天童不免下箇注脚、差之毫釐、失之千里。會也打草驚蛇、不會也焼錢引鬼。荒田不揀老俱胝、只今信手拈來底。

Old Buddha Hongzhi, of Mount Tiantong in the Qingyuan Prefecture of the Great Song, in a convocation, addressed the assembly, saying,[6]

Proposed:

A monk asked Zhaozhou, "How about when the king requested saindhava?"[7]

Zhaozhou bowed with hands folded.

Xuedou commented, "He requested salt, and he offered him a horse."[8]

The Master said,[9]

Xuedou was a maestro a hundred years ago; Zhaozhou was an old buddha a hundred twenty years old. If Zhaozhou's right, Xuedou isn't; if Xuedou's right, Zhaozhou isn't. So, tell me, in the end, how about it? Tiantong can't avoid adding a note:

To miss by a hair is to fail by a thousand miles.
Understanding it is beating the weeds to scare the snake;
Not understanding it is burning money to summon the spirit.
Old Juzhi, unconcerned with the abandoned field,
Just now casually bringing it up.[10]

[74:5] {2:255}

先師古佛上堂のとき、よのつねにいはく、宏智古佛。しかあるを、宏智古佛を古佛と相見せる、ひとり先師古佛のみなり。宏智のとき、徑山の大慧禪師宗杲といふあり、南嶽の遠孫なるべし。大宋一國の天下おもはく、大慧は宏智にひとしかるべし、あまりさへ、宏智よりもその人なり、とおもへり。このあやまりは、大宋國内の道俗、ともに疏學にして、道眼いまだあきらかならず、知人のあきらめなし、知己のちからなきによりてなり。

---

6 **Old Buddha Hongzhi, of Mount Tiantong in the Qingyuan Prefecture of the Great Song** (*Daisō Keigenfu Tendōzan Wanshi kobutsu* 大宋慶元府天童山宏智古佛): I.e., the Caodong 曹洞 master Hongzhi Zhengjue 宏智正覺 (1091-1157). The passage is quoted from the *Hongzhi chanshi guanglu* 宏智禪師廣錄 (T.2001.48:51c7-13).

7 **Zhaozhou** (*Jōshū* 趙州): I.e., Zhaozhou Congshen 趙州從諗 (778-897).

8 **Xuedou** (*Setchō* 雪竇): I.e., Xuedou Zhijian 雪竇智鑑 (1105-1192).

9 **The Master** (*shi* 師): I.e., Hongzhi.

10 **Old Juzhi** (*rō Gutei* 老俱胝): I.e., Wuzhou Juzhi 婺州俱胝 (dates unknown), Tang-dynasty Chan master famous for holding up one finger in answer to everything.

My former master, the Old Buddha, when he addressed a convocation, always spoke of "Old Buddha Hongzhi."[11] Yet, it was my former master, the Old Buddha, alone who encountered Buddha Hongzhi as an old buddha. At the time of Hongzhi, there was a certain Zonggao, Chan Master Dahui of Mount Jing, who was a distant descendant of Nanyue.[12] Everyone throughout the Great Song thought that Dahui was the equal of Hongzhi; worse, they thought he was "that person," even more than Hongzhi.[13] This error was due to the fact that both the clergy and laity in the Land of the Great Song are lax in learning, have yet to open the eye of the way, lack the clarity to know people and the power to know themselves.

[74:6]

宏智のあぐるところ、眞箇の立志あり。趙州古佛曲躬叉手、の道理を參學すべし。正當恁麼時、これ王、索仙陀婆なりやいなや、臣、奉仙陀婆なりやいなや。雪竇の索鹽奉馬、の宗旨を參學すべし。いはゆる索鹽奉馬、ともに王、索仙陀婆なり、臣、索仙陀婆なり。世尊、索仙陀婆、迦葉、破顔微笑なり。初祖、索仙陀婆、四子、馬・鹽・水・器を奉ず。馬・鹽・水・器の、すなはち索仙陀婆なるとき、奉馬・奉水する關棙子、學すべし。

There is real resolve in what Hongzhi raises. We should study the principle of *Old Buddha Zhaozhou's "bowing with hands folded."* At the moment he does this, is this "*the king requesting saindhava*" or not? Is it "*the minister offering him saindhava*" or not? And we should study the essential point of Xuedou's "*he requested salt, and he offered him a horse.*" This "*requesting salt and offering a horse*" is both "*the king requesting saindhava*" and "*the minister requesting saindhava.*" It is *the World-Honored One requesting saindhava*, and *Kāśyapa breaking into a smile.*[14] *The First Ancestor requests saindhava*, and his four disciples offer him a horse, salt, water, and a vessel.[15] We should study the pivotal point of offering a horse or offering water, at the time when the horse, the salt, the water, and the vessel are themselves "requesting *saindhava.*"

---

11 **My former master, the Old Buddha** (*senshi kobutsu* 先師古佛): I.e., Tiantong Rujing 天童如淨 (1162-1227).

12 **Zonggao, Chan Master Dahui of Mount Jing** (*Kinzan no Daie zenji Sōkō* 徑山の大慧禪師宗杲): I.e., the Linji 臨濟 master Dahui Zonggao 大慧宗杲 (1089-1163), in the lineage from Nanyue Huairang 南嶽懷讓 (677-744).

13 **"that person"** (*sono hito* その人): I.e., "a person of substance," "a real person"; an expression occurring several times in the *Shōbōgenzō*.

14 **Kāśyapa breaking into a smile** (*Kashō hagan mishō* 迦葉破顔微笑): Allusion to the famous story of the first transmission of the treasury of the true dharma eye on Vulture Peak, when the Buddha held up a flower, and Mahākāśyapa smiled; see Supplementary Notes, s.v. "Break into a smile."

15 **The First Ancestor** (*shoso* 初祖): Reference to the first ancestor in China, Bodhidharma, who famously asked four disciples for their understandings of his teachings.

* * * * *

[74:7]
南泉一日見鄧隠峰來、遂指淨缾曰、淨缾即境、缾中有水、不得動著境、與老僧將水來。峰遂將缾水、向南泉面前瀉。泉即休。

One day, on seeing Deng Yinfeng approaching, Nanquan pointed at a water pitcher and said, "The water pitcher is an object; inside the pitcher there is water.[16] *Without moving the object, bring this old monk the water."*

Feng thereupon poured the water in the pitcher in front of Nanquan.

Quan desisted.

[74:8] {2:256}
すでにこれ南泉索水、徹底海枯。隠峰奉器、缾漏傾湫。しかもかくのごとくなりといへども、境中有水、水中有境を參學すべし。動水也未、動境也未。

Clearly, this is,[17]
Nanquan requested the water:
Right to the bottom, the ocean dried up.[18]
Yinfeng offered the vessel:
The pitcher spilled, the lake overturned.[19]

Be that as it may, we should study "*inside the object there is water,*" *inside the water there is an object. Has he moved the water or not? Has he moved the object or not?*

---

16 **Nanquan** (*Nansen* 南泉): I.e., Nanquan Puyuan 南泉普願 (748-835). "Deng Yinfeng" 鄧隠峰 refers to Wutaishan Yinfeng 五臺山隠峰 (dates unknown). Their anecdote occurs, e.g., at *Liandeng huiyao* 聯燈會要, ZZ.136:516b13-15; also recorded at *shinji Shōbōgenzō* 眞字正法眼藏, DZZ.5:160, case 64.

17 **Clearly, this is** (*sude ni kore* すでにこれ): Dōgen's comment here takes the form of a Chinese quatrain.

18 **Right to the bottom, the ocean dried up** (*tettei kai ko* 徹底海枯): Likely, reflecting the words, quoted in "Shōbōgenzō ganzei" 正法眼藏眼睛, of Tiantong Rujing 天童如淨 (1162-1227)*;* see Supplementary Notes, s.v. "Gouge out Bodhidharma's eye." "The ocean dried up" (*kai ko* 海枯) is a common trope in Chan literature occurring several times in Dōgen's writing, typically in play on the lines by the Five Dynasties poet Du Xunhe 杜荀鶴:

海枯終見底、人死不知心。
When the ocean dries up, we finally see the bottom;
When a person dies, we do not know his mind.

19 **The pitcher spilled, the lake overturned** (*byō ro kei shū* 缾漏傾湫): This phrase is often understood to mean "the pitcher spilled, forming a pool." More likely, it reflects a common expression praising great power: "to overturn lakes and topple peaks" (*kei shū tō gaku* 傾湫倒嶽).

* * * * *

[74:9]

香嚴襲燈大師、因僧問、如何是王索仙陀婆。嚴云、過遮邊來。僧過去。嚴云、鈍置殺人。

Great Master Xideng of Xiangyan was once asked by a monk, "What is 'the king requested saindhava'?"[20]

Yan said, "Come over here."

The monk went over.

Yan said, "You're making a total fool of people."

[74:10]

しばらくとふ、香嚴道底の、過遮邊來、これ索仙陀婆なりや、奉仙陀婆なりや、試請道看。ちなみに、僧過遮邊去せる、香嚴の索底なりや、香嚴の奉底なりや、香嚴の本期なりや。もし本期にあらずば、鈍置殺人といふべからず。もし本期ならば、鈍置殺人なるべからず。香嚴一期の盡力道底なりといへども、いまだ喪身失命をまぬかれず。たとへばこれ、敗軍之將さらに武勇をかたる。おほよそ説黄道黒、頂顆眼睛、おのれづから仙陀婆の索・奉、審審細細なり。拈拄杖、擧拂子、たれかしらざらんといひぬべし。しかあれども、膠柱調絃するともがらの分上にあらず。このともがら、膠柱調絃をしらざるがゆえに、分上にあらざるなり。

Let me just ask a bit. Xiangyan's saying, "*Come over here*" — was this requesting *saindhava*, or was it offering *saindhava*? *Try saying something.* Then, *the monk's going over there* — was this what Xiangyan requested? Was it what Xiangyan offered? Was it what Xiangyan expected? If it was not what Xiangyan expected, he would not have said, "*You're making a total fool of people*"; if it was what he expected, he would not have been "*making a total fool of people.*" While it may be something said with all the strength of Xiangyan's whole life, he could not avoid *forfeiting his body and losing his life.*[21] It is the defeated general still talking of his valor.[22]

---

20 **Great Master Xideng of Xiangyan** (*Kyōgen Shūtō daishi* 香嚴襲燈大師): I.e., Xiangyan Zhixiang (d. 898). This incident can be found (together with the Zhaozhou case discussed by Hongzhi in section 4, above) at *Biyan lu* 碧巖錄, T.2003.48:216c23-25.

21 **forfeiting his body and losing his life** (*sōshin shitsumyō* 喪身失命): A fixed expression for dying; perhaps best known from the famous problem, recorded in Dōgen's *shinji Shōbōgenzō* 眞字正法眼藏 (DZZ.5:254, case 243), of the man hanging by his teeth over a thousand-foot cliff who is asked the meaning of Bodhidharma's arrival from the west: "If he opens his mouth to answer, he forfeits his body and loses his life." See Supplementary Notes, s.v. "Forfeit one's body and lose one's life."

22 **the defeated general still talking of his valor** (*haigun shi shō sara ni buyū o kataru* 敗軍之將さらに武勇をかたる): From the saying (found in the *Shiji* 史記, Huai Yin hou liezhuan 淮陰侯列傳, KR.2a0001.500.870a):

In general, *the crown of the head and the eyes talking of the yellow and speaking of the black* are themselves the requesting and the offering of *saindhava* in all their details.[23] *Taking up the staff, holding up the whisk* — who would say they do not understand this?[24] Nevertheless, this is not a status shared by the types that *glue the stops and tune the strings.*[25] Because these types do not know what "*gluing the stops and tuning the strings*" is, they do not share this status.

* * * * *

[74:11] {2:257}

世尊一日陞座、文殊白槌云、諦觀法王法、法王法如是。世尊下座。

One day, the World-Honored One ascended his seat.[26] *Mañjuśrī sounded the mallet and said, "Behold the dharma of the King of the Dharma. Such is the dharma of the King of the Dharma." The World-Honored One descended his seat.*

[74:12]

雪竇山明覺禪師重顕云、列聖叢中作者知、法王法令不如斯。衆中若有仙陀客、何必文殊下一槌。

Zhongxian, Chan Master Mingjue of Mount Xuedou, said,[27]

An adept among the assembled sages
Knows the Dharma King's law's not so.
Were a saindhava person in the assembly,
Why need Mañjuśrī strike the mallet?

敗軍之將、不可以言勇。
The defeated general ought not talk of valor.

23 **talking of the yellow and speaking of the black** (*sekkō dōkoku* 説黄道黒): I.e., discussing heaven ("black") and earth ("yellow"); here probably the teachings of the Chan masters.

24 **Taking up the staff, holding up the whisk** (*nen shūjō ko hossu* 拈拄杖擧拂子): Classic gestures of the Chan master. See Supplementary Notes, s.v. "Staff," "Whisk."

25 **glue the stops and tune the strings** (*kōchū chōgen* 膠柱調絃): An idiomatic expression for inflexibility; gluing down the moveable bridges that enable changes in pitch on a stringed instrument.

26 **The World-Honored One** (*Seson* 世尊): Paralleling case number 92, *Biyan lu* 碧巖錄, T.2003.48:216b18-19.

27 **Zhongxian, Chan Master Mingjue of Mount Xuedou** (*Setchōzan Myōkaku zenji Jūken* 雪竇山明覺禪師重顕): I.e., Xuedou Zhongxian 雪竇重顯, quoting his verse also found at case 92 of the *Biyan lu* 碧巖錄 (T.2003.48:216c7-10).

[74:13]

しかあれば、雪竇道は、一槌、もし渾身無孔ならんがごとくは、下了・未下、ともに脱落無孔ならん。もしかくのごとくならんは、一槌、すなはち仙陀婆なり。すでに恁麼人ならん、これ、列聖一叢仙陀客なり。このゆえに、法王法如是なり。使得十二時、これ索仙陀姿なり。被十二時使、これ索仙陀婆なり。索拳頭奉拳頭すべし、索拂子奉拂子すべし。

Thus, what Xuedou says is that, when the mallet is a whole body without holes, whether struck or not, it is without holes sloughed off.[28] When it is like this, the mallet is itself *saindhava*; when they are already such a person, the entire group of assembled sages is *saindhava* people.[29] Therefore, "*such is the dharma of the King of the Dharma.*" To "*employ the twelve times*" — this is "requesting *saindhava*"; to "*be employed by the twelve times*" — this is "requesting *saindhava*."[30] We should *request a fist and offer a fist*; we should *request a staff and offer a staff.*

* * * * *

[74:14]

しかあれども、いま大宋國の諸山にある長老と稱するともがら、仙陀婆すべて夢也未見在なり。苦哉苦哉、祖道陵夷なり。苦學おこたらざれ、佛祖の命脈、まさに嗣續すべし。たとへば、如何是佛といふがごとき、即心是佛と道取する、その宗旨いかん。これ仙陀婆にあらざらんや。即心是佛といふは、たれといふぞ、と審細に參究すべし。たれかしらん、仙陀婆の築著磕著なることを。

Nevertheless, those types that call themselves elders at the various mountains of the Land of the Great Song have never seen *saindhava* even in their dreams.[31] Painful, painful — the erosion of the way of the

---

28 **a whole body without holes** (*konjin muku* 渾身無孔): Often taken to mean "complete, without flaw"; more likely, reflecting the common expression "an iron hammer without holes" (*muku tettsui* 無孔鐵槌) — i.e., a hammer head with no hole for a handle; hence, as we might say, something one "can't get a handle on." The exact sense of the novel expression "without holes sloughed off" (*datsuraku muku* 脱落無孔; i.e., "[something in which] being without holes has been sloughed off"[?]) is uncertain; perhaps, something like "[a mallet that] transcends itself as a mallet without holes." For the use of "slough off" (*datsuraku* 脱落), see Supplementary Notes, s.v. "Slough off."

29 **when they are already such a person** (*sude ni inmo nin naran* すでに恁麼人ならん): Allusion to the well-known saying attributed to Yunju Daoying 雲居道膺 (d. 902); see Supplementary Notes, s.v. "Such a person."

30 **to "employ the twelve times"** (*shitoku jūni ji* 使得十二時); **to "be employed by the twelve times"** (*hi jūni ji shi* 被十二時使): From the popular saying, frequently cited in the *Shōbōgenzō*, attributed to Zhaozhou 趙州; see Supplementary Notes, s.v. "Employ the twelve times."

31 **various mountains** (*shozan* 諸山): Also read *shosan*. A term for the major Buddhist monasteries.

ancestors. Do no neglect hard study; we should carry on the vital artery of the buddhas and ancestors. For example, when one asks, "*What is a buddha,*" and another says, "*This mind itself is the buddha,*" what does this mean? Is this not *saindhava*? We should study in detail of whom it is said "*this mind itself is the buddha*"? Who knows of *saindhava*'s hitting and banging?[32]

正法眼藏王索仙陀婆第七十四
Treasury of the True Dharma Eye
The King Requests Saindhava
Number 74

[Ryūmonji MS:]
爾時寛元三年十月二十二日、在越州大佛寺示衆
Presented to the assembly at Daibutsu Monastery, Esshū; twenty-second day, tenth month, third year of Kangen [12 November 1245]

32 ***saindhava*'s hitting and banging** (*sendaba no chikujaku katsujaku naru koto* 仙陀婆の築著磕著なること): Perhaps meaning something like, "how the various meanings of *saindhava* knock against each other." See Supplementary Notes, s.v. "Hitting and banging."

Treasury of the True Dharma Eye

Number 75

Leaving Home

Shukke

出家

Leaving Home

Shukke

Introduction

This short chapter was presented to the assembly in the autumn of 1246 at Eiheiji. It represents the final text of the seventy-five-chapter *Shōbōgenzō* and is found in the ninety-five-chapter Honzan edition as number 82 (or 83 in the Iwanami and Shūmuchō versions). A fragment has also been preserved as number 3 in the third fascicle of the twenty-eight-text *Himitsu* collection.

As its title indicates, the text deals with the topic of going forth from the household life into the Buddhist monastic order. Through comments on several canonical passages, Dōgen argues here, as he does elsewhere, that joining the order and taking its precepts are necessary conditions for inclusion in his tradition of buddhas and ancestors. He also argues that, when properly understood, the ultimate goal of the Buddhist path, unsurpassed awakening, is already fulfilled at the beginning of the path in the very act of leaving home and receiving the precepts.

Dōgen explores the topic of leaving home at much greater length in the "Shukke kudoku" 出家功徳 chapter of the twelve-chapter *Shōbōgenzō*.

正法眼藏第七十五
Treasury of the True Dharma Eye
Number 75
出家
Leaving Home

[75:1] {2:259}

禪苑清規云、三世諸佛、皆曰出家成道。西天二十八祖、唐土六祖、傳佛心印、盡是沙門。蓋以嚴淨毘尼、方能洪範三界。然則參禪問道、戒律爲先。既非離過防非、何以成佛作祖。受戒之法、應備三衣・鉢具並新淨衣物。如無新衣、浣染令淨、入壇受戒、不得借衣鉢。一心専注、愼勿異緣。像佛形儀、具佛戒律、得佛受用、此非小事、豈可軽心。若借衣鉢、雖登壇受戒、並不得戒。若不曾受、一生爲無戒之人。濫厠空門、虚受信施。初心入道、法律未諳、師匠不言、陷人於此。今茲苦口、敢望銘心。既受聲聞戒、應受菩薩戒、此入法之漸也。

In the Rules of Purity for the Chan Park, *it is said,*[1]

The buddhas of the three times all speak of leaving home and attaining the way. The twenty-eight ancestors of Sindh in the West and the six ancestors of the Land of the Tang who transmitted the seal of the buddha mind were all śramaṇas. *For it is only by the strict purity of the vinaya that one can be a great model for the three realms. This being the case, in studying Chan and inquiring about the way, the precepts are considered primary. If one has not freed oneself from transgressions and warded off impropriety, how can one attain buddhahood or become an ancestor?*

With regard to the procedure for receiving the precepts, one should be prepared with the three robes, pātra *utensil, and new clean clothing.*[2] *If one does not have new robes, purify the clothing by washing and dyeing. When entering the platform and receiving the precepts, one may not borrow robes and* pātra. *Concentrate single-mindedly and be careful to avoid thoughts of extraneous matters. To emulate a buddha's appearance and deportment, to equip oneself with a buddha's precepts,*

1 ***Rules of Purity for the Chan Park*** (*Zennen shingi* 禪苑清規): Quoting the entirety of the opening section of the text, on "receiving the precepts" (*jukai* 受戒) (*Chanyuan qinggui* 禪苑清規, ZZ.111:877a4-13).

2 ***pātra* utensil** (*hatsugu* 鉢具): I.e., monk's eating bowl; taking *hatsugu* 鉢具 as synonymous with *hou* 鉢盂 ("*pātra* bowl"). Some readers take it as "*pātra* and seating cloth" (*zagu* 座具), though the subsequent discussion makes no mention of the latter.

to obtain a buddha's rewards — these are not trifling matters; how could one take them lightly?[3] *If one borrows robes and pātra, even though one mounts the platform and receives the precepts, one will not actually obtain the precepts. If one does not receive them again, one will go through one's entire life as a person without the precepts, mingling improperly with the followers of emptiness and accepting in vain the donations of the faithful.*[4] *Beginners who enter the way are not fully acquainted with the rules. If ordination teachers do not tell them, they allow people to fall into this error. This is said in earnest, trusting it will be engraved on the mind. Once one has received the śrāvaka precepts, one should receive the bodhisattva precepts; this is the progression for entering the dharma.*[5]

[75:2] {2:260}

あきらかにしるべし、諸佛諸祖の成道、ただこれ出家受戒のみなり、諸佛諸祖の命脈、ただこれ出家受戒のみなり。いまだかつて出家せざるものは、ならびに佛祖にあらざるなり。佛をみ、祖をみるとは、出家受戒するなり。

It should be clear that the attainment of the way of the buddhas and the ancestors is only by those who leave home and receive the precepts; the vital artery of the buddhas and the ancestors is only of those who leave home and receive the precepts. None of those who have never left home is a buddha or ancestor. "To see a buddha," "to see an ancestor" means to leave home and receive the precepts.

[75:3]

摩訶迦葉、随順世尊、志求出家、冀度諸有。佛言善來比丘、鬚髮自落、袈裟著體。

---

3 **to obtain a buddha's rewards** (*toku butsu juyū* 得佛受用): The exact sense of the term *juyū* 受用 here is uncertain. Some readers take it as referring to the buddha's "reward body" (*juyū shin* 受用身; S. *sambhoga-kāya*) that is the product of the bodhisattva's merit; but, in the context here, it would seem more likely a reference to the more mundane benefits (of alms, prestige, etc.) enjoyed by a buddha.

4 **mingling improperly with the followers of emptiness and accepting in vain the donations of the faithful** (*ranshi kūmon, kyoju shinse* 濫厠空門、虛受信施): "Followers of emptiness" here refers to the monastic order, as followers of the doctrine of emptiness. Perhaps the unordained are said to "accept in vain" (*kyoju* 虛受) the alms of the faithful in the sense that donations made to them do not result in the merit that accrues to gifts to a bhikṣu.

5 ***śrāvaka* precepts** (*shōmon kai* 聲聞戒); **bodhisattva precepts** (*bosatsu kai* 菩薩戒): I.e., the full precepts (*gusoku kai* 具足戒) of the bhikṣu and *bhikṣuṇī* (in East Asia, typically 250 rules for the monk and 348 for the nun); and the precepts applicable to both lay and monastic (in East Asia, typically the ten grave and forty-eight minor rules of the *Brahma's Net Sūtra* (*Fanwang jing* 梵網經, T.1484).

Mahākāśyapa, following the World-Honored One, sought to leave home in hopes of delivering beings.[6] *When the Buddha said, "Welcome, bhikṣu," his beard and hair fell off by themselves, and a kāṣāya cloaked his body.*

[75:4]

ほとけを學して諸有を解脱するとき、みな出家受戒する勝躅、かくのごとし。

Whenever someone studies the buddha and is liberated from existences, the outstanding examples of leaving home and receiving the precepts are all like this.

[75:5]

大般若經第三日、佛世尊言、若菩薩摩訶薩、作是思惟、我於何時、當捨國位、出家之日、即成無上正等菩提、還於是日、轉妙法輪、即令無量無數有情、遠塵離垢、生淨法眼、復令無量無數有情、永盡諸漏、心慧解脱、亦令無量無數有情、皆於無上正等菩提、得不退轉。是菩薩摩訶薩、欲成斯事、應學般若波羅蜜。

In the Great Prajñā Sūtra*, roll 3, it is said that the Buddha, the World-Honored One said,*[7]

Suppose there were a bodhisattva-mahāsattva *who had this thought:*

On the very day when at some point I abandon my position as ruler of the country and leave home, I shall attain unsurpassed, perfect bodhi. Again, on that very day, I shall turn the wheel of the wondrous dharma, thereby causing incalculable, innumerable sentient beings to distance themselves from dust and separate themselves from filth, and to produce the pure dharma eye; and further, I shall cause incalculable, innumerable sentient beings forever to exhaust the contaminants and bring their minds to wisdom and liberation; and I shall cause incalculable, innumerable sentient beings all to attain non-regression from unsurpassed, perfect bodhi.

This bodhisattva-mahāsattva*, desiring to accomplish these things, should study the prajñā-pāramitā.*

---

6 **Mahākāśyapa** (*Makakashō* 摩訶迦葉): From the *Jingde chuandeng lu* 景德傳燈錄 (T.2076.51:206a2-3). The miracle described here is a common trope in Buddhist texts.

in hopes of delivering beings (*ki do shou* 冀度諸有): Taking the term *shou* 諸有 here as equivalent to "sentient beings" (*ujō* 有情; S. *sattva*); Dōgen's comment in the next section, *shou o gedatsu suru* 諸有を解脱する (rendered, "liberated from existences"), seems to take it in a more metaphysical sense, as "all the existences" (*u* 有; S. *bhava*) (to which beings are subject).

7 ***Great Prajñā Sūtra*** (*Dai hannya kyō* 大般若經): From Xuanzang's 玄奘 translation of the *Great Perfection of Wisdom Sūtra* (*Da bore poluomi jing* 大般若波羅蜜多經, T.220.5:16b10-16).

[75:6] {2:261}

おほよそ無上菩提は、出家受戒のとき満足するなり、出家の日にあらざれば成滿せず。しかあればすなはち、出家之日を拈來して、成無上菩提の日を現成せり、成無上菩提の日を拈出する、出家の日なり。この出家の翻筋斗する、轉妙法輪なり。この出家、すなはち無數有情をして無上菩提を不退轉ならしむるなり。しるべし、自利利他ここに滿足して、阿耨菩提不退不轉なるは、出家受戒なり。成無上菩提、かへりて出家の日を成菩提するなり。まさにしるべし、出家の日は、一異を超越せるなり。出家の日のうちに、三阿僧祇劫を修證するなり。出家之日のうちに、住無邊劫海、轉妙法輪するなり。出家の日は、謂如食頃にあらず、六十小劫にあらず、三際を超越せり、頂顊を脱落せり。出家の日は、出家の日を超越せるなり。しかもかくのごとくなりといへども、籠籠打破すれば、出家の日、すなはち出家の日なり。成道の日、すなはち成道の日なり。

In short, unsurpassed bodhi is brought to fulfillment at the time one leaves home and receives the precepts; it is not fulfilled except on the day one leaves home. Thus, in taking up "the day we leave home," we realize the day we "attain unsurpassed bodhi"; and to bring out the day we attain unsurpassed bodhi is [to bring out] the day we leave home. The flipping of this leaving home is the "turning of the wheel of the wondrous dharma."[8] This leaving home itself causes innumerable sentient beings not to regress from unsurpassed bodhi. It should be clear that fulfilling here the benefiting of self and benefiting of others and not regressing from *anuttara-bodhi* are leaving home and receiving the precepts. Attaining unsurpassed bodhi, conversely, makes the day one leaves home attain bodhi. We should realize that the day one leaves home transcends oneness and difference. Within the day one leaves home, one practices and verifies for the three *asaṃkhyeya-kalpas*; within the day one leaves home, one *dwells in the limitless ocean of kalpas, "turning the wheel of the wondrous dharma."*[9] The day one leaves home is not "like the time of a meal"; it is not "sixty minor kalpas."[10] It has transcended the three

8 **The flipping of this leaving home** (*kono shukke no honkinto suru* この出家の翻筋斗する): The "flip" (or "somersault"; *honkinto* 翻筋斗) here is intransitive (i.e., the act of leaving home); a common image in Chan texts for vigorous activity.

9 **the three *asaṃkhyeya-kalpas*** (*san asōgi kō* 三阿僧祇劫): "Three incalculable æons," the traditional calculation of the time it takes to complete the bodhisattva path to unsurpassed bodhi.

dwells in the limitless ocean of kalpas (*jū muhen kō kai* 住無邊劫海): A phrase expressing the bodhisattva's willingness to remain indefinitely in saṃsāra in order to liberate beings; from the *Ratnakūṭa-sūtra* (*Da baoji jing* 大寶積經, T.310.11:208c18):

爲利一衆生、住無邊劫海。

For the benefit of a single living being,
He dwells in a limitless ocean of kalpas.

10 **"like the time of a meal"** (*inyo jiki kyō* 謂如食頃); **"sixty minor kalpas"** (*rokujū shōkō* 六十小劫): From the expression "sixty minor kalpas are like the time of a meal"

junctures; it has sloughed off the crown of the head.[11] The day one leaves home has transcended the day one leaves home. Still, though this is so, when the nets and cages are broken, the day one leaves home is precisely the day one leaves home; the day one attains the way is precisely the day one attains the way.

[75:7] {2:262}

大論第十三曰、佛在祇桓、有酔婆羅門、來至佛所、欲作比丘。佛勅諸比丘、與剃頭著袈裟。酒醒驚怪、見身變異忽爲比丘、即便走去。諸比丘問擧佛、何以聽酔婆羅門、而作比丘、而今歸去。佛言、此婆羅門、無量劫中、無出家心、今因酔後、暫發微心、爲此縁故、後出家。如是種種因縁。出家破戒、猶勝在家持戒、以在家戒、不爲解脱。

In the Great Treatise, roll 13, it is said,[12]

When the Buddha was staying in Jetavana, there was a drunken brahman, who came to the Buddha seeking to become a bhikṣu. The Buddha ordered the bhikṣus to shave his head and put him in a kāṣāya. When the brahman sobered up, he was astonished and appalled to see that he had suddenly been transformed into a bhikṣu and immediately ran off. The bhikṣus asked the Buddha, "Why did you permit a drunken brahman to become a bhikṣu? And now, he's returned home."

The Buddha said, "For innumerable kalpas, that brahman had no thought of leaving home. But now, because he became drunk, he briefly had a bit of that thought. Due to this karmic connection, he will later leave home."

There are various causes and conditions like this.

One who leaves home and violates the precepts is still superior to a householder who keeps the precepts; for the householder's precepts are not for the sake of liberation.

(*rokujū shōkō inyo jiki kyō* 六十小劫謂如食頃); from the *Lotus Sūtra* account (*Miaofa lianhua jing* 妙法蓮華經, T.262.9:4a23-27) of the preaching of the sūtra by the past Buddha Candrasūryapradīpa, which took sixty minor kalpas but was experienced by the audience as merely the length of a meal.

11 **transcended the three junctures** (*sansei o chōotsu seri* 三際を超越せり): I.e., gone beyond "the three times" (*sansei* 三世), or periods, of past, present, and future.

sloughed off the crown of the head (*chōnei o datsuraku seri* 頂𩕳を脱落せり): An unusual image. The term *chōnei* 頂𩕳 ("crown of the head") regularly serves as synecdoche for the person; hence, the sense here may be "freed from one's identity." See Supplementary Notes, s.v. "Crown of the head."

12 ***Great Treatise*** (*Dairon* 大論): This entire section represents a quotation from the *Zhiguan fuxing zhuanhong jue* 止觀輔行傳弘決 (T.1912.46:214b9-17), by Zhanran 湛然 (711-782), which itself quotes the *Dazhidu lun* 大智度論 (T.1509.25:161b17-23).

[75:8] {2:263}

佛敕の宗旨、あきらかにしりぬ、佛化はただ出家、それ根本なり、いまだ出家せざるは、佛法にあらず。如來在世、もろもろの外道、すでにみづからが邪道をすてて、佛法に歸依するとき、かならずまづ出家をこふしなり。世尊、あるひはみづから善來比丘とさづけまします、あるひは諸比丘に敕して剃頭鬚髮、出家受戒せしめましますに、ともに出家受戒の法、たちまちに具足せしなり。

The essential point of the Buddha's order is obvious: in the Buddha's propagation, simply leaving home is fundamental; not having left home is not the buddha dharma. When the Tathāgata was in the world, when various followers of other paths voluntarily abandoned completely their false ways and took refuge in the buddha dharma, invariably the first thing they did was request to leave home. The World-Honored One either conferred this on them himself, saying, "Welcome, bhikṣu," or he ordered the bhikṣus to shave their beard and hair, and have them leave home and receive the precepts. In either case, the procedure for leaving home and receiving the precepts was immediately provided.

[75:9]

しるべし、佛化すでに身心にかうぶらしむるとき、頭髮自落し、袈裟覆體するなり。もし諸佛いまだ聽許しましまさざるには、鬚髮剃除せられず、袈裟覆體せられず、佛戒受得せられざるなり。しかあればすなはち、出家受戒は、諸佛如來の親受記なり。

We should realize that, once one receives the Buddha's propagation in body and mind, one's hair falls off by itself, and a *kāṣāya* covers one's body. So long as the buddhas have not approved it, beard and hair are not shaved off, the *kāṣāya* does not cover the body, and the buddha precepts are not received. This being the case, leaving home and receiving the precepts is personally receiving the prophecy of the buddhas, the tathāgatas.[13]

[75:10]

釋迦牟尼佛言、諸善男子、如來見諸衆生樂於小法、德薄垢重者、爲是人説我小出家、得阿耨多羅三藐三菩提。然我實成佛已來、久遠若斯。但以方便教化衆生、令入佛道、作如是説。

Buddha Śākyamuni said,[14]

Good sons, when the Tathāgata sees living beings who delight in lesser teachings, their merits meager and their impurities severe, for these

---

13 **personally receiving the prophecy of the buddhas, the tathāgatas** (*shobutsu nyorai no shin juki* 諸佛如來の親受記): I.e., receiving a prediction of one's future attainment of buddhahood, a necessary step in traditional accounts of the bodhisattva path.

14 **Buddha Śākyamuni** (*Shakamuni butsu* 釋迦牟尼佛): From the *Lotus Sūtra* (*Miaofa lianhua jing* 妙法蓮華經, T.262.9:42c5-9).

people, I say that I left home as a youth and attained anuttara-samyak-saṃbodhi. However, since I actually attained buddhahood it has been as long as this.[15] *It is only by expedient means to teach and convert living beings and cause them to enter the way of the buddhas that I say this.*

[75:11]

しかあれば、久遠實成は、我小出家なり。得阿耨多羅三藐三菩提は、我小出家なり。我小出家を擧拈するに、德薄垢重の樂小法する衆生、ならびに我小出家するなり。我小出家の説法を見聞參學するところに、見佛阿耨多羅三藐三菩提なり。樂小法の衆生を救度するとき、爲是人説、我小出家、得阿耨多羅三藐三菩提なり。

Thus, "actually attained long ago" is "I left home as a youth." "Attained *anuttara-samyak-saṃbodhi*" is "I left home as a youth." When we take up "I left home as a youth," the living beings who delight in lesser teachings, "their merits meager and their impurities severe," are all undertaking "I left home as a youth." Where we hear and study the dharma talk of "I left home as a youth," we see *anuttara-samyak-saṃbodhi*. When we save living beings who delight in lesser teachings, this is "for *these people, I say that I left home as a youth and attained anuttara-samyak-saṃbodhi.*"

[75:12] {2:264}

しかもかくのごとくなりといふとも、畢竟じてとふべし、出家功德、それいくらばかりなるべきぞ。かれにむかふていふべし、頂顆許なり。

Still, while it may be like this, in the end, we should ask, "Just how great is the merit of leaving home?" To that we should say, "About the size of the crown of the head."

正法眼藏出家第七十五
Treasury of the True Dharma Eye
Leaving Home
Number 75

15 **as long as this** (*kūon nyakushi* 久遠若斯): I.e., as long as the example, previously given in the *Lotus Sūtra*, of a period longer than an inconceivably large number of kalpas.

[Ryūmonji MS:]

爾時寛元四年丙午九月十五日、在越宇永平寺示衆

Presented to the assembly at Eihei Monastery, Etsuu; fifteenth day, ninth month of the senior fire year of the horse, the fourth year of Kangen [25 October 1246][16]

正慶癸酉孟夏第二日、於馬州菟東莊終書寫了。伏願世世結良緣頓入諸佛無上道矣。永平末流菩薩比丘道源

Finished copying at Utsuka Estate, Mashū; second day, early summer [fourth month], junior water year of the chicken, the second year of Shōkei [16 May 1333].[17] *Humbly requesting favorable karmic connections in life after life so as directly to enter the unsurpassed way of the buddhas. A distant descendant of Eihei, Bodhisattva Bhikṣu Dōgen.*[18]

天文十六丁未林鐘初五、能州在悳德精舍而書寫了也。燒香九頓，哲囱賢衲拜

Finished copying at Kōtoku Vihāra, Noshū, as the monastery bell sounds the fifth hour, junior fire year of the sheep, sixteenth year of Tenbun [1547]. Burning incense and nine bows, reverently, patch-robed Tessō Ken[19]

[*Himitsu* MS:]

古出家ノ後、有御龍草本、以之可書改之、仍可破之

There is his draft manuscript that postdates the old "Shukke"; use it to update this and then destroy it.[20]

---

16 The *Himitsu* 秘密 MS shares an identical colophon.

17 **Mashū** 馬州: I.e., Tajima Province.

18 **Bodhisattva Bhikṣu Dōgen** (*bosatsu biku Dōgen* 菩薩比丘道源): Likely, a transcribing error for Tsūgen 通源 (d.u.).

19 **Tessō Ken** 喆囱賢: I.e., Tessō Hōken 喆囱芳賢, copyist of the Ryūmonji 龍門寺 MS (d. 1551).

20 The authorship, date, precise meaning, and implications of this note remain unknown.

The Sōtō Zen Text Project *Shōbōgenzō*

Volume I
The Seventy-five-Chapter Compilation, Part 1

1. The Realized Kōan *Genjō kōan* 現成公案
2. Mahā-prajñā-pāramitā *Maka hannya haramitsu* 摩訶般若波羅蜜
3. Buddha Nature *Busshō* 佛性
4. Studying the Way with Body and Mind *Shinjin gakudō* 身心學道
5. This Mind Itself Is the Buddha *Soku shin ze butsu* 即心是佛
6. Deportment of the Practicing Buddha *Gyōbutsu iigi* 行佛威儀
7. One Bright Pearl *Ikka myōju* 一顆明珠
8. The Mind Cannot Be Got *Shin fukatoku* 心不可得
9. The Old Buddha Mind *Kobutsushin* 古佛心
10. Great Awakening *Daigo* 大悟
11. Principles of Seated Meditation *Zazen gi* 坐禪儀
12. Needle of Seated Meditation *Zazen shin* 坐禪箴
13. Ocean Seal Samādhi *Kaiin zanmai* 海印三昧
14. Sky Flowers *Kūge* 空華
15. Radiance *Kōmyō* 光明

Volume II
The Seventy-five-Chapter Compilation, Part 2

16A. Sustained Practice, Part 1 *Gyōji jō* 行持上
16B. Sustained Practice, Part 2 *Gyōji ge* 行持下
17. Such *Inmo* 恁麼
18. Avalokiteśvara *Kannon* 觀音
19. The Old Mirror *Kokyō* 古鏡
20. Sometimes *Uji* 有時
21. Prediction *Juki* 授記
22. Full Function *Zenki* 全機
23. The Moon *Tsuki* 都機
24. Painted Cake *Gabyō* 畫餅
25. Sound of the Stream, Form of the Mountain *Keisei sanshoku* 谿聲山色
26. Beyond the Buddha *Butsu kōjō ji* 佛向上事
27. Talking of a Dream within a Dream *Muchū setsumu* 夢中説夢
28. Making a Bow and Getting the Marrow *Raihai tokuzui* 禮拜得髓
29. The Mountains and Waters Sūtra *Sansui kyō* 山水經
30. Sūtra Reading *Kankin* 看經

Volume III
The Seventy-five-Chapter Compilation, Part 3

31. Do No Evil *Shoaku makusa* 諸惡莫作
32. Transmitting the Robe *Den'e* 傳衣
33. Sayings *Dōtoku* 道得
34. The Teachings of the Buddhas *Bukkyō* 佛教
35. Spiritual Powers *Jinzū* 神通
36. The Arhat *Arakan* 阿羅漢

Volume IV
The Seventy-five-Chapter Compilation, Part 4

Volume V
The Seventy-five-Chapter Compilation, Part 5

Volume VI
The Twelve-Chapter Compilation

Volume VII
Supplementary Chapters, Variant Texts

Supplementary Chapters

Variant Texts

Volume VIII

